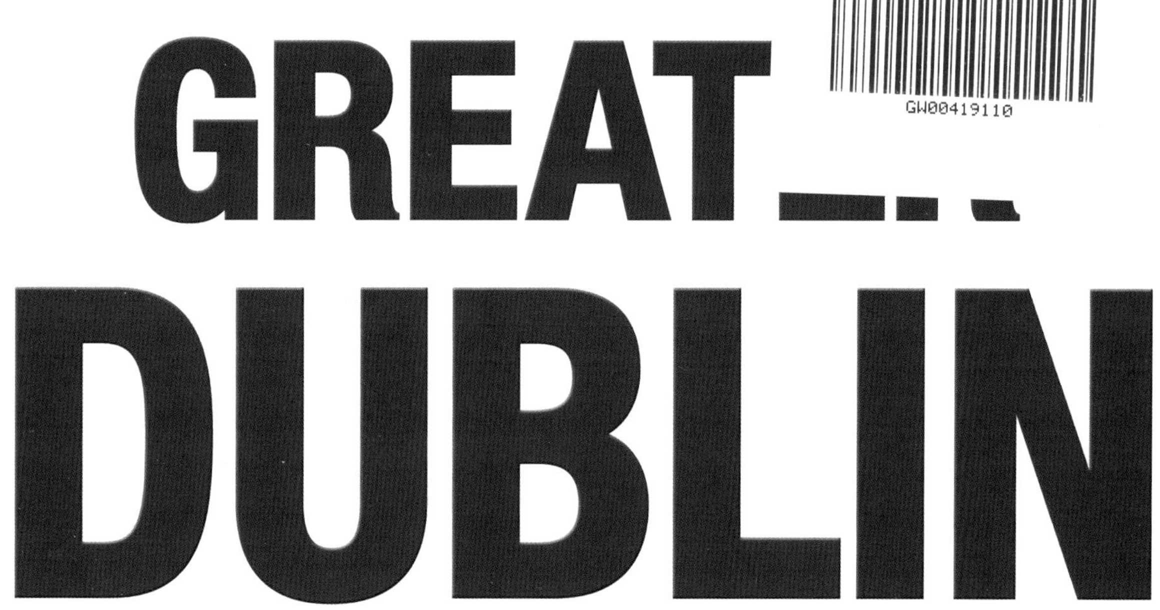

GREAT DUBLIN

GW00419110

Contents

Motorway / under construction

Tunnelled motorway

N6 National primary road

N55 National secondary road

R95 Regional road

Other road

Track

Ferry

City boundary

Railway / Station

Dublin Luas tramway / Station
JERVIS

Bus / Coach station

P Car park

Lake / River

GSS Garda Síochána (police) station

i Tourist information centre

+ Church

PO Lib Public service building (appropriate name shown)

Leisure / Tourism

Shopping

Administration / Law

Health / Hospital

Education

Notable building

Built up area

Park / Garden / Sports ground / Public open space

Cemetery

0   0.25   0.5   0.75   1 km
0   1/4   1/2 mile

Scale 1:14,400 4.4 inches (11.2cm) to 1 mile / 6.9cm to 1km

Published by Collins
An imprint of HarperCollins*Publishers*
77-85 Fulham Palace Road, Hammersmith, London W6 8JB

www.collins.co.uk

Copyright © HarperCollins*Publishers* Ltd 2005

Collins® is a registered trademark of HarperCollins*Publishers* Limited

Mapping generated from Collins Bartholomew digital databases

Based on Ordnance Survey Ireland by permission of the Government. © Government of Ireland.

Printed in China.

SI11961 / NDB

e-mail: roadcheck@harpercollins.co.uk

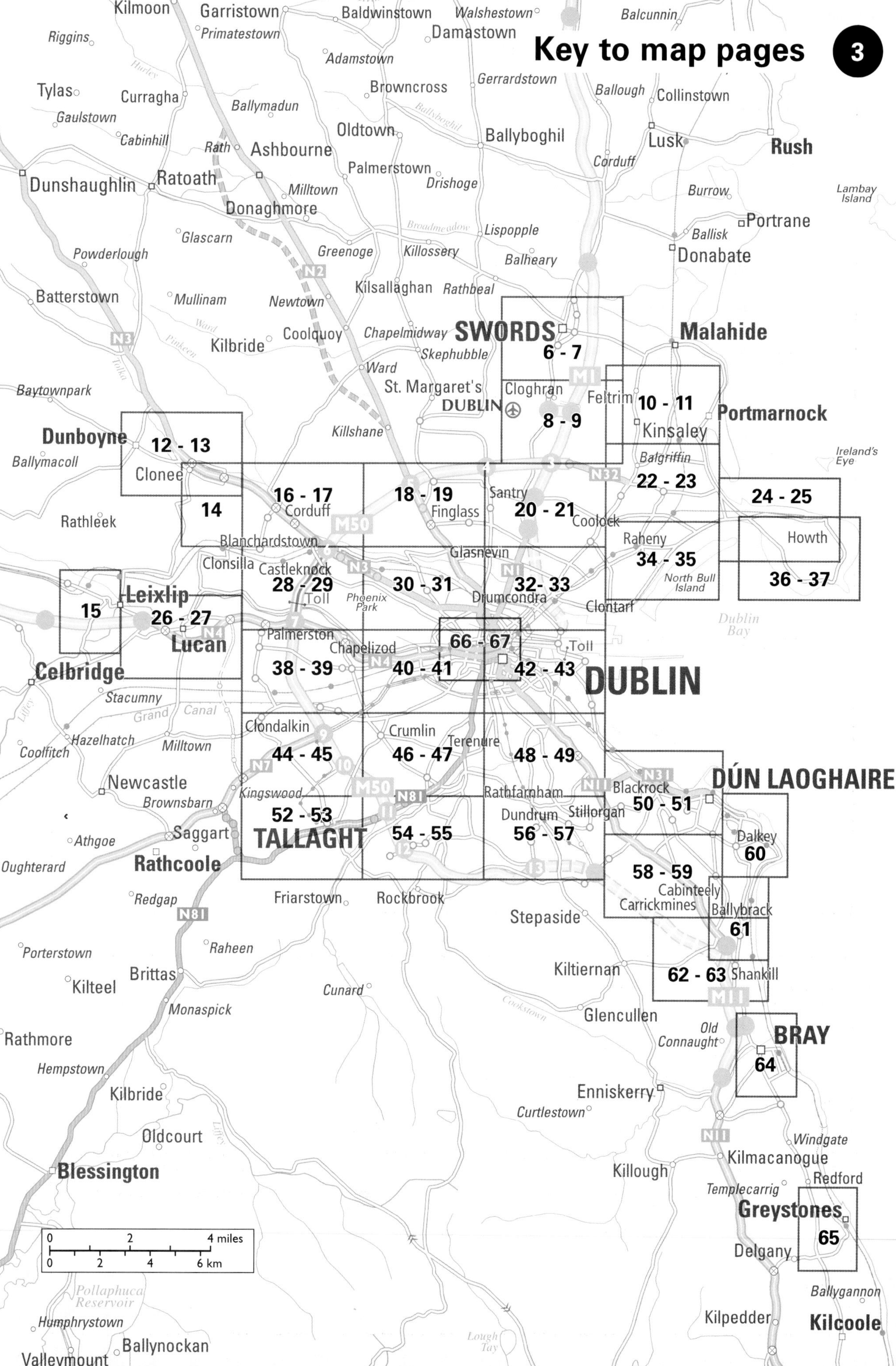

Riggins
Kilmoon
Garristown
Baldwinstown
Walshestown
Balcunnin
Tylas
Curragha
Primatestown
Damastown
Gaulstown
Ballymadun
Adamstown
Gerrardstown
Ballough
Collinstown
Cabinhill
Rath
Ashbourne
Oldtown
Browncross
Rush
Powderlough
Ratoath
Milltown
Palmerstown
Ballyboghil
Lusk
Dunshaughlin
Donaghmore
Drishoge
Burrow
Lambay Island
Glascarn
Greenoge
Killossery
Ballisk
Portrane
Batterstown
Mullinam
Newtown
Kilsallaghan
Rathbeal
Balheary
Donabate
Kilbride
Coolquoy
Chapelmidway
SWORDS
Malahide
Baytownpark
Ward
St. Margaret's
Skephubble
6 - 7
Dunboyne
Killshane
DUBLIN
Cloghran
Feltrim
10 - 11
Portmarnock
Ballymacoll
12 - 13
8 - 9
Kinsaley
Clonee
Balgriffin
Ireland's Eye
Rathleek
14
16 - 17
18 - 19
Santry
22 - 23
24 - 25
Corduff
Finglass
20 - 21
Coolock
Blanchardstown
Raheny
Howth
Leixlip
Clonsilla
Glasnevin
34 - 35
36 - 37
15
26 - 27
28 - 29
Castleknock
30 - 31
32- 33
North Bull Island
Lucan
Toll
Drumcondra
Clontarf
Celbridge
Phoenix Park
Dublin Bay
Stacumny
Palmerston
66 - 67
Toll
Hazelhatch
Grand Canal
Chapelizod
Coolfitch
Milltown
38 - 39
40 - 41
42 - 43
DUBLIN
Clondalkin
Crumlin
Newcastle
Terenure
48 - 49
DÚN LAOGHAIRE
Brownsbarn
44 - 45
46 - 47
Rathfarnham
Blackrock
Kingswood
Dundrum
Stillorgan
50 - 51
Saggart
52 - 53
54 - 55
56 - 57
Dalkey
Athgoe
Rathcoole
TALLAGHT
60
Oughterard
58 - 59
Cabinteely
Redgap
Friarstown
Rockbrook
Carrickmines
Ballybrack
Porterstown
Stepaside
61
Brittas
Raheen
Kilteel
Kiltiernan
62 - 63
Shankill
Rathmore
Cunard
Hempstown
Glencullen
BRAY
Kilbride
Old Connaught
64
Oldcourt
Enniskerry
Blessington
Curtlestown
Kilmacanogue
Windgate
Killough
Redford
Templecarrig
Greystones
65
Delgany
0   2   4 miles
0   2   4   6 km
Pollaphuca Reservoir
Ballygannon
Humphrystown
Kilpedder
Kilcoole
Valleymount
Ballynockan
Lough Tay

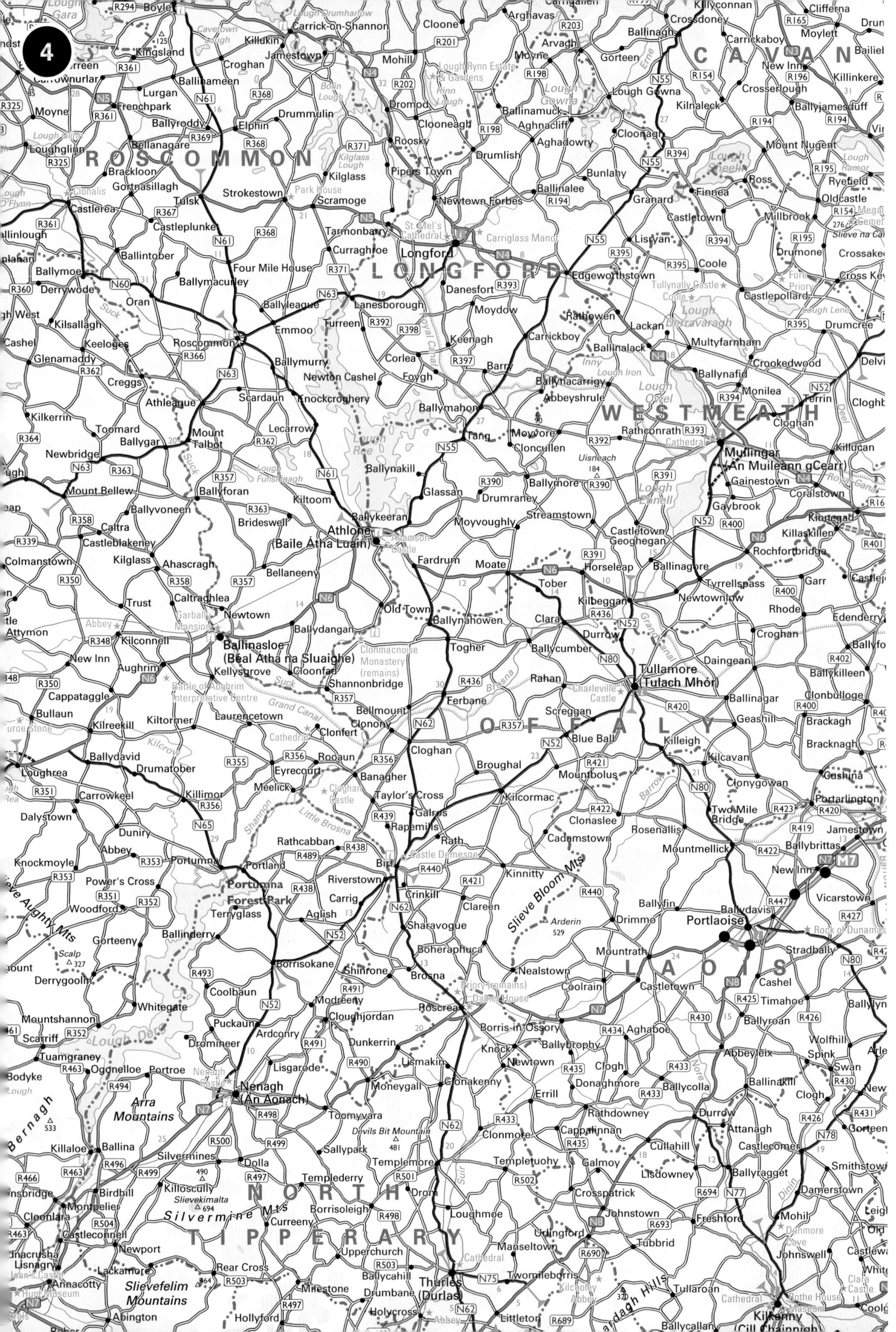
ROSCOMMON
LONGFORD
CAVAN
WESTMEATH
OFFALY
LAOIS
NORTH TIPPERARY
Boyle
Carrick-on-Shannon
Cloone
Arghavas
Crossdoney
Killyconnan
Clifferna
Moylett
Bailieborough
Kingsland
Killukin
Jamestown
Mohill
Arvagh
Moyne
Gorteen
Ballinagh
Carrickaboy
New Inn
Killinkere
Carrownurlar
Croghan
Ballinameen
Lurgan
Frenchpark
Dromod
Ballinamuck
Lough Gowna
Kilnaleck
Crosserlough
Ballyjamesduff
Moyne
Ballyroddy
Elphin
Drummulin
Clooneagh
Aghnacliff
Cloonagh
Loughglinn
Bellanagare
Roosky
Drumlish
Aghadowry
Mount Nugent
Brackloon
Kilglass
Pipers Town
Bunlahy
Ross
Ryefield
Gortnasillagh
Clonalis
Tulsk
Strokestown
Park House
Scramoge
Newtown Forbes
Ballinalee
Granard
Finnea
Oldcastle
Castlerea
Castleplunket
Tarmonbarry
St. Mel's Cathedral
Carriglass Manor
Castletown
Millbrook
Ballintober
Curraghroe
Longford
Lisryan
Drumone
Crossakeel
Ballymoe
Four Mile House
Ballymacurley
Coole
Edgeworthstown
Cross Keys
Derrywode
Oran
Ballyleague
Lanesborough
Danesfort
Tullynally Castle
Castlepollard
Kilsallagh
Emmoo
Turreen
Moydow
Rathowen
Lackan
Lough Derravaragh
Drumcree
Roscommon
Keenagh
Carrickboy
Ballinalack
Multyfarnham
Cashel
Keeloges
Glenamaddy
Ballymurry
Corlea
Barry
Ballynafid
Crookedwood
Delvin
Creggs
Newton Cashel
Foygh
Ballynacarrigy
Abbeyshrule
Lough Owel
Monilea
Terrin
Athleague
Scardaun
Knockcroghery
Ballymahon
Kilkerrin
Toomard
Mount Talbot
Lecarrow
Tang
Moyvore
Cloncullen
Rathconrath
Cathedral
Mullingar (An Muileann gCearr)
Cloghan
Killucan
Ballygar
Newbridge
Lough Ree
Ballynakill
Uisneach
Gainestown
Coralstown
Mount Bellew
Ballyforan
Lough Funshinagh
Kiltoom
Glassan
Drumraney
Ballymore
Lough Ennell
Ballyvoneen
Brideswell
Ballykeeran
Moyvoughly
Streamstown
Gaybrook
Kinnegad
Caltra
Castleblakeney
Athlone (Baile Átha Luain)
Adamson Castle
Castletown Geoghegan
Killaskillen
Rochfortbridge
Colmanstown
Kilglass
Ahascragh
Bellaneeny
Fardrum
Moate
Horseleap
Ballinagore
Tober
Tyrrellspass
Garr
Castlejordan
Trust
Caltraghlea
Newtown
Old Town
Kilbeggan
Newtownlow
Rhode
Garbally Mansion
Ballynahowen
Clara
Edenderry
Attymon
Abbey
Kilconnell
Ballinasloe (Béal Átha na Sluaighe)
Ballydangan
Durrow
Croghan
New Inn
Aughrim
Kellysgrove
Clonmacnoise Monastery (remains)
Cloonfad
Togher
Ballycumber
Daingean
Ballykilleen
Tullamore (Tulach Mhór)
Battle of Aughrim Interpretative Centre
Shannonbridge
Rahan
Charleville Castle
Clonbullogue
Cappataggle
Bullaun
Ferbane
Ballinagar
Brackagh
Kilreekill
Kiltormer
Laurencetown
Bellmount
Clonony
Screggan
Geashill
Turoe Stone
Clonfert
Blue Ball
Bracknagh
Loughrea
Ballydavid
Drumatober
Eyrecourt
Rooaun
Cloghan
Broughal
Killeigh
Kilcavan
Meelick
Banagher
Mountbolus
Clonygowan
Cushina
Carrowkeel
Killimor
Cloghan Castle
Taylor's Cross
Kilcormac
Portarlington
Dalystown
Galros
Rapemills
Clonaslee
Two Mile Bridge
Rosenallis
Jamestown
Duniry
Little Brosna
Rathcabban
Rath
Cadamstown
Ballybrittas
Abbey
Mountmellick
Knockmoyle
Portumna
Portland
Birr
Castle Demesne
Kinnitty
New Inn
Power's Cross
Portumna Forest Park
Riverstown
Slieve Bloom Mts
Vicarstown
Woodford
Terryglass
Carrig
Crinkill
Clareen
Ballyfin
Ballydavis
Slieve Aughty Mts
Aglish
Sharavogue
Arderin
Drimmo
Portlaoise
Rock of Dunamase
Ballinderry
Gorteeny
Scalp
Boheraphuca
Mountrath
Stradbally
Mount
Derrygoolin
Borrisokane
Shinrone
Brosna
Nealstown
Cashel
Coolbaun
Priory (remains)
Castletown
Coolrain
Timahoe
Whitegate
Modreeny
Damer House
Ballyroan
Ballylynan
Mountshannon
Puckaun
Cloughjordan
Roscrea
Borris-in-Ossory
Aghaboe
Scarriff
Lough Derg
Ardcrony
Dromineer
Dunkerrin
Ballybrophy
Wolfhill
Tuamgraney
Knock
Newtown
Abbeyleix
Spink
Arles
Lisgarode
Lismakin
Clogh
Swan
Bodyke
Ogonelloe
Portroe
Nenagh Castle
Nenagh (An Aonach)
Moneygall
Clonakenny
Donaghmore
Ballycolla
Ballinakill
Arra Mountains
Erill
Clogh
Newtown
Toomyvara
Rathdowney
Durrow
Bernagh
Devils Bit Mountain
Cappalinnan
Attanagh
Gorteen
Killaloe
Ballina
Silvermines
Dolla
Sallypark
Clonmore
Cullahill
Castlecomer
Templemore
Templetuohy
Galmoy
Lisdowney
Smithstown
Birdhill
Killoscully
Templederry
Ballyragget
Slievekimalta
Drom
Crosspatrick
Damerstown
Ballina
Montpelier
Silvermine Mts
Borrisoleigh
Loughmoe
Johnstown
Freshford
Mohil
Leighlinbridge
Cloonlara
Curreeny
Urlingford
Dunmore Cave
Castleconnell
Newport
Upperchurch
Manseltown
Tubbrid
Johnswell
Castlewarren
Lisnagry
Lackamore
Rear Cross
Ballycahill
Cathedral
Twomileborris
Kilcooley Abbey
Slieveardagh Hills
Tullaroan
Clara Castle
Annacotty
Slievefelim Mountains
Milestone
Thurles (Durlas)
Drumbane
Holycross
Abbey
Littleton
Cathedral
Rothe House Museum
Kilkenny (Cill Chainnigh)
Abington
Hollyford
Ballycallan
Hunt Museum
King John's Castle
Coolgreany
R294
R361
R325
N5
N61
R368
R369
R371
R202
N4
R201
R203
R198
N55
R154
R196
R165
R194
R195
R154
R367
N61
R368
N60
R360
R363
N63
R392
R398
R397
R393
R395
R394
R194
N63
R366
R362
R364
R363
R357
N61
R390
N55
R392
R393
R391
R358
R339
R350
R358
R357
N6
R436
N52
N80
R400
R401
R402
R348
R350
N6
R357
R436
R420
R356
R355
N62
R357
R421
N52
N80
R423
R420
R419
R422
N65
R351
R356
R439
R438
R489
R353
R440
R421
R447
R427
N7
M7
R351
R352
R438
N62
R440
N52
R493
R491
N52
N7
R434
R430
R425
R426
N8
R352
R491
R490
R435
R433
R433
R430
R463
R494
N7
R498
N62
R433
R435
R426
R431
N78
R500
R499
R496
R463
R466
R499
R497
R501
R502
R694
N77
R504
R498
R693
N8
R690
R503
N75
R503
R497
N62
R689

Scale

| 0 | 5 | 10 | 15 kilometres |
| 0 | 3 | 6 | 9 miles |

Road distances shown in blue
are in miles

DUBLIN (Baile Átha Cliath)

DUBLIN CITY

Drogheda (Droichead Átha)

Dún Laoghaire

Bray (Bré)

Wicklow (Cill Mhantáin)

Arklow (An tInbhear Mór)

Carlow (Ceatharlach)

Naas (An Nás)

Newbridge (Droichead Nua)

Navan (An Uaimh)

Kells (Ceanannus Mór)

To Douglas 2¾ – 4¾ hrs (summer only)
To Liverpool 4 – 8 hrs
To Holyhead 1¾ – 3¼ hrs

LOUTH

MEATH

FINGAL

SOUTH DUBLIN

DÚN LAOGHAIRE RATHDOWN

KILDARE

WICKLOW

CARLOW

Wicklow Mts.

National Park

Wicklow Mountain

Lugnaquilla Mountain 926

Mullaghcleevaun 850

Djouce Mountain 886

Great Sugar Loaf 506

Dundalk Bay

Dunany Point

Clogher Head

Lambay Island

Ireland's Eye

Howth Castle Gardens

Dublin Bay

Talbot Botanic Gardens

Avondale Forest Park

Mount Usher Gardens

Wicklow Head

Ardmore Point

Brittas Bay

Mizen Head

Kilmichael Point

Bog of Allen

The Curragh

Blessington Lakes

Russborough House

Powerscourt House

Glendalough Visitor Centre

Meeting of The Waters

National Maritime Museum

James Joyce Tower

St Brigid's Cathedral

Dún a'Rí Forest Park

Place names include: Blackrock, Dromiskin, Castlebellingham, Annagassan, Togher, Port, Clogherhead, Termonfeckin, Baltray, Bettystown, Laytown, Julianstown, Gormanstown, Balbriggan, Skerries, Naul, Damastown, Lusk, Rush, Portrane, Donabate, Malahide, Portmarnock, Howth, Coolock, Clontarf, Swords, Donaghmore, Ashbourne, Ratoath, Kilbride, Dunboyne, Clonee, Blanchardstown, Maynooth, Leixlip, Lucan, Palmerston, Clondalkin, Tallaght, Rathfarnham, Terenure, Stillorgan, Dalkey, Ballybrack, Shankill, Enniskerry, Kilmacanogue, Greystones, Delgany, Kilcoole, Newcastle, Newtownmountkennedy, Roundwood, Tomdarragh, Annamoe, Laragh, Glendalough, Rathnew, Glenealy, Ashford, Rathdrum, Redcross, Avoca, Aughrim, Woodenbridge, Johnstown, Ferrybank, Greenan, Aghavannagh, Knockananna, Moyne, Hacketstown, Rathvilly, Tullow, Tinahely, Coolgreany, Courtown, Riverchapel, Gorey, Clogh, Craanford, Carnew, Knockbrandon, Coolattin, Shillelagh, Crosspatrick, Killinierin, Inch, Castletown, Ballon, Fenagh, Myshall, Clonegal, Bunclody, Mount Leinster, Goresbridge, Leighlin, Carlow, Graigue, Tullow, Kilkea, Timolin, Moone, Castledermot, Graney, Baltinglass, Stratford, Donard, Rathdangan, Kiltegan, Grangeford, Bridgeland, Tinahely, Kildavin, Ballyroebuck, Clohamon, Camolin

Rivers/features: Boyne, Blackwater, Dee, Glyde, Liffey, Barrow, Slaney, Avonmore, Avonbeg, Avoca

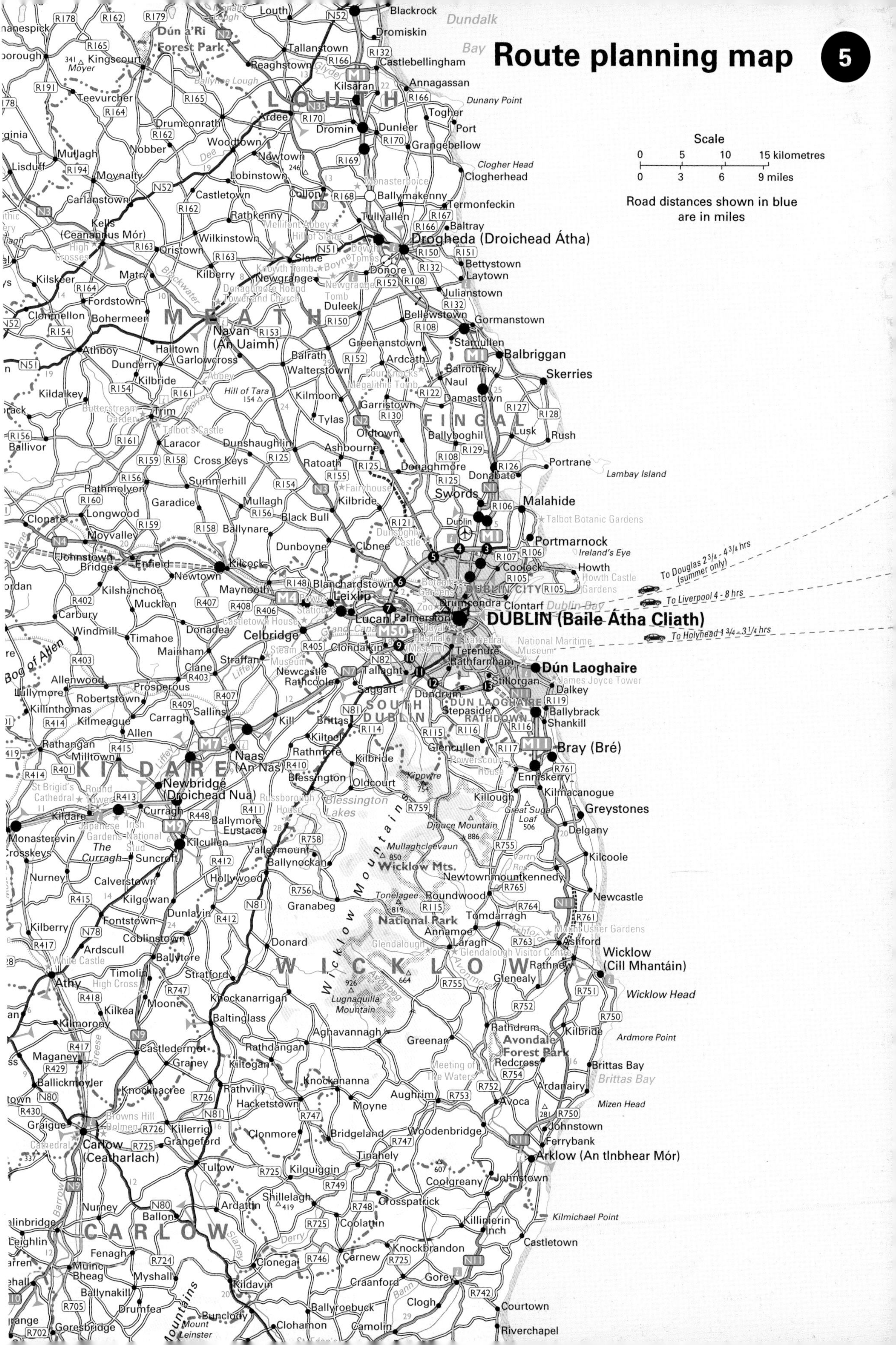

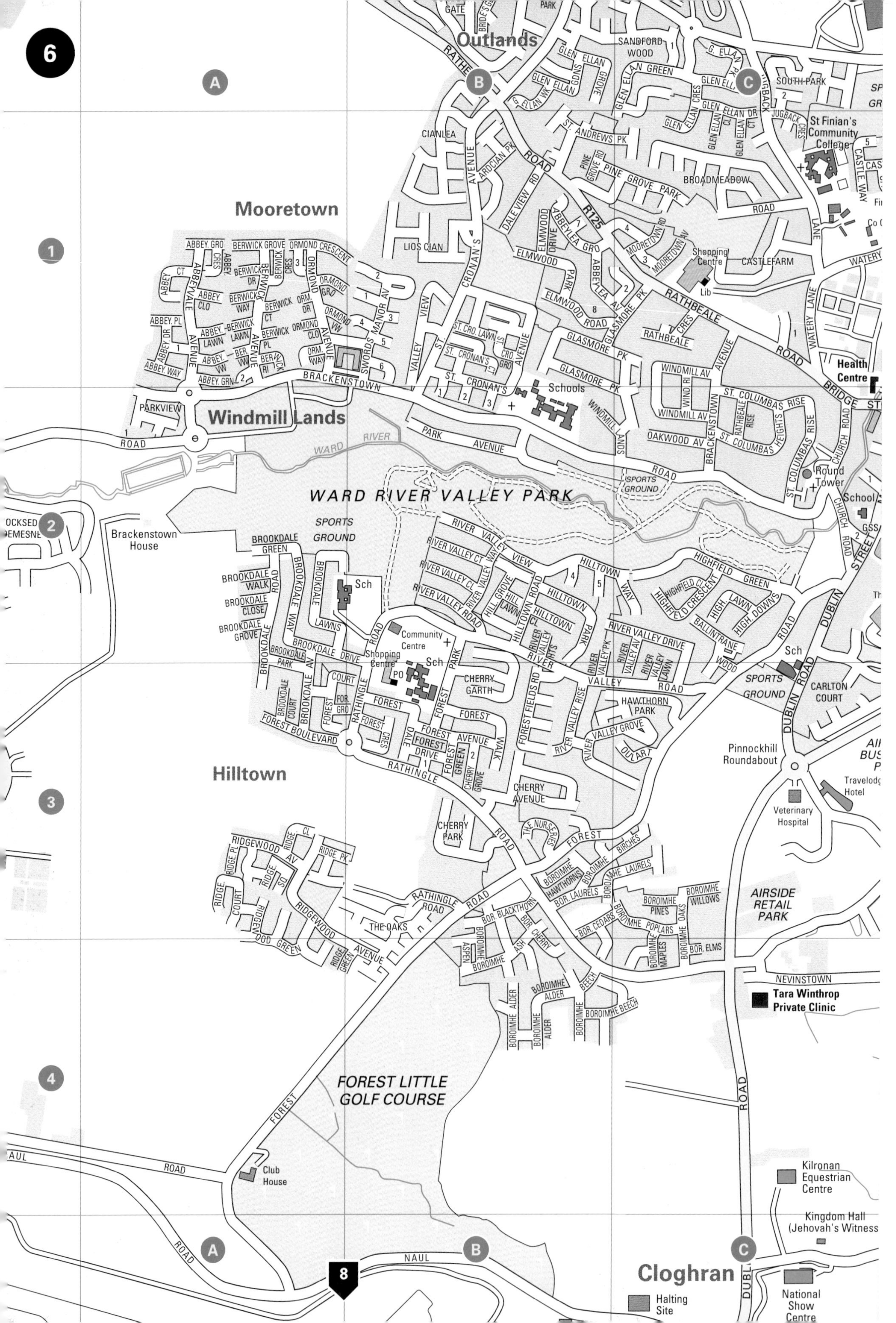
A
B
C
1
2
3
4
Outlands
Mooretown
Windmill Lands
WARD RIVER VALLEY PARK
WARD RIVER
SPORTS GROUND
Brackenstown House
Hilltown
FOREST LITTLE GOLF COURSE
Club House
Cloghran
Halting Site
National Show Centre
Kingdom Hall (Jehovah's Witness
Kilronan Equestrian Centre
Tara Winthrop Private Clinic
NEVINSTOWN
AIRSIDE RETAIL PARK
Veterinary Hospital
Travelodge Hotel
Pinnockhill Roundabout
CARLTON COURT
Round Tower
School
Health Centre
St Finian's Community College
Shopping Centre
Lib
Schools
Community Centre
Sch
PO
SANDFORD WOOD
GLEN ELLAN GREEN
SOUTH PARK
BROADMEADOW
ROAD
CASTLEFARM
RATHBEALE ROAD
RATHBEALE CRES
WINDMILL AV
BRACKENSTOWN AVENUE
ST. COLUMBAS RISE
OAKWOOD AV
BRACKENSTOWN ROAD
PARK AVENUE
CIANLEA
LIOS CIAN
CRONAN'S
VALLEY VIEW
ELMWOOD ROAD
GLASMORE PK
ABBEY GRO
BERWICK GROVE
ORMOND CRESCENT
SWORDS MANOR AV
ORMOND AVENUE
ABBEYVALE AVENUE
PARKVIEW
RIVER VALLEY VIEW
HILLTOWN WAY
HIGHFIELD GREEN
HIGHFIELD CRESCENT
RIVER VALLEY DRIVE
RIVER VALLEY ROAD
BALLINTRANE WOOD
BROOKDALE GREEN
BROOKDALE WALK
BROOKDALE CLOSE
BROOKDALE GROVE
BROOKDALE LAWNS
BROOKDALE DRIVE
FOREST BOULEVARD
RATHINGLE ROAD
FOREST AVENUE
FOREST WALK
CHERRY GARTH
CHERRY AVENUE
CHERRY PARK
HAWTHORN PARK
VALLEY GROVE
FOREST FIELDS RD
RIDGEWOOD AV
RIDGEWOOD AVENUE
RIDGE COURT
RIDGEWOOD GREEN
RIDGE GREEN
THE OAKS
THE NURSERIES
FOREST ROAD
BOROIMHE LAURELS
BOROIMHE WILLOWS
BOROIMHE PINES
BOROIMHE POPLARS
BOROIMHE OAKS
BOR. ELMS
BOROIMHE MAPLES
BOROIMHE ASPEN
BOROIMHE ALDER
BOROIMHE BEECH
NAUL ROAD
DUBLIN ROAD
DUBLIN STREET
CHURCH ROAD
R125

8

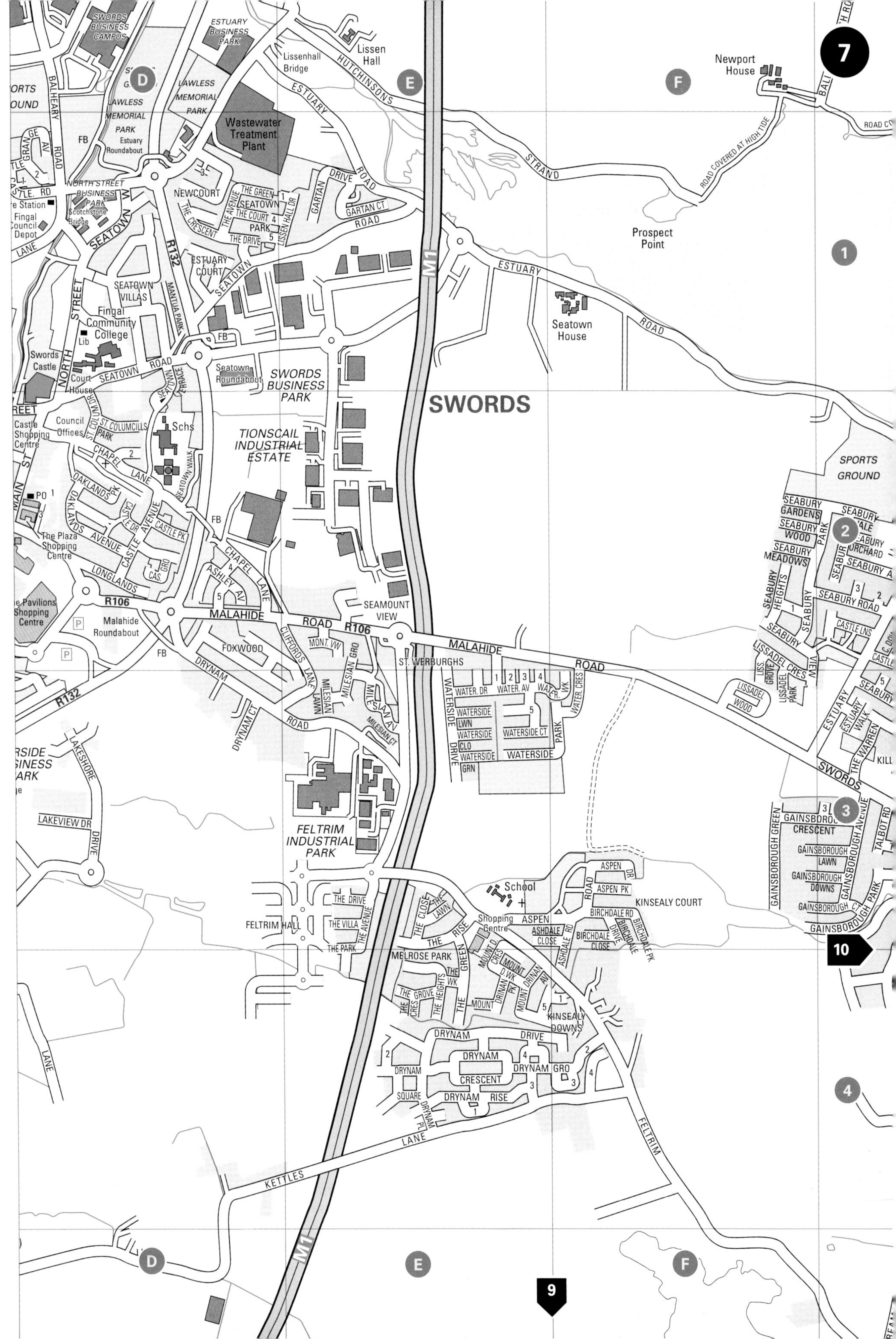

7
SWORDS
Swords Business Campus
Estuary Business Park
Lissen Hall
Lissenhall Bridge
Hutchinsons
Estuary
Newport House
Lawless Memorial Park
Wastewater Treatment Plant
Estuary Roundabout
Newcourt
North Street Business Park
Scotchstone Bridge
Fingal Council Depot
Strand
Road covered at high tide
Prospect Point
Gartan Drive
Gartan Ct
Estuary Road
Estuary Court
Seatown Villas
Seatown House
Fingal Community College
Lib
Swords Castle
Court House
Seatown Road
Seatown Roundabout
Swords Business Park
Tionscail Industrial Estate
Council Offices
Castle Shopping Centre
Schs
Chapel Lane
Oaklands Avenue
Castle Avenue
The Plaza Shopping Centre
Pavilions Shopping Centre
Malahide Roundabout
Malahide Road
R106
R132
M1
Seamount View
St. Werburghs
Foxwood
Cliffords Lane
Milesian Lawn
Drynam Road
Drynam Ct
Waterside
Waterside Drive
Sports Ground
Seabury Gardens
Seabury Wood
Seabury Meadows
Seabury Heights
Seabury Road
Lissadel Wood
Swords Road
Gainsborough Crescent
Gainsborough Lawn
Gainsborough Downs
Talbot Rd
Lakeshore Drive
Lakeview Dr
Feltrim Industrial Park
Feltrim Hall
The Drive
The Villa
The Park
The Avenue
School
Kinsealy Court
Shopping Centre
Aspen
Ashdale Close
Birchdale Close
Birchdale Pk
Melrose Park
Mount Drinan
Kinsealy Downs
Drynam Drive
Drynam Crescent
Drynam Gro
Drynam Rise
Drynam Square
Drynam Pl
Kettles Lane
Feltrim
Lane
10
9

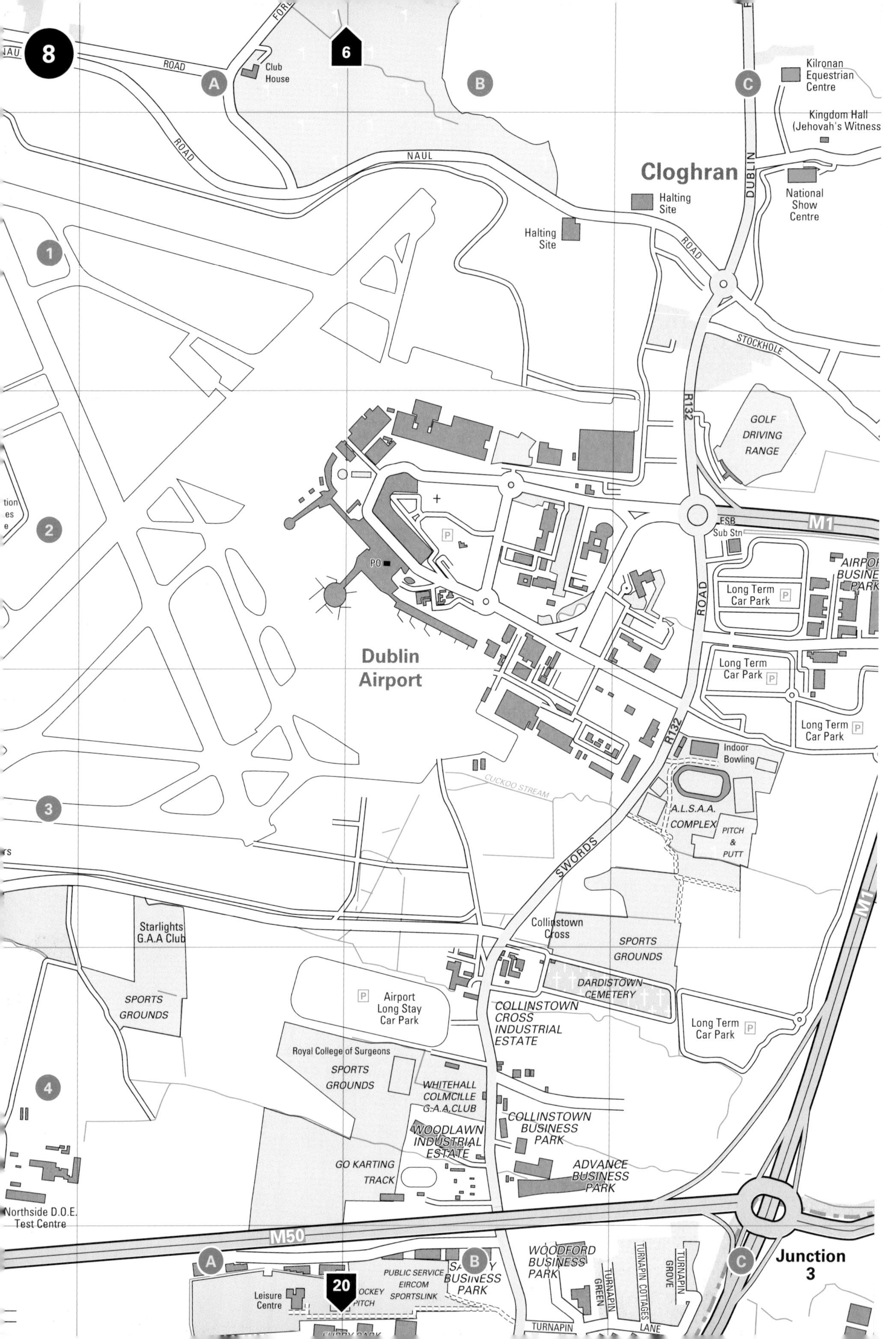
8
6
20
ROAD
Club House
NAUL
ROAD
Kilronan Equestrian Centre
Kingdom Hall (Jehovah's Witness)
Cloghran
DUBLIN
Halting Site
National Show Centre
Halting Site
ROAD
STOCKHOLE
R132
GOLF DRIVING RANGE
M1
ESB Sub Stn
Long Term Car Park
PO
ROAD
Dublin Airport
Long Term Car Park
Long Term Car Park
R132
Indoor Bowling
CUCKOO STREAM
A.L.S.A.A. COMPLEX
PITCH & PUTT
SWORDS
Collinstown Cross
SPORTS GROUNDS
Starlights G.A.A Club
DARDISTOWN CEMETERY
Airport Long Stay Car Park
COLLINSTOWN CROSS INDUSTRIAL ESTATE
Long Term Car Park
SPORTS GROUNDS
Royal College of Surgeons
SPORTS GROUNDS
WHITEHALL COLMCILLE G.A.A.CLUB
COLLINSTOWN BUSINESS PARK
WOODLAWN INDUSTRIAL ESTATE
GO KARTING TRACK
ADVANCE BUSINESS PARK
Northside D.O.E. Test Centre
M50
WOODFORD BUSINESS PARK
TURNAPIN GREEN
TURNAPIN COTTAGES
GROVE
TURNAPIN
LANE
Junction 3
PUBLIC SERVICE EIRCOM SPORTSLINK
BUSINESS PARK
Leisure Centre
TURNAPIN

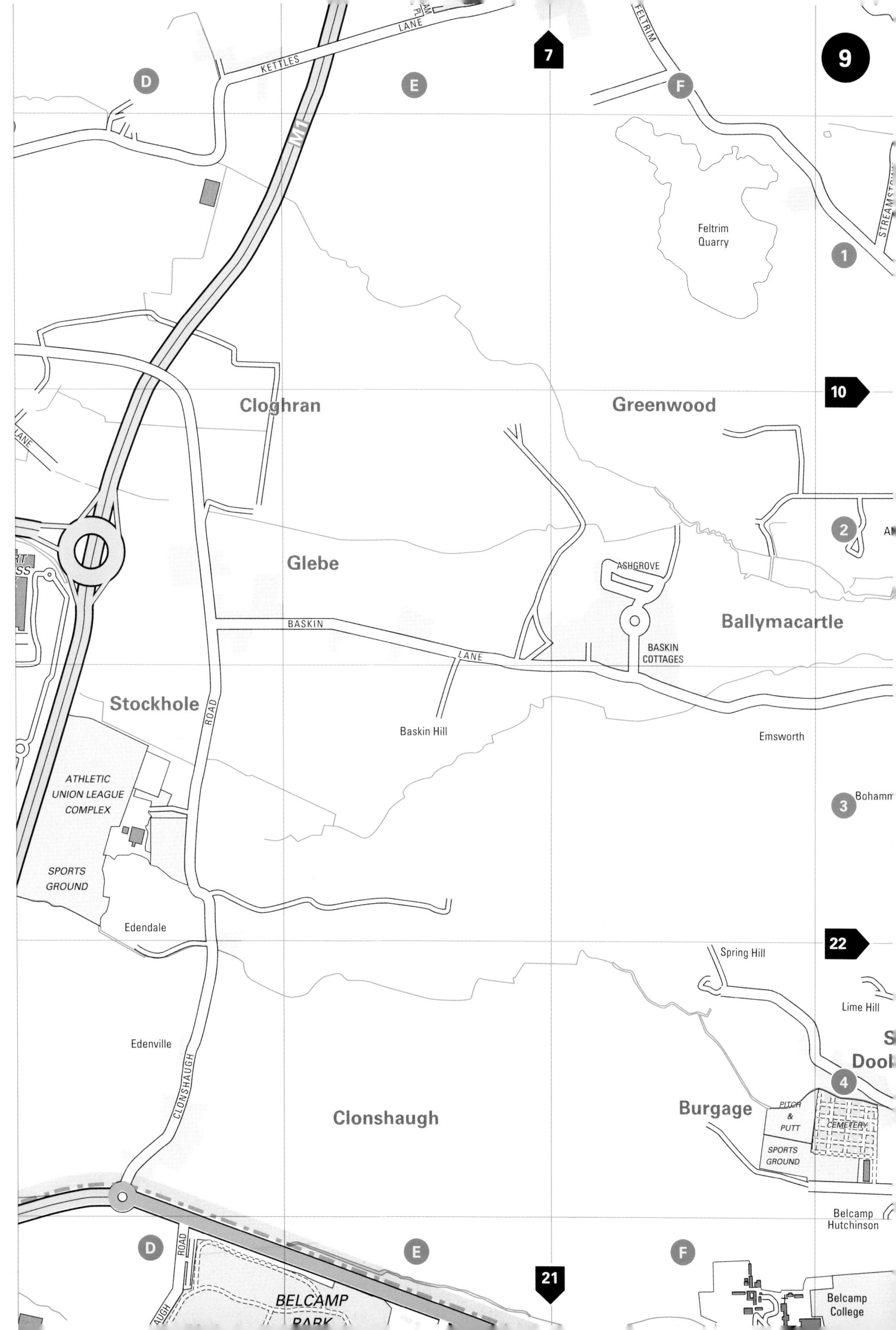
9
7
10
22
21
D
E
F
1
2
3
4
KETTLES
LANE
FELTRIM
M1
Feltrim Quarry
Cloghran
Greenwood
Glebe
ASHGROVE
BASKIN
LANE
BASKIN COTTAGES
Ballymacartle
Stockhole
ROAD
Baskin Hill
Emsworth
ATHLETIC UNION LEAGUE COMPLEX
SPORTS GROUND
Edendale
Spring Hill
Lime Hill
Edenville
CLONSHAUGH
Clonshaugh
Burgage
PITCH & PUTT
CEMETERY
SPORTS GROUND
Belcamp Hutchinson
ROAD
BELCAMP
Belcamp College

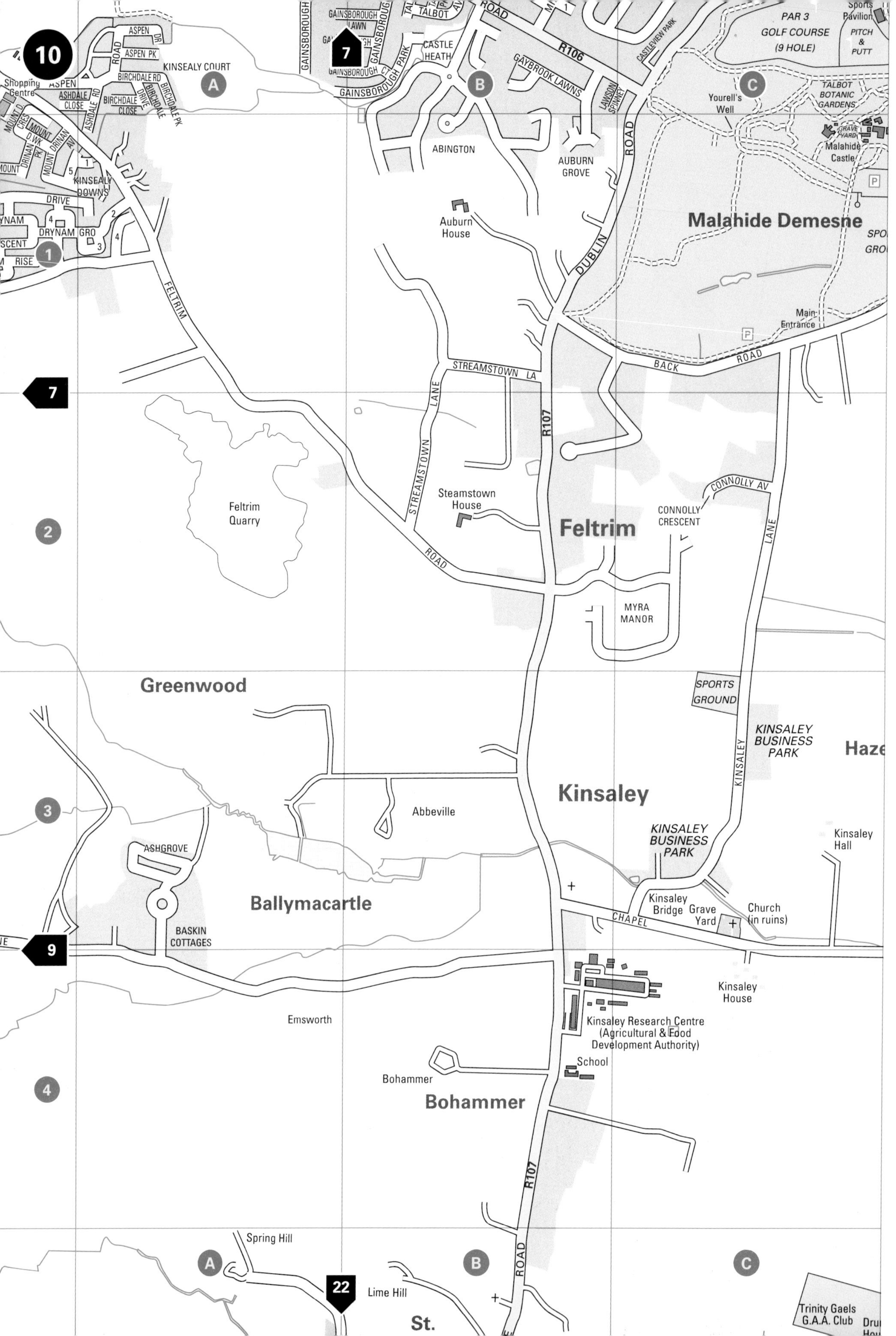
10
7
Malahide Demesne
PAR 3 GOLF COURSE (9 HOLE)
PITCH & PUTT
Sports Pavilion
TALBOT BOTANIC GARDENS
Yourell's Well
Malahide Castle
Main Entrance
KINSEALY COURT
Shopping Centre
ASPEN
ASPEN DR
ASPEN PK
ASHDALE CLOSE
ASHDALE RD
BIRCHDALE RD
BIRCHDALE CLOSE
BIRCHDALE DRIVE
BIRCHDALE PK
KINSEALY DOWNS
DRIVE
DRYNAM GRO
RISE
GAINSBOROUGH
GAINSBOROUGH LAWN
GAINSBOROUGH PARK
TALBOT
CASTLE HEATH
GAYBROOK LAWNS
LAWSON SPINNEY
CASTLEVIEW PARK
R106
ABINGTON
AUBURN GROVE
Auburn House
DUBLIN ROAD
FELTRIM
STREAMSTOWN LA
STREAMSTOWN LANE
BACK ROAD
R107
Feltrim Quarry
Steamstown House
Feltrim
CONNOLLY AV
CONNOLLY CRESCENT
ROAD
MYRA MANOR
Greenwood
SPORTS GROUND
KINSALEY BUSINESS PARK
KINSALEY LANE
Haze
Kinsaley
Abbeville
KINSALEY BUSINESS PARK
Kinsaley Hall
ASHGROVE
Ballymacartle
Kinsaley Bridge
Grave Yard
Church (in ruins)
CHAPEL
BASKIN COTTAGES
9
Kinsaley House
Emsworth
Kinsaley Research Centre (Agricultural & Food Development Authority)
School
Bohammer
Bohammer
Spring Hill
22
Lime Hill
St.
Trinity Gaels G.A.A. Club
A
B
C
1
2
3
4

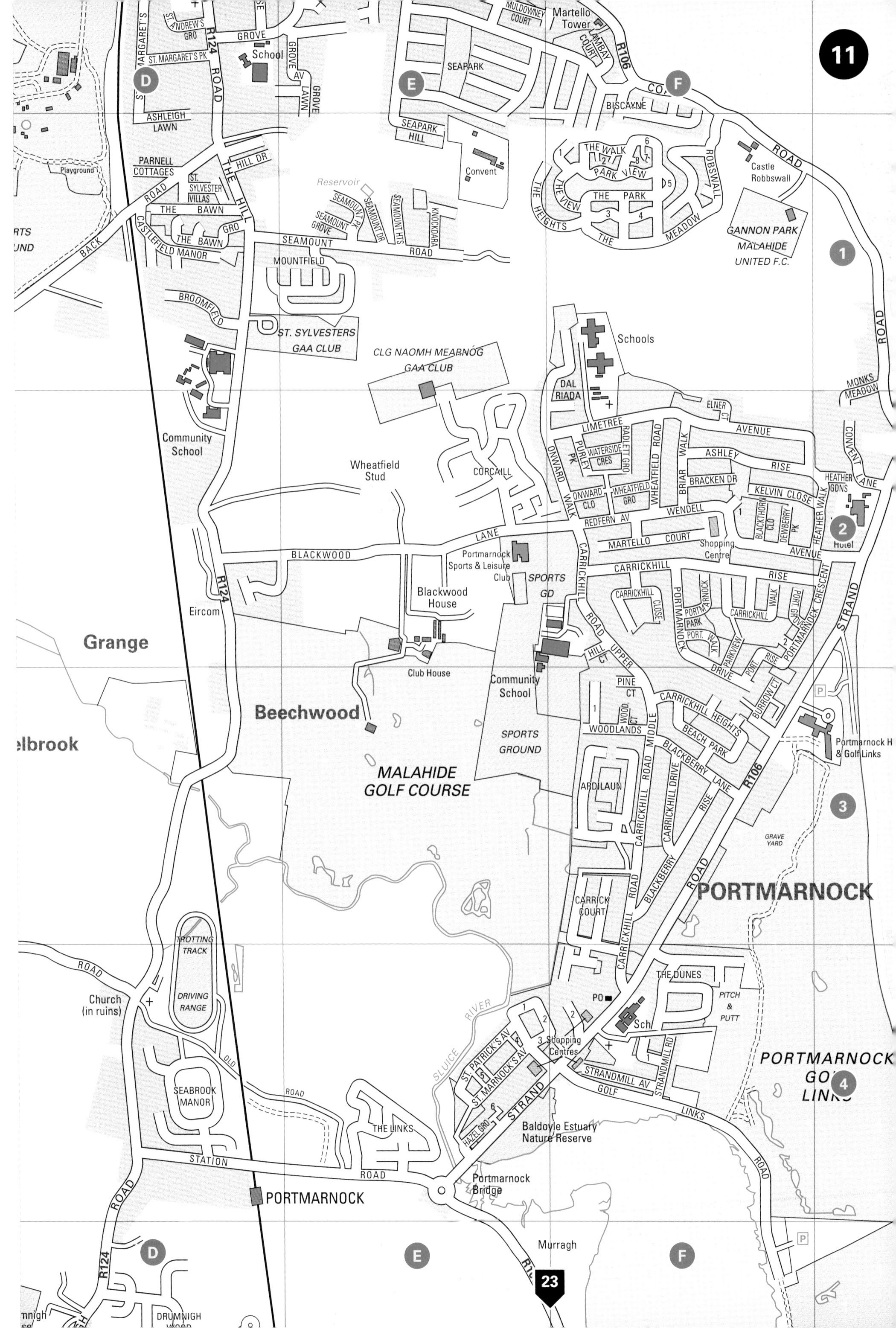
11
D
E
F
Grange
Beechwood
MALAHIDE GOLF COURSE
PORTMARNOCK
PORTMARNOCK GOLF LINKS
Baldoyle Estuary Nature Reserve
Portmarnock Bridge
Murragh
Martello Tower
Castle Robbswall
GANNON PARK MALAHIDE UNITED F.C.
Convent
School
Schools
Community School
ST. SYLVESTERS GAA CLUB
CLG NAOMH MEARNÓG GAA CLUB
Wheatfield Stud
Blackwood House
Club House
Portmarnock Sports & Leisure Club
SPORTS GD
SPORTS GROUND
Shopping Centre
Hotel
Portmarnock Hotel & Golf Links
Eircom
Church (in ruins)
TROTTING TRACK
DRIVING RANGE
PITCH & PUTT
GRAVE YARD
Shopping Centres
PO
Sch
Reservoir
Playground
R124
R106
SEAPARK
SEAPARK HILL
MULDOWNEY COURT
LAMBAY COURT
BISCAYNE
THE WALK
PARK VIEW
THE VIEW
THE PARK
THE HEIGHTS
THE MEADOW
ROBSWALL
ST. ANDREW'S GRO
ST. MARGARET'S PK
ASHLEIGH LAWN
PARNELL COTTAGES
ST. SYLVESTER VILLAS
THE BAWN
THE HILL
HILL DR
CASTLEFIELD MANOR
SEAMOUNT ROAD
SEAMOUNT PK
SEAMOUNT DR
SEAMOUNT HTS
SEAMOUNT GROVE
KNOCKDARA
MOUNTFIELD
BROOMFIELD
BACK ROAD
BLACKWOOD LANE
CORCAILL
DAL RIADA
LIMETREE AVENUE
ELNER CT
ASHLEY RISE
MONKS MEADOW
CONVENT LANE
HEATHER GDNS
HEATHER WALK
KELVIN CLOSE
BLACKTHORN CLO
DEWBERRY PK
WENDELL AVENUE
REDFERN AV
MARTELLO COURT
ONWARD WALK
ONWARD CLO
PURLEY PK
WATERSIDE CRES
RADLETT GRO
WHEATFIELD ROAD
WHEATFIELD GRO
BRIAR WALK
BRACKEN DR
CARRICKHILL ROAD
CARRICKHILL RISE
CARRICKHILL CLOSE
CARRICKHILL WALK
PORT GRO
PORTMARNOCK CRESCENT
PORTMARNOCK DRIVE
PORTMARNOCK PARK
PORT. WALK
PARKVIEW
PORT. RISE
BURROW CT
HILL CT
UPPER
PINE CT
WOOD. CT
CARRICKHILL HEIGHTS
BEACH PARK
WOODLANDS
ARDILAUN
CARRICKHILL ROAD MIDDLE
CARRICKHILL DRIVE
BLACKBERRY LANE
BLACKBERRY RISE
STRAND ROAD
CARRICK COURT
THE DUNES
STRANDMILL RD
STRANDMILL AV
GOLF LINKS ROAD
ST. PATRICK'S AV
ST. MARNOCK'S AV
HAZEL GRO
STRAND
SLUICE RIVER
OLD ROAD
SEABROOK MANOR
THE LINKS
STATION ROAD
PORTMARNOCK
DRUMNIGH WOOD
23

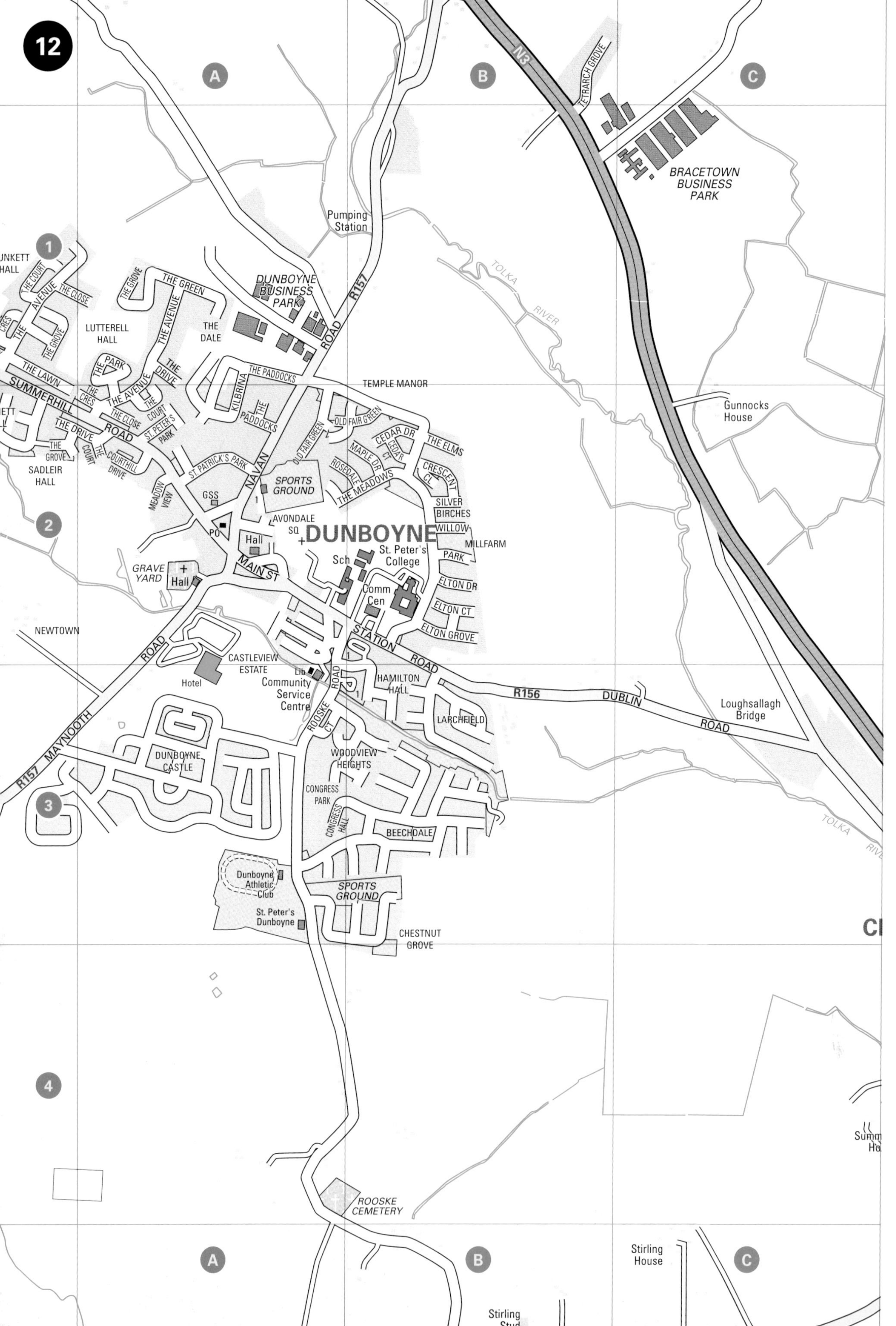

A B C

1

PLUNKETT HALL

THE COURT
THE AVENUE
THE CLOSE
THE GROVE
CRES
THE GROVE

LUTTERELL HALL

THE GROVE
THE AVENUE
THE PARK
THE AVENUE
THE DRIVE
THE DALE

THE GREEN

DUNBOYNE BUSINESS PARK

Pumping Station

NAVAN ROAD

R157

TOLKA

RIVER

BRACETOWN BUSINESS PARK

Gunnocks House

SUMMERHILL ROAD
THE LAWN
ETT
THE CRES
THE CLOSE
THE COURT
THE DRIVE
THE COURT
THE GROVE
SADLEIR HALL
COURTHILL DRIVE
MEADOW VIEW

THE PADDOCKS

KILBRINA
ST PETER'S PARK
ST PATRICK'S PARK
THE PADDOCKS
OLD FAIR GREEN
NAVAN
GSS
1
PO
Hall
AVONDALE SQ

TEMPLE MANOR

OLD FAIR GREEN
CEDAR DR
CEDAR
MAPLE DR
ROSEDALE
THE MEADOWS
THE ELMS
CRESCENT CL
SILVER BIRCHES
WILLOW PARK
MILLFARM

2

DUNBOYNE
St. Peter's College
Sch
Comm Cen

ELTON DR
ELTON CT
ELTON GROVE

GRAVE YARD
Hall

NEWTOWN

MAIN ST

STATION ROAD

MAYNOOTH ROAD
R157

Hotel

CASTLEVIEW ESTATE

Lib
Community Service Centre

ROOSKE CT
ROOSKE

ROAD

HAMILTON HALL

LARCHFIELD

R156 DUBLIN ROAD

Loughsallagh Bridge

TOLKA River

DUNBOYNE CASTLE

WOODVIEW HEIGHTS

CONGRESS PARK
Congress Hall

BEECHDALE

3

Dunboyne Athletic Club

St. Peter's Dunboyne

SPORTS GROUND

CHESTNUT GROVE

CH

4

Summ Ho

ROOSKE CEMETERY

Stirling House

A B C

Stirling Stud

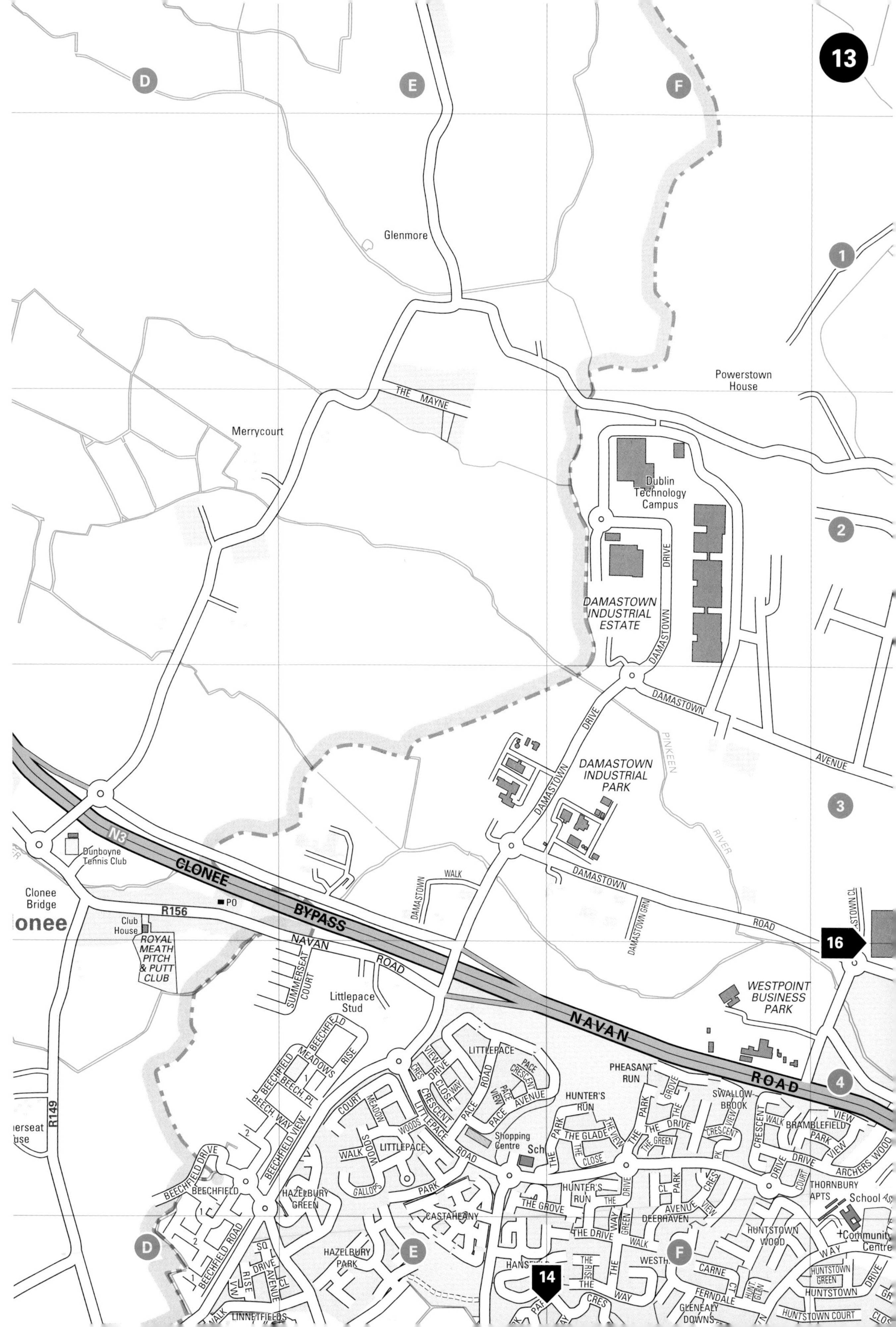

D E F

1

Glenmore

Powerstown House

THE MAYNE

Merrycourt

Dublin Technology Campus

2

DAMASTOWN INDUSTRIAL ESTATE

DAMASTOWN DRIVE

DAMASTOWN AVENUE

PINKEEN

RIVER

DAMASTOWN INDUSTRIAL PARK

DAMASTOWN DRIVE

3

N3

CLONEE BYPASS

Dunboyne Tennis Club

Clonee Bridge

onee

Club House

R156

PO

ROYAL MEATH PITCH & PUTT CLUB

R149

NAVAN ROAD

SUMMERSEAT COURT

DAMASTOWN WALK

DAMASTOWN GRN

DAMASTOWN ROAD

16

WESTPOINT BUSINESS PARK

DAMASTOWN CL

NAVAN ROAD

4

erseat use

Littlepace Stud

BEECHFIELD MEADOWS

RISE

BEECH PL

BEECHFIELD VIEW

BEECH WAY

BEECHFIELD DRIVE

BEECHFIELD

1 2

HAZELBURY GREEN

SQ DRIVE RISE VW

BEECHFIELD ROAD

LINNETFIELDS

2

COURT MEADOW

WOODS WALK

GALLOPS WALK

PARK

HAZELBURY PARK

CASTAHEANY

LITTLEPACE VIEW DRS CLOSE WAY

CRESCENT

LITTLEPACE WOODS

LITTLEPACE

LITTLEPACE ROAD

LITTLEPACE

PACE ROAD

PACE VIEW

PACE CRESCENT

PACE AVENUE

Shopping Centre Sch

HUNTER'S RUN

THE GLADE

THE CLOSE

HUNTER'S RUN

THE GROVE

THE DRIVE

THE WAY

HANSF

THE RISE

THE CRES

THE WAY

WESTH

PHEASANT RUN

THE PARK

THE GREEN

THE PK

CL PARK

THE CL

AVENUE

DEERHAVEN

CARNE

FERNDALE

GLENEALY DOWNS

SWALLOW BROOK

CRESCENT

THE DRIVE

THE DRIVE

WALK

VIEW

BRAMBLEFIELD PARK

ARCHERS WOOD

THORNBURY APTS

School

+Community Centre

HUNTSTOWN WOOD

HUNTSTOWN GREEN

WAY

HUNTSTOWN COURT

HUNTSTOWN

CLOS

DRIVE

14

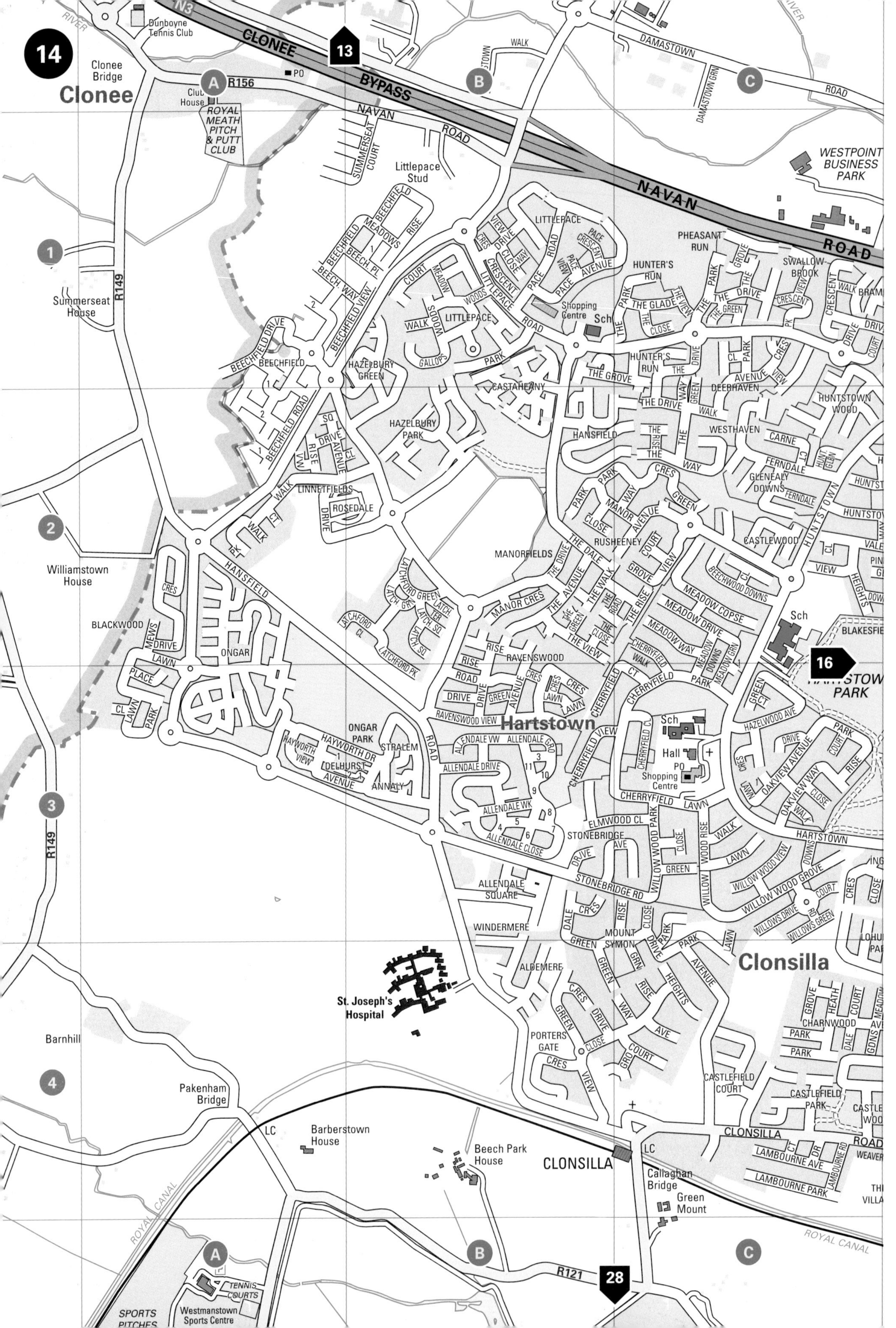
14
13
16
28
A
B
C
1
2
3
4
Clonee
Clonee Bridge
Dunboyne Tennis Club
N3
CLONEE BYPASS
R156
PO
Club House
ROYAL MEATH PITCH & PUTT CLUB
NAVAN ROAD
NAVAN ROAD
DAMASTOWN
DAMASTOWN GRN
ROAD
WALK
WESTPOINT BUSINESS PARK
SUMMERSEAT COURT
Littlepace Stud
R149
Summerseat House
Williamstown House
BEECHFIELD MEADOWS
BEECHFIELD RISE
BEECH PL
BEECH WAY
BEECHFIELD VIEW
BEECHFIELD DRIVE
BEECHFIELD
BEECHFIELD ROAD
HAZELBURY GREEN
HAZELBURY PARK
LITTLEPACE
LITTLEPACE CRESCENT
LITTLEPACE ROAD
LITTLEPACE WOODS
LITTLEPACE GALLOPS
LITTLEPACE MEADOW
LITTLEPACE COURT
LITTLEPACE WALK
PACE ROAD
PACE CRESCENT
PACE AVENUE
PACE VIEW
Shopping Centre
Sch
PHEASANT RUN
HUNTER'S RUN
THE GLADE
THE CLOSE
THE GREEN
THE DRIVE
THE PARK
SWALLOW-BROOK
CASTAHEANY
HUNTER'S RUN
THE GROVE
DEERHAVEN
HANSFIELD
WESTHAVEN
CARNE
HUNTSTOWN WOOD
FERNDALE
GLENEALY DOWNS
HUNTSTOWN
CASTLEWOOD
LINNETFIELDS
ROSEDALE
MANORFIELDS
RUSHEENEY
THE DALE
THE AVENUE
THE WALK
THE RISE
MEADOW COPSE
MEADOW DRIVE
MEADOW WAY
MEADOW DOWNS
BEECHWOOD DOWNS
BLAKESFIELD
HARTSTOWN PARK
BLACKWOOD
MEWS
DRIVE
LAWN
PLACE
CL
PARK
CRES
ONGAR
HANSFIELD ROAD
LATCHFORD GREEN
LATCHFORD CL
LATCHFORD PK
LATCH SQ
MANOR CRES
RAVENSWOOD
RAVENSWOOD VIEW
Hartstown
ONGAR PARK
HAYWORTH DR
HAYWORTH VIEW
DELHURST AVENUE
STRALEM
ANNALY
ALLENDALE VW
ALLENDALE GRO
ALLENDALE DRIVE
ALLENDALE WK
ALLENDALE CLOSE
ALLENDALE SQUARE
CHERRYFIELD
CHERRYFIELD VIEW
CHERRYFIELD WALK
CHERRYFIELD CL
CHERRYFIELD LAWN
Hall
PO
HAZELWOOD AVE
OAKVIEW AVENUE
OAKVIEW WAY
HARTSTOWN
ELMWOOD CL
STONEBRIDGE AVE
STONEBRIDGE RD
WILLOW WOOD PARK
WILLOW WOOD RISE
WILLOW WOOD VIEW
WILLOW WOOD GROVE
WILLOW WOOD GREEN
WILLOWS DRIVE
WILLOWS GREEN
WINDERMERE
MOUNT SYMON
ALDEMERE
Clonsilla
St. Joseph's Hospital
PORTERS GATE
Barnhill
CHARNWOOD
CASTLEFIELD COURT
CASTLEFIELD PARK
CLONSILLA ROAD
LAMBOURNE AVE
LAMBOURNE PARK
LAMBOURNE RD
Pakenham Bridge
LC
Barberstown House
Beech Park House
CLONSILLA
Callaghan Bridge
Green Mount
ROYAL CANAL
R121
TENNIS COURTS
SPORTS PITCHES
Westmanstown Sports Centre

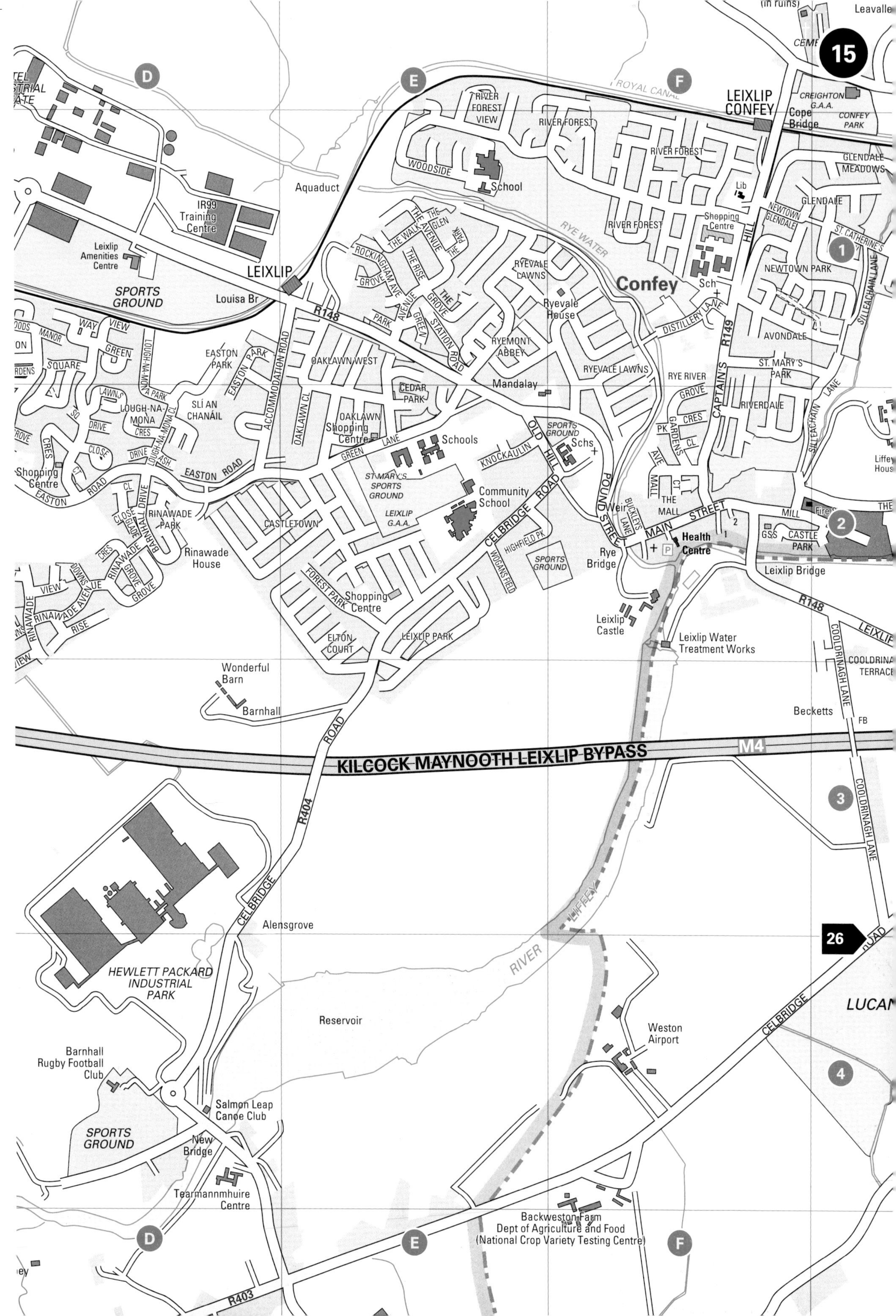
LEIXLIP CONFEY
Cope Bridge
ROYAL CANAL
CREIGHTON G.A.A.
CONFEY PARK
RIVER FOREST VIEW
RIVER FOREST
WOODSIDE
School
Aquaduct
IR99 Training Centre
Leixlip Amenities Centre
LEIXLIP
SPORTS GROUND
Louisa Br
R148
RYE WATER
Confey
Shopping Centre
Sch
Lib
GLENDALE MEADOWS
GLENDALE
NEWTOWN GLENDALE
ST. CATHERINE'S
NEWTOWN PARK
SILLEACHAIN LANE
AVONDALE
ST. MARY'S PARK
RIVERDALE
DISTILLERY LANE
CAPTAIN'S HILL
R149
RYE RIVER GROVE
RYEVALE LAWNS
Ryevale House
RYEMONT ABBEY
Mandalay
THE WALK
THE AVENUE
THE GLEN
THE PARK
THE RISE
THE GROVE
ROCKINGHAM GROVE
ROCKINGHAM AVE
STATION ROAD
OAKLAWN WEST
OAKLAWN CL
OAKLAWN Shopping Centre
CEDAR PARK
ACCOMMODATION ROAD
EASTON PARK
EASTON ROAD
SLÍ AN CHANÁIL
LOUGH-NA-MONA
Shopping Centre
Schools
ST MARY'S SPORTS GROUND
LEIXLIP G.A.A.
Community School
KNOCKAULIN
OLD HILL
SPORTS GROUND
Schs
POUND STREET
Weir
BUCKLEYS LANE
MAIN STREET
Health Centre
THE MALL
GARDENS
Rye Bridge
CASTLETOWN
CELBRIDGE ROAD
HIGHFIELD PK
WOGANSFIELD
SPORTS GROUND
FOREST PARK
Shopping Centre
ELTON COURT
LEIXLIP PARK
RINAWADE PARK
Rinawade House
RINAWADE AVENUE
BARNHALL DRIVE
Leixlip Castle
Leixlip Water Treatment Works
MILL
CASTLE PARK
GSS
Leixlip Bridge
COOLDRINAGH LANE
COOLDRINAGH TERRACE
Becketts
FB
Wonderful Barn
Barnhall
KILCOCK MAYNOOTH LEIXLIP BYPASS
M4
R404
CELBRIDGE ROAD
Alensgrove
HEWLETT PACKARD INDUSTRIAL PARK
RIVER LIFFEY
Reservoir
Weston Airport
CELBRIDGE ROAD
LUCAN
Barnhall Rugby Football Club
SPORTS GROUND
Salmon Leap Canoe Club
New Bridge
Tearmannmhuire Centre
Backweston Farm Dept of Agriculture and Food (National Crop Variety Testing Centre)
R403
D
E
F
1
2
3
4

26

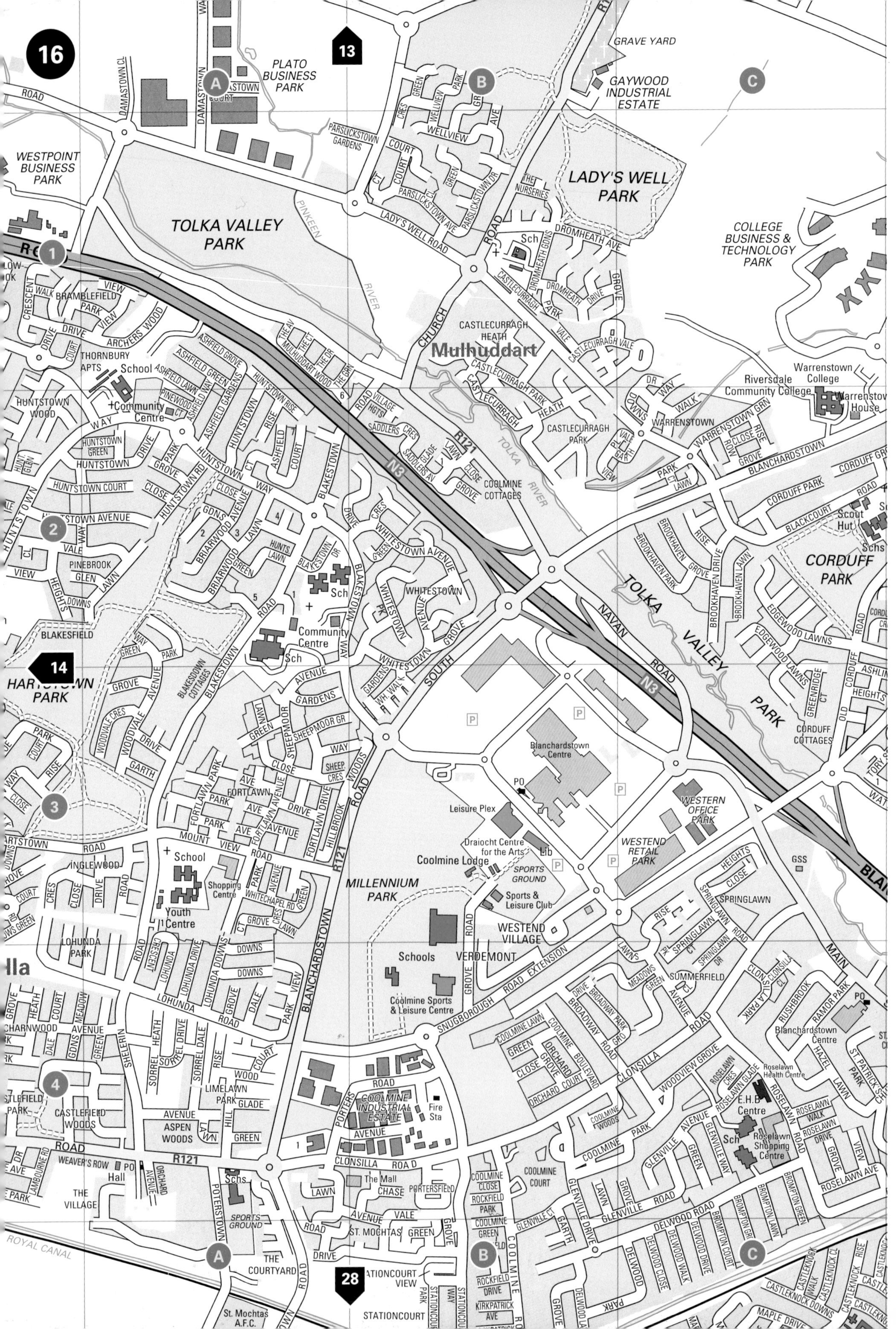

13
14
28
A
B
C
1
2
3
4
PLATO BUSINESS PARK
GRAVE YARD
GAYWOOD INDUSTRIAL ESTATE
WESTPOINT BUSINESS PARK
LADY'S WELL PARK
TOLKA VALLEY PARK
COLLEGE BUSINESS & TECHNOLOGY PARK
Mulhuddart
CASTLECURRAGH HEATH
Warrenstown College
Riversdale Community College
Warrenstown House
WARRENSTOWN
CASTLECURRAGH PARK
COOLMINE COTTAGES
TOLKA RIVER
PINKEEN RIVER
THORNBURY APTS
School
Community Centre
HUNTSTOWN WOOD
HUNTSTOWN AVENUE
HUNTSTOWN COURT
PINEBROOK
BLAKESFIELD
HARTSTOWN PARK
BLAKESDOWN COTTAGES
WHITESTOWN
WHITESTOWN AVENUE
Sch
N3
R121
NAVAN ROAD
TOLKA VALLEY PARK
CORDUFF PARK
CORDUFF COTTAGES
Scout Hut
Blanchardstown Centre
PO
Leisure Plex
Draiocht Centre for the Arts
Lib
Coolmine Lodge
SPORTS GROUND
Sports & Leisure Club
WESTERN OFFICE PARK
WESTEND RETAIL PARK
WESTEND VILLAGE
MILLENNIUM PARK
Schools
VERDEMONT
Coolmine Sports & Leisure Centre
SNUGBOROUGH ROAD EXTENSION
BLANCHARDSTOWN ROAD
MAIN
Shopping Centre
Youth Centre
LOHUNDA PARK
FORTLAWN
SPRINGLAWN
SUMMERFIELD
COOLMINE INDUSTRIAL ESTATE
Fire Sta
The Mall
PORTERSFIELD
COOLMINE COURT
Blanchardstown Centre
Roselawn Health Centre
E.H.B Centre
Roselawn Shopping Centre
CASTLEFIELD WOODS
ASPEN WOODS
WEAVER'S ROW
Hall
THE VILLAGE
Schs
SPORTS GROUND
ROYAL CANAL
THE COURTYARD
STATIONCOURT VIEW
STATIONCOURT
St. Mochtas A.F.C.
ST. MOCHTAS
CLONSILLA ROAD
GLENVILLE ROAD
DELWOOD ROAD
CASTLEKNOCK DOWNS
MAPLE DRIVE
GSS

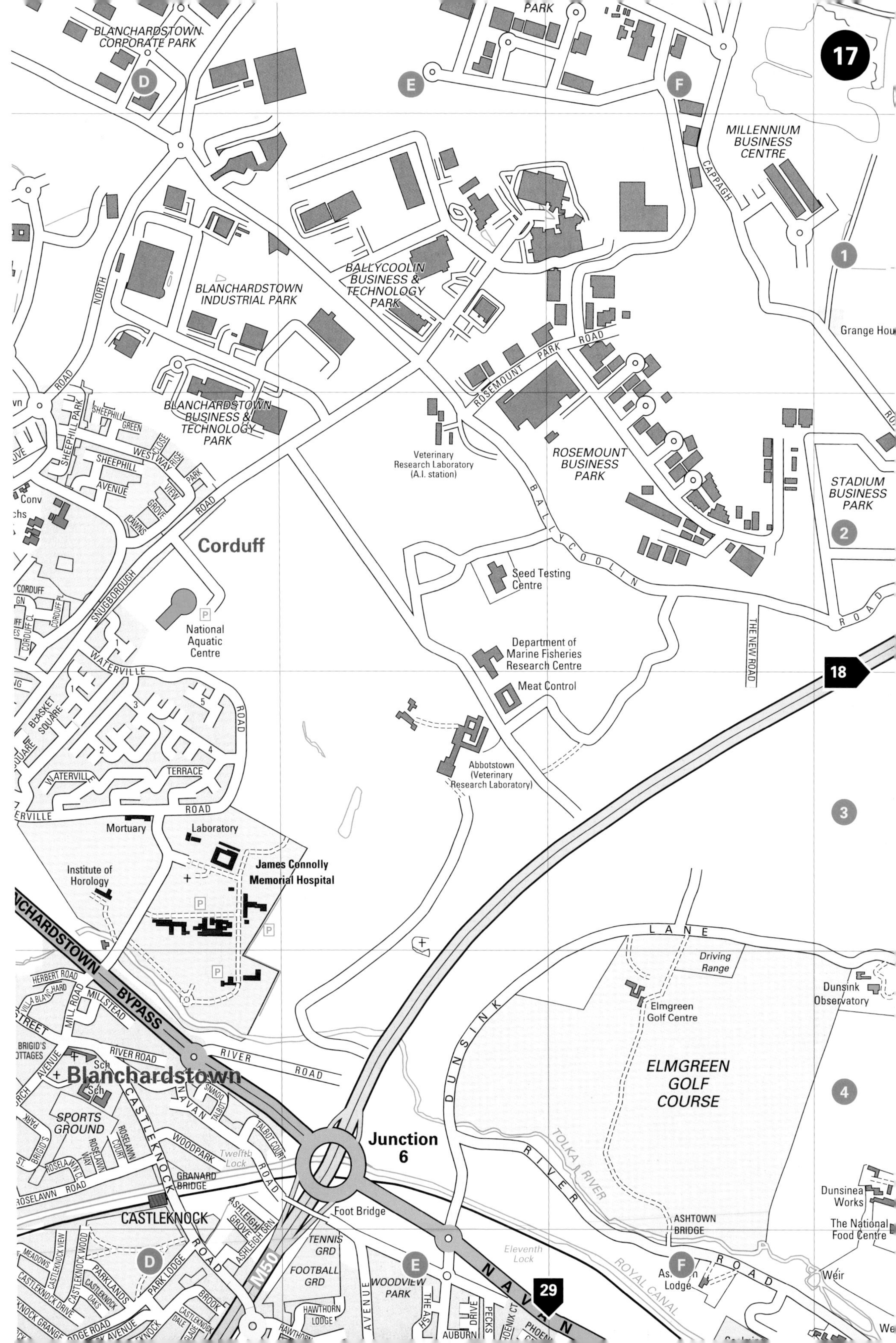

BLANCHARDSTOWN CORPORATE PARK

D

E

F

PARK

MILLENNIUM BUSINESS CENTRE

CAPPAGH

1

BALLYCOOLIN BUSINESS & TECHNOLOGY PARK

BLANCHARDSTOWN INDUSTRIAL PARK

ROSEMOUNT PARK ROAD

Grange Hou

NORTH ROAD

BLANCHARDSTOWN BUSINESS & TECHNOLOGY PARK

SHEEPHILL PARK

SHEEPHILL GREEN

WESTWAY

SHEEPHILL AVENUE

CLOSE

PARK

VIEW

GROVE

LAWNS

ROAD

Veterinary Research Laboratory (A.I. station)

ROSEMOUNT BUSINESS PARK

BALLYCOOLIN

STADIUM BUSINESS PARK

2

ROAD

THE NEW ROAD

Conv

chs

Corduff

SNUGBOROUGH ROAD

P

National Aquatic Centre

Seed Testing Centre

CORDUFF PL

CORDUFF

WATERVILLE

BASKET SQUARE

1

2

3

4

Department of Marine Fisheries Research Centre

Meat Control

18

CL

SGN

WATERVILLE ROAD

WATERVILL TERRACE

WATERVILLE ROAD

Abbotstown (Veterinary Research Laboratory)

3

TERVILLE

Mortuary

Laboratory

Institute of Horology

+

P

James Connolly Memorial Hospital

P

P

LANE

Driving Range

Dunsink Observatory

BLANCHARDSTOWN

BYPASS

DUNSINK

Elmgreen Golf Centre

Herbert Road

HERBERT ROAD

VILLA BLANCHARD

MILL ROAD

MILLSTEAD

STREET

BRIGID'S COTTAGES

AVENUE

RIVER ROAD

RIVER ROAD

Blanchardstown

Sch

NAVAN

Sch

SNAMOO

ELMGREEN GOLF COURSE

4

ARCH

SPORTS GROUND

ST BRIGID'S

ROSELAWN WAY

ROSELAWN

ROSELAWN ROAD

CASTLEKNOCK ROAD

ROSEMANN COURT

WOODPARK

Twelfth Lock

GRANARD BRIDGE

Junction 6

TALBOT COURT

DUNSINK

TOLKA RIVER

Dunsinea Works

The National Food Centre

CASTLEKNOCK

D

Park Lodge

MEADOWS

CASTLEKNOCK VIEW

PARKLANDS

CASTLEKNOCK DRIVE

CASTLEKNOCK OAKS

CASTLEKNOCK GRANGE

LODGE ROAD

KNOCK AVENUE

CASTLEKNOCK DALE

ASHLEIGH GROVE

ASHLEIGH GREEN

ASHLEIGH LAWN

BROOK

HAWTHORN LODGE

HAWTHORN

ROAD

M50

AVENUE

THE EAST

Foot Bridge

TENNIS GRD

FOOTBALL GRD

E

WOODVIEW PARK

NAVAN

29

Eleventh Lock

ASHTOWN BRIDGE

As n Lodge

F

ROAD

Weir

ROYAL CANAL

PECKS

PHOENIX

DRIVE

AUBURN

RIVER

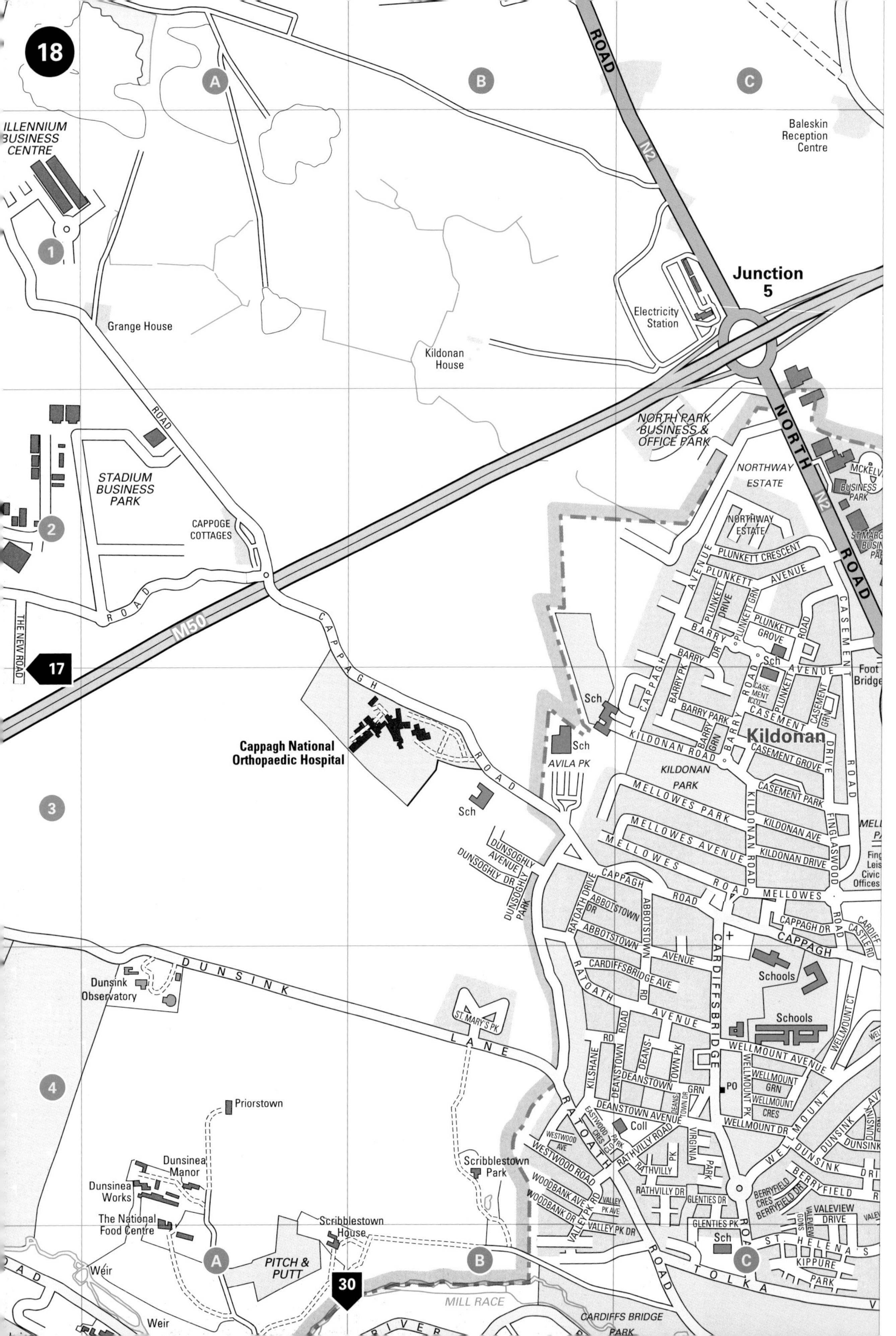

A   B   C

ILLENNIUM
BUSINESS
CENTRE

1

Grange House

Kildonan
House

Baleskin
Reception
Centre

Junction
5

Electricity
Station

NORTH PARK
BUSINESS &
OFFICE PARK

ROAD

N2

NORTH ROAD

NORTHWAY
ESTATE

MCKELV
BUSINESS
PA

STADIUM
BUSINESS
PARK

CAPPOGE
COTTAGES

ROAD

ROAD

M50

THE NEW ROAD

17

2

NORTHWAY
ESTATE

PLUNKETT CRESCENT

AVENUE

PLUNKETT DRIVE

AVENUE

PLUNKETT GRN

PLUNKETT GROVE

BARRY

BARRY PK

BARRY DR

PLUNKETT ROAD

CASE. MENT ECG

CASEMENT AVENUE

Sch

CASEMENT GRN

CASEMENT DRIVE

Kildonan

ST MARG
BUSINESS
PA

Foot
Bridge

CAPPAGH
ROAD

Sch

Sch

AVILA PK

CAPPAGH ROAD

Sch

Cappagh National
Orthopaedic Hospital

Sch

DUNSOGHLY AVENUE

DUNSOGHLY DR

DUNSOGHLY PARK

KILDONAN ROAD

BARRY PARK

BARRY GRN

KILDONAN
PARK

MELLOWES PARK

MELLOWES AVENUE

CASEMENT GROVE

CASEMENT PARK

KILDONAN AVE

KILDONAN DRIVE

MELLOWES ROAD

KILDONAN ROAD

FINGLASWOOD ROAD

MELLE
PA

Fing
Leis
Civic
Offices

3

CAPPAGH DR

CAPPAGH

MELLOWES

CAPPAGH ROAD

RATOATH DRIVE

ABBOTSTOWN DR

ABBOTSTOWN

ABBOTSTOWN
AVENUE

CARDIFFSBRIDGE AVE

CARDIFFSBRIDGE RD

CARDIFFSBRIDGE AVENUE

Schools

Schools

CARDIFF
CASTLE R

DUNSINK

Dunsink
Observatory

LANE

ST. MARY'S PK

RATOATH

KILSHANE RD

DEANSTOWN RD

DEANSTOWN

DEANS-
TOWN PK

DEANSTOWN GRN

WELLMOUNT AVENUE

PO

WELLMOUNT
GRN

WELLMOUNT
CRES

WELLMOUNT DR

WELLMOUNT CT

DUNSINK DRI

DUNSINK

DUNSINK

4

Priorstown

DEANSTOWN AVENUE

Coll

EASTWOOD CRES

WESTWOOD AVE

WESTWOOD ROAD

RATHVILLY RD

RATHVILLY

RATHVILLY PK

RATHVILLY DR

VIRGINIA PARK

GLENTIES DR

BERRYFIELD CRES

BERRYFIELD DRI

VALEVIEW GDNS

VALEVIEW DRIVE

AVI

Dunsinea
Manor

Dunsinea
Works

The National
Food Centre

Scribblestown
Park

Scribblestown
House

WOODBANK AVE

WOODBANK DR

VALLEY PK AVE

VALLEY PK RD

VALLEY PK DR

GLENTIES PK

Sch

ST. HELENA'S
PARK

KIPPURE
PARK

VALE

ROA

A

PITCH &
PUTT

30

B

MILL RACE

C

TOLKA

Weir

Weir

RIVER

CARDIFFS BRIDGE
PARK

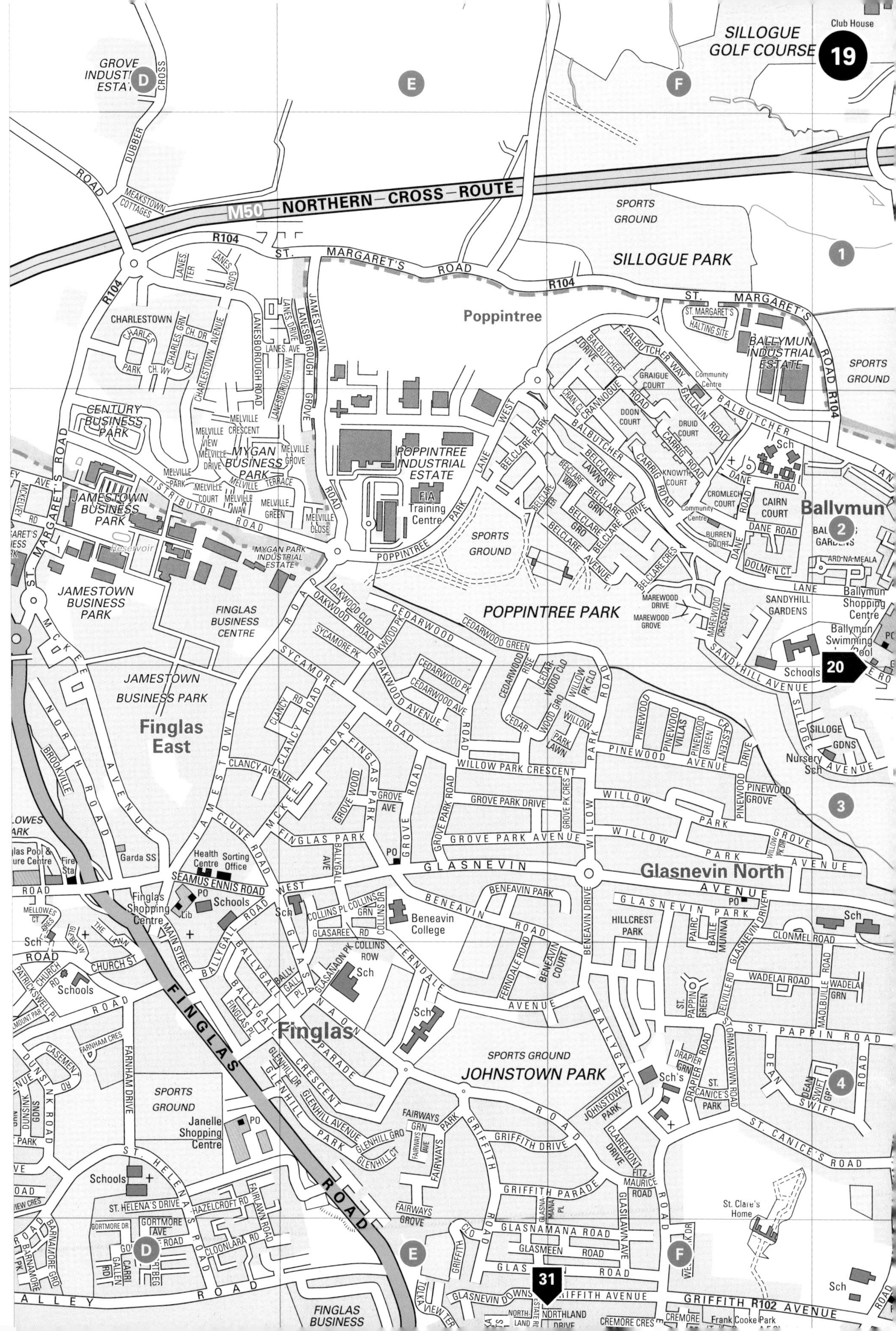

19
SILLOGUE GOLF COURSE
Club House
GROVE INDUSTRIAL ESTATE
D
E
F
1
2
3
4
DUBBER CROSS
ROAD
MEAKSTOWN COTTAGES
M50 NORTHERN CROSS ROUTE
R104
ST. MARGARET'S ROAD
SPORTS GROUND
SILLOGUE PARK
Poppintree
CHARLESTOWN
CHARLES PARK
CHARLESTOWN AVENUE
LANESBOROUGH ROAD
LANES DRIVE
LANES. AVE
LANESBOROUGH GROVE
JAMESTOWN
ST. MARGARET'S HALTING SITE
BALLYMUN INDUSTRIAL ESTATE
BALBUTCHER WAY
BALBUTCHER DRIVE
GRAIGUE COURT
Community Centre
CENTURY BUSINESS PARK
MELVILLE CRESCENT
MELVILLE VIEW
MELVILLE DRIVE
MYGAN BUSINESS PARK
MELVILLE GROVE
MELVILLE TERRACE
MELVILLE PARK
MELVILLE COURT
MELVILLE WAY
MELVILLE GREEN
MELVILLE CLOSE
POPPINTREE INDUSTRIAL ESTATE
FIA Training Centre
CRANNOGUE ROAD
DOON COURT
DRUID COURT
GALLAUN ROAD
BALBUTCHER LANE
CARRIG ROAD
KNOWTH COURT
CROMLECH COURT
DANE ROAD
CAIRN COURT
Ballymun
Sch
BELCLARE PARK
BELCLARE LAWNS
BELCLARE GRN
BELCLARE GRO
BELCLARE DRIVE
BELCLARE AVENUE
BELCLARE CRES
BELCLARE WAY
BELCLARE TER
JAMESTOWN BUSINESS PARK
DISTRIBUTOR ROAD
Reservoir
MYGAN PARK INDUSTRIAL ESTATE
POPPINTREE PARK
SPORTS GROUND
BURREN COURT
DOLMEN CT
ARD NA MEALA
SANDYHILL GARDENS
Ballymun Shopping Centre
Ballymun Swimming Pool
MAREWOOD DRIVE
MAREWOOD GROVE
MAREWOOD CRESCENT
SANDYHILL AVENUE
Schools
20
FINGLAS BUSINESS CENTRE
OAKWOOD CLO
OAKWOOD ROAD
OAKWOOD PK
SYCAMORE PK
CEDARWOOD
CEDARWOOD GREEN
CEDARWOOD RISE
CEDARWOOD PK
CEDARWOOD AVE
OAKWOOD AVENUE
WILLOW PK CLO
WILLOW PARK LAWN
WILLOW PARK ROAD
PINEWOOD
PINEWOOD VILLAS
PINEWOOD GREEN
PINEWOOD CRESCENT
PINEWOOD DRIVE
PINEWOOD AVENUE
PINEWOOD GROVE
SILLOGE GDNS
SILLOGE AVENUE
Nursery Sch
MCKEE
NORTH ROAD
BROOKVILLE
SYCAMORE ROAD
CLANCY ROAD
CLANCY AVENUE
Finglas East
JAMESTOWN ROAD
FINGLAS PARK
GROVEWOOD
GROVE AVE
GROVE ROAD
WILLOW PARK CRESCENT
GROVE PARK ROAD
GROVE PARK DRIVE
GROVE PK CRES
WILLOW PARK
WILLOW GROVE
GROVE PARK AVENUE
WILLOW PARK AVENUE
Glasnevin North
GLASNEVIN AVENUE
CLUNE ROAD
Health Centre
Sorting Office
Garda SS
Fire Sta
SEAMUS ENNIS ROAD
FINGLAS PARK
BALLYGALL AVE
PO
Finglas Shopping Centre
Lib
Schools
MAIN STREET
BALLYGALL ROAD WEST
COLLINS PL
COLLINS GRN
COLLINS DR
GLASAREE RD
COLLINS ROW
Beneavin College
BENEAVIN PARK
BENEAVIN ROAD
BENEAVIN DRIVE
BENEAVIN COURT
FERNDALE ROAD
FERNDALE AVENUE
HILLCREST PARK
GLASNEVIN PARK
PAIRC BAILE MUNNA
GLASNEVIN DRIVE
CLONMEL ROAD
WADELAI ROAD
WADELAI GRN
MAOLBUILLE ROAD
ST. PAPPIN GREEN
DELVILLE RD
STORMANSTOWN ROAD
ST. PAPPIN ROAD
GLASANAON PK
Sch
FINGLAS ROAD
CHURCH ST
THE LANE
PATRICKSWELL PL
CHURCH RD
Schools
FARNHAM CRES
FARNHAM DRIVE
CASEMENT RD
DUNSINK ROAD
BALLYGALL PL
FINGLAS PL
Finglas
NAOMH PARADE
GLENHILL DR
GLENHILL CRESCENT
GLENHILL AVENUE
GLENHILL PARK
GLENHILL GRO
GLENHILL CT
SPORTS GROUND
JOHNSTOWN PARK
JOHNSTOWN PARK
BALLYGALL ROAD
Sch's
DRAPIER GRN
DRAPIER ROAD
ST. CANICE'S PARK
DEAN SWIFT ROAD
DEAN SWIFT GRN
ST. CANICE'S ROAD
SPORTS GROUND
Janelle Shopping Centre
FAIRWAYS GRN
FAIRWAYS AVE
FAIRWAYS PARK
FAIRWAYS
FAIRWAYS GROVE
GRIFFITH ROAD
GRIFFITH DRIVE
CLAREMONT DRIVE
FITZMAURICE ROAD
GRIFFITH PARADE
GLASILAWN AVE
ST. HELENA'S ROAD
ST. HELENA'S DRIVE
HAZELCROFT RD
FAIRLAWN RD
CLOONLARA RD
GORTMORE AVE
GORTMORE DR
BARNAMORE GRO
BARNAMORE PK
CARRIGALLEN
ROAD
GLASNAMANA ROAD
GLASNAMANA PL
GLASMEEN ROAD
GLASILAWN ROAD
St. Clare's Home
Sch
GRIFFITH CLO
GLASNEVIN DOWNS
31
GRIFFITH AVENUE
R102
NORTHLAND DRIVE
CREMORE CRES
CREMORE
Frank Cooke Park
FINGLAS BUSINESS
TOLKA VIEW TER
ALLEY ROAD

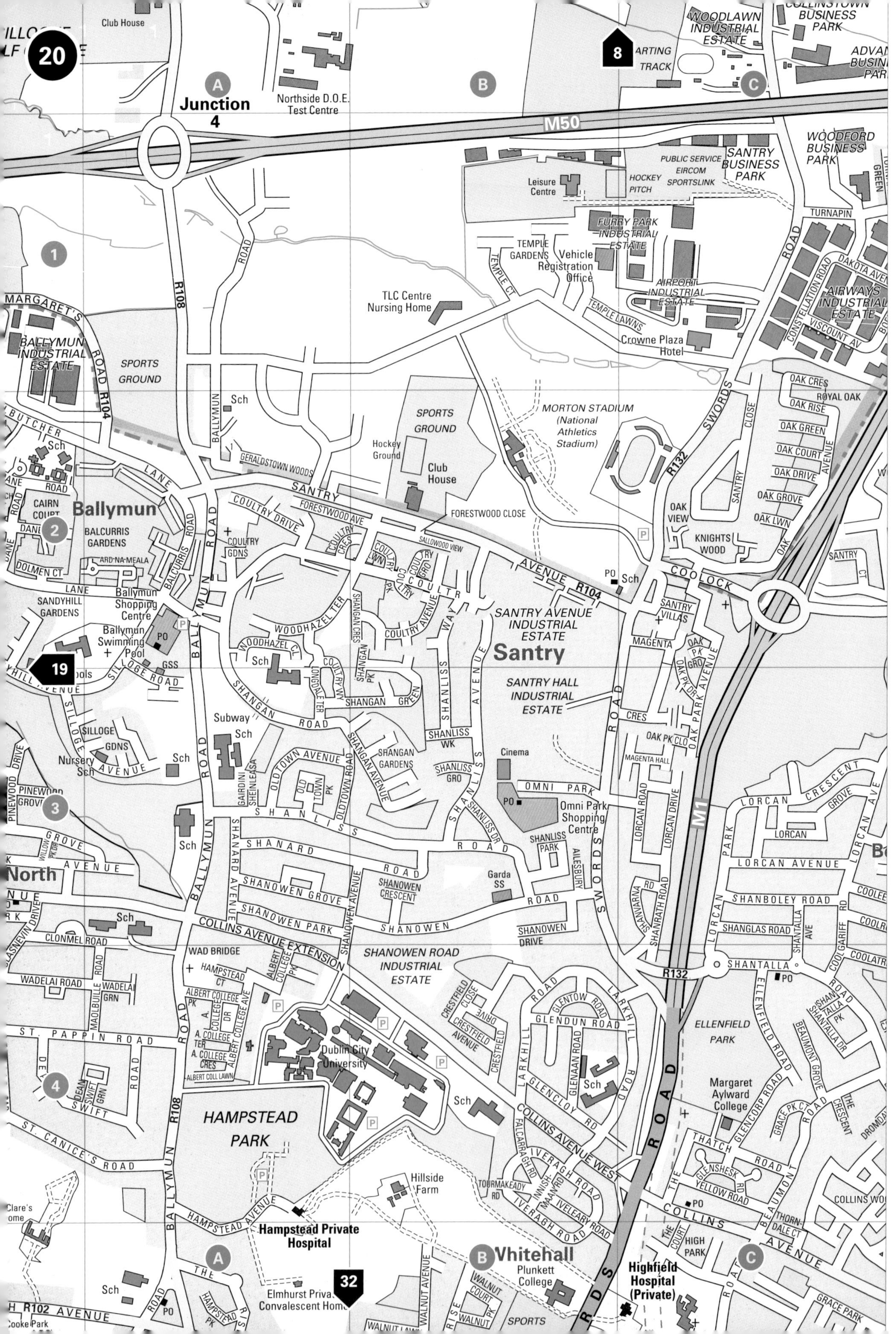
Junction 4
M50
Northside D.O.E. Test Centre
Club House
WOODLAWN INDUSTRIAL ESTATE
COLLINSTOWN BUSINESS PARK
KARTING TRACK
SANTRY BUSINESS PARK
WOODFORD BUSINESS PARK
PUBLIC SERVICE EIRCOM SPORTSLINK
HOCKEY PITCH
Leisure Centre
FURRY PARK INDUSTRIAL ESTATE
TEMPLE GARDENS
Vehicle Registration Office
AIRPORT INDUSTRIAL ESTATE
AIRWAYS INDUSTRIAL ESTATE
TLC Centre Nursing Home
Crowne Plaza Hotel
BALLYMUN INDUSTRIAL ESTATE
SPORTS GROUND
MORTON STADIUM (National Athletics Stadium)
Hockey Ground
Club House
Ballymun
Santry
SANTRY AVENUE INDUSTRIAL ESTATE
SANTRY HALL INDUSTRIAL ESTATE
Ballymun Shopping Centre
Ballymun Swimming Pool
Cinema
Omni Park Shopping Centre
Garda SS
SHANOWEN ROAD INDUSTRIAL ESTATE
Dublin City University
HAMPSTEAD PARK
Hillside Farm
Hampstead Private Hospital
Elmhurst Private Convalescent Home
Whitehall
Plunkett College
Highfield Hospital (Private)
ELLENFIELD PARK
Margaret Aylward College
North
M1
R108
R104
R132
R102
SWORDS ROAD
BALLYMUN ROAD
COLLINS AVENUE
COLLINS AVENUE EXTENSION
COLLINS AVENUE WEST
SANTRY AVENUE
COOLOCK LANE
SHANGAN ROAD
SHANLISS ROAD
SHANARD ROAD
SHANOWEN ROAD
LORCAN AVENUE
ST. PAPPIN ROAD
ST. CANICE'S ROAD
HAMPSTEAD AVENUE
19
8
32

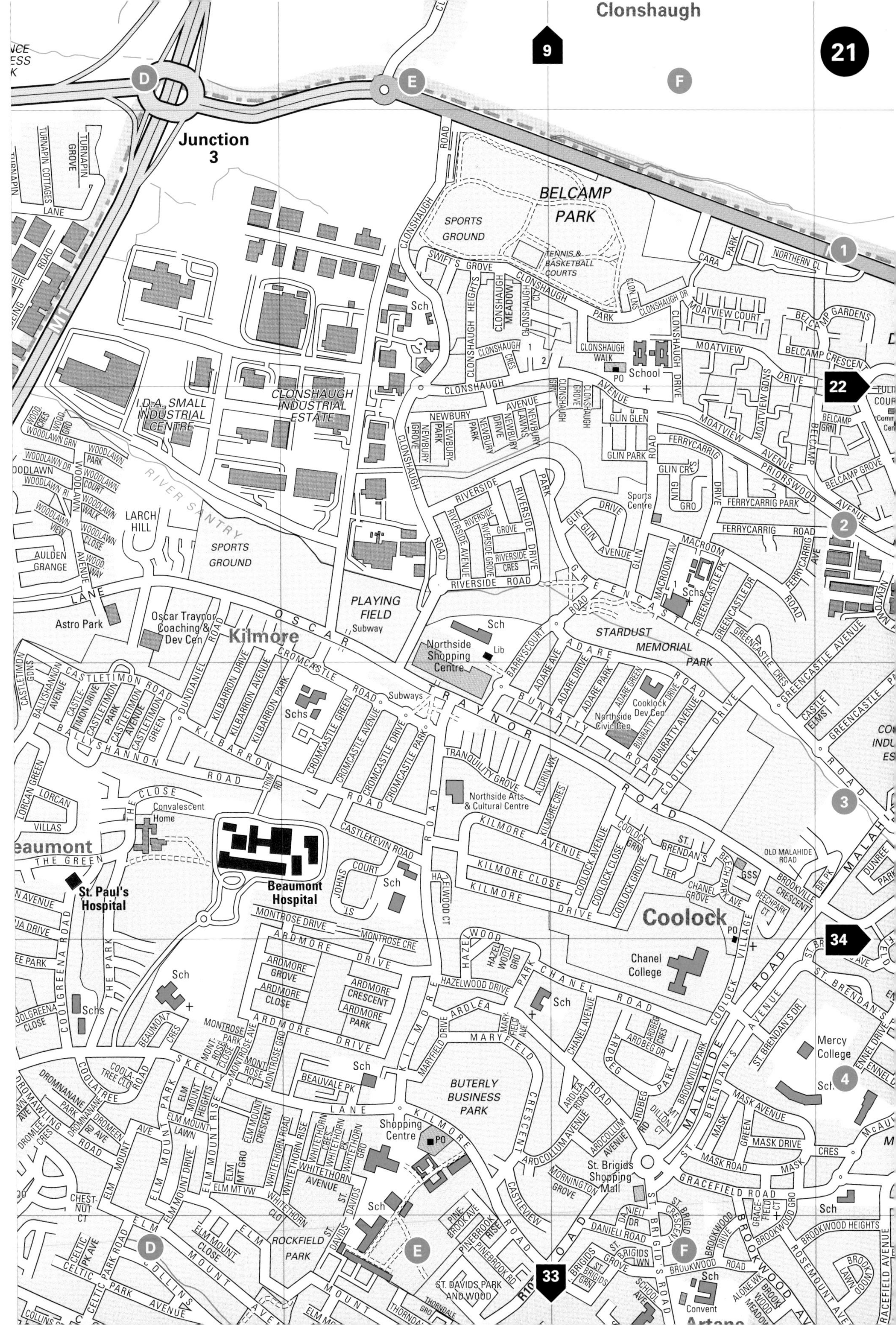
Clonshaugh
9
21
D
E
F
Junction 3
M1
BELCAMP PARK
SPORTS GROUND
TENNIS & BASKETBALL COURTS
TURNAPIN GROVE
TURNAPIN COTTAGES
LANE
CLONSHAUGH ROAD
SWIFT'S GROVE
CLONSHAUGH HEIGHTS
CLONSHAUGH MEADOW
CLONSHAUGH CT
CLONSHAUGH PARK
CLONSHAUGH DR
CLON LNS
CARA PARK
NORTHERN CL
MOATVIEW COURT
BELCAMP GARDENS
Sch
CLONSHAUGH CRES
CLONSHAUGH WALK
PO
School
CLONSHAUGH DRIVE
MOATVIEW
BELCAMP CRESCENT
22
MOATVIEW GDNS
DRIVE
CLONSHAUGH AVENUE
CLONSHAUGH INDUSTRIAL ESTATE
I.D.A. SMALL INDUSTRIAL CENTRE
NEWBURY GROVE
NEWBURY PARK
NEWBURY DRIVE
NEWBURY AVENUE
NEWBURY LAWNS
CLONSHAUGH GROVE
GLIN GLEN
GLIN PARK
GLIN ROAD
FERRYCARRIG
MOATVIEW AVENUE
BELCAMP GRN
BELCAMP
PRIORSWOOD AVENUE
BELCAMP GROVE
RIVER SANTRY
WOODLAWN CRES
WOODLAWN GRO
WOODLAWN GRN
WOODLAWN DR
WOODLAWN PARK
WOODLAWN COURT
WOODLAWN WALK
WOODLAWN VIEW
WOODLAWN CLOSE
WOODLAWN WAY
WOODLAWN AVENUE
LARCH HILL
SPORTS GROUND
RIVERSIDE
RIVERSIDE AVENUE
RIVERSIDE GROVE
RIVERSIDE DRIVE
RIVERSIDE CRES
RIVERSIDE ROAD
PARK
GLIN CRES
GLIN GRO
GLIN DRIVE
GLIN AVENUE
Sports Centre
FERRYCARRIG DRIVE
FERRYCARRIG PARK
FERRYCARRIG ROAD
FERRYCARRIG AVE
MACROOM
MACROOM AV
GREENCASTLE PK
GREENCASTLE DR
GREENCASTLE ROAD
Schs
AULDEN GRANGE
LANE
Astro Park
Oscar Traynor Coaching & Dev Cen
PLAYING FIELD
Subway
Kilmore
OSCAR TRAYNOR ROAD
Northside Shopping Centre
Sch
Lib
BARRYSCOURT
ADARE AVE
ADARE DRIVE
ADARE PARK
ADARE GREEN
ADARE
STARDUST MEMORIAL PARK
GREENCASTLE CRES
GREENCASTLE AVENUE
CASTLETIMON GDNS
BALLYSHANNON AVENUE
CASTLETIMON ROAD
CASTLETIMON DRIVE
CASTLETIMON PARK
CASTLETIMON AVENUE
CASTLETIMON GREEN
DUNDANIEL ROAD
KILBARRON DRIVE
KILBARRON AVENUE
KILBARRON PARK
CROMCASTLE ROAD
Schs
CROMCASTLE GREEN
CROMCASTLE AVENUE
CROMCASTLE DRIVE
CROMCASTLE PARK
Subways
BUNRATTY ROAD
Cooklock Dev Cen
Northside Civic Cen
BUNRATTY DRIVE
BUNRATTY AVENUE
COOLOCK DRIVE
CASTLE ELMS
GREENCASTLE
BALLYSHANNON ROAD
KILBARRON ROAD
TRIM RD
TRANQUILITY GROVE
ALDRIN WK
Northside Arts & Cultural Centre
KILMORE CRES
COOLOCK ROAD
3
LORCAN GREEN
LORCAN
VILLAS
THE CLOSE
Convalescent Home
Beaumont
THE GREEN
St. Paul's Hospital
Beaumont Hospital
CASTLEKEVIN ROAD
ST. JOHNS COURT
Sch
HAZELWOOD CT
KILMORE AVENUE
KILMORE CLOSE
KILMORE DRIVE
COOLOCK AVENUE
COOLOCK CLOSE
COOLOCK GROVE
COOLOCK GRN
ST. BRENDAN'S TER
BEECH PARK AVE
CHANEL GROVE
GSS
OLD MALAHIDE ROAD
BROOKVILLE CRESCENT
BEECHPARK CT
BR. PK
DUNREE PARK
Coolock
PO
COOLOCK VILLAGE
34
MONTROSE DRIVE
MONTROSE CRE
ARDMORE DRIVE
ARDMORE GROVE
ARDMORE CLOSE
ARDMORE CRESCENT
ARDMORE PARK
HAZELWOOD
HAZELWOOD GRO
HAZELWOOD DRIVE
Chanel College
CHANEL ROAD
ST. BRENDAN'S AVE
ST. BRENDAN'S DR
Mercy College
COOLGREENA ROAD
THE PARK
Sch
Schs
COOLGREENA CLOSE
BEAUMONT CRES
MONTROSE PARK
MONTROSE CLOSE
MONTROSE AVE
MONTROSE GRO
MONTROSE CT
ARDMORE DRIVE
KILMORE ROAD
ARDLEA ROAD
MARYFIELD DRIVE
MARYFIELD AVE
MARYFIELD CRESCENT
Sch
CHANEL AVENUE
ARDBEG ROAD
ARDBEG DR
ARDBEG CRES
ARDBEG PARK
BROOKVILLE PARK
MALAHIDE ROAD
4
Sch
COOLATREE CLO
COOLATREE
DROMNANANE PARK
DROMAWLING
DROMLEE CRES
DROMEEN AVE
SKELLY'S LANE
ELM MOUNT PARK
ELM MOUNT HEIGHTS
ELM MOUNT LAWN
ELM MOUNT RISE
ELM MOUNT CRESCENT
ELM MOUNT DRIVE
ELM MOUNT AVE
ELM MT GRO
ELM MT VW
BEAUVALE PK
WHITETHORN RISE
WHITETHORN CRES
WHITETHORN PK
WHITETHORN GRO
WHITETHORN AVENUE
WHITETHORN CLO
BUTERLY BUSINESS PARK
Shopping Centre
PO
ARDLEA ROAD
ARDCOLLUM AVENUE
ST. BRIGIDS Shopping Mall
MASK AVENUE
MASK GREEN
MASK DRIVE
MASK ROAD
MASK CRES
GRACEFIELD ROAD
GRACEFIELD CT
BROOKWOOD GRO
Sch
BROOKWOOD HEIGHTS
CHESTNUT CT
CELTIC PK AVE
CELTIC PARK ROAD
CELTIC PARK AVENUE
ELM MOUNT CLOSE
ELM MOUNT ROAD
COLLINS
ROCKFIELD PARK
ST. DAVIDS
Sch
PINEBROOK AVE
PINEBROOK RISE
PINEBROOK RD
CASTLEVIEW
MORNINGTON GROVE
DANIELI DR
DANIELI ROAD
ST. BRIGIDS CRESCENT
ST. BRIGIDS GROVE
ST. BRIGIDS LWN
ST. BRIGIDS GRN
ST. BRIGID'S ROAD
BROOKWOOD DRIVE
BROOKWOOD ROAD
BROOKWOOD AV
ROSEMOUNT AV
BROOKWOOD LAWN
GRACEFIELD AVENUE
ALONE WK
BROOKWOOD MEADOW
Sch
Convent
SCHOOL AVE
ST. DAVIDS PARK AND WOOD
33
THORNDALE GRO
MOUNT

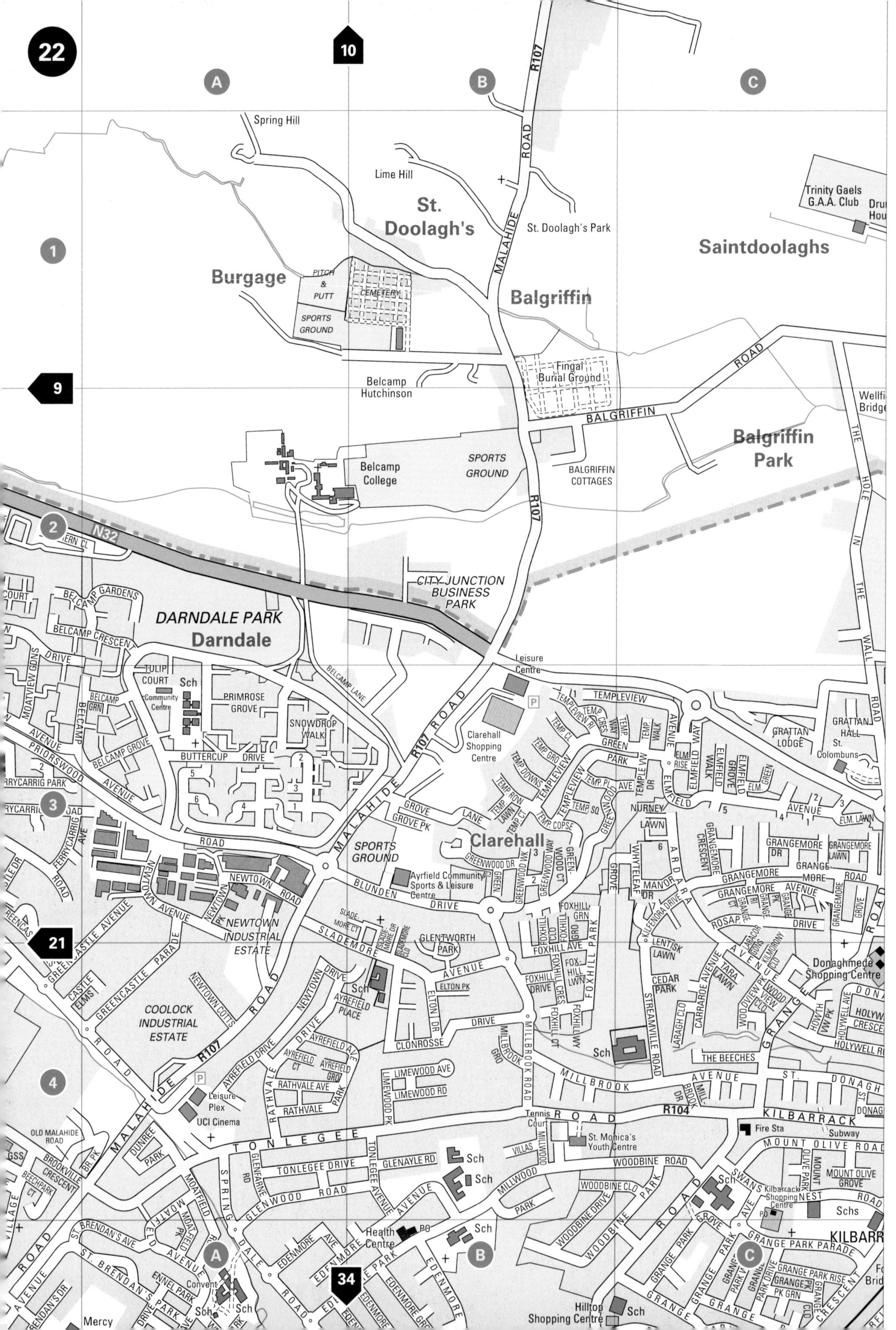
10
A
B
C
R107
Spring Hill
Lime Hill
St. Doolagh's
St. Doolagh's Park
Trinity Gaels G.A.A. Club
Saintdoolaghs
Burgage
PITCH & PUTT
CEMETERY
SPORTS GROUND
Balgriffin
MALAHIDE ROAD
Fingal Burial Ground
BALGRIFFIN ROAD
9
Belcamp Hutchinson
Belcamp College
SPORTS GROUND
BALGRIFFIN COTTAGES
Balgriffin Park
THE HOLE IN THE WALL ROAD
N32
CITY JUNCTION BUSINESS PARK
DARNDALE PARK
Darndale
BELCAMP GARDENS
BELCAMP CRESCENT
TULIP COURT
Sch
Community Centre
PRIMROSE GROVE
SNOWDROP WALK
BELCAMP LANE
Leisure Centre
Clarehall Shopping Centre
TEMPLEVIEW
BUTTERCUP DRIVE
PRIORSWOOD ROAD
BELCAMP GROVE
BELCAMP AVENUE
R107 ROAD
GROVE LANE
GROVE PK
Clarehall
SPORTS GROUND
Ayrfield Community Sports & Leisure Centre
BLUNDEN DRIVE
NEWTOWN ROAD
NEWTOWN AVENUE
NEWTOWN INDUSTRIAL ESTATE
21
GREENCASTLE AVENUE
GREENCASTLE PARADE
COOLOCK INDUSTRIAL ESTATE
SLADEMORE AVENUE
GLENTWORTH PARK
ELTON PK
ELTON DR
CLONROSSE DRIVE
AYREFIELD PLACE
FOXHILL AVE
FOXHILL DRIVE
FOXHILL PARK
MILLBROOK ROAD
MILLBROOK AVENUE
STREAMVILLE ROAD
THE BEECHES
GRANGEMORE AVENUE
GRANGEMORE ROAD
Donaghmede Shopping Centre
HOLYWELL CRESCENT
ELMFIELD AVENUE
ELMFIELD WAY
GRATTAN LODGE
GRATTAN HALL
St. Colombuns
KILBARRACK ROAD
Fire Sta
Subway
MOUNT OLIVE ROAD
MOUNT OLIVE GROVE
Kilbarrack Shopping Centre
Schs
4
OLD MALAHIDE ROAD
Leisure Plex
UCI Cinema
RATHVALE AVE
LIMEWOOD AVE
TONLEGEE ROAD
TONLEGEE DRIVE
GLENAYLE RD
GLENWOOD ROAD
Tennis Court
St. Monica's Youth Centre
WOODBINE ROAD
R104
Health Centre
PO
Convent
Mercy
34
Hilltop Shopping Centre
GRANGE PARK PARADE
KILBARRACK

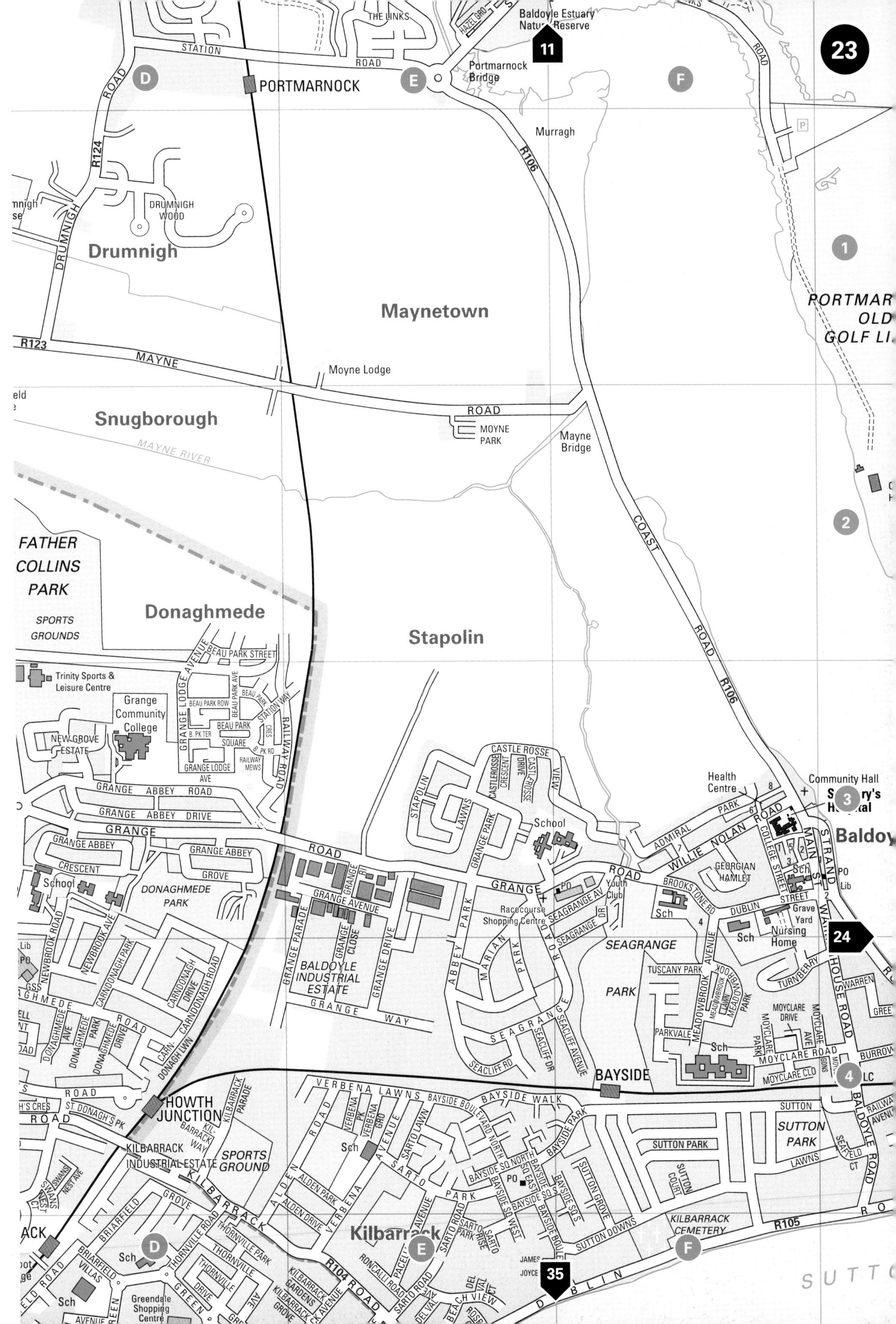

Baldoyle Estuary Nature Reserve
11
PORTMARNOCK
Portmarnock Bridge
Murragh
Drumnigh
DRUMNIGH WOOD
Maynetown
PORTMARNOCK OLD GOLF LI
Moyne Lodge
Snugborough
MOYNE PARK
Mayne Bridge
MAYNE RIVER
FATHER COLLINS PARK
SPORTS GROUNDS
Donaghmede
Stapolin
Trinity Sports & Leisure Centre
Grange Community College
NEW GROVE ESTATE
Health Centre
Community Hall
Baldoy
School
Youth Club
Racecourse Shopping Centre
GEORGIAN HAMLET
Grave Yard
Nursing Home
24
SEAGRANGE PARK
DONAGHMEDE PARK
BALDOYLE INDUSTRIAL ESTATE
BAYSIDE
HOWTH JUNCTION
KILBARRACK INDUSTRIAL ESTATE
SPORTS GROUND
SUTTON PARK
Kilbarrack
KILBARRACK CEMETERY
Greendale Shopping Centre
35
SUTTO
R106
R123
R124
R104
R105
STATION ROAD
MAYNE ROAD
COAST ROAD
GRANGE ROAD
DUBLIN ROAD

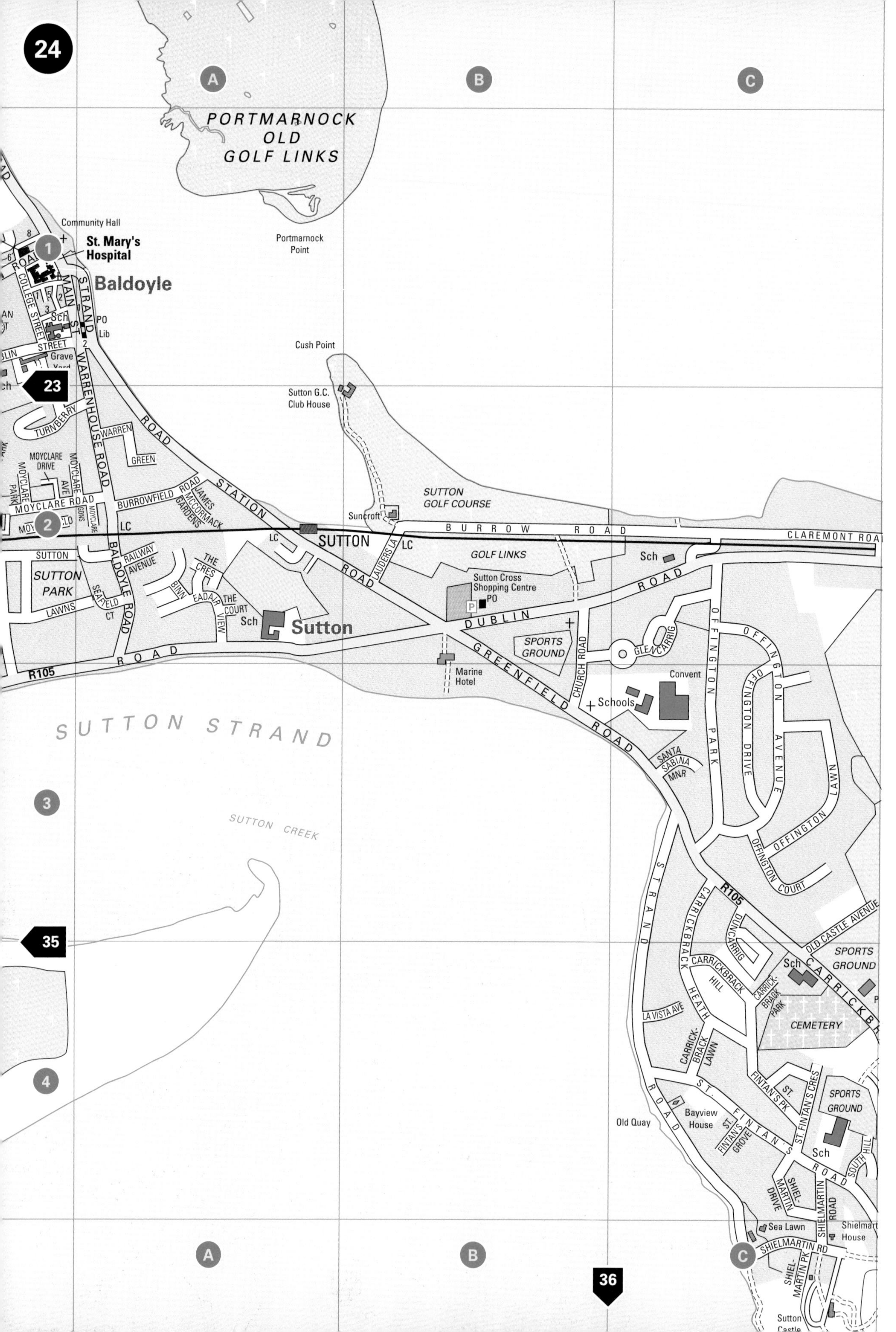

A

B

C

PORTMARNOCK
OLD
GOLF LINKS

Portmarnock
Point

Community Hall

Cush Point

St. Mary's
Hospital

Baldoyle

Sutton G.C.
Club House

PO
Lib

Grave
Yard

23

SUTTON
GOLF COURSE

TURNBERRY

WARREN
GREEN

MOYCLARE
DRIVE

MOYCLARE ROAD

BURROWFIELD

JAMES McCORMACK GARDENS

STATION

ROAD

Suncroft

Sutcroft

BURROW   ROAD

CLAREMONT ROAD

MOY

LC

SUTTON

LC

GOLF LINKS

Sch

SUTTON
PARK

RAILWAY AVENUE

BALDOYLE ROAD

THE CRES

SEAFELD

BINN

EADAR VIEW

THE COURT

Sch

Sutton

LAUDERS LA

LC

Sutton Cross
Shopping Centre

P   PO

CHURCH ROAD

ROAD

Sch

GLEN CARRIG

Convent

OFFINGTON PARK

OFFINGTON DRIVE

OFFINGTON AVENUE

OFFINGTON LAWN

LAWNS

ROAD

R105

SPORTS
GROUND

DUBLIN

GREENFIELD   ROAD

Marine
Hotel

Schools

SANTA
SABINA
MNR

OFFINGTON COURT

SUTTON   STRAND

SUTTON CREEK

STRAND

CARRICKBRACK

OLD CASTLE AVENUE

CARRICKBRACK HILL

DUNCARRIG

CARRICK-BRACK PARK

Sch

CARRICKBR

R105

SPORTS
GROUND

35

LA VISTA AVE

CARRICKBRACK HEATH

CEMETERY

CARRICK-BRACK LAWN

ROAD

ST. FINTAN'S

ST. FINTAN'S CRES

SPORTS
GROUND

4

Old Quay

Bayview
House

ST. FINTAN'S PK

ST. FINTAN'S GROVE

Sch

SOUTH HILL

ROAD

SHIELMARTIN DRIVE

SHIEL-MARTIN ROAD

SHIELMARTIN ROAD

Sea Lawn

Shielmart
House

SHIEL-MARTIN PK

C

SHIELMARTIN RD

Sutton
Castle

A

B

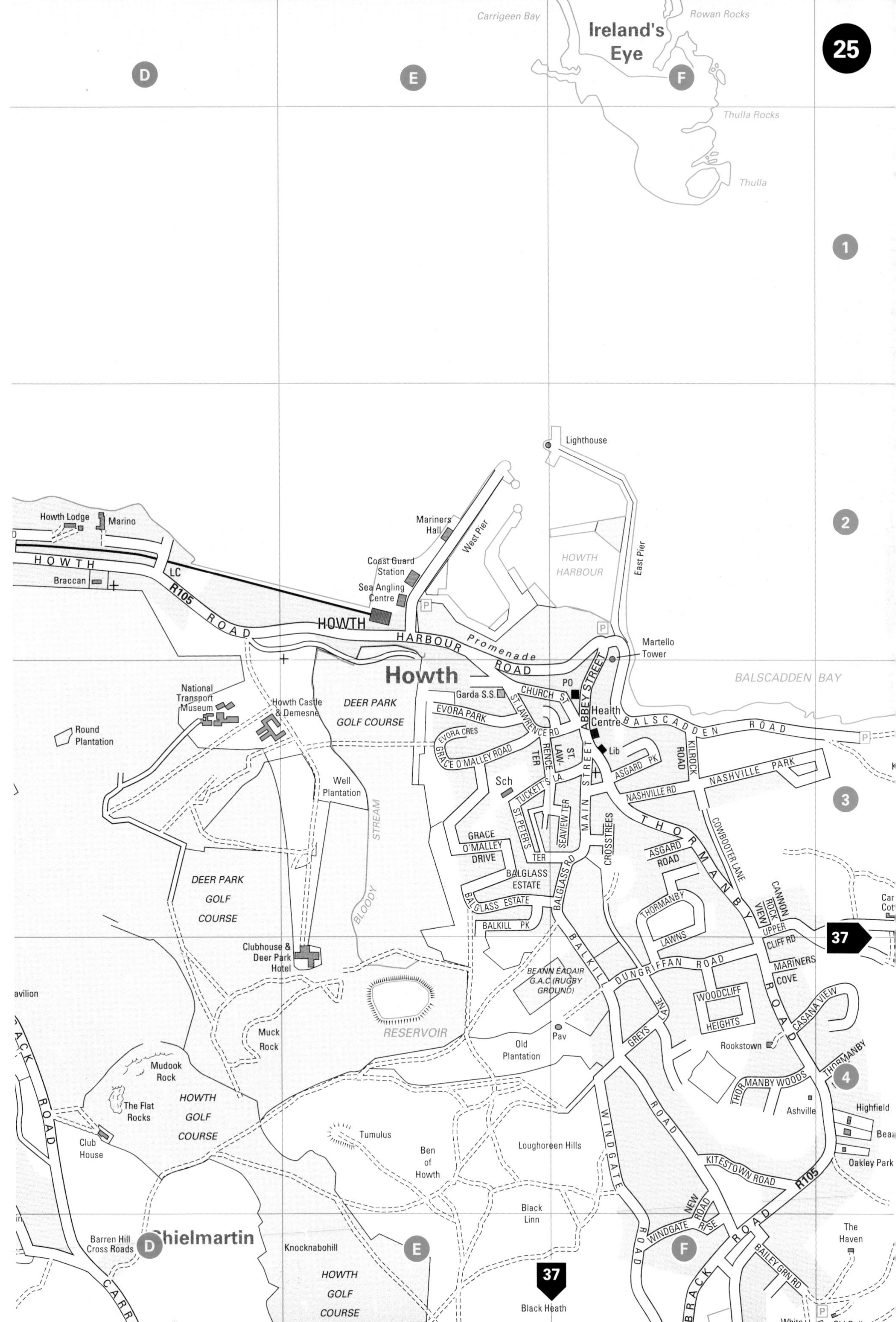

Carrigeen Bay
Rowan Rocks

Ireland's Eye

Thulla Rocks

Thulla

D   E   F

1

2

Lighthouse

Howth Lodge Marino

Mariners Hall

West Pier

HOWTH HARBOUR

East Pier

H O W T H
Braccan
R105 R O A D
LC

Coast Guard Station

Sea Angling Centre

P

HOWTH

HARBOUR ROAD

Promenade

P

Martello Tower

BALSCADDEN BAY

P

Howth

National Transport Museum

Howth Castle & Demesne

DEER PARK GOLF COURSE

Round Plantation

Garda S.S.

Evora Park

Evora Cres

GRACE O'MALLEY ROAD

Well Plantation

PO
CHURCH ST.
ST. LAWRENCE RD
ABBEY STREET
Health Centre
BALSCADDEN ROAD
Lib
KILROCK ROAD
NASHVILLE PARK
ASGARD PK
NASHVILLE RD
MAIN STREET
LAW-RENCE
TER
Sch
TUCKETT'S LA
ST. PETER'S TER
SEAVIEW TER

3

GRACE O'MALLEY DRIVE

BLOODY STREAM

DEER PARK GOLF COURSE

BALGLASS ESTATE
BALGLASS ESTATE
BALKILL PK
BALKILL RD
CROSSTREES
ASGARD ROAD
THORMANBY ROAD

COWBOOTERLANE

CANNON ROCK VIEW
UPPER CLIFF RD
MARINERS COVE

Car Cot

37

Clubhouse & Deer Park Hotel

BEANN EADAIR G.A.C (RUGBY GROUND)

THORMANBY LAWNS

DUNGRIFFAN ROAD

WOODCLIFF HEIGHTS

CASANA VIEW

avilion

Muck Rock

RESERVOIR

Old Plantation

Pav

GREYS LANE

Rookstown

THORMANBY WOODS

THORMANBY

4

BACK ROAD

Mudook Rock

The Flat Rocks

HOWTH GOLF COURSE

Ashville

Highfield
Bea
Oakley Park

Club House

Tumulus

Ben of Howth

Loughoreen Hills

WINDGATE ROAD

KITESTOWN ROAD

R105 ROAD

Shielmartin

Barren Hill Cross Roads

D

Knocknabohill

E

Black Linn

Black Heath

F

NEW ROAD
WINDGATE RISE

BRACK ROAD

BAILEY GRN RD

The Haven

White
Old Baily

P

HOWTH GOLF COURSE

37

Black Heath

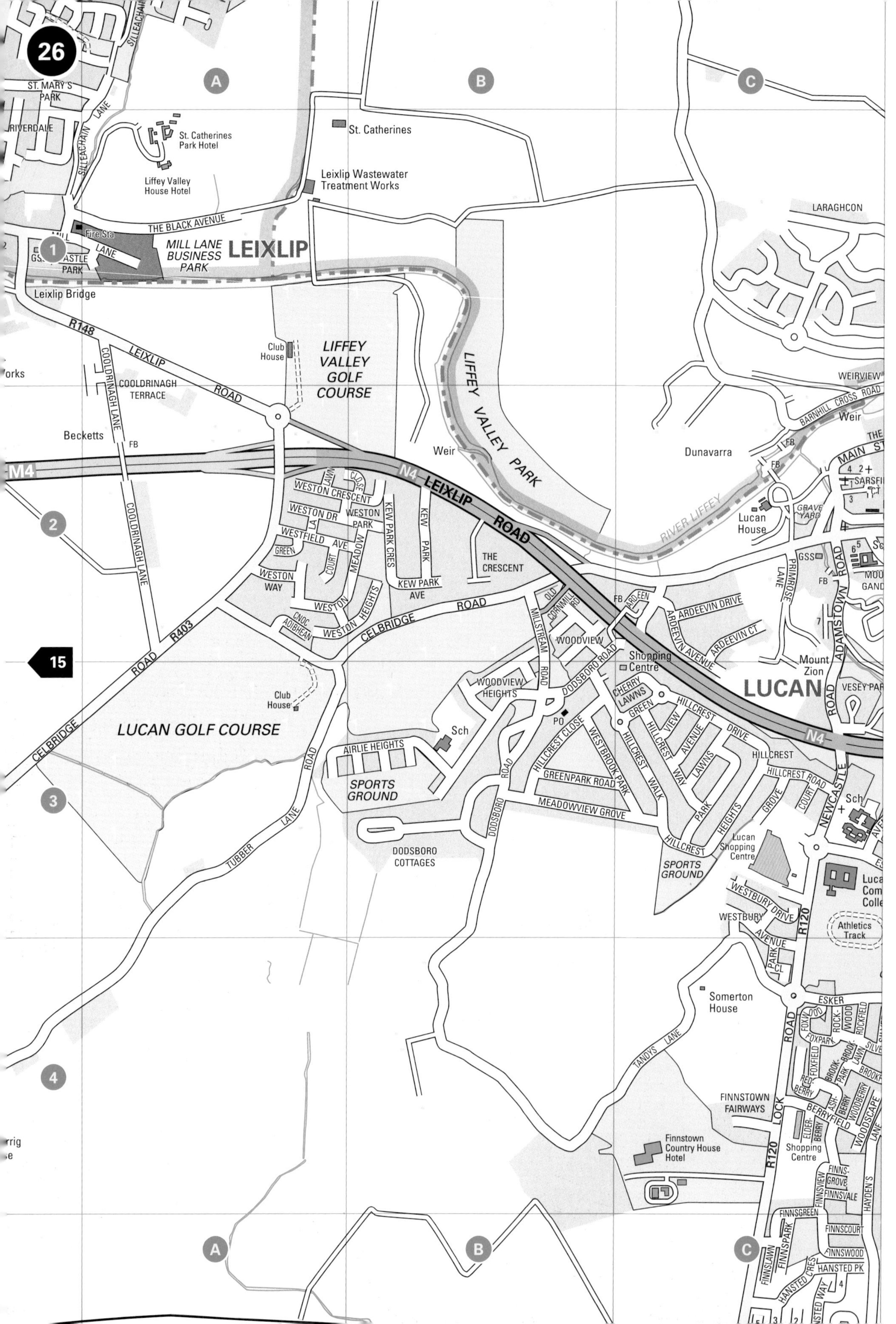

A

B

C

ST. MARY'S PARK

RIVERDALE

St. Catherines Park Hotel

St. Catherines

Leixlip Wastewater Treatment Works

Liffey Valley House Hotel

LARAGHCON

THE BLACK AVENUE

Fire Sta

MILL LANE BUSINESS PARK

LEIXLIP

1

orks

GS

MILL LANE

CASTLE PARK

Leixlip Bridge

R148

LEIXLIP

COOLDRINAGH LANE

COOLDRINAGH TERRACE

ROAD

Club House

LIFFEY VALLEY GOLF COURSE

LIFFEY VALLEY PARK

WEIRVIEW

BARNHILL CROSS ROAD

Weir

THE MAIN ST

Becketts

FB

Weir

Dunavarra

SARSFI

Lucan House

GRAVE YARD

Lucan House

GSS

MO GAND

M4

2

COOLDRINAGH LANE

N4

LEIXLIP ROAD

RIVER LIFFEY

WESTON CRESCENT

LAWN

CLOSE

WESTON PARK

KEW PARK CRES

KEW PARK

PRIMROSE LANE

ADAMSTOWN ROAD

WESTON DR

WESTFIELD AVE

GREEN

MEADOW

THE CRESCENT

Woodview

ARDEEVIN DRIVE

ARDEEVIN AVENUE

ARDEEVIN CT

FB

7

LUCAN

R403

ROAD

WESTON WAY

COURT

WESTON HEIGHTS

CNOC AOIBHEAN

WESTON

CELBRIDGE

ROAD

MILLSTREAM ROAD

CORNMILL RD

OLD

Shopping Centre

CHERRY LAWNS

GREEN

HILLCREST VIEW

HILLCREST AVENUE

Mount Zion

VESEY PAR

15

Club House

LUCAN GOLF COURSE

CEL BRIDGE

ROAD

Woodview Heights

Sch

WOODVIEW HEIGHTS

DODSBORO ROAD

PO

HILLCREST CLOSE

WESTBROOK PARK

HILLCREST WALK

HILLCREST WAY

LAWNS

DRIVE

PARK

HILLCREST

HILLCREST ROAD

HILLCREST

HILLCREST COURT

GROVE

Sch

NEWCASTLE

R120

N4

3

TUBBER LANE ROAD

AIRLIE HEIGHTS

SPORTS GROUND

DODSBORO ROAD

GREENPARK ROAD

MEADOWVIEW GROVE

HEIGHTS

SPORTS GROUND

Lucan Shopping Centre

Luca Com Coll

Athletics Track

DODSBORO COTTAGES

WESTBURY DRIVE

WESTBURY AVENUE

PARK CL

R120

Somerton House

ESKER ROAD

ROCK FOXDO

ROCK WOOD

ROCKFIELD

SILVE

4

rrig se

TANDYS LANE

FINNSTOWN FAIRWAYS

FOXPAR

FOXHELD

RED BERRY

ASH

BERRYFIELD

BROOK

PARK BROOK

LAWN

BROOK

ELDER BERRY

WOODBERRY

WOODSCAPE

Finnstown Country House Hotel

LOCK

R120

Shopping Centre

FINNS GROVE

FINNSVIEW

FINNSVALE

HAYDEN S

FINNSLAWN

FINNSPARK

FINNSGREEN

FINNSCOURT

FINNSWOOD

HANSTED S

HANSTED CRES

HANSTED PK

A

B

C

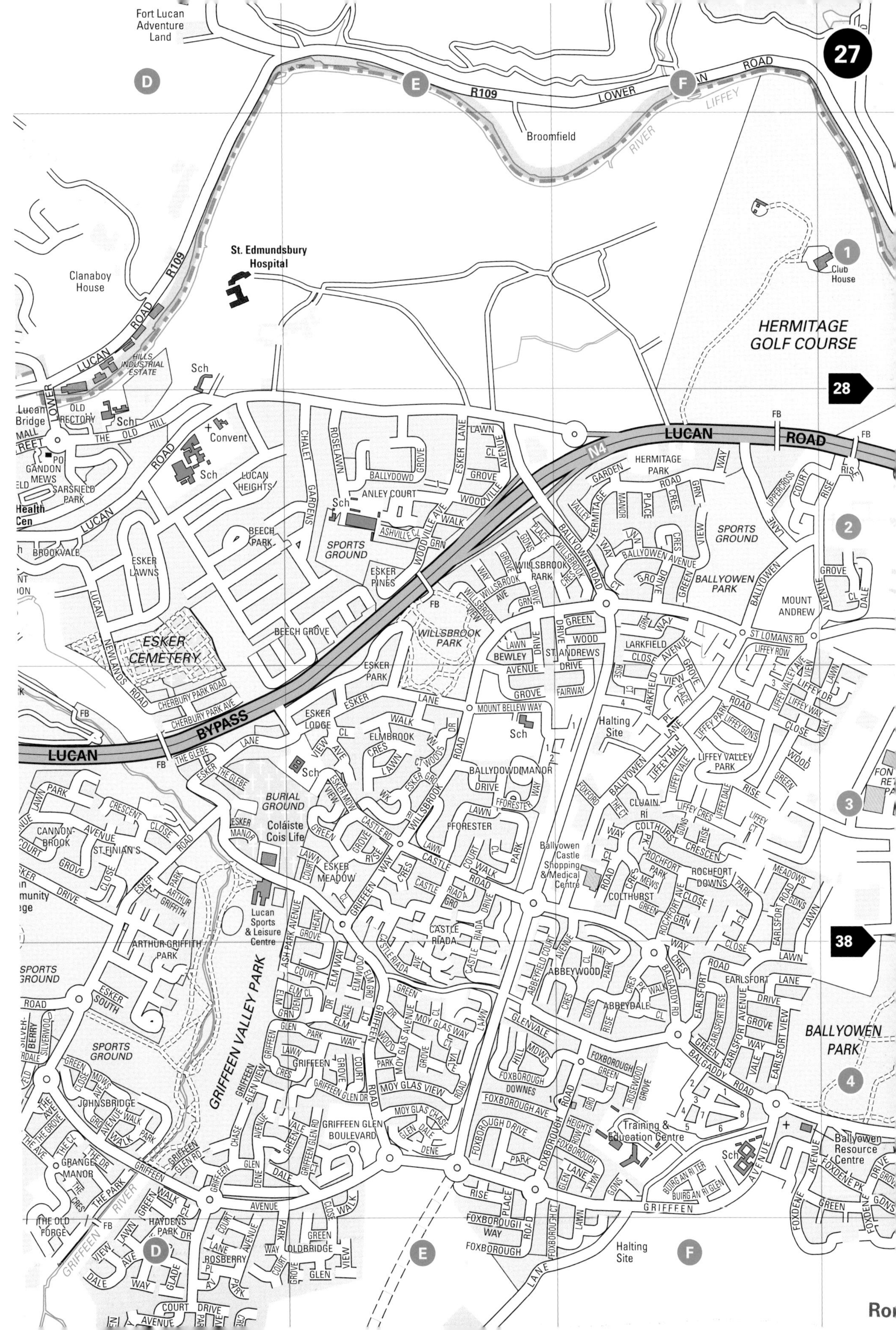
27
Fort Lucan
Adventure
Land
R109
LOWER
LUCAN ROAD
LIFFEY
RIVER
Broomfield
Clanaboy
House
St. Edmundsbury
Hospital
Club
House
HERMITAGE
GOLF COURSE
28
HILLS
INDUSTRIAL
ESTATE
Sch
Lucan
Bridge
OLD
RECTORY
THE OLD HILL
Convent
GANDON
MEWS
SARSFIELD
PARK
Health
Cen
LUCAN
HEIGHTS
CHALET
GARDENS
ROSELAWN
BALLYDOWD GROVE
ESKER LANE
LAWN
CL
AVENUE
GROVE
ANLEY COURT
WOODVILLE
WALK
ASHVILLE CL
SPORTS
GROUND
ESKER
PINES
BEECH
PARK
BROOKVALE
ESKER
LAWNS
N4
LUCAN ROAD
FB
HERMITAGE
PARK
GARDEN
VALLEY
MANOR
PLACE
CRES
GRN
VIEW
WAY
BALLYOWEN AVENUE
BALLYOWEN
PARK
UPPERCROSS
COURT
RISE
LANE
MOUNT
ANDREW
GROVE
DALE
WILLSBROOK
PARK
BALLYOWEN ROAD
WILLSBROOK
VIEW
BEECH GROVE
ESKER
CEMETERY
NEWLANDS
ROAD
CHERBURY PARK ROAD
CHERBURY PARK AVE
LUCAN
BYPASS
ESKER
PARK
ESKER LANE
BEWLEY
AVENUE
GREEN
WOOD
ST. ANDREWS
DRIVE
FAIRWAY
LARKFIELD
CLOSE
AVENUE
VIEW
PLACE
ST LOMANS RD
LIFFEY ROW
LIFFEY VALLEY AVE
LIFFEY DR
LIFFEY WAY
CLOSE
WALK
MOUNT BELLEW WAY
Halting
Site
ESKER
LODGE
ELMBROOK
CRES
LAWN
WALK
THE GLEBE
Sch
BURIAL
GROUND
Coláiste
Cois Life
BALLYDOWD MANOR
DRIVE
FFORESTER
LIFFEY PARK
LIFFEY GDNS
LIFFEY VALLEY
PARK
LIFFEY HALL
LIFFEY VALE
CLUAIN
RÍ
COLTHURST
CRESCENT
ROCHFORT
PARK
ROCHFORT
DOWNS
MEADOWS
CANNON-
BROOK
CRESCENT
ST. FINIAN'S
CLOSE
ESKER MANOR
ESKER
MEADOW
CASTLE RD
Ballyowen
Castle
Shopping
&Medical
Centre
COLTHURST
ROCHFORT AVE
Lucan
Sports
& Leisure
Centre
ARTHUR GRIFFITH
PARK
CASTLE
RIADA
ABBEYWOOD
EARLSFORT
LANE
DRIVE
GROVE
SPORTS
GROUND
ESKER
SOUTH
GRIFFEEN VALLEY PARK
ASH PARK AVENUE
ELM WAY
MOY GLAS AVENUE
MOY GLAS WAY
ABBEYDALE
BALGADDY RD
EARLSFORT RISE
EARLSFORT AVENUE
EARLSFORT VIEW
BALLYOWEN
PARK
38
SILVERWOOD
SPORTS
GROUND
JOHNSBRIDGE
GRIFFEEN
MOY GLAS VIEW
MOY GLAS CHASE
GLENVALE
FOXBOROUGH
DOWNES
FOXBOROUGH AVE
FOXBOROUGH
GREEN
ROSEWOOD
GROVE
Training &
Education Centre
BALGADDY
ROAD
Ballyowen
Resource
Centre
GRANGE
MANOR
GRIFFEEN GLEN RD
GRIFFEEN GLEN
BOULEVARD
FOXBOROUGH DRIVE
HEIGHTS
BUIRG AN RÍ TER
BUIRG AN RÍ GLEN
GRIFFEEN
FOXDENE
GREEN
GDNS
THE OLD
FORGE
HAYDENS
PARK
GRIFFEEN RIVER
ROSBERRY
OLDBRIDGE
GLEN
FOXBOROUGH
WAY
FOXBOROUGH CT
Halting
Site
LANE
COURT
DRIVE
AVENUE
Ro

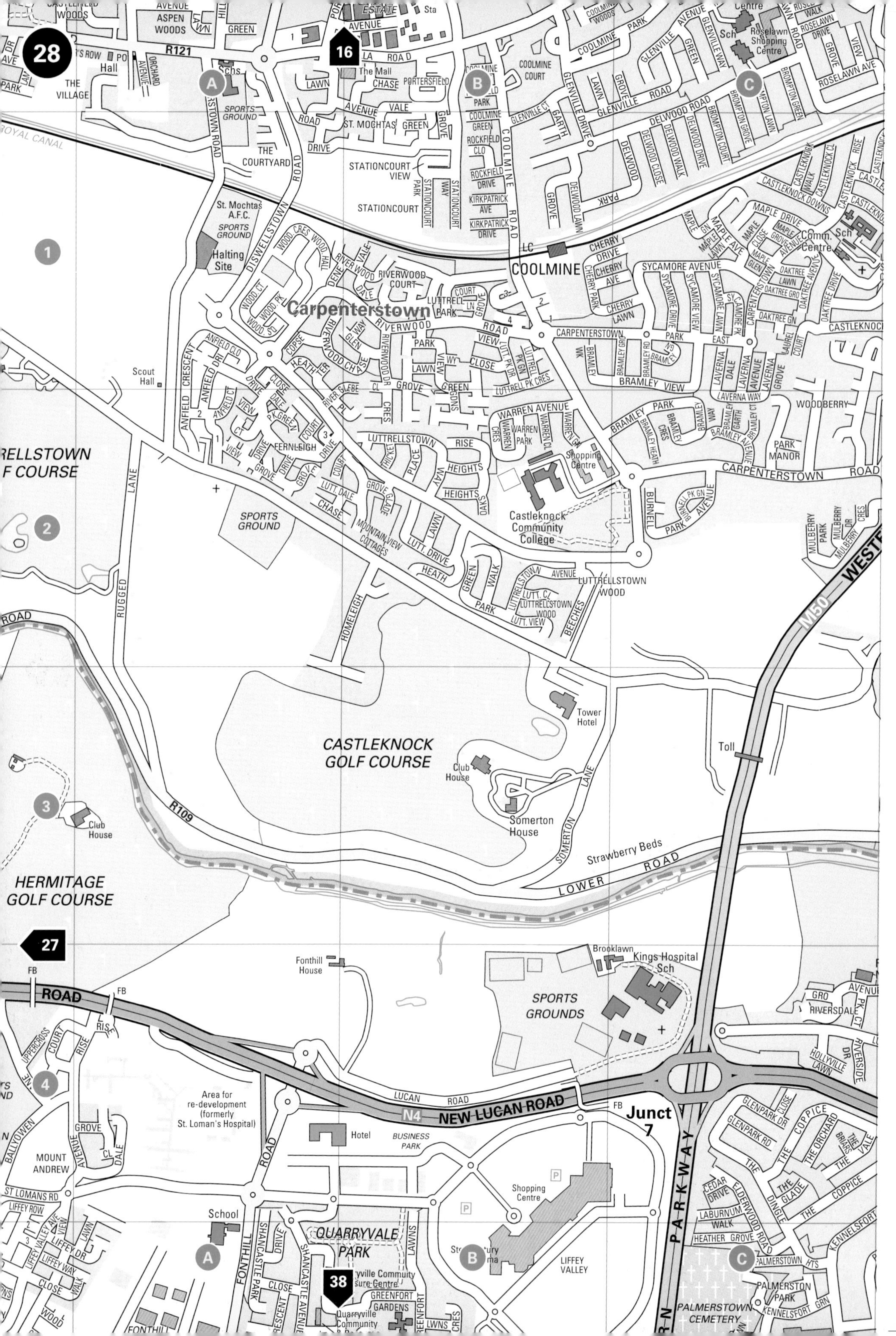
16
27
38
The Village
Aspen Woods
R121
The Mall
Royal Canal
Diswellstown Road
The Courtyard
Stationcourt
Stationcourt View
Coolmine Court
Coolmine Road
Coolmine
Roselawn Shopping Centre
Glenville Road
Delwood Road
Castleknock Downs
Maple Drive
Sycamore Avenue
Cherry Drive
Comm. Centre
St. Mochtas A.F.C.
Sports Ground
Halting Site
Carpenterstown
Riverwood Road
Carpenterstown Road
Bramley View
Warren Avenue
Shopping Centre
Castleknock Community College
Luttrellstown Wood
Woodberry
Park Manor
Scout Hall
Rugged Lane
Sports Ground
Mountain View Cottages
Homeleigh
Luttrellstown Golf Course
Castleknock Golf Course
Tower Hotel
Club House
Somerton House
Somerton Lane
Toll
M50
Western
R109
Strawberry Beds
Lower Road
Hermitage Golf Course
Club House
Fonthill House
Brooklawn
Kings Hospital Sch
Sports Grounds
Area for re-development (formerly St. Loman's Hospital)
Lucan Road
N4
New Lucan Road
Junct 7
Parkway
Hotel
Business Park
Shopping Centre
Liffey Valley
School
Quarryvale Park
Mount Andrew
St Lomans Rd
Liffey Row
Riversdale
Hollyville Lawn
Glenpark Dr
The Coppice
The Orchard
The Dingle
Elderwood Road
Heather Grove
Laburnum Walk
Palmerstown Hts
Palmerston Park
Palmerstown Cemetery
Kennelsfort Grn

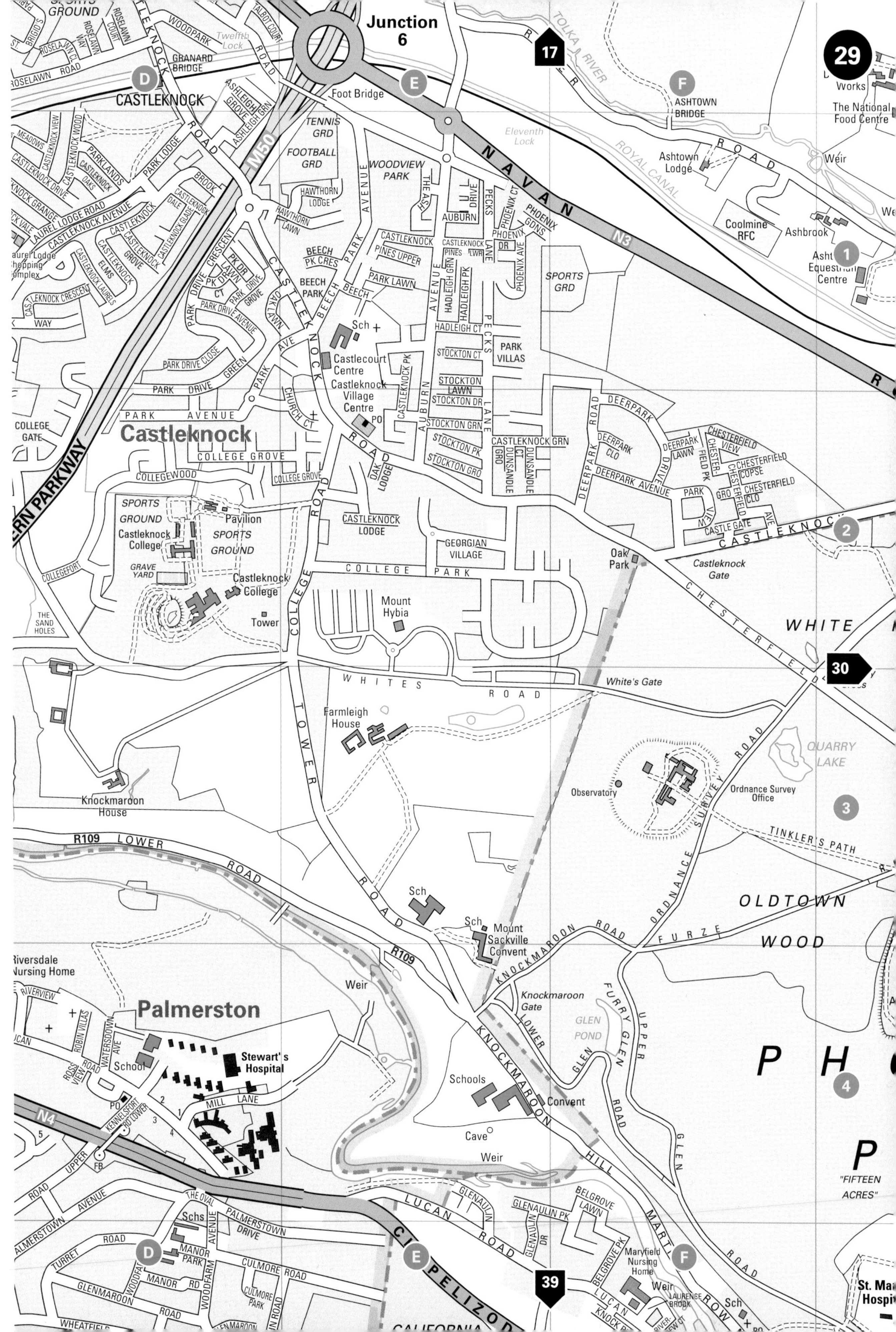

Junction 6
17
D
E
F
CASTLEKNOCK
Foot Bridge
ASHTOWN BRIDGE
Works
The National Food Centre
Twelfth Lock
Eleventh Lock
TOLKA RIVER
ROYAL CANAL
NAVAN ROAD
N3
M50
WESTERN PARKWAY
Ashtown Lodge
Weir
Coolmine RFC
Ashbrook
Ashtown Equestrian Centre
1
GRANARD BRIDGE
ROSELAWN ROAD
ASHLEIGH GROVE
ASHLEIGH GRN
TENNIS GRD
FOOTBALL GRD
WOODVIEW PARK
HAWTHORN LODGE
HAWTHORN LAWN
CASTLEKNOCK ROAD
PARK LODGE
PARKLANDS
LAUREL LODGE ROAD
CASTLEKNOCK AVENUE
Laurel Lodge Shopping Complex
CASTLEKNOCK CRESCENT
CASTLEKNOCK PINES UPPER
BEECH PK CRES
BEECH PARK
PARK LAWN
AUBURN
PECKS LANE
PHOENIX CT
PHOENIX GDNS
PHOENIX DR
PHOENIX AVE
SPORTS GRD
HADLEIGH GRN
HADLEIGH PK
HADLEIGH CT
STOCKTON CT
PARK VILLAS
STOCKTON LAWN
STOCKTON DR
STOCKTON GRN
STOCKTON PK
STOCKTON GRO
Sch
Castlecourt Centre
Castleknock Village Centre
PO
PARK DRIVE CRESCENT
PARK DRIVE AVENUE
PARK DRIVE CLOSE
PARK DRIVE GREEN
PARK AVENUE
CHURCH CT
COLLEGE GATE
Castleknock
COLLEGE GROVE
COLLEGEWOOD
OAK LODGE
CASTLEKNOCK LODGE
CASTLEKNOCK GRN
DUNSANDLE GRO
DUNSANDLE CT
DEERPARK ROAD
DEERPARK CLO
DEERPARK LAWN
DEERPARK DRIVE
DEERPARK AVENUE
CHESTERFIELD VIEW
CHESTERFIELD COPSE
CHESTERFIELD CLO
CHESTERFIELD AVE
PARK VIEW
CASTLE GATE
CASTLEKNOCK
2
SPORTS GROUND
Pavilion
Castleknock College
GRAVE YARD
Tower
GEORGIAN VILLAGE
COLLEGE PARK
Oak Park
Castleknock Gate
CHESTERFIELD
WHITE
30
COLLEGEFORT
THE SAND HOLES
Mount Hybia
WHITES ROAD
White's Gate
Farmleigh House
TOWER ROAD
QUARRY LAKE
Observatory
Ordnance Survey Office
SURVEY ROAD
3
TINKLER'S PATH
Knockmaroon House
R109
LOWER ROAD
OLDTOWN
WOOD
Mount Sackville Convent
FURZE ROAD
ORDNANCE
KNOCKMAROON ROAD
Riversdale Nursing Home
RIVERVIEW
Weir
Palmerston
Knockmaroon Gate
GLEN POND
FURRY GLEN
UPPER GLEN ROAD
LOWER GLEN ROAD
KNOCKMAROON HILL
P H
4
ROBIN VILLAS
WATERSDOWN AVE
School
Stewart's Hospital
MILL LANE
Schools
Convent
Cave
ROSS VIEW
PO
KENNELSPORT RD LOWER
N4
FB
UPPER
P
"FIFTEEN ACRES"
THE OVAL
PALMERSTOWN AVENUE
PALMERSTOWN DRIVE
Schs
MANOR PARK
MANOR RD
WOODFARM AVENUE
CULMORE ROAD
CULMORE PARK
GLENMAROON ROAD
TURRET ROAD
WHEATFIELD
LUCAN ROAD
GLENAULIN
GLENAULIN PK
GLENAULIN DR
BELGROVE LAWN
BELGROVE PK
Maryfield Nursing Home
MARTIN'S ROW
LAURENCE BROOK
CHAPELIZOD
CALIFORNIA
39
St. Mary's Hospital

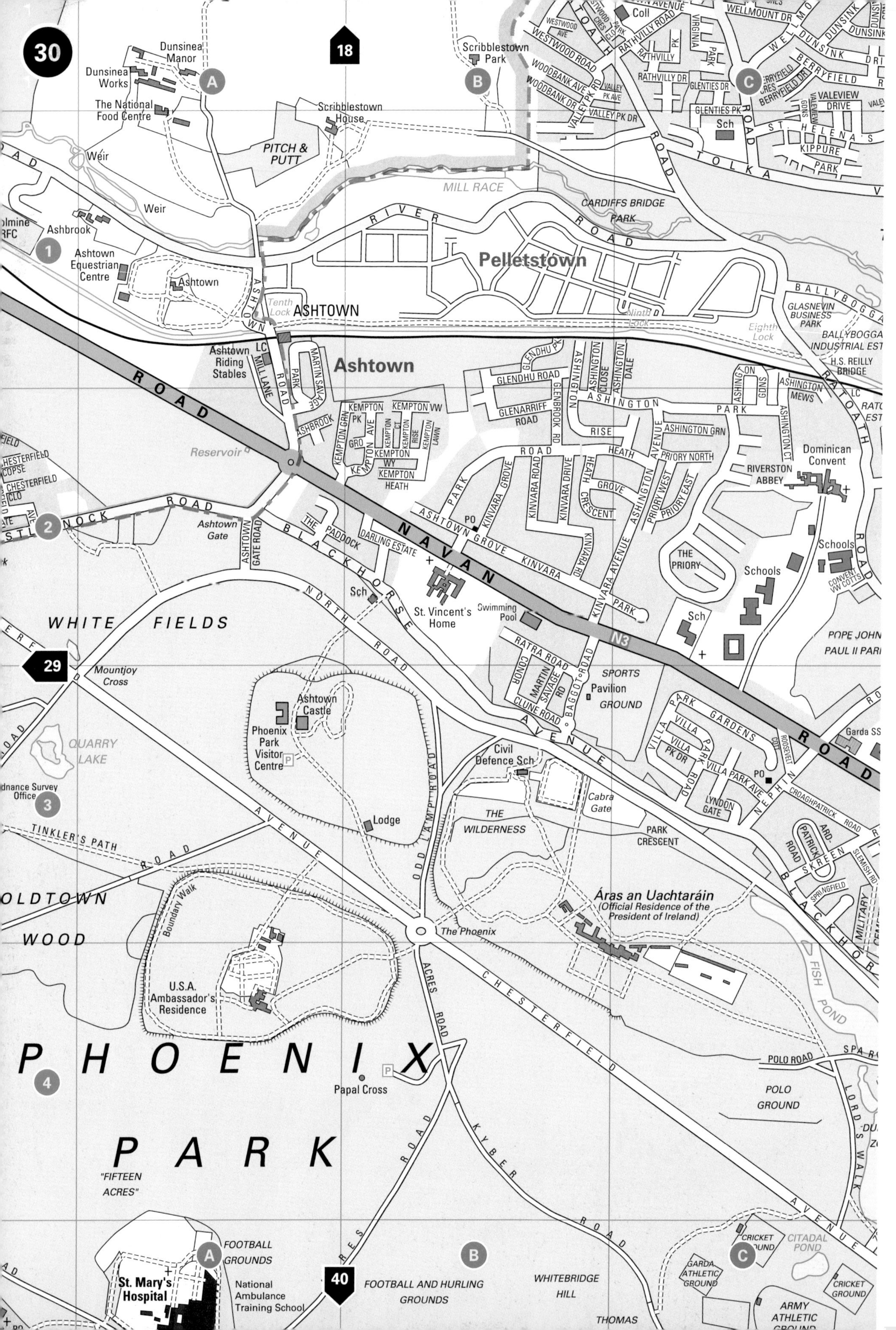

Dunsinea Manor

Dunsinea Works

A

The National Food Centre

18

Scribblestown Park

B

Scribblestown House

PITCH & PUTT

Coll

WESTWOOD AVE
WESTWOOD ROAD
WOODBANK ROAD
WOODBANK AVE
WOODBANK DR

WELLMOUNT DR
WELLMOUNT ROAD

RATHVILLY ROAD
RATHVILLY PK
RATHVILLY DR

VIRGINIA PARK

DUNSINK
DUNSINK

VALLEY
PK AVE
VALLEY
PK DR

GLENTIES DR
GLENTIES DR
GLENTIES PK

BERRYFIELD
CRES
BERRYFIELD DR
BERRYFIELD RD

VALEVIEW
DRIVE

C

Sch

ST. HELENAS
KIPPURE
PARK

MILL RACE

Weir

Weir

RIVER

ROAD

CARDIFFS BRIDGE
PARK

Pelletstown

BALLYBOGGA

GLASNEVIN
BUSINESS
PARK

BALLYBOGGAN
INDUSTRIAL EST.

H.S. REILLY
BRIDGE

RATOATH

Ninth
Lock

Eighth
Lock

TOLKA

olmine
RFC

Ashbrook

1

Ashtown Equestrian Centre

Ashtown

Tenth Lock

ASHTOWN

ASHTOWN

Ashtown Riding Stables

LC

MILL LANE

MARTIN SAVAGE
PARK

ROAD

Ashtown

Ashbrook

KEMPTON
GRN
KEMPTON
GRO
KEMPTON

KEMPTON VW
KEMPTON
AVE
KEMPTON
CT
KEMPTON
RISE
KEMPTON
WY
KEMPTON
HEATH

KEMPTON
LAWN

GLENDHU PK

GLENDHU ROAD

GLENARRIFF
ROAD

GLENBORG ROAD

ASHINGTON
CLOSE
ASHINGTON
DALE

ASHINGTON
GDNS

ASHINGTON

ASHINGTON
MEWS

LC

ROAD

Reservoir

2 NOCK ROAD

Ashtown Gate

THE
PADDOCK

Ashtown Gate

DARLING ESTATE

BLACKHORSE

Darling Estate

Sch

St. Vincent's Home

NAVAN

ASHTOWN GROVE

KINVARA GROVE

KINVARA ROAD

KINVARA DRIVE

PO

KINVARA

Swimming Pool

ASHINGTON
RISE
ASHINGTON
HEATH

PRIORY NORTH

GROVE

PRIORY WEST
PRIORY EAST

ASHINGTON GRN

ASHINGTON
AVENUE

RIVERSTON
ABBEY

Dominican
Convent

Schools

Schools

CONVENT
VW COTTS

WHITE FIELDS

NORTH

ROAD

Mountjoy Cross

29

Ashtown Castle

Phoenix Park Visitor Centre
P

KINVARA
CRESCENT

KINVARA
PARK

THE PRIORY

Sch

ROAD

POPE JOHN
PAUL II PARK

RATRA ROAD

MARTIN
SAVAGE
ROAD

CLUNE ROAD

BAGGOT ROAD

SPORTS
Pavilion
GROUND

Garda SS

VILLA
PARK
GARDENS

VILLA
PARK

VILLA
VILLA
PK DR
VILLA PARK AVE

ROOSEVELT
COTT

PO

ROAD

CROAGHPATRICK ROAD

LYNDON
GATE

ROAD

ance Survey
Office

3

OLDTOWN

WOOD

TINKLER'S PATH

AVENUE

ROAD

QUARRY
LAKE

Boundary Walk

Lodge

Civil Defence Sch

ODD LAMP ROAD

Cabra
Gate

THE
WILDERNESS

PARK
CRESCENT

PATRICK
ROAD

SLEMISH RD
SPRINGFIELD
ARD.

4

PHOENIX

U.S.A. Ambassador's Residence

Papal Cross
P

ACRES

ROAD

CHESTERFIELD

The Phoenix

Áras an Uachtaráin
(Official Residence of the
President of Ireland)

AVENUE

BLACKHORSE

FISH
POND

Polo Road

POLO
GROUND

SPAR

LORD'S WALK

DU

PARK

"FIFTEEN
ACRES"

A

FOOTBALL
GROUNDS

**St. Mary's
Hospital**

40

National Ambulance Training School

RES

ROAD

KYBER

ROAD

FOOTBALL AND HURLING
GROUNDS

B

WHITEBRIDGE
HILL

THOMAS

AVENUE

CHESTERFIELD
COPSE

CHESTERFIELD
CLO

Cricket
Ground

C

CITADAL
POND

GARDA
ATHLETIC
GROUND

Cricket
GROUND

ARMY
ATHLETIC
GROUND

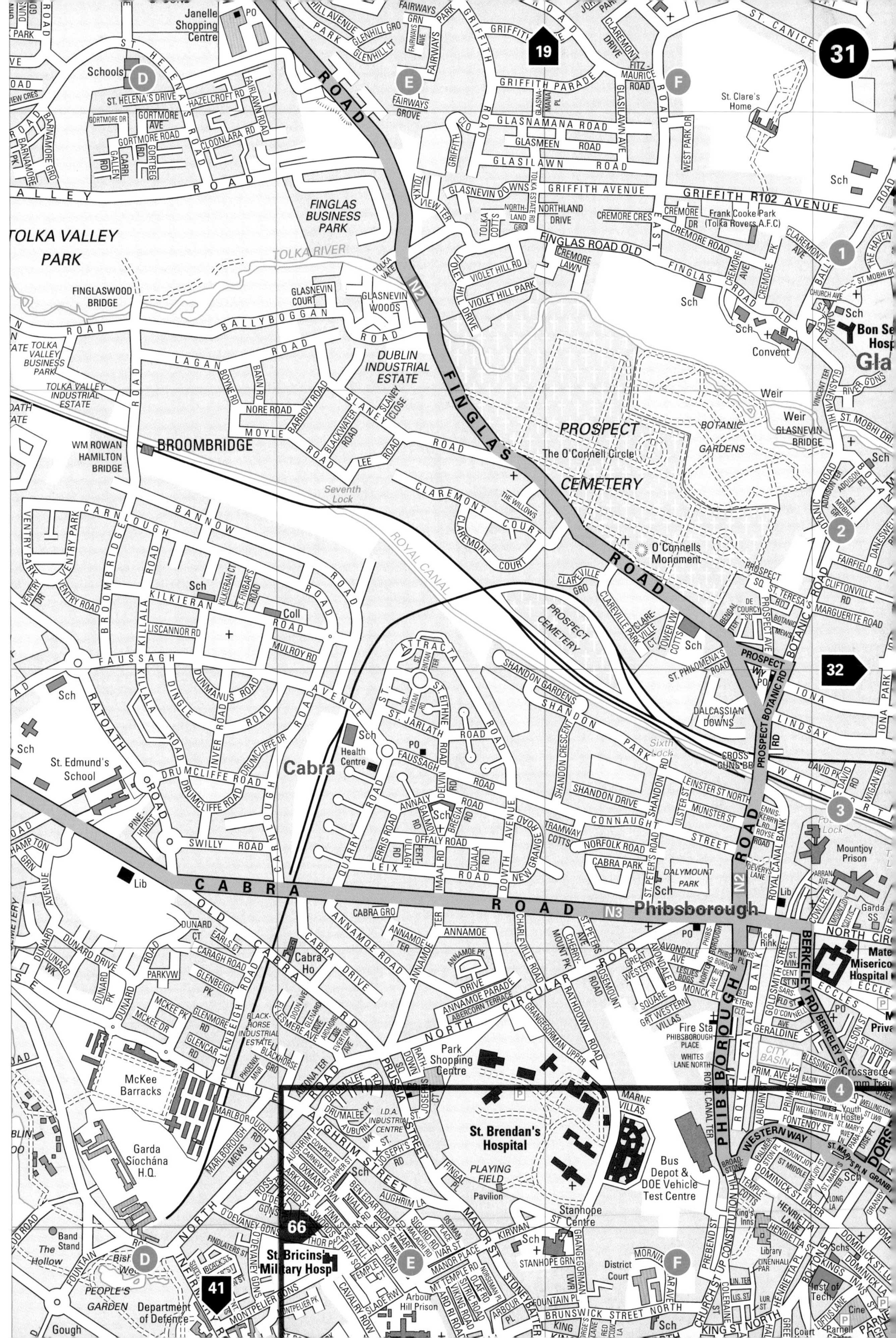

31
19
32
66
41
TOLKA VALLEY PARK
FINGLAS BUSINESS PARK
DUBLIN INDUSTRIAL ESTATE
PROSPECT CEMETERY
BOTANIC GARDENS
BROOMBRIDGE
Cabra
Phibsborough
FINGLAS ROAD
CABRA ROAD
PHIBSBOROUGH ROAD
GRIFFITH AVENUE
ROYAL CANAL
TOLKA RIVER
St. Brendan's Hospital
McKee Barracks
Garda Síochána H.Q.
St. Bricins Military Hosp
Mountjoy Prison
Arbour Hill Prison

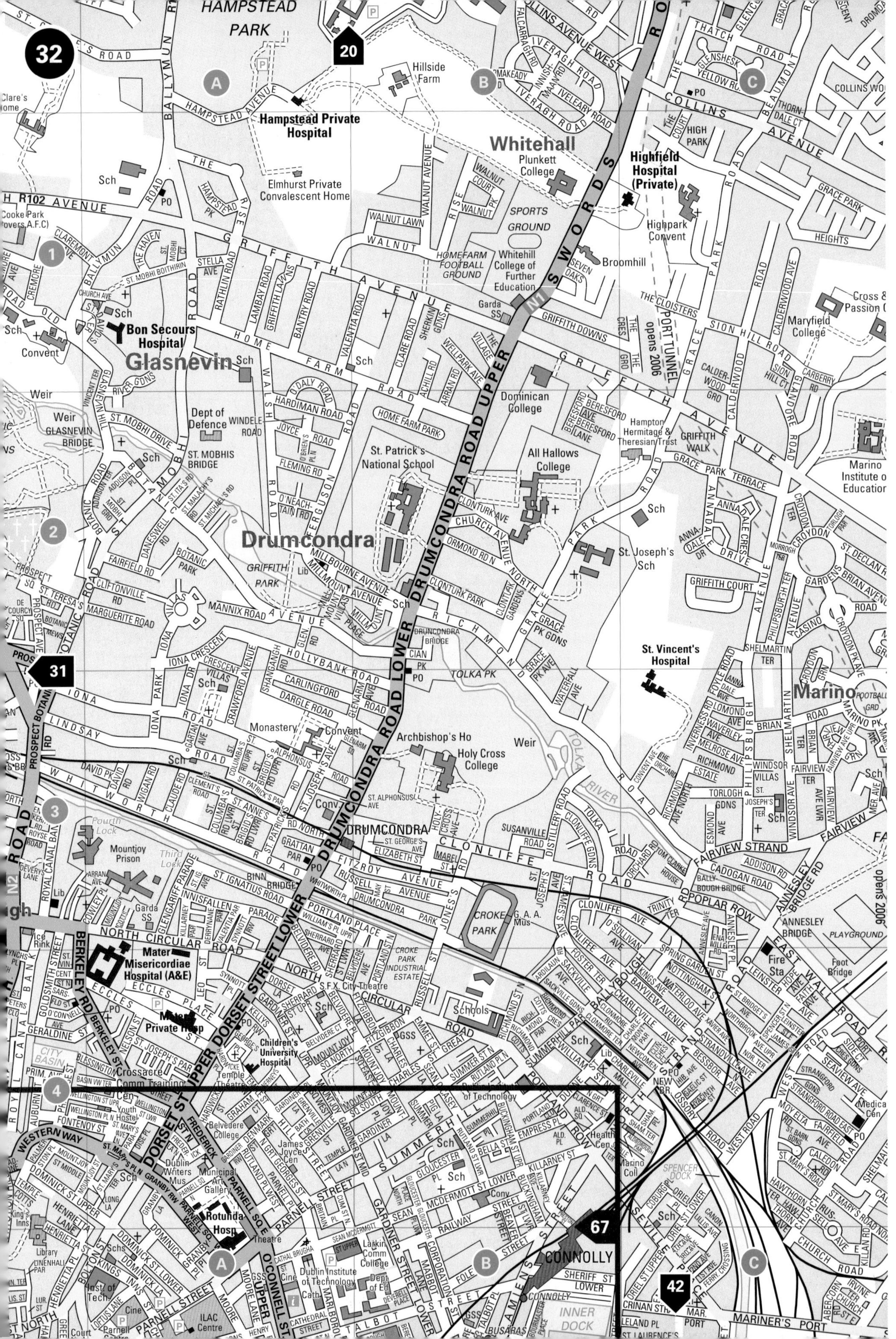
HAMPSTEAD
PARK
20
A
B
C
1
2
3
4
31
67
42
Hampstead Private Hospital
Hillside Farm
Elmhurst Private Convalescent Home
Whitehall
Plunkett College
Highfield Hospital (Private)
Highpark Convent
SPORTS GROUND
HOMEFARM FOOTBALL GROUND
Whitehill College of Further Education
Broomhill
SWORDS ROAD
N1
Garda SS
Bon Secours Hospital
Glasnevin
Convent
Sch
PO
Lib
Weir
GLASNEVIN BRIDGE
Dept of Defence
ST. MOBHIS BRIDGE
Dominican College
All Hallows College
Hampton Hermitage & Theresian Trust
Cross & Passion Coll
Maryfield College
Marino Institute of Education
St. Patrick's National School
Drumcondra
GRIFFITH PARK
DRUMCONDRA ROAD UPPER
DRUMCONDRA ROAD LOWER
St. Joseph's Sch
St. Vincent's Hospital
Marino
TOLKA PK
Archbishop's Ho
Holy Cross College
Monastery
Convent
TOLKA RIVER
DRUMCONDRA
PORT TUNNEL opens 2006
Mountjoy Prison
Fourth Lock
Third Lock
ROYAL CANAL BANK
N2
Mater Misericordiae Hospital (A&E)
Mater Private Hosp
Children's University Hospital
CROKE PARK
G. A. A. Mus
CROKE PARK INDUSTRIAL ESTATE
S.F.X. City Theatre
Schools
Ice Rink
CITY BASIN
Crossacre Comm Training Cen
Temple Theatre
Belvedere College
James Joyce Cen
Dublin Writers Mus
Municipal Art Gallery
Rotunda Hosp
Theatre
Larkin Comm College
Dublin Institute of Technology
Dept of Ed
Cath
Cine
King's Inns
Library
ILAC Centre
CONNOLLY
INNER DOCK
SPENCER DOCK
BUSARAS
Health Cen
Marino Coll
Fire Sta
Medical Cen
Foot Bridge
PLAYGROUND
ANNESLEY BRIDGE
BALLYBOUGH BRIDGE
BINN BRIDGE
DRUMCONDRA BRIDGE
GRIFFITH AVENUE
COLLINS AVENUE
HOME FARM ROAD
IVERAGH ROAD
BALLYMUN ROAD
WALNUT AVENUE
ST. MOBHI ROAD
BOTANIC ROAD
MANNIX ROAD
IONA ROAD
LINDSAY ROAD
WHITWORTH ROAD
CLONLIFFE ROAD
RICHMOND ROAD
GRACE PARK ROAD
PHILIPSBURGH AVENUE
FAIRVIEW STRAND
NORTH CIRCULAR ROAD
PORTLAND PLACE
DORSET STREET UPPER
DORSET STREET LOWER
ECCLES STREET
BERKELEY RD
WESTERN WAY
PARNELL STREET
O'CONNELL ST UPPER
GARDINER STREET LOWER
SUMMERHILL
SEAN McDERMOTT ST LOWER
EAST WALL ROAD
NORTH STRAND ROAD
SEVILLE PLACE
MARINER'S PORT
SHERIFF ST LOWER
AMIENS STREET
TALBOT ST
CATHEDRAL STREET
BOLTON ST
DOMINICK ST LOWER
HENRIETTA ST
KINGS INNS ST
RICHMOND ESTATE
FAIRVIEW
CLONTARF ROAD

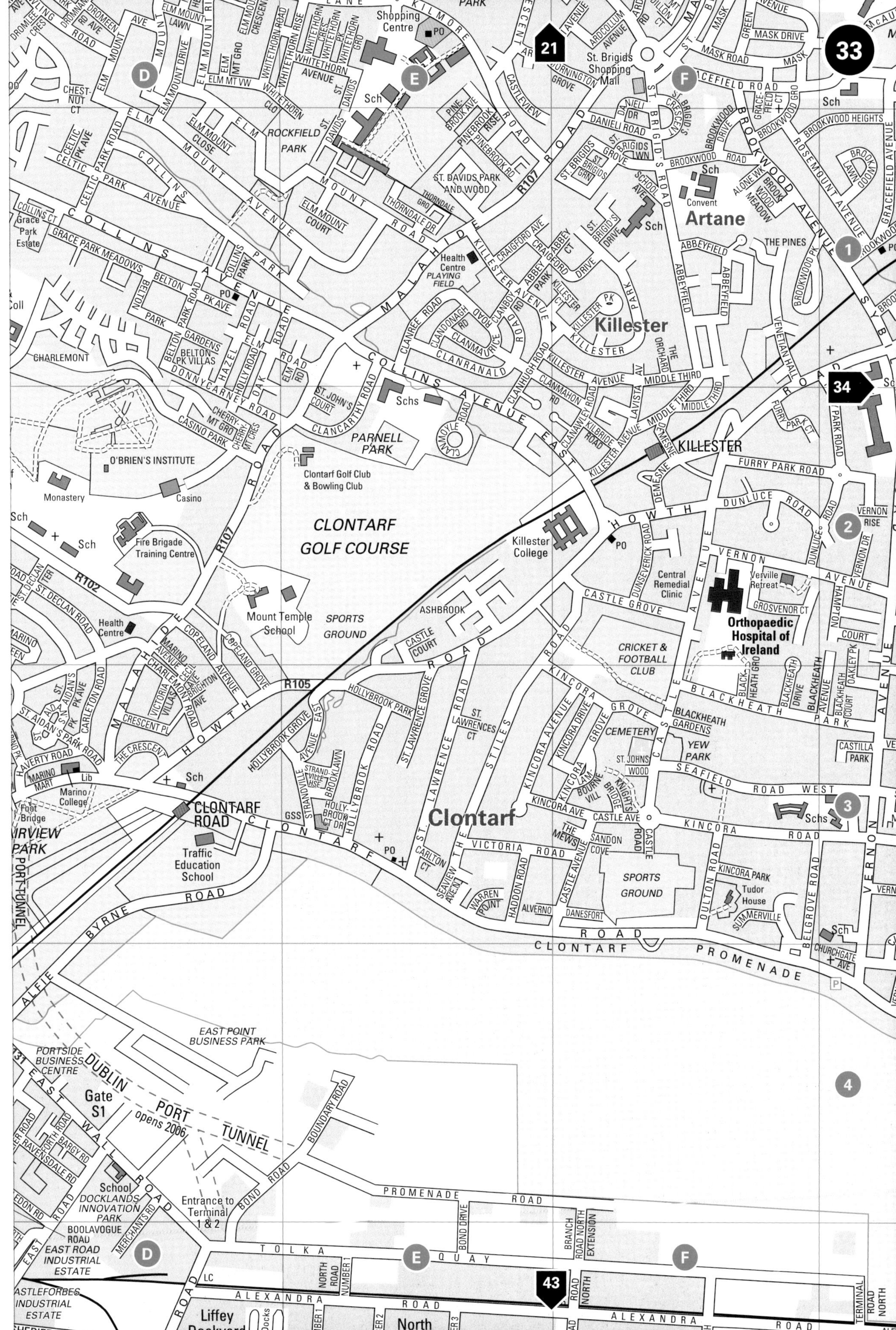
33
21
34
43
D
E
F
1
2
3
4
Shopping Centre
PO
KILMORE
PARK
Sch
WHITETHORN AVENUE
ROCKFIELD PARK
St. Brigids Shopping Mall
MASK ROAD
MASK DRIVE
GRACEFIELD ROAD
BROOKWOOD HEIGHTS
BROOKWOOD AVENUE
ROSEMOUNT AVENUE
GRACEFIELD AVENUE
CHEST-NUT CT
ELM MOUNT CLOSE
ELM MOUNT COURT
ELM MOUNT DRIVE
CELTIC PARK AVENUE
COLLINS PARK AVENUE
COLLINS AVENUE
Grace Park Estate
GRACE PARK MEADOWS
BELTON PARK ROAD
BELTON PARK GARDENS
BELTON PK VILLAS
DONNYCARNEY ROAD
CHARLEMONT
CASINO PARK
O'BRIEN'S INSTITUTE
Monastery
Casino
ST. DAVIDS PARK AND WOOD
THORNDALE DR
MALAHIDE ROAD
R107
Health Centre
PLAYING FIELD
DANIELI ROAD
BROOKWOOD ROAD
ST. BRIGIDS ROAD
Convent
Artane
THE PINES
ABBEYFIELD
KILLESTER AVENUE
KILLESTER PARK
Killester
MIDDLE THIRD
CLANRANALD
CLANMAURICE
CLANCARTHY ROAD
Schs
PARNELL PARK
Clontarf Golf Club & Bowling Club
CLONTARF GOLF COURSE
KILLESTER
FURRY PARK ROAD
DUNLUCE ROAD
VERNON RISE
VERNON AVENUE
Killester College
HOWTH ROAD
PO
Central Remedial Clinic
Verville Retreat
GROSVENOR CT
Orthopaedic Hospital of Ireland
CASTLE GROVE
ASHBROOK
CASTLE COURT
Fire Brigade Training Centre
R102
ST. DECLAN ROAD
Health Centre
Mount Temple School
SPORTS GROUND
CRICKET & FOOTBALL CLUB
BLACKHEATH PARK
BLACKHEATH GARDENS
CEMETERY
YEW PARK
SEAFIELD ROAD WEST
KINCORA ROAD
KINCORA AVENUE
R105
HOLLYBROOK PARK
HOLLYBROOK ROAD
ST. LAWRENCE ROAD
STILES ROAD
CASTILLA PARK
Schs
Marino College
CLONTARF ROAD
Traffic Education School
Clontarf
VICTORIA ROAD
CLONTARF ROAD
CLONTARF PROMENADE
SPORTS GROUND
Tudor House
KINCORA PARK
BELGROVE ROAD
OULTON ROAD
HADDON ROAD
BYRNE ROAD
ALFIE
PORT TUNNEL
EAST POINT BUSINESS PARK
PORTSIDE BUSINESS CENTRE
DUBLIN PORT TUNNEL opens 2006
Gate S1
EAST WALL ROAD
BOUNDARY ROAD
School
DOCKLANDS INNOVATION PARK
Entrance to Terminal 1 & 2
BOND ROAD
PROMENADE ROAD
BOND DRIVE
BRANCH ROAD NORTH EXTENSION
TOLKA QUAY
EAST ROAD INDUSTRIAL ESTATE
CASTLEFORBES INDUSTRIAL ESTATE
ALEXANDRA ROAD
Liffey Dockyard
North
TERMINAL ROAD NORTH

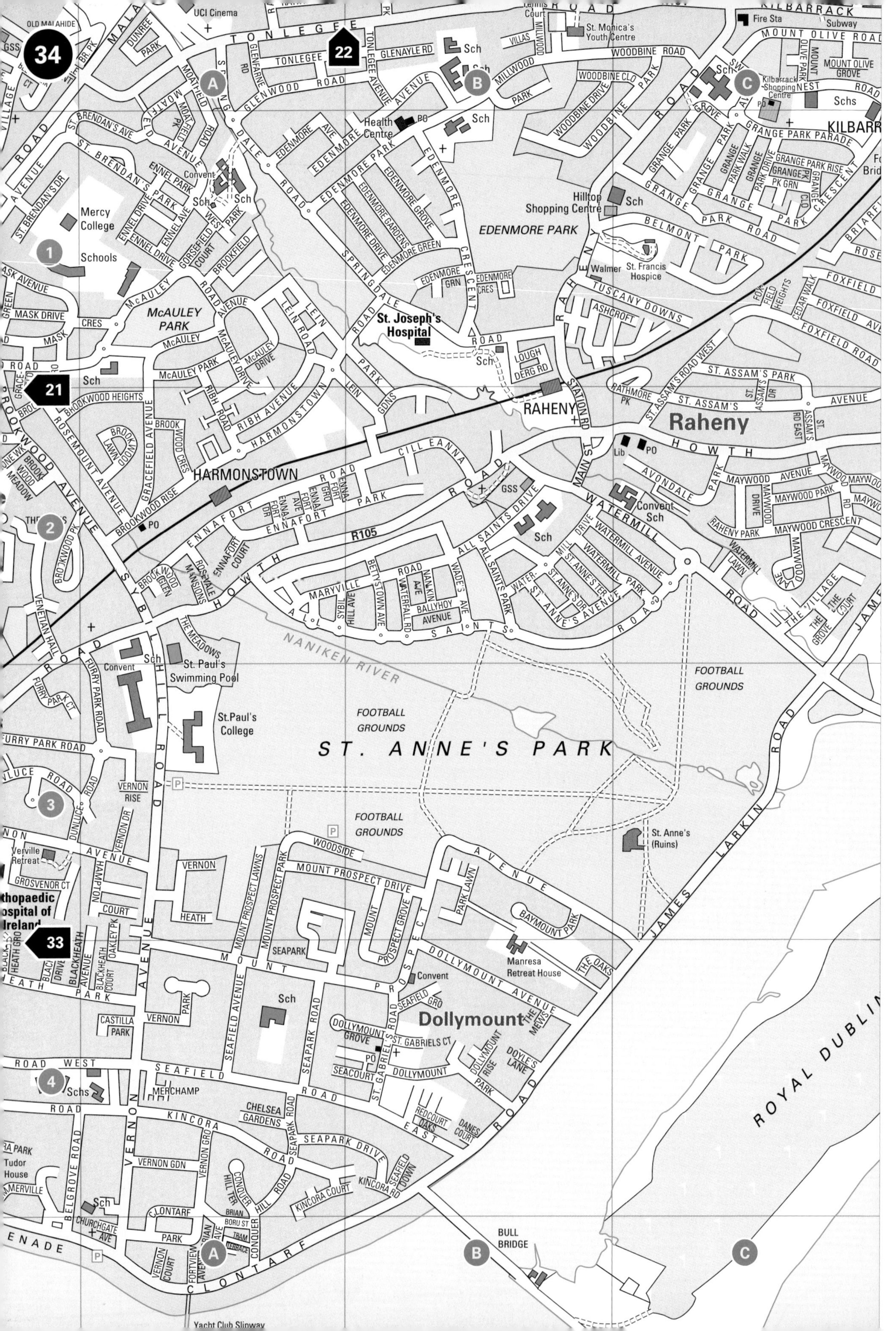
34
22
21
33
A
B
C
1
2
3
4
UCI Cinema
St. Monica's Youth Centre
Fire Sta
Subway
KILBARRACK
MOUNT OLIVE ROAD
MOUNT OLIVE GROVE
Kilbarrack Shopping Centre
Schs
TONLEGEE
TONLEGEE ROAD
TONLEGEE AVENUE
GLENAYLE RD
GLENFARNE RD
GLENWOOD ROAD
WOODBINE ROAD
WOODBINE CLO
WOODBINE DRIVE
WOODBINE PARK
MILLWOOD PARK
Health Centre
PO
Sch
Convent
Mercy College
Schools
ST. BRENDAN'S AVE
ST. BRENDAN'S PARK
ST. BRENDAN'S DR
MOATFIELD AVENUE
ENNEL PARK
ENNEL DRIVE
ENNEL AVE
GORSEFIELD COURT
BROOKFIELD
EDENMORE AVE
EDENMORE PARK
EDENMORE DRIVE
EDENMORE GARDENS
EDENMORE GROVE
EDENMORE GREEN
EDENMORE GRN
EDENMORE CRES
EDENMORE CRESCENT
EDENMORE PARK
SPRINGDALE ROAD
GRANGE PARK PARADE
GRANGE PARK RISE
GRANGE PARK WALK
GRANGE PARK DRIVE
GRANGE PARK ROAD
GRANGE PARK CRESCENT
Hilltop Shopping Centre
BELMONT PARK
Walmer
St. Francis Hospice
TUSCANY DOWNS
ASHCROFT
FOXFIELD
FOXFIELD AVE
FOXFIELD ROAD
CEDAR WALK
McAULEY PARK
MASK AVENUE
MASK DRIVE
McAULEY ROAD
McAULEY AVENUE
McAULEY DRIVE
LEIN ROAD
LEIN PARK
LEIN GDNS
St. Joseph's Hospital
LOUGH DERG RD
ST. ASSAM'S PARK
ST. ASSAM'S AVENUE
ST. ASSAM'S ROAD WEST
ST. ASSAM'S RD EAST
RATHMORE PK
RAHENY
Raheny
STATION RD
MAIN ST
HOWTH ROAD
Lib
BROOKWOOD HEIGHTS
BROOKWOOD AVENUE
BROOKWOOD RISE
BROOKWOOD PK
ROSEMOUNT AVENUE
GRACEFIELD AVENUE
RIBH AVENUE
RIBH ROAD
HARMONSTOWN ROAD
HARMONSTOWN
CILL EANNA
ENNAFORT ROAD
ENNAFORT PARK
ENNAFORT DR
ENNAFORT COURT
R105
GSS
ALL SAINTS DRIVE
ALL SAINTS PARK
ALL SAINTS ROAD
WATERMILL ROAD
WATERMILL AVENUE
WATERMILL PARK
WATERMILL DRIVE
WATERMILL LAWN
ST. ANNE'S AVENUE
AVONDALE PARK
Convent Sch
MAYWOOD AVENUE
MAYWOOD PARK
MAYWOOD CRESCENT
MAYWOOD DRIVE
RAHENY PARK
THE VILLAGE
THE COURT
THE GROVE
MARYVILLE ROAD
BETTYSTOWN AVE
WATERFALL RD
BALLYHOY AVENUE
WADE'S AVE
SYBIL HILL AVE
SYBIL HILL ROAD
NANIKEN RIVER
THE MEADOWS
St. Paul's Swimming Pool
St.Paul's College
FURRY PARK ROAD
FURRY PARK CT
FOOTBALL GROUNDS
ST. ANNE'S PARK
St. Anne's (Ruins)
JAMES LARKIN ROAD
VERNON RISE
VERNON AVENUE
VERNON HEATH
VERNON PARK
DUNLUCE ROAD
Verville Retreat
GROSVENOR CT
HAMPTON COURT
WOODSIDE
MOUNT PROSPECT DRIVE
MOUNT PROSPECT AVENUE
MOUNT PROSPECT PARK
MOUNT PROSPECT LAWNS
MOUNT PROSPECT GROVE
PARK LAWN
BAYMOUNT PARK
Manresa Retreat House
THE OAKS
DOLLYMOUNT AVENUE
Dollymount
THE MEWS
SEAPARK
SEAPARK ROAD
SEAPARK DRIVE
SEAFIELD AVENUE
SEAFIELD ROAD EAST
SEAFIELD ROAD WEST
SEAFIELD GRO
SEAFIELD DOWN
DOLLYMOUNT GROVE
DOLLYMOUNT PARK
DOLLYMOUNT RISE
ST. GABRIELS CT
ST. GABRIEL'S ROAD
DOYLE'S LANE
SEACOURT
REDCOURT OAKS
DANES COURT
CASTILLA PARK
BLACKHEATH AVENUE
BLACKHEATH COURT
BLACKHEATH DRIVE
BLACKHEATH PARK
OAKLEY PK
Orthopaedic Hospital of Ireland
MERCHAMP
CHELSEA GARDENS
KINCORA ROAD
KINCORA COURT
KINCORA RD
VERNON GDN
VERNON GRO
CONQUER HILL ROAD
HILLTER
CLONTARF PARK
CLONTARF ROAD
BRIAN AVE
BORU ST
TRAM TERRACE
FORTVIEW AVENUE
VERNON COURT
CHURCHGATE AVE
BELGROVE ROAD
Tudor House
PROMENADE
BULL BRIDGE
ROYAL DUBLIN
Yacht Club Slipway

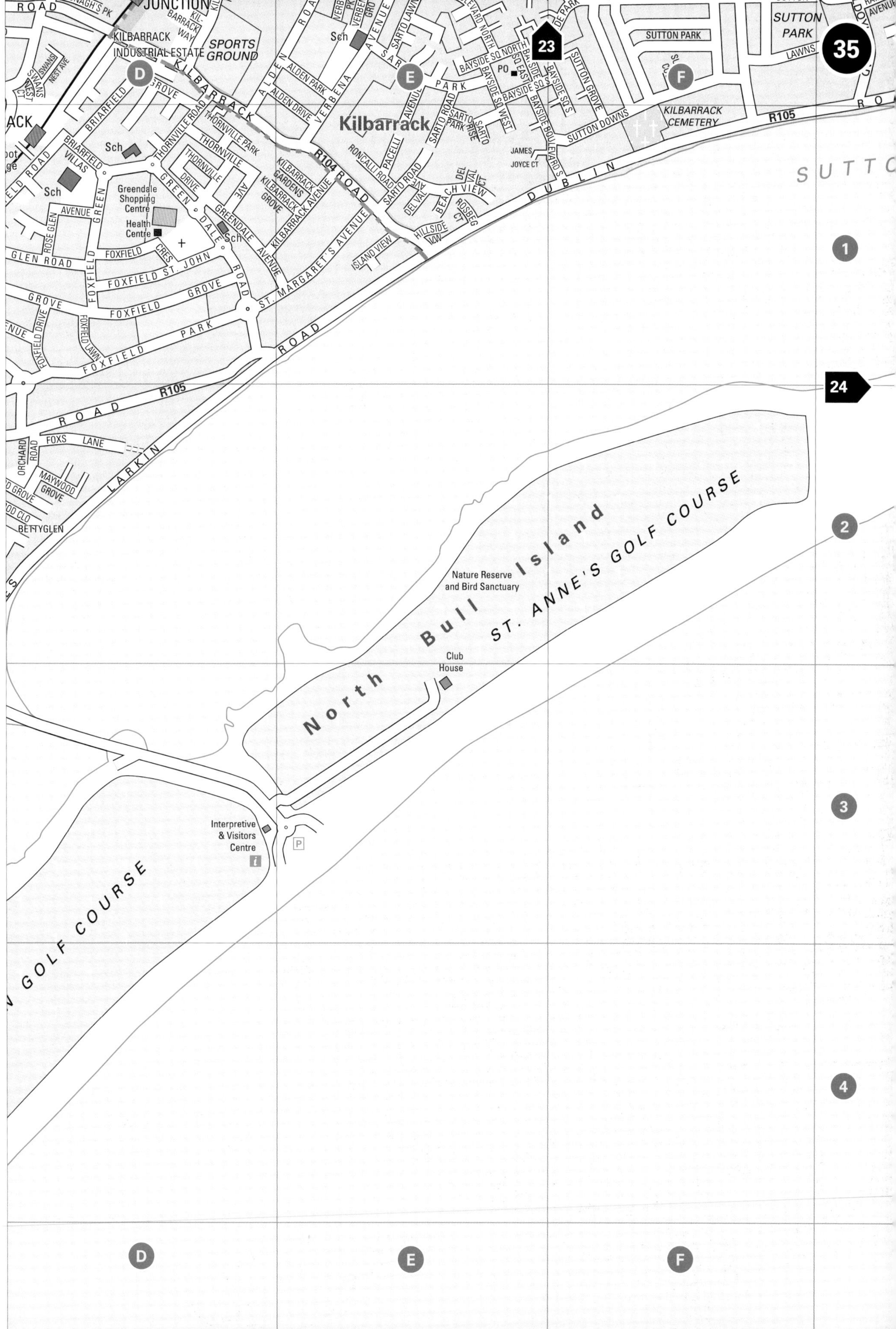
35
23
24
JUNCTION
KILBARRACK INDUSTRIAL ESTATE
SPORTS GROUND
Kilbarrack
KILBARRACK CEMETERY
SUTTON PARK
SUTTON DOWNS
SUTTON GROVE
Greendale Shopping Centre
Health Centre
Sch
PO
JAMES JOYCE CT
KILBARRACK ROAD
R104 ROAD
R105
DUBLIN ROAD
ST. MARGARET'S AVENUE
FOXFIELD ST. JOHN
FOXFIELD GROVE
FOXFIELD PARK
FOXFIELD DRIVE
FOXFIELD LAWN
FOXS LANE
ORCHARD ROAD
MAYWOOD GROVE
BETTYGLEN
LARKIN ROAD
GREENDALE AVENUE
BRIARFIELD VILLAS
THORNVILLE ROAD
THORNVILLE PARK
THORNVILLE DRIVE
KILBARRACK GARDENS
KILBARRACK GROVE
KILBARRACK AVENUE
ALDEN PARK
ALDEN DRIVE
VERBENA AVENUE
SARTO ROAD
SARTO PARK
SARTO RISE
SARTO LAWN
RONCALLI ROAD
PACELLI AVENUE
DEL VAL AVE
DEL VAL CT
BEACH VIEW
ROSBEG CT
HILLSIDE VW
ISLAND VIEW
BAYSIDE SQ. NORTH
BAYSIDE SQ. EAST
BAYSIDE SQ. WEST
BAYSIDE SQ. S
BAYSIDE BOULEVARD S
GLEN ROAD
ROSE GLEN
SUTTON
North Bull Island
Nature Reserve and Bird Sanctuary
ST. ANNE'S GOLF COURSE
Club House
Interpretive & Visitors Centre
GOLF COURSE
D
E
F
1
2
3
4

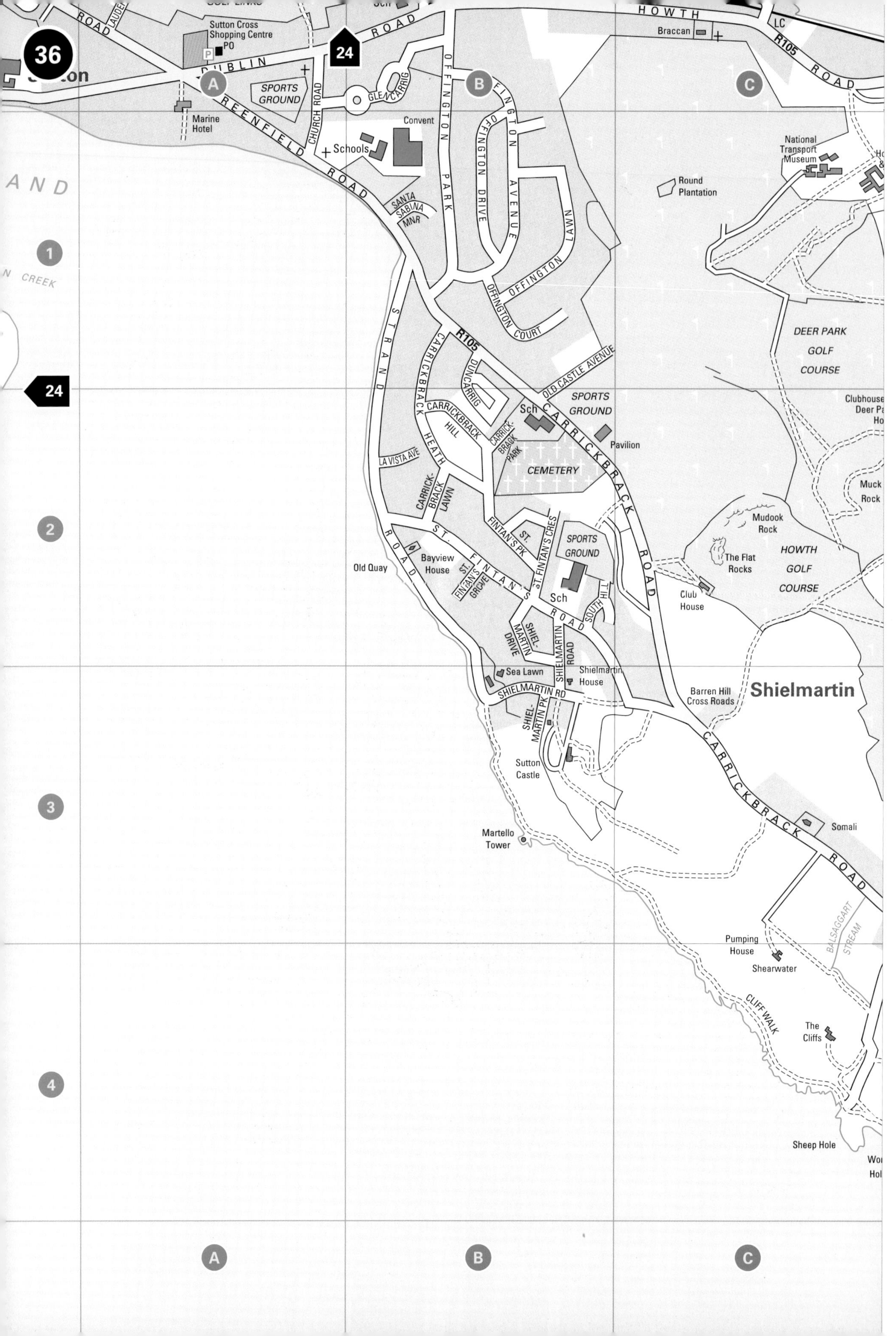

ROAD
LAUDE

Sutton Cross
Shopping Centre
PO
P

HOWTH
Braccan
R105 ROAD
LC

A
B
C

Sutton

Marine
Hotel

SPORTS
GROUND

DUBLIN ROAD

GREENFIELD ROAD

CHURCH ROAD

GLENCARRIG

OFFINGTON PARK

ROAD

Convent

Schools

SANTA
SABINA
MNR

OFFINGTON DRIVE

FINGTON AVENUE

OFFINGTON LAWN

OFFINGTON COURT

National
Transport
Museum

AND

CREEK

1

24

STRAND ROAD

CARRICKBRACK

DUNCARRIG

R105

CARRICKBRACK
HILL

LA VISTA AVE

HEATH

CARRICK-
BRACK
PARK

OLD CASTLE AVENUE

Sch

SPORTS
GROUND

CARRICKBRACK ROAD

Pavilion

Round
Plantation

DEER PARK
GOLF
COURSE

Clubhouse
Deer Pa
Ho

CEMETERY

Muck
Rock

2

Old Quay

Bayview
House

CARRICK-
BRACK
LAWN

ST. FINTAN'S ROAD

FINTAN'S PK

ST. FINTAN'S GROVE

FINTAN'S

ST FINTAN'S CRES

ST

SPORTS
GROUND

Sch

SOUTH HILL

SHIEL-
MARTIN
ROAD

SHIELMARTIN ROAD

Mudook
Rock

The Flat
Rocks

Club
House

HOWTH
GOLF
COURSE

Sea Lawn

SHIELMARTIN RD

SHIEL-
MARTIN PK

SHIEL-
MARTIN
DRIVE

Shielmartin
House

Barren Hill
Cross Roads

Shielmartin

CARRICKBRACK ROAD

3

Sutton
Castle

Martello
Tower

Somali

Pumping
House

Shearwater

BALSAGGART STREAM

4

CLIFF WALK

The
Cliffs

Sheep Hole

Wo
Hol

A
B
C

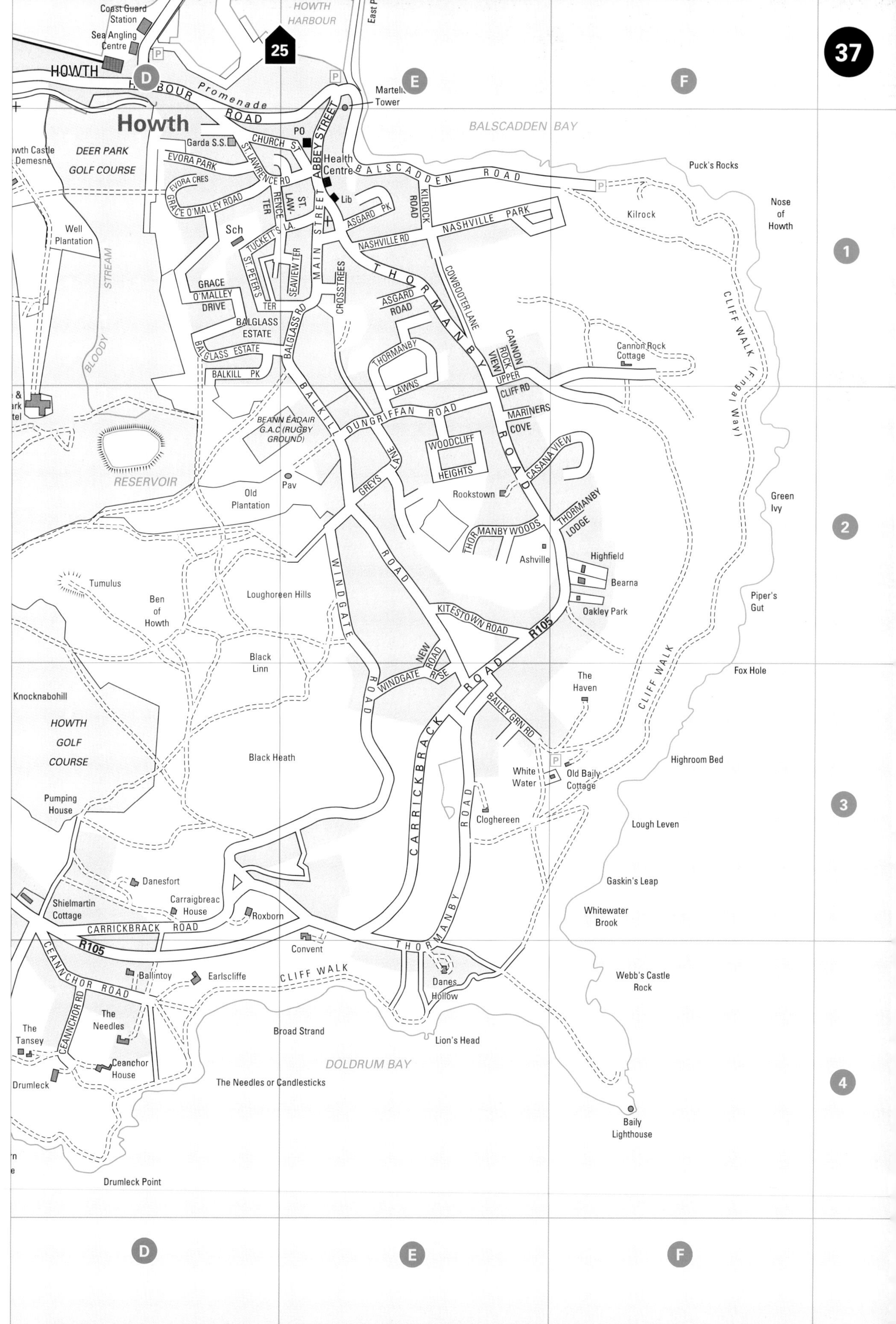

Coast Guard Station
Sea Angling Centre
HOWTH HARBOUR
25
HOWTH
HARBOUR ROAD
Promenade
Howth
Martello Tower
BALSCADDEN BAY
Howth Castle Demesne
DEER PARK GOLF COURSE
Garda S.S.
CHURCH ST
PO
ABBEY STREET
Health Centre
BALSCADDEN ROAD
Puck's Rocks
EVORA PARK
ST. LAWRENCE RD
EVORA CRES
GRACE O'MALLEY ROAD
Lib
ASGARD PK
KILROCK ROAD
Kilrock
Nose of Howth
Well Plantation
Sch
TUCKETT'S LA.
ST. LAWRENCE TER
MAIN STREET
NASHVILLE PARK
NASHVILLE RD
STREAM
ST. PETER'S TER
SEAVIEW TER
CROSSTREES
THORMANBY ROAD
COWBOOTER LANE
GRACE O'MALLEY DRIVE
ASGARD ROAD
CLIFF WALK (Fingal Way)
BALGLASS ESTATE
BALGLASS RD
BLOODY
CANNON ROCK VIEW
Cannon Rock Cottage
THORMANBY LAWNS
UPPER CLIFF RD
BALKILL PK
BALKILL
DUNGRIFFAN ROAD
MARINERS COVE
BEANN EADAIR G.A.C (RUGBY GROUND)
WOODCLIFF HEIGHTS
CASANA VIEW
RESERVOIR
Pav
Old Plantation
GREYS LANE
Rookstown
THORMANBY LODGE
Green Ivy
THORMANBY WOODS
Ashville
Highfield
Bearna
Tumulus
Ben of Howth
Loughoreen Hills
WINDGATE ROAD
KITESTOWN ROAD
Oakley Park
Piper's Gut
R105
Black Linn
NEW ROAD
WINDGATE RISE
Fox Hole
The Haven
CLIFF WALK
Knocknabohill
HOWTH GOLF COURSE
BAILEY GRN RD
Black Heath
Highroom Bed
White Water
Old Baily Cottage
Pumping House
CARRICKBRACK ROAD
Cloghereen
Lough Leven
Danesfort
Gaskin's Leap
Shielmartin Cottage
Carraigbreac House
Roxborn
Whitewater Brook
CARRICKBRACK ROAD
THORMANBY
Convent
CEANNCHOR ROAD
Ballintoy
Earlscliffe
CLIFF WALK
Danes Hollow
Webb's Castle Rock
CEANNCHOR RD
The Needles
The Tansey
Broad Strand
Lion's Head
DOLDRUM BAY
Ceanchor House
Drumleck
The Needles or Candlesticks
Baily Lighthouse
Drumleck Point
D
E
F
1
2
3
4

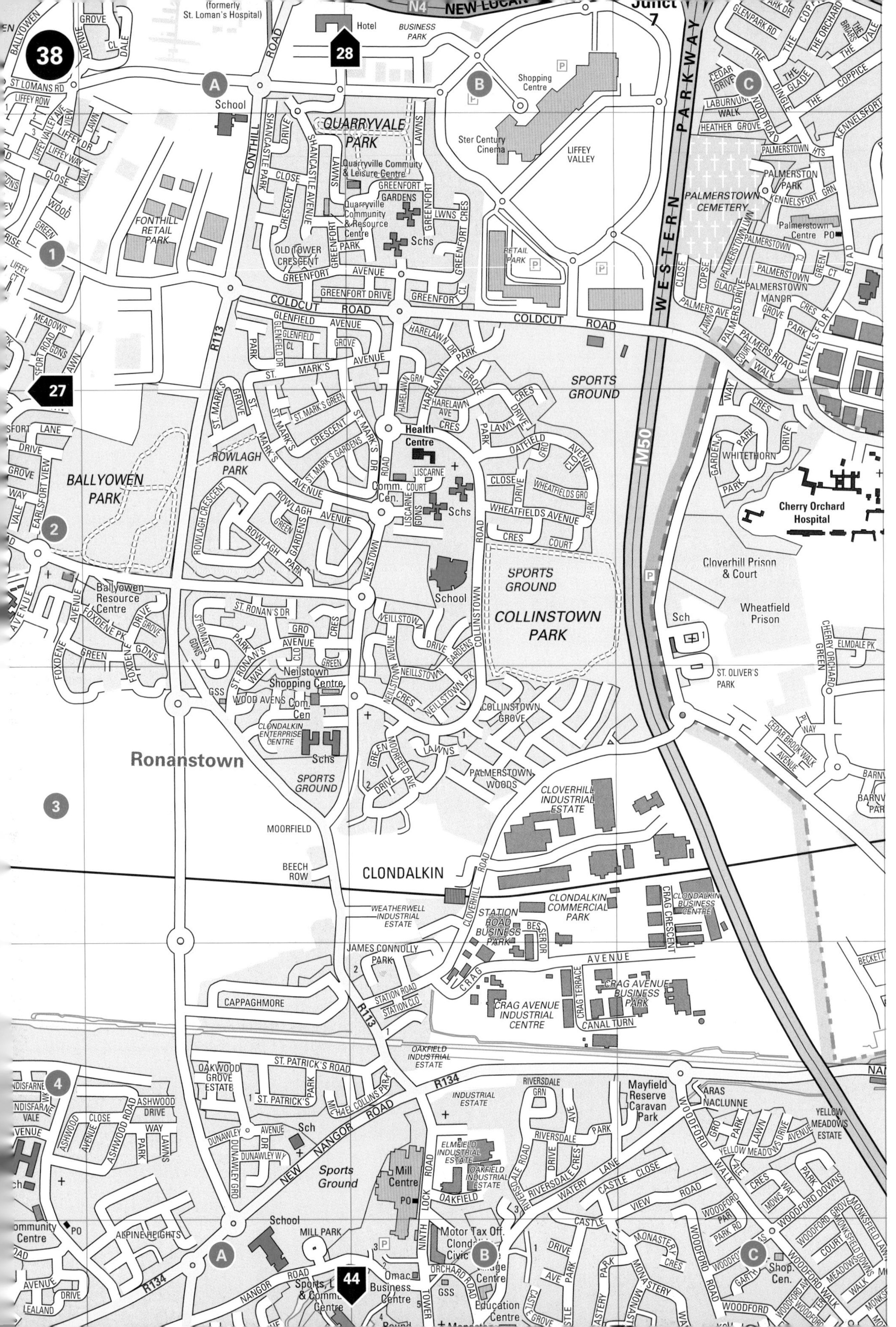

Ronanstown
CLONDALKIN
BALLYOWEN PARK
COLLINSTOWN PARK
QUARRYVALE PARK
ROWLAGH PARK
LIFFEY VALLEY
Shopping Centre
Ster Century Cinema
FONTHILL RETAIL PARK
PALMERSTOWN CEMETERY
Cherry Orchard Hospital
Cloverhill Prison & Court
Wheatfield Prison
SPORTS GROUND
Health Centre
Comm. Cen.
Neilstown Shopping Centre
CLONDALKIN ENTERPRISE CENTRE
CLOVERHILL INDUSTRIAL ESTATE
CLONDALKIN COMMERCIAL PARK
CLONDALKIN BUSINESS CENTRE
STATION ROAD BUSINESS PARK
WEATHERWELL INDUSTRIAL ESTATE
CRAG AVENUE INDUSTRIAL CENTRE
CRAG AVENUE BUSINESS PARK
OAKFIELD INDUSTRIAL ESTATE
Mayfield Reserve Caravan Park
Mill Centre
Motor Tax Off.
Ballyowen Resource Centre
Quarryville Community & Leisure Centre
Palmerstown Centre
COLDCUT ROAD
NEW NANGOR ROAD
WESTERN PARKWAY
M50
N4 NEW LUCAN
R113
R134
ST. PATRICK'S ROAD
CAPPAGHMORE
MOORFIELD
BEECH ROW
PALMERSTOWN WOODS
COLLINSTOWN GROVE
WOODFORD

28
27
44

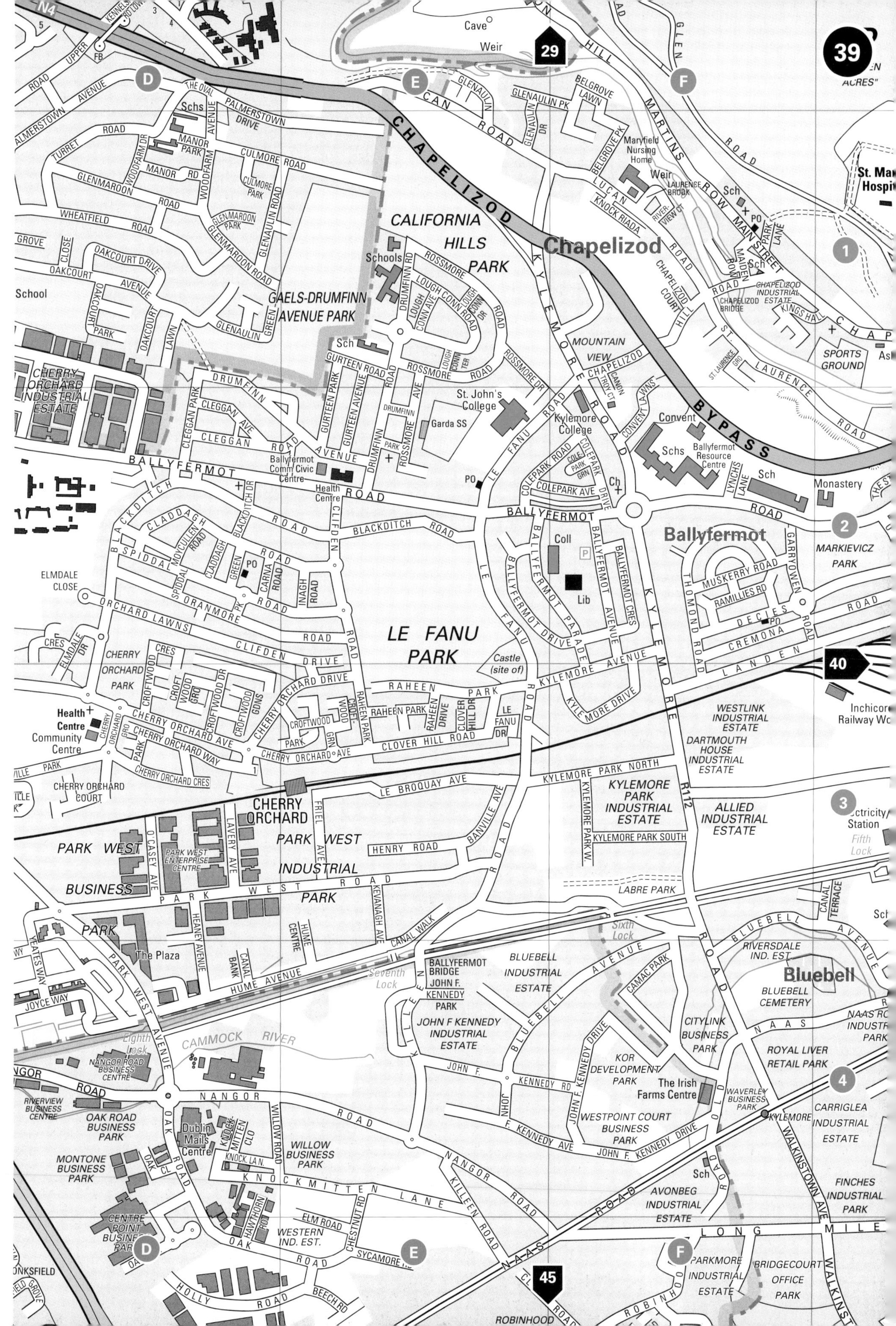

39
29
40
45
Cave
Weir
Chapelizod
CHAPELIZOD BYPASS
CALIFORNIA HILLS PARK
GAELS-DRUMFINN AVENUE PARK
LE FANU PARK
Ballyfermot
Bluebell
Kylemore College
St. John's College
Garda SS
Ballyfermot Comm Civic Centre
Health Centre
Maryfield Nursing Home
Convent
Ballyfermot Resource Centre
Monastery
MARKIEVICZ PARK
Coll
Lib
Castle (site of)
CHERRY ORCHARD INDUSTRIAL ESTATE
CHERRY ORCHARD PARK
CHERRY ORCHARD
Community Centre
ELMDALE CLOSE
School
Schools
MOUNTAIN VIEW
CHAPELIZOD INDUSTRIAL ESTATE
CHAPELIZOD BRIDGE
SPORTS GROUND
St. Mary's Hospital
Inchicore Railway Works
WESTLINK INDUSTRIAL ESTATE
DARTMOUTH HOUSE INDUSTRIAL ESTATE
KYLEMORE PARK INDUSTRIAL ESTATE
ALLIED INDUSTRIAL ESTATE
Electricity Station
Fifth Lock
Sixth Lock
Seventh Lock
Eighth Lock
PARK WEST BUSINESS PARK
PARK WEST INDUSTRIAL PARK
PARK WEST ENTERPRISE CENTRE
The Plaza
BALLYFERMOT BRIDGE
JOHN F. KENNEDY PARK
JOHN F KENNEDY INDUSTRIAL ESTATE
BLUEBELL INDUSTRIAL ESTATE
RIVERSDALE IND. EST.
BLUEBELL CEMETERY
CITYLINK BUSINESS PARK
KOR DEVELOPMENT PARK
The Irish Farms Centre
WESTPOINT COURT BUSINESS PARK
ROYAL LIVER RETAIL PARK
NAAS ROAD INDUSTRIAL PARK
WAVERLEY BUSINESS PARK
CARRIGLEA INDUSTRIAL ESTATE
AVONBEG INDUSTRIAL ESTATE
FINCHES INDUSTRIAL PARK
PARKMORE INDUSTRIAL ESTATE
BRIDGECOURT OFFICE PARK
NANGOR ROAD BUSINESS CENTRE
RIVERVIEW BUSINESS CENTRE
OAK ROAD BUSINESS PARK
MONTONE BUSINESS PARK
Dublin Mails Centre
WILLOW BUSINESS PARK
WESTERN IND. EST.
CENTRE POINT BUSINESS PARK
CAMMOCK RIVER
PALMERSTOWN AVENUE
PALMERSTOWN DRIVE
CHAPELIZOD HILL ROAD
MARTINS ROW
MAIN STREET
LUCAN ROAD
KYLEMORE ROAD
BALLYFERMOT ROAD
LE FANU ROAD
CHERRY ORCHARD AVE
CLOVER HILL ROAD
KYLEMORE AVENUE
LE BROQUAY AVE
KYLEMORE PARK NORTH
KYLEMORE PARK SOUTH
LABRE PARK
PARK WEST ROAD
PARK WEST AVENUE
HUME AVENUE
CANAL WALK
BLUEBELL AVENUE
NAAS ROAD
NANGOR ROAD
OAK ROAD
KNOCKMITTEN LANE
LONG MILE
WALKINSTOWN AVE
JOHN F. KENNEDY DRIVE
JOHN F. KENNEDY AVE
ST. LAURENCE ROAD
GURTEEN ROAD
ROSSMORE ROAD
DRUMFINN ROAD
CLEGGAN ROAD
BLACKDITCH ROAD
CLIFDEN ROAD
ORANMORE ROAD
ORCHARD LAWNS
RAHEEN PARK
LANDEN ROAD
CREMONA ROAD
MUSKERRY ROAD
THOMOND ROAD
GARRYOWEN ROAD
GLENMAROON ROAD
WHEATFIELD ROAD
CULMORE ROAD
OAKCOURT AVENUE
R112
KYLEMORE
ROBINHOOD ROAD
HOLLY ROAD
BEECH RD
ELM ROAD
SYCAMORE RD
CHESTNUT RD
JOYCE WAY
YEATES WAY
MONKSFIELD

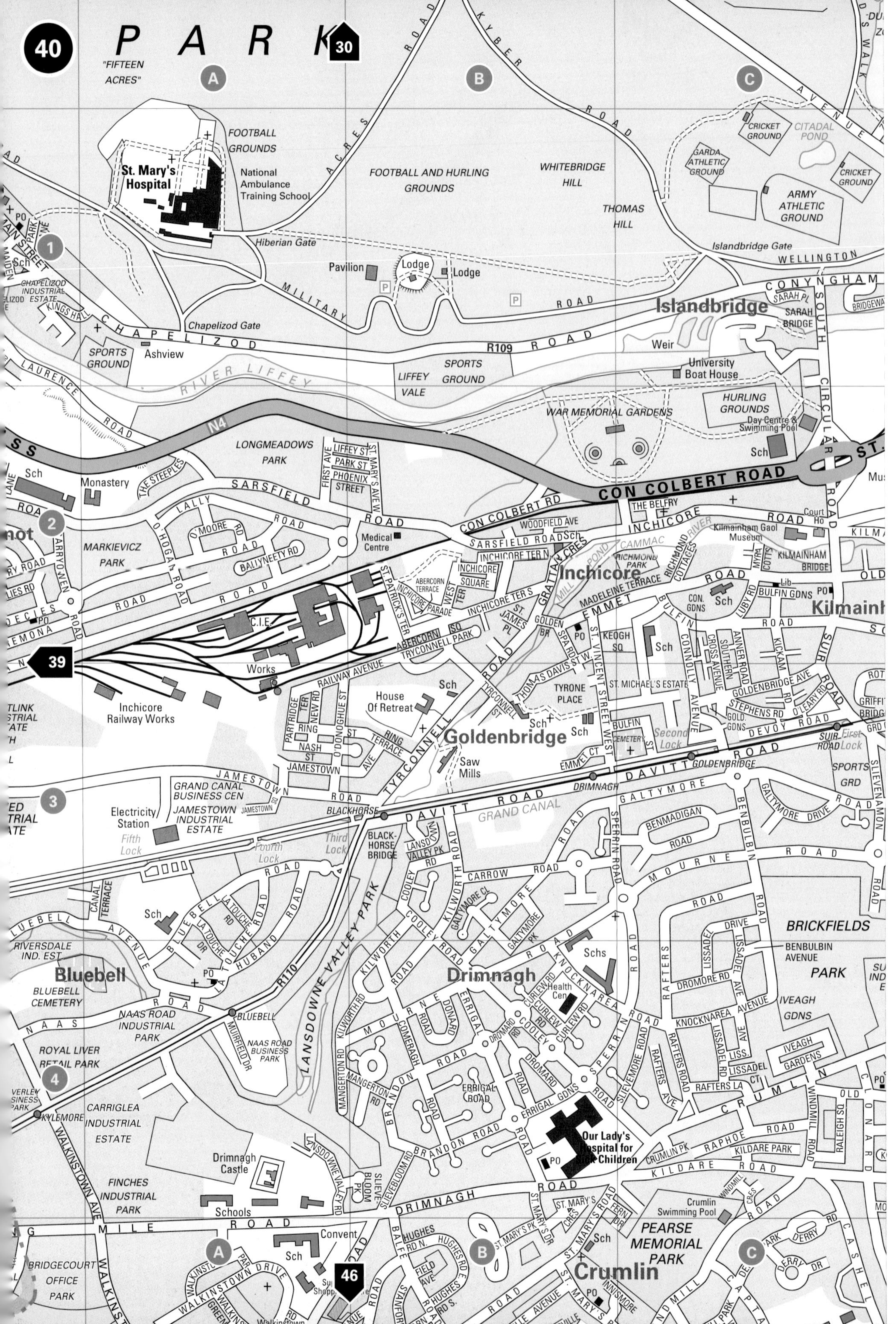

"FIFTEEN ACRES"

A

B

C

FOOTBALL GROUNDS

St. Mary's Hospital

National Ambulance Training School

FOOTBALL AND HURLING GROUNDS

WHITEBRIDGE HILL

THOMAS HILL

CRICKET GROUND

CITADAL POND

GARDA ATHLETIC GROUND

CRICKET GROUND

ARMY ATHLETIC GROUND

CHAPELIZOD INDUSTRIAL ESTATE

Kings Hall

CHAPELIZOD ROAD

Chapelizod Gate

Hiberian Gate

MILITARY ROAD

Pavilion

Lodge

Lodge

R109 ROAD

Islandbridge Gate

WELLINGTON

CONYNGHAM ROAD

Islandbridge

Sarah Bridge

SOUTH CIRCULAR ROAD

Weir

University Boat House

SPORTS GROUND

Ashview

RIVER LIFFEY

LIFFEY VALE

SPORTS GROUND

WAR MEMORIAL GARDENS

HURLING GROUNDS

Day Centre & Swimming Pool

Sch

LAURENCE ROAD

N4

LONGMEADOWS PARK

LIFFEY ST.

PARK ST.

MARY'S AVE.

FIRST AVE.

PHOENIX STREET

CON COLBERT ROAD

THE BELFRY

Court Ho.

Sch

Monastery

THE STEEPLES

SARSFIELD ROAD

CON COLBERT RD.

WOODFIELD AVE.

INCHICORE

Kilmainham Gaol Museum

KILMAINHAM BRIDGE

Kilmainh

Sch

MARKIEVICZ PARK

O'MOORE RD.

LALLY ROAD

BALLYNEETY RD.

SARSFIELD ROAD

Sch

INCHICORE TERR.

INCHICORE SQUARE

RICHMOND PARK

RICHMOND COTTAGES

Lib

KILMAINHAM

2

O'HOGAN RD.

Medical Centre

ABERCORN TERRACE

INCHICORE TERS.

GRATTAN CRES.

MILL

CAMMAC

CON. GDNS.

BULFIN GDNS.

ROAD

DECIES RD.

ROAD

ST. PATRICK'S TER.

INCHICORE PARADE

INCHICORE TERS.

ST. JAMES PL.

GOLDEN BR.

EMMET ROAD

MADELEINE TERRACE

LUBY RD.

Sch

39

C.I.E.

ABERCORN SQ.

TRYCONNELL PARK

THOMAS DAVIS ST. W.

PO

KEOGH SQ.

CONNOLLY AVE.

SOUTHERN

KICKAM RD.

ROT GRIFFI

Works

INCHICORE

Inchicore Railway Works

PARTRIDGE TER.

NEW RD.

RAILWAY AVENUE

Sch

TYRONE PLACE

ST. VINCENT STREET WEST

ST. MICHAEL'S ESTATE

CROSS AVENUE

GOLDENBRIDGE AVE.

STEPHENS RD.

O'LEARY RD.

BRIDG

RING TER.

NASH ST.

O'DONOGHUE ST.

RING TERRACE

House Of Retreat

Goldenbridge

TYRONNELL ST.

BULFIN CEMETERY

Second Lock

GOLD. GDNS.

DEVOY RD.

SUIR ROAD

SUIR First Lock

JAMESTOWN

JAMESTOWN ROAD

Saw Mills

EMMET CT.

SPORTS GRD.

3

Electricity Station

GRAND CANAL BUSINESS CEN

JAMESTOWN INDUSTRIAL ESTATE

JAMESTOWN

BLACKHORSE

DAVITT ROAD

DRIMNAGH ROAD

GALTYMORE

GOLDENBRIDGE

SLIEVENAMON

ED STRIAL ATE

Fifth Lock

Fourth Lock

Third Lock

BLACK-HORSE BRIDGE

LANSD VALLEY PK.

GRAND CANAL

DAVITT ROAD

SPERRIN ROAD

GALTYMORE DRIVE

BENMADIGAN ROAD

LISSADEL AVE.

GALTYMORE ROAD

ROAD

CANAL TERRACE

Sch

BLUEBELL RD.

LATOUCHE RD.

LATOUCHE DR.

LATOUCHE ROAD

HUBAND ROAD

R110

COOLEY ROAD

KILWORTH RD.

CARROW ROAD

MOURNE ROAD

BENBULBIN ROAD

RAFTERS ROAD

BRICKFIELDS

BENBULBIN AVENUE

IVEAGH GDNS.

PARK

Bluebell

BLUEBELL CEMETERY

NAAS ROAD INDUSTRIAL PARK

PO

Bluebell

COOLEY ROAD

KILWORTH RD.

GALTYMORE PK.

KNOCKNAREA ROAD

Schs

Health Cen

DROMORE RD.

LISSADEL AVENUE

KNOCKNAREA AVENUE

LISS. AVE.

LISSADEL CT.

IVEAGH GARDENS

RIVERSDALE IND. EST.

LAURENCE AVENUE

NAAS ROAD BUSINESS PARK

MANGERTON RD.

ERRIGAL GDNS.

DROMARD AVE.

COOLEY RD.

CURLEW RD.

DROMARD RD.

SPERRIN ROAD

RAFTERS AVE.

RAFTERS LA.

LISSADEL

CRUMLIN ROAD

WINDMILL

4

ROYAL LIVER RETAIL PARK

VERLEY SINESS PARK

KYLEMORE

CARRIGLEA INDUSTRIAL ESTATE

WALKINSTOWN AVE.

BRANDON ROAD

COMERAGH ROAD

ERRIGAL ROAD

CURLEW RD.

Our Lady's Hospital for Sick Children

PO

CRUMLIN PK.

KILDARE PARK

RAPHOE ROAD

WINDMILL CRES.

OLD

RALEIGH SQ.

CASH

PO

FINCHES INDUSTRIAL PARK

Drimnagh Castle

Schools

LANSDOWNE VALLEY ROAD

SLIEVE BLOOM PK.

DRIMNAGH ROAD

BRANDON ROAD

ST. MARY'S RD.

KILDARE ROAD

Crumlin Swimming Pool

PEARSE MEMORIAL PARK

CAPTA

CONARD

DERRY

BRIDGECOURT OFFICE PARK

MILE ROAD

WALKINSTOWN

WALKINSTOWN DRIVE

WALKINS GREEN

Convent

Sch

46

Sub Shopp

HUGHES RD. N.

HUGHES RD.

FIELD AVE.

STANFORD

ST. MARY'S PK.

ST. MARY'S CRES.

ST. MARY'S TER.

Sch

Crumlin

INNISMORE

DERRY DR.

A

B

C

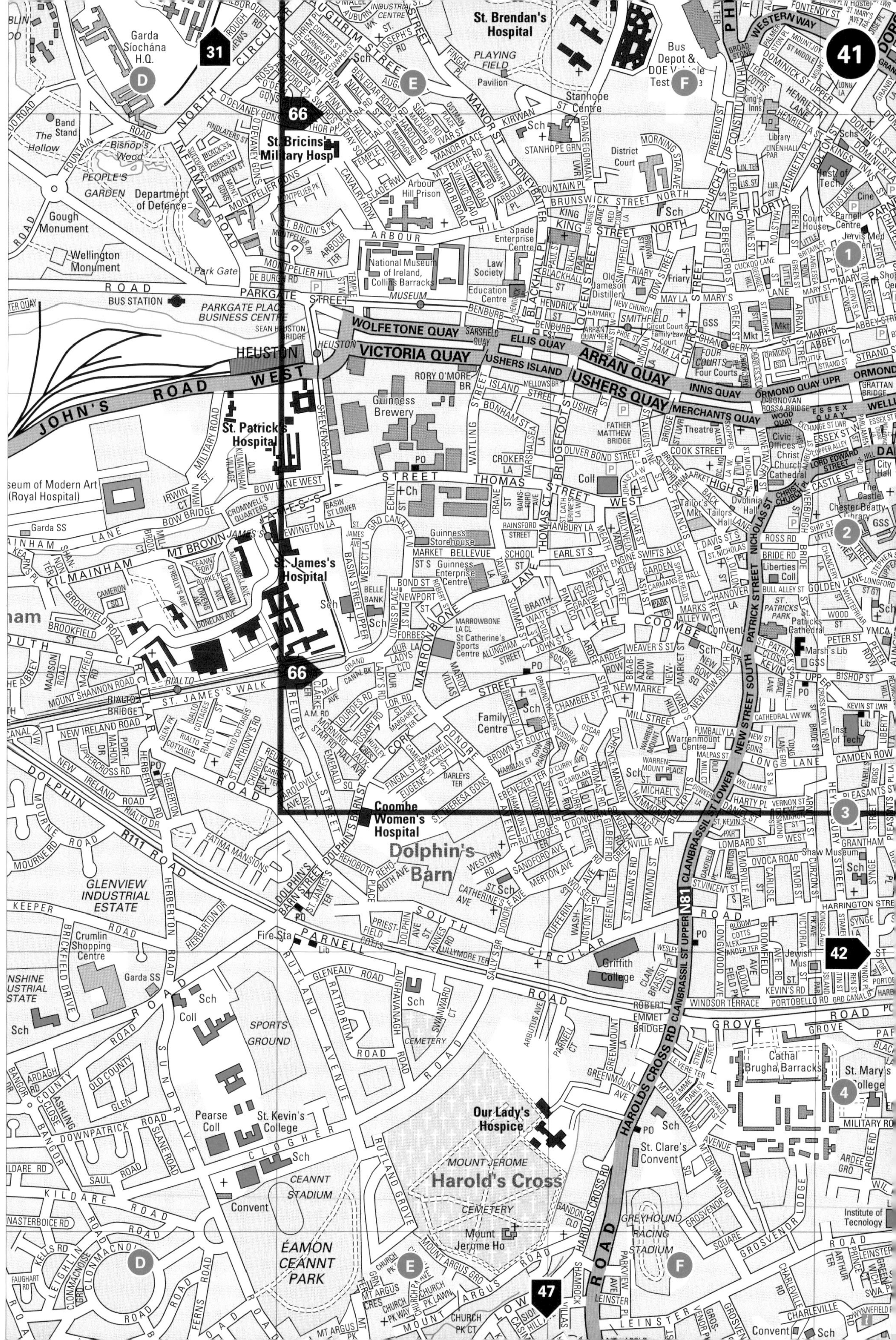

41
31
66
42
47
D
E
F
1
2
3
4
Garda Síochána H.Q.
St. Brendan's Hospital
PLAYING FIELD
Pavilion
Bus Depot & DOE Vehicle Test Centre
Stanhope Centre
St. Bricins' Military Hosp
Band Stand
The Hollow
Bishop's Wood
PEOPLE'S GARDEN
Department of Defence
Gough Monument
Wellington Monument
Park Gate
Arbour Hill Prison
District Court
Spade Enterprise Centre
Law Society
Education Centre
National Museum of Ireland, Collins Barracks
MUSEUM
Old Jameson Distillery
Friary
Circuit Court & Family law Court
FOUR COURTS
Four Courts
Library
Court House
Parnell Centre
Jervis Med Centre
Inst of Tech
Cine
Mkt
GSS
BUS STATION
PARKGATE PLACE BUSINESS CENTRE
HEUSTON
SEAN HEUSTON BRIDGE
WOLFE TONE QUAY
VICTORIA QUAY
ELLIS QUAY
ARRAN QUAY
USHERS ISLAND
USHERS QUAY
INNS QUAY
ORMOND QUAY UPR
MERCHANTS QUAY
WOOD QUAY
ESSEX QUAY
ST. JOHN'S ROAD WEST
RORY O'MORE BR
MELLOWS BR
FATHER MATTHEW BRIDGE
O'DONOVAN ROSSA BRIDGE
GRATTAN BRIDGE
Guinness Brewery
St. Patrick's Hospital
Museum of Modern Art (Royal Hospital)
Garda SS
Theatre
Civic Offices
Christ Church Cathedral
City Hall
The Castle
Chester Beatty Library
Coll
Dvblinia Hall
Tailors Hall
Tailor's Mkt
Guinness Storehouse
Guinness Enterprise Centre
St. James's Hospital
Liberties Coll
St. Patrick's Park
St. Patricks Cathedral
Marsh's Lib
YMCA
Inst of Tech
Lib
Convent
Warrenmount Centre
Family Centre
MARROWBONE LA CL St Catherine's Sports Centre
Coombe Women's Hospital
Dolphin's Barn
Shaw Museum
Jewish Mus
Griffith College
GLENVIEW INDUSTRIAL ESTATE
Crumlin Shopping Centre
Garda SS
Fire Sta
Lib
SPORTS GROUND
CEMETERY
Cathal Brugha Barracks
St. Mary's College
Our Lady's Hospice
MOUNT JEROME
Harold's Cross
CEMETERY
Mount Jerome Ho
St. Clare's Convent
GREYHOUND RACING STADIUM
Pearse Coll
St. Kevin's College
CEANNT STADIUM
Convent
ÉAMON CEANNT PARK
Institute of Tecnology
ROBERT EMMET BRIDGE
N81
R111
CLANBRASSIL ST UPPER
CLANBRASSIL ST LOWER
NEW STREET SOUTH
PATRICK STREET
NICHOLAS ST
HAROLDS CROSS RD
SOUTH CIRCULAR ROAD
DOLPHIN ROAD
CRUMLIN ROAD
SUNDRIVE ROAD
KILMAINHAM
THOMAS STREET
JAMES'S STREET
THE COOMBE
ST. JAMES'S WALK
CORK STREET
DONORE AVENUE
MANOR STREET
STONEYBATTER
KING STREET NORTH
BRUNSWICK STREET NORTH
NORTH CIRCULAR ROAD
INFIRMARY ROAD
CONYNGHAM ROAD
PARKGATE STREET
BENBURB ST
SMITHFIELD
CHURCH STREET
CONSTITUTION HILL
HENRIETTA ST
BOLTON ST
DOMINICK ST UPPER
CAPEL ST
MARY ST
ABBEY ST
HIGH ST
LORD EDWARD STREET
CASTLE ST
BRIDE RD
BRIDE ST
HEYTESBURY STREET
CAMDEN ROW
LONG LANE
GRANTHAM ST
HARRINGTON STREET
PORTOBELLO RD
GROVE ROAD
LEINSTER RD
MOUNT ARGUS RD
KIMMAGE ROAD LOWER
GRD CANAL PL
MARROWBONE LANE
BASIN STREET UPPER
ST. ANTHONY'S RD
HERBERTON RD
RIALTO BRIDGE
MOUNTSHANNON ROAD
BROOKFIELD ROAD
EMMET RD
BOW LANE WEST
IRWIN ST
MOUNT BROWN
OLD COUNTY GLEN
KILDARE RD
CLOGHER ROAD
RUTLAND GROVE
RUTLAND AVENUE
RATHDRUM
GLENEALY ROAD
AUGHAVANAGH ROAD
SLANE ROAD
DOWNPATRICK ROAD
GROSVENOR SQUARE
MILITARY ROAD
CHARLEVILLE RD

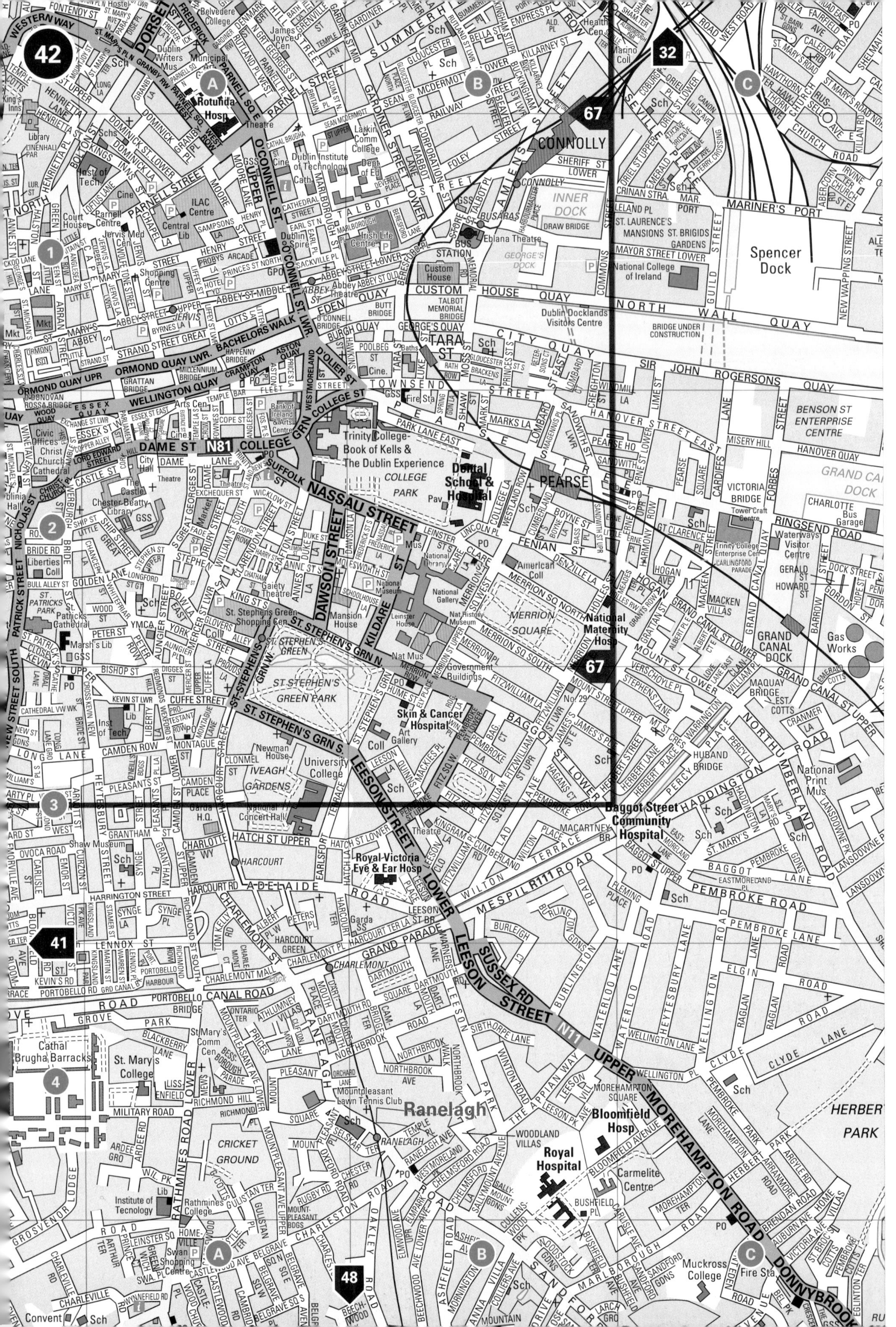
A
B
C
1
2
3
4
32
67
41
48
WESTERN WAY
DORSET ST
FREDERICK ST N
PARNELL SQ E
PARNELL STREET
Rotunda Hosp
Dublin Writers Mus
Municipal Gallery
Belvedere College
James Joyce Cen
SUMMERHILL
GARDINER STREET LOWER
O'CONNELL ST. UPPER
O'CONNELL ST. LWR.
Dublin Institute of Technology
Larkin Comm College
Dept of Ed
CONNOLLY
SHERIFF ST LOWER
INNER DOCK
GEORGE'S DOCK
Spencer Dock
MARINER'S PORT
MAYOR STREET LOWER
National College of Ireland
ST. LAURENCE'S MANSIONS
ST. BRIGIDS GARDENS
Custom House
BUSARAS
Eblana Theatre
BUS STATION
CUSTOM HOUSE QUAY
NORTH WALL QUAY
Dublin Docklands Visitors Centre
BRIDGE UNDER CONSTRUCTION
CITY QUAY
SIR JOHN ROGERSONS QUAY
TALBOT MEMORIAL BRIDGE
TARA ST
ILAC Centre
Central Lib
Court House
Jervis Med Cen
Jervis Shopping Centre
HENRY STREET
ABBEY STREET MIDDLE
ABBEY STREET LOWER
Abbey Theatre
Irish Life Centre
Dublin Spire
GPO
BACHELORS WALK
ORMOND QUAY UPR
ORMOND QUAY LWR.
WELLINGTON QUAY
ASTON QUAY
EDEN QUAY
BURGH QUAY
GEORGE'S QUAY
D'OLIER ST
TOWNSEND STREET
PEARSE STREET
PEARSE
HA'PENNY BRIDGE
MILLENNIUM BRIDGE
GRATTAN BRIDGE
O'DONOVAN ROSSA BRIDGE
O'CONNELL BRIDGE
BUTT BRIDGE
ESSEX QUAY
Civic Offices
Christ Church Cathedral
Dublinia
DAME ST
N81
COLLEGE GRN
Bank of Ireland & Arts Centre
Arts Cen
City Hall
The Castle
Chester Beatty Library
Trinity College - Book of Kells & The Dublin Experience
COLLEGE PARK
Dental School & Hospital
NASSAU STREET
DAWSON STREET
KILDARE ST
GRAFTON STREET
National Library
National Museum
National Gallery
Nat History Museum
Leinster House
Mansion House
Gaiety Theatre
St. Stephens Green Shopping Cen
ST STEPHEN'S GREEN PARK
ST. STEPHEN'S GRN N.
ST. STEPHEN'S GRN S.
Government Buildings
MERRION SQUARE
MERRION SQ NORTH
MERRION SQ SOUTH
American Coll
National Maternity Hosp
FENIAN ST
Skin & Cancer Hospital
FITZWILLIAM SQ
BAGGOT ST LOWER
Newman House
University College
IVEAGH GARDENS
National Concert Hall
Garda H.Q.
Shaw Museum
HARCOURT
Royal Victoria Eye & Ear Hosp
LEESON STREET LOWER
Baggot Street Community Hospital
MACARTNEY BR
MESPIL R11 ROAD
BENSON ST ENTERPRISE CENTRE
HANOVER QUAY
GRAND CANAL DOCK
VICTORIA BRIDGE
Tower Craft Centre
RINGSEND ROAD
Bus Garage
Waterways Visitor Centre
Trinity College Enterprise Cen
Gas Works
GRAND CANAL DOCK
GRAND CANAL ST UPPER
GRAND CANAL ST LOWER
MACKEN VILLAS
MAQUAY BRIDGE
HUBAND BRIDGE
NORTHUMBERLAND ROAD
National Print Mus
HADDINGTON ROAD
PEMBROKE ROAD
Inst of Tech
Lib
PATRICK STREET
NEW STREET SOUTH
ST. PATRICKS PARK
St. Patricks Cathedral
Marsh's Lib
Liberties Coll
CAMDEN ROW
LONG LANE
HARRINGTON STREET
ADELAIDE ROAD
GRAND PARADE
CHARLEMONT
CHARLEMONT MALL
PORTOBELLO
PORTOBELLO RD
GROVE PARK
Cathal Brugha Barracks
St. Mary's College
MILITARY ROAD
RATHMINES ROAD LOWER
Rathmines College
Institute of Tecnology
CRICKET GROUND
Mountpleasant Lawn Tennis Club
Ranelagh
RANELAGH
SUSSEX RD
LEESON STREET UPPER
N11
MOREHAMPTON ROAD
DONNYBROOK
Bloomfield Hosp
Royal Hospital
Carmelite Centre
WOODLAND VILLAS
HERBERT PARK
Muckross College
Fire Sta
Swan Shopping Centre
Convent
BEECHWOOD
ELGIN ROAD
CLYDE ROAD
WELLINGTON LANE
WATERLOO LANE
BURLINGTON ROAD

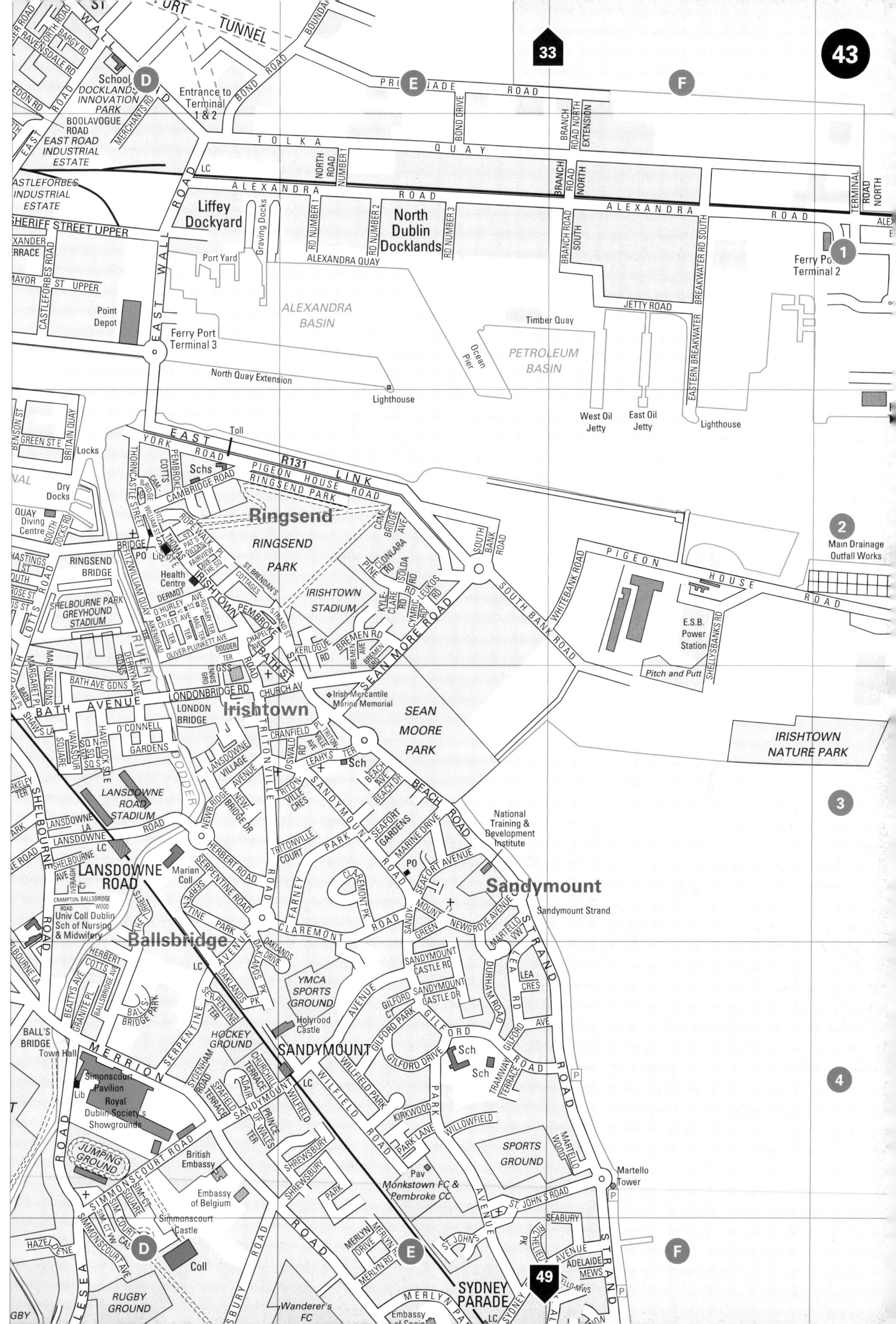

TUNNEL

PROMENADE ROAD

D School DOCKLANDS INNOVATION PARK

E

F

Entrance to Terminal 1 & 2

BOOLAVOGUE ROAD
EAST ROAD INDUSTRIAL ESTATE

TOLKA QUAY

BOND DRIVE

BRANCH ROAD NORTH EXTENSION

CASTLEFORBES INDUSTRIAL ESTATE

ALEXANDRA ROAD

LC

RD NUMBER 1

RD NUMBER 2

RD NUMBER 3

BRANCH ROAD NORTH

ALEXANDRA ROAD

SHERIFF STREET UPPER

Liffey Dockyard

North Dublin Docklands

BRANCH ROAD SOUTH

BREAKWATER RD SOUTH

ALEXANDER TERRACE

Graving Docks

Alexandra Quay

Ferry Port Terminal 2

1

MAYOR ST UPPER

CASTLEFORBES RD

Port Yard

JETTY ROAD

Point Depot

ALEXANDRA BASIN

Timber Quay

EASTERN BREAKWATER

SHELLYBANKS RD

Ferry Port Terminal 3

Ocean Pier

PETROLEUM BASIN

North Quay Extension

West Oil Jetty

East Oil Jetty

Lighthouse

GREEN ST E

Locks

EAST ROAD

Toll

R131 LINK

Lighthouse

2

Main Drainage Outfall Works

BRITAIN QUAY

Dry Docks

PIGEON HOUSE ROAD

RINGSEND PARK

SOUTH BANK ROAD

PIGEON HOUSE ROAD

QUAY Diving Centre

DOCKS RD

York Road

Schs

CAMBRIDGE ROAD

THORNCASTLE STREET

Ringsend

RINGSEND PARK

WHITEBANK ROAD

HASTINGS ST

RINGSEND BRIDGE

PO

Health Centre

RIVER DODDER

PEMBROKE

IRISHTOWN STADIUM

SEAN MOORE ROAD

E.S.B. Power Station

ROSE ST

SHELBOURNE PARK GREYHOUND STADIUM

DERMOT

BATHS

Pitch and Putt

MARGARET PL

BATH AVENUE GDNS

LONDONBRIDGE RD

Irishtown

Irish Mercantile Marine Memorial

CHURCH AV

SEAN MOORE PARK

IRISHTOWN NATURE PARK

LONDON BRIDGE

BATH AVENUE

O'CONNELL GARDENS

3

HAVELOCK SQ

Lansdowne Village

LANSDOWNE ROAD STADIUM

NEWBRIDGE DR

Sch

BEACH ROAD

National Training & Development Institute

LANSDOWNE ROAD

LANSDOWNE LA

HERBERT ROAD

TRITONVILLE COURT

SEAFORT GARDENS

Marine Drive

Sandymount

LANSDOWNE LC

Marian Coll

SERPENTINE ROAD

FARNEY ROAD

SANDYMOUNT ROAD

PO

Seafort Avenue

Sandymount Strand

CRAMPTON BALLSBRIDGE ROAD

BALLSBRIDGE WOOD

Univ Coll Dublin Sch of Nursing & Midwifery

SERPENTINE PARK

CLAREMONT ROAD

SANDYMOUNT GREEN

NEWGROVE AVENUE

STRAND ROAD

Ballsbridge

SERPENTINE AVENUE

OAKLANDS DRIVE

YMCA SPORTS GROUND

Holyrood Castle

AVENUE

SANDYMOUNT CASTLE RD

SANDYMOUNT CASTLE DR

DURHAM ROAD

LEA RD

LEA CRES

BALL'S BRIDGE

MERRION ROAD

Town Hall

HOCKEY GROUND

SANDYMOUNT

GILFORD PARK

GILFORD CT

GILFORD ROAD

GILFORD DRIVE

Sch

TRAMWAY TERRACE

P

Simonscourt Pavilion Royal Dublin Society's Showgrounds

Lib

WILFIELD ROAD

WILFIELD

KIRKWOOD

WILLFIELD PARK

PARK LANE

WILLOWFIELD

Sch

MARTELLO WOOD

4

British Embassy

SHREWSBURY PARK

SPORTS GROUND

Martello Tower

JUMPING GROUND

Embassy of Belgium

Simonscourt Castle

SHREWSBURY ROAD

Pav Monkstown FC & Pembroke CC

ST JOHN'S ROAD

SEABURY

P

D

Coll

RUGBY GROUND

SIMMONSCOURT ROAD

Wanderer's FC

MERLYN DRIVE

MERLYN RD

E

ST JOHN'S

MERLYN PARK

SYDNEY PARADE

ADELAIDE MEWS

F

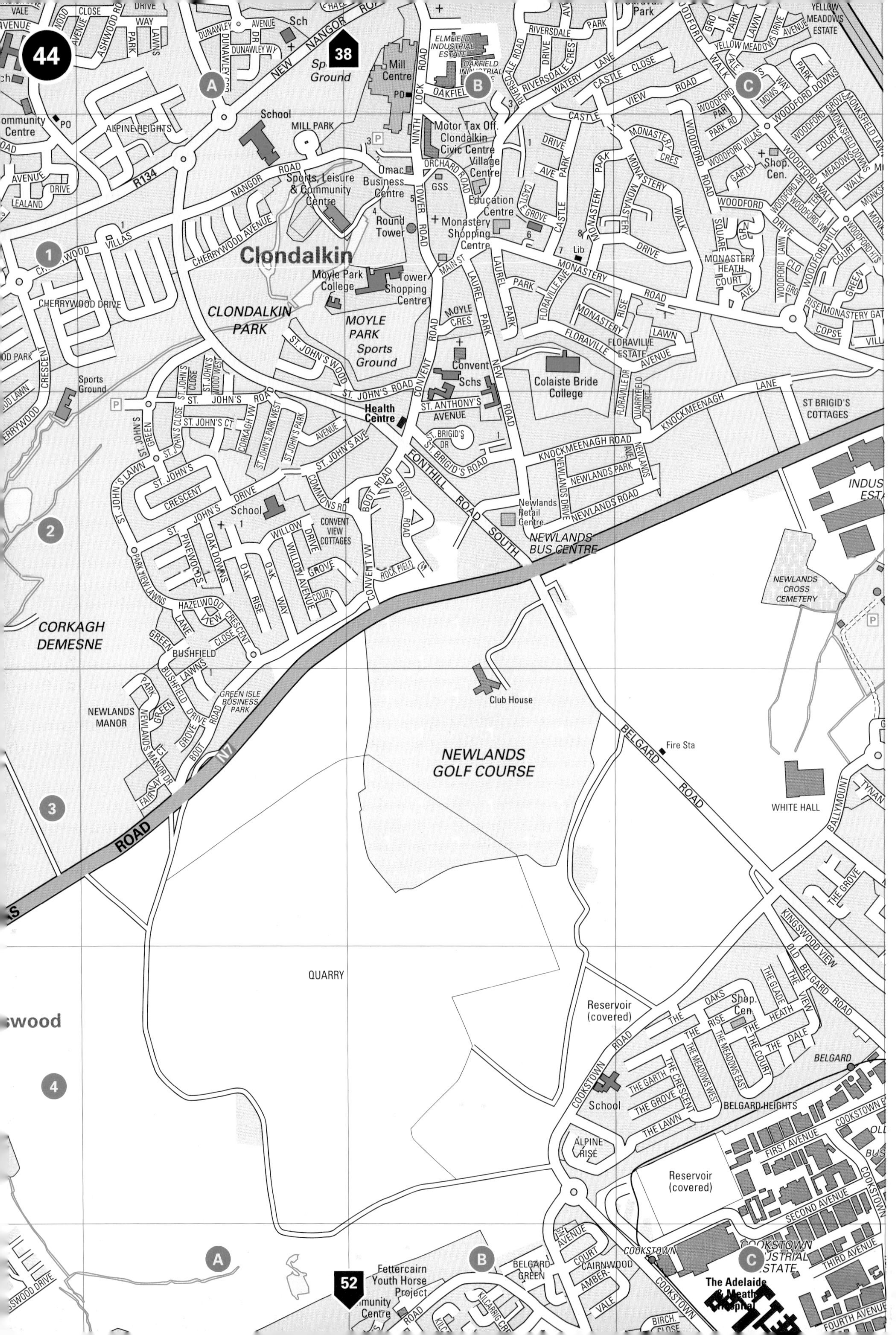
Clondalkin
CLONDALKIN PARK
MOYLE PARK Sports Ground
Mill Centre
Round Tower
Monastery Shopping Centre
Tower Shopping Centre
Moyle Park College
Sports, Leisure & Community Centre
Motor Tax Off. Clondalkin Civic Centre
Village Centre
Education Centre
Omac Business Centre
Colaiste Bride College
Convent Schs
Health Centre
Newlands Retail Centre
NEWLANDS BUS CENTRE
CORKAGH DEMESNE
NEWLANDS MANOR
GREEN ISLE BUSINESS PARK
NEWLANDS GOLF COURSE
Club House
Fire Sta
QUARRY
NEWLANDS CROSS CEMETERY
WHITE HALL
ST BRIGID'S COTTAGES
FLORAVILLE ESTATE
ELMFIELD INDUSTRIAL ESTATE
OAKFIELD INDUSTRIAL ESTATE
YELLOW MEADOWS ESTATE
ALPINE HEIGHTS
MILL PARK
Reservoir (covered)
BELGARD HEIGHTS
BELGARD
COOKSTOWN INDUSTRIAL ESTATE
The Adelaide & Meath Hospital
Fettercairn Youth Horse Project
NEW NANGOR ROAD
R134
NANGOR ROAD
N7
ROAD
BELGARD ROAD
FONTHILL ROAD SOUTH
KNOCKMEENAGH LANE
KNOCKMEENAGH ROAD
MONASTERY ROAD
CONVENT ROAD
NEW ROAD
TOWER ROAD
ST. JOHN'S ROAD
COOKSTOWN ROAD
OLD BELGARD ROAD
KINGSWOOD VIEW
38
52

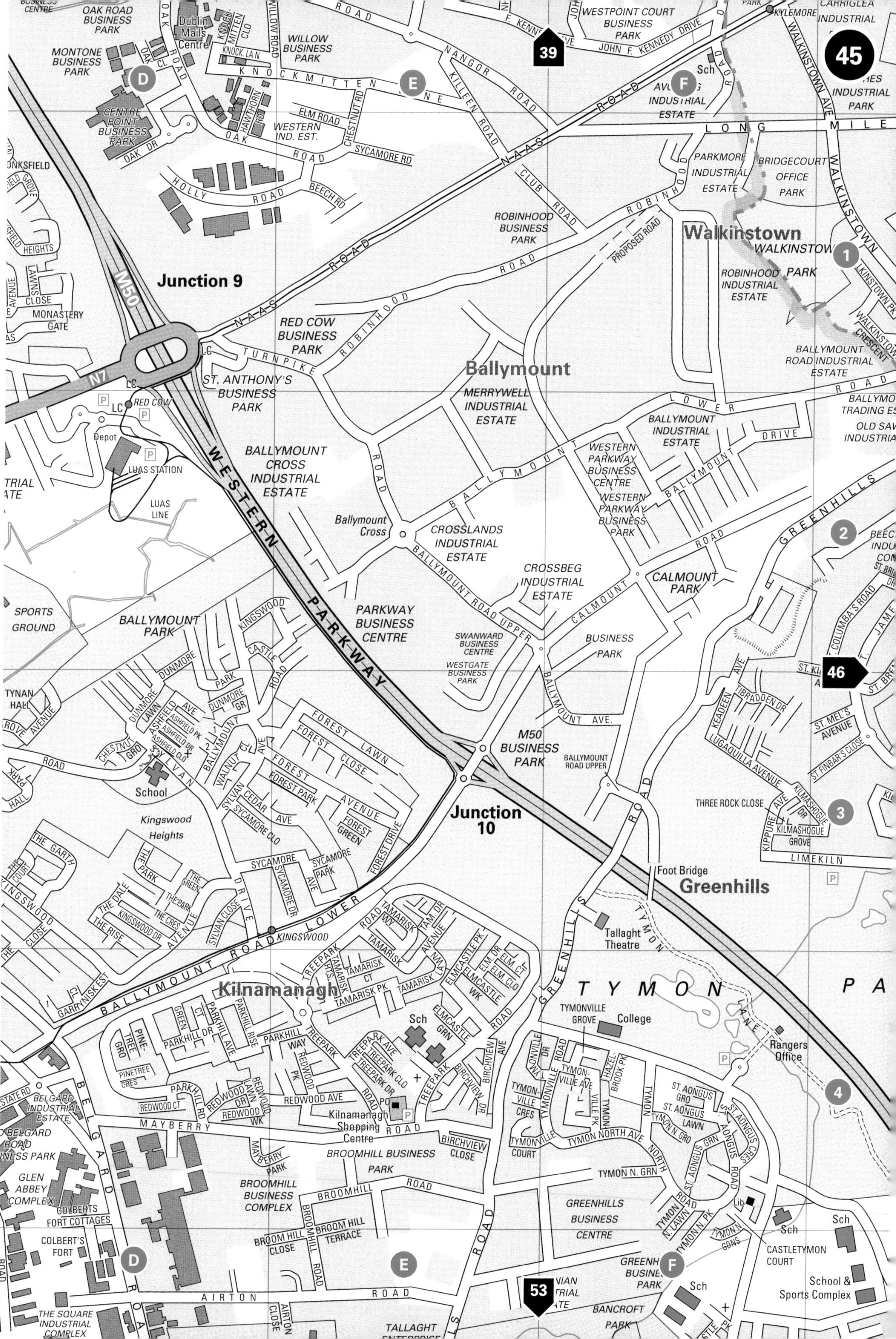
Junction 9
Ballymount
Walkinstown
Junction 10
Greenhills
Kilnamanagh
TYMON PA
M50
N7
NAAS ROAD
WESTERN PARKWAY
LONG MILE
RED COW BUSINESS PARK
ST. ANTHONY'S BUSINESS PARK
BALLYMOUNT CROSS INDUSTRIAL ESTATE
MERRYWELL INDUSTRIAL ESTATE
CROSSLANDS INDUSTRIAL ESTATE
CROSSBEG INDUSTRIAL ESTATE
PARKWAY BUSINESS CENTRE
CALMOUNT PARK
M50 BUSINESS PARK
ROBINHOOD BUSINESS PARK
ROBINHOOD INDUSTRIAL ESTATE
PARKMORE INDUSTRIAL ESTATE
BRIDGECOURT OFFICE PARK
WESTERN IND. EST.
WILLOW BUSINESS PARK
OAK ROAD BUSINESS PARK
MONTONE BUSINESS PARK
CENTRE POINT BUSINESS PARK
BALLYMOUNT PARK
SPORTS GROUND
LUAS STATION
Tallaght Theatre
Kilnamanagh Shopping Centre
BROOMHILL BUSINESS PARK
BROOMHILL BUSINESS COMPLEX
GREENHILLS BUSINESS CENTRE
Rangers Office
College
39
46
53

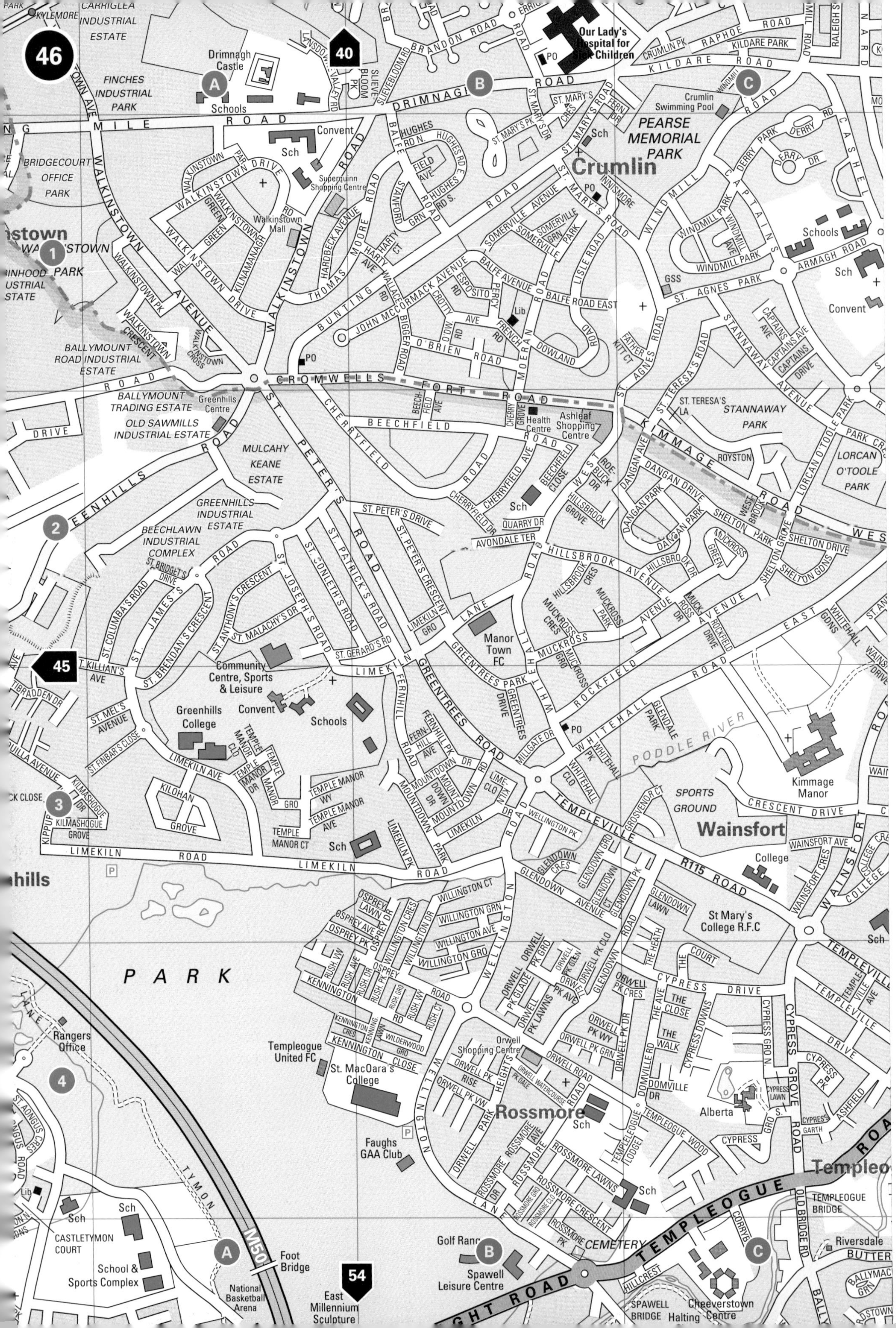

46
40
45
54
A
B
C
1
2
3
4
KYLEMORE
CARRIGLEA INDUSTRIAL ESTATE
FINCHES INDUSTRIAL PARK
Drimnagh Castle
Schools
Convent
Sch
Superquinn Shopping Centre
Walkinstown Mall
BRIDGECOURT OFFICE PARK
WALKINSTOWN PARK
BALLYMOUNT ROAD INDUSTRIAL ESTATE
BALLYMOUNT TRADING ESTATE
OLD SAWMILLS INDUSTRIAL ESTATE
Greenhills Centre
MULCAHY KEANE ESTATE
GREENHILLS INDUSTRIAL ESTATE
BEECHLAWN INDUSTRIAL COMPLEX
Our Lady's Hospital for Sick Children
PO
Crumlin Swimming Pool
PEARSE MEMORIAL PARK
Crumlin
Lib
Schools
GSS
Convent
Health Centre
Ashleaf Shopping Centre
STANNAWAY PARK
LORCAN O'TOOLE PARK
Manor Town FC
Community Centre, Sports & Leisure
Greenhills College
Convent
Schools
Kimmage Manor
SPORTS GROUND
Wainsfort
College
St Mary's College R.F.C
PODDLE RIVER
PARK
Rangers Office
Templeogue United FC
St. MacDara's College
Faughs GAA Club
Orwell Shopping Centre
Rossmore
Alberta
Golf Range
Spawell Leisure Centre
Foot Bridge
National Basketball Arena
East Millennium Sculpture
CASTLETYMON COURT
School & Sports Complex
Templeogue
TEMPLEOGUE BRIDGE
Riversdale
SPAWELL BRIDGE
Halting
Cheeverstown Centre
CEMETERY
M50
LONG MILE ROAD
DRIMNAGH ROAD
KILDARE ROAD
CRUMLIN ROAD
WALKINSTOWN AVENUE
WALKINSTOWN ROAD
CROMWELLS FORT ROAD
ST. PETER'S ROAD
GREENHILLS ROAD
KIMMAGE ROAD WEST
LIMEKILN ROAD
LIMEKILN LANE
GREENTREES ROAD
WHITEHALL ROAD
TEMPLEVILLE ROAD
R115 ROAD
WELLINGTON ROAD
CYPRESS DRIVE
CYPRESS GROVE ROAD
TEMPLEOGUE ROAD
KNOCKLYON ROAD
ST. AGNES ROAD
WINDMILL ROAD
ARMAGH ROAD

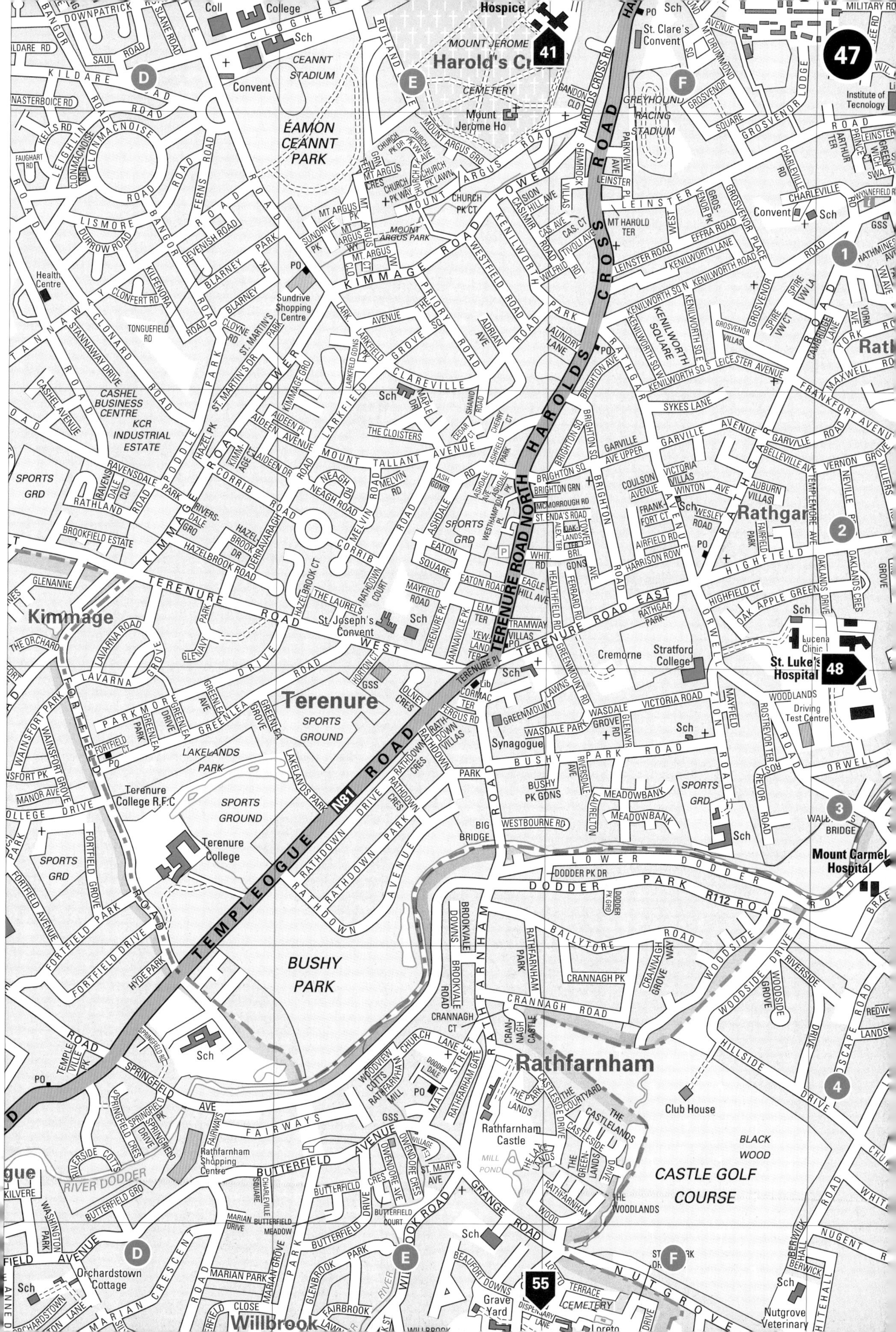

Harold's Cross
Hospice
Mount Jerome Cemetery
41
Mount Jerome Ho
College
Coll
Convent
Ceannt Stadium
Éamon Ceannt Park
St. Clare's Convent
Greyhound Racing Stadium
Military Rd
Institute of Tecnology
Harolds Cross Road
Clogher Road
Kildare Road
Clonmacnoise Road
Sundrive Road
Mount Argus Road
Kimmage Road Lower
Leinster Road
Grosvenor Square
Kenilworth Square
Rathgar Road
Harolds Cross Road
Terenure Road North
Sundrive Shopping Centre
Health Centre
Stannaway Road
Cashel Business Centre
KCR Industrial Estate
Sports Grd
Kimmage
Rathgar
Garville Avenue
Highfield Road
Frankfort Avenue
Terenure Road East
Terenure Road West
St. Joseph's Convent
Cremorne
Stratford College
Lucena Clinic
St. Luke's Hospital
48
Driving Test Centre
Orwell Road
Zion Road
Terenure
Sports Ground
Lakelands Park
Terenure College R.F.C
Terenure College
Templeogue Road
N81
Synagogue
Bushy Park Road
Dodder Park Road
R112
Mount Carmel Hospital
Bushy Park
Rathfarnham
Rathfarnham Castle
Castle Golf Course
Black Wood
Club House
Hillside Drive
Rathfarnham Shopping Centre
Butterfield Avenue
River Dodder
Orchardstown Cottage
Willbrook
Grave Yard
Cemetery
Nutgrove Veterinary
55
Fortfield Road
Springfield Ave
Fairways
Grange Road
Nutgrove

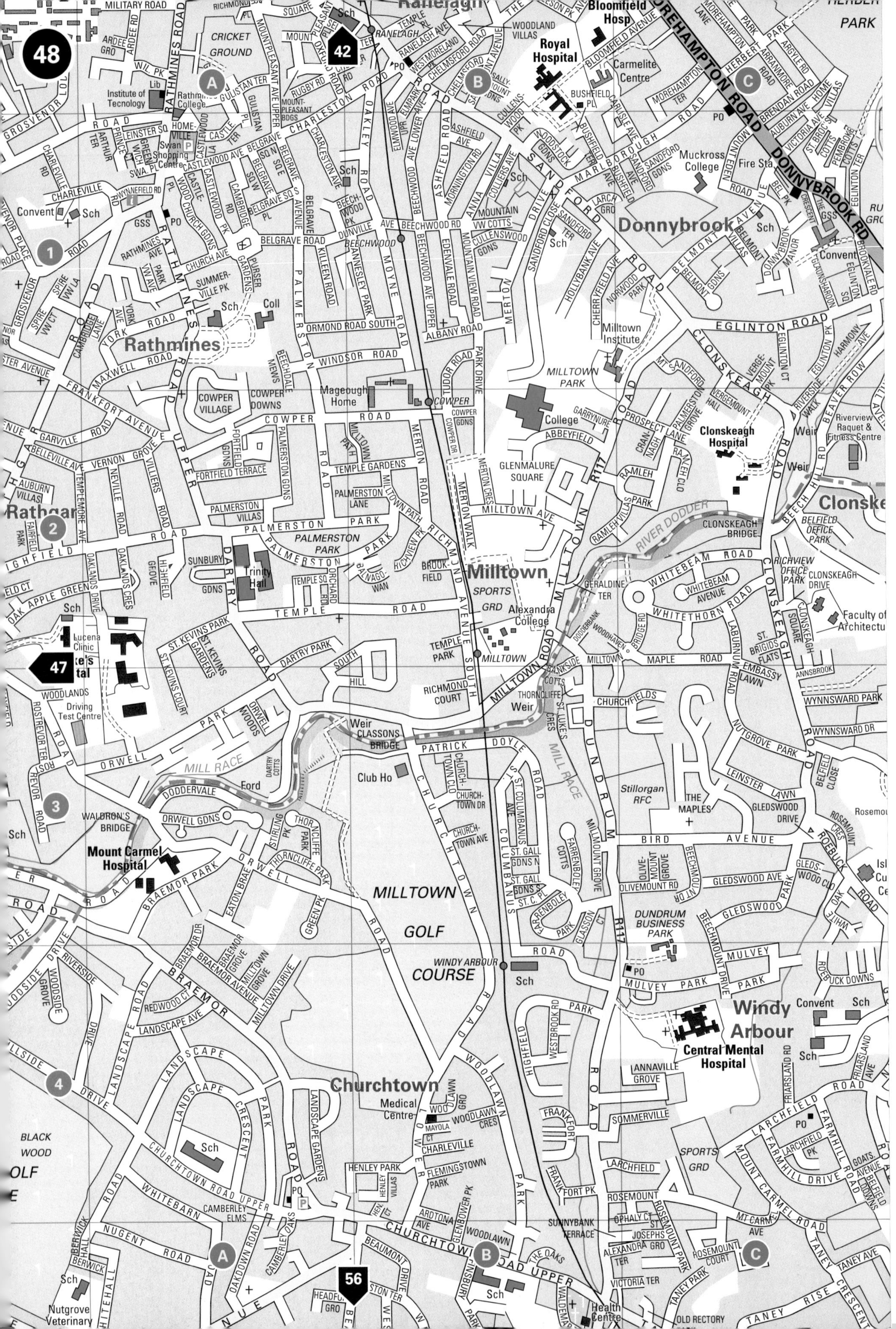
Ranelagh
42
47
56
A
B
C
1
2
3
4
HERBERT PARK
MILITARY ROAD
CRICKET GROUND
Institute of Tecnology
Rathmines College
Swan Shopping Centre
Bloomfield Hosp
Royal Hospital
Carmelite Centre
MOREHAMPTON ROAD
DONNYBROOK RD
Muckross College
Fire Sta.
Donnybrook
Convent
Rathmines
RATHMINES ROAD UPPER
CHARLESTON ROAD
BELGRAVE ROAD
BEECHWOOD
SANDFORD ROAD
MARLBOROUGH ROAD
EGLINTON ROAD
CLONSKEAGH ROAD
Milltown Institute
MILLTOWN PARK
College
GLENMALURE SQUARE
Clonskeagh Hospital
Riverview Raquet & Fitness Centre
Clonskeagh
BEECH HILL RD
Rathgar
CAMBRIDGE LANE
YORK ROAD
MAXWELL ROAD
FRANKFORT AVENUE
COWPER VILLAGE
COWPER DOWNS
COWPER ROAD
Mageough Home
ORMOND ROAD SOUTH
WINDSOR ROAD
ALBANY ROAD
PALMERSTON ROAD
PALMERSTON PARK
TEMPLE GARDENS
MILLTOWN ROAD
Trinity Hall
DARTRY ROAD
TEMPLE ROAD
Milltown
SPORTS GRD
Alexandra College
RIVER DODDER
CLONSKEAGH BRIDGE
WHITEBEAM ROAD
WHITETHORN ROAD
MAPLE ROAD
Faculty of Architecture
Lucena Clinic
Driving Test Centre
DARTRY PARK
MILLTOWN
RICHMOND COURT
Weir
CLASSONS BRIDGE
PATRICK DOYLE ROAD
MILL RACE
ORWELL PARK
Club Ho
Ford
DODDERVALE
WALDRON'S BRIDGE
Mount Carmel Hospital
BRAEMOR PARK
ORWELL ROAD
MILLTOWN GOLF COURSE
WINDY ARBOUR
CHURCHTOWN ROAD
DUNDRUM ROAD
R117
Stillorgan RFC
THE MAPLES
BIRD AVENUE
GLEDSWOOD AVE
DUNDRUM BUSINESS PARK
MULVEY PARK
Windy Arbour
Central Mental Hospital
Convent
Sch
BRAEMOR ROAD
LANDSCAPE ROAD
Churchtown
Medical Centre
BLACK WOOD
CHURCHTOWN ROAD UPPER
NUGENT ROAD
WHITEBARN ROAD
WOODLAWN PARK
FRANKFORT
SOMMERVILLE
SPORTS GRD
LARCHFIELD ROAD
MOUNT CARMEL ROAD
TANEY CRESCENT
Health Centre
Nutgrove Veterinary
OLD RECTORY

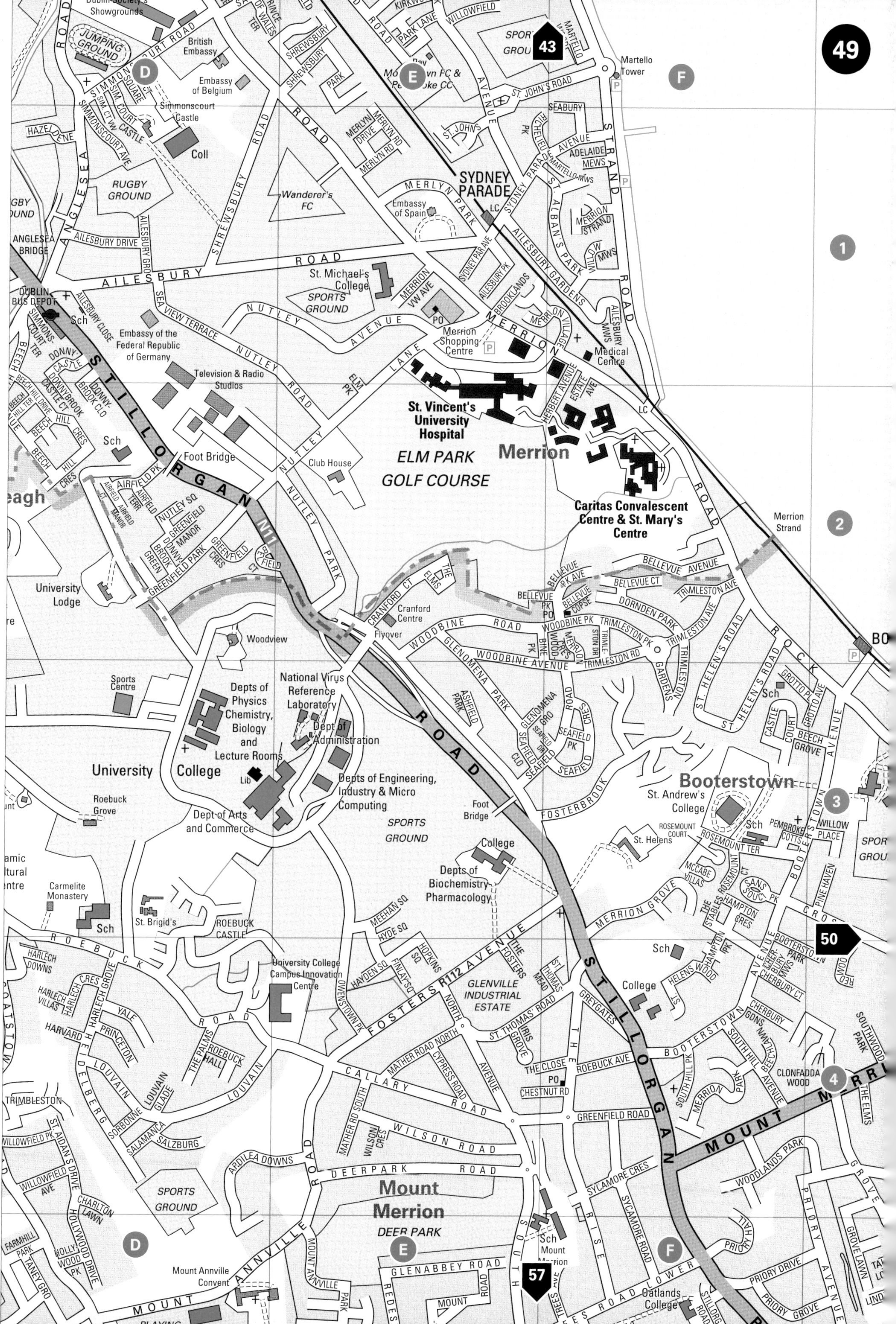

Merrion
Booterstown
Mount Merrion
University College
ELM PARK GOLF COURSE
St. Vincent's University Hospital
Caritas Convalescent Centre & St. Mary's Centre
STILLORGAN ROAD
N11
MERRION ROAD
ROCK ROAD
STRAND ROAD
AILESBURY ROAD
NUTLEY LANE
MOUNT MERRION AVENUE
FOSTERS AVENUE
R112
ROEBUCK ROAD
MOUNT ANNVILLE
SYDNEY PARADE
Martello Tower
Merrion Strand
Merrion Shopping Centre
Television & Radio Studios
Embassy of the Federal Republic of Germany
British Embassy
Embassy of Belgium
Embassy of Spain
Simmonscourt Castle
RUGBY GROUND
Wanderer's FC
St. Michael's College
SPORTS GROUND
Foot Bridge
Flyover
Club House
Cranford Centre
Woodview
National Virus Reference Laboratory
Depts of Physics Chemistry, Biology and Lecture Rooms
Dept of Administration
Depts of Engineering, Industry & Micro Computing
Dept of Arts and Commerce
Depts of Biochemistry Pharmacology
GLENVILLE INDUSTRIAL ESTATE
University College Campus Innovation Centre
Roebuck Castle
Carmelite Monastery
St. Brigid's
St. Andrew's College
Oatlands College
Mount Anville Convent
DEER PARK
CLONFADDA WOOD
University Lodge
DUBLIN BUS DEPOT
ANGLESEA BRIDGE
43
50
57

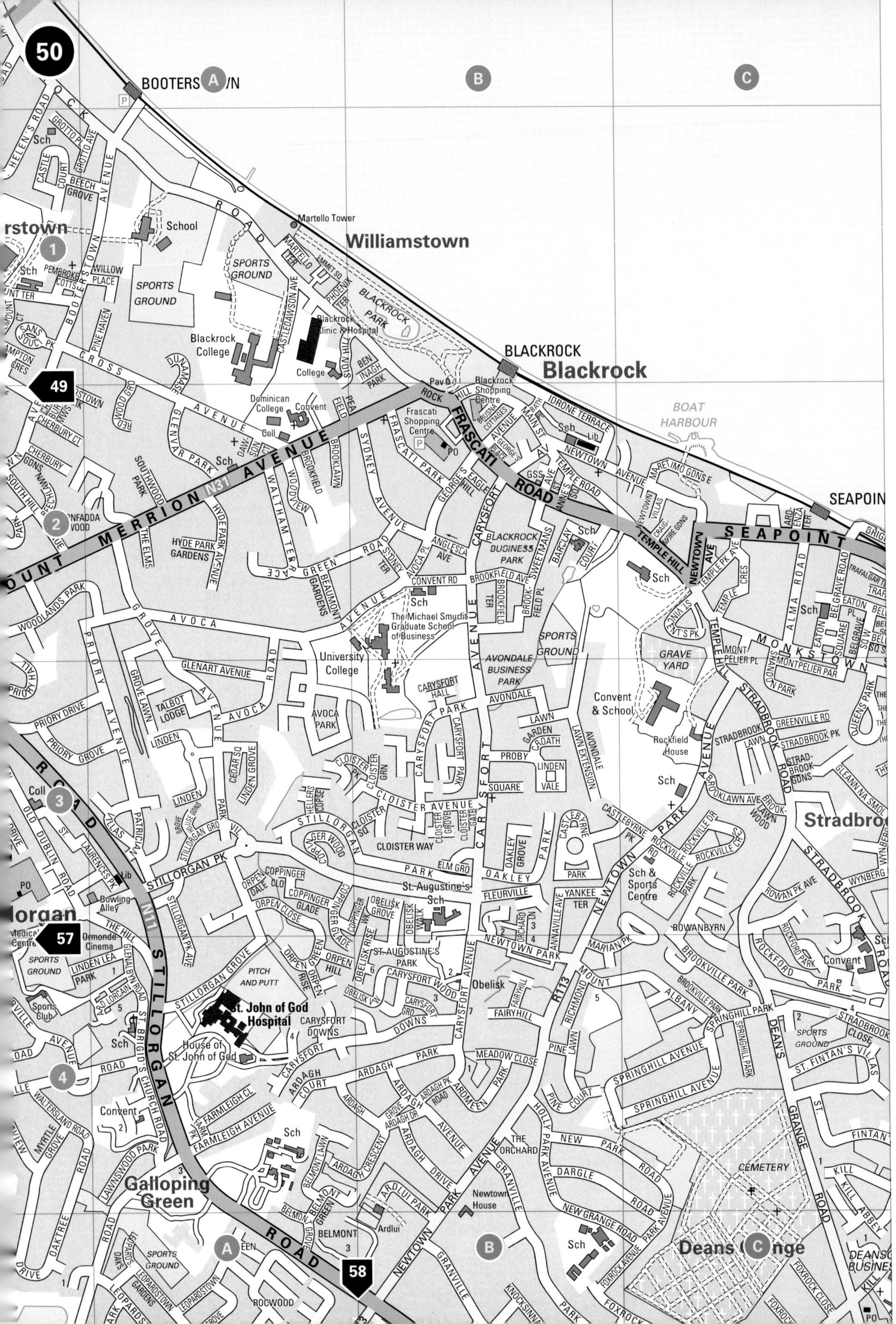
Williamstown
Blackrock
BLACKROCK
Martello Tower
Blackrock College
Blackrock Clinic & Hospital
BLACKROCK PARK
SPORTS GROUND
School
Dominican College
Convent
Frascati Shopping Centre
Blackrock Shopping Centre
BOAT HARBOUR
SEAPOINT
MERRION AVENUE
N31
FRASCATI ROAD
TEMPLE HILL
SEAPOINT
MONKSTOWN
University College
The Michael Smurfit Graduate School of Business
AVOCA PARK
CARYSFORT HALL
BLACKROCK BUSINESS PARK
AVONDALE BUSINESS PARK
GRAVE YARD
Convent & School
Rockfield House
Stradbrook
STILLORGAN ROAD
N11
St. John of God Hospital
House of St. John of God
PITCH AND PUTT
Galloping Green
Obelisk
Newtown House
CEMETERY
Deans Grange
Ormonde Cinema
Bowling Alley
Sch & Sports Centre
49
57
58

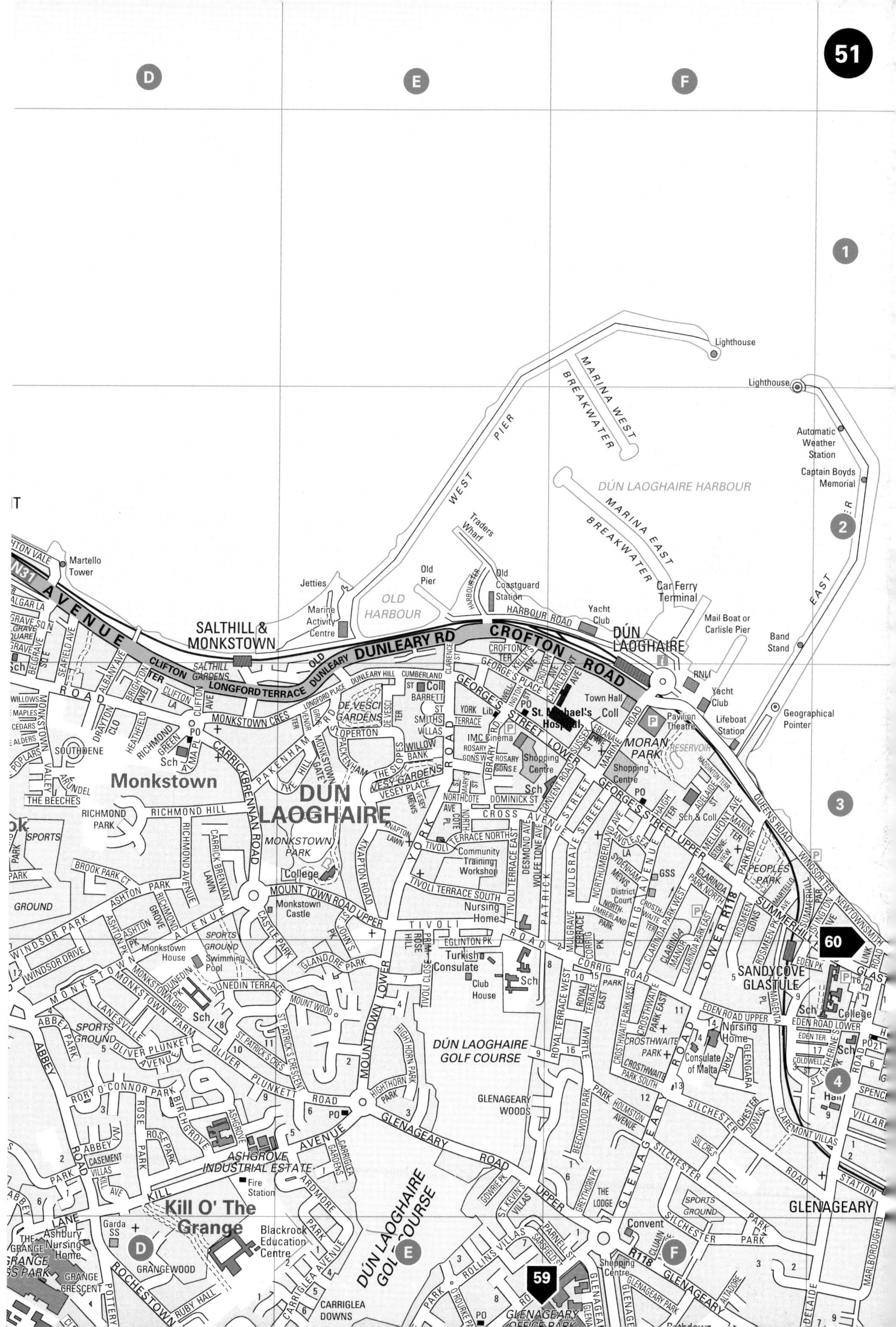

D E F

1

2

3

4

Lighthouse

Lighthouse

Automatic Weather Station

Captain Boyds Memorial

DÚN LAOGHAIRE HARBOUR

MARINA WEST BREAKWATER

WEST PIER

MARINA EAST BREAKWATER

EAST PIER

Mail Boat or Carlisle Pier

Band Stand

Geographical Pointer

Martello Tower

TRAFALGAR VALE
N31
AVENUE

Traders Wharf

Jetties

Marine Activity Centre

Old Pier

Old Harbour

Old Coastguard Station

HARBOUR ROAD

Car Ferry Terminal

Yacht Club

DÚN LAOGHAIRE

RNLI

Yacht Club

Lifeboat Station

SALTHILL & MONKSTOWN

CLIFTON TER

LONGFORD TERRACE

CLIFTON GARDENS

SALTHILL PLACE

OLD DUNLEARY **DUNLEARY RD**

CROFTON ROAD

CROFTON TER

Town Hall

Coll

Pavilion Theatre

RESERVOIR

Monkstown

MONKSTOWN CRES

DE VESCI GARDENS

DE VESCI TER

VESEY PLACE

VESEY MEWS

St. Michael's Hospital

IMC Cinema

Library

York Terrace

Shopping Centre

MORAN PARK

Shopping Centre

PO

Sch & Coll

PEOPLES PARK

DÚN LAOGHAIRE

RICHMOND PARK

RICHMOND HILL

CARRICKBRENNAN ROAD

PAKENHAM

MONKSTOWN PARK

College

Monkstown Castle

Community Training Workshop

CROSS AVE

Nursing Home

QUEENS ROAD

WINDSOR TER

NEWTOWNSMITH

60

GLAS

SANDYCOVE GLASTULE

College

Nursing Home

Consulate of Malta

SPORTS GROUND

Monkstown House

Swimming Pool

Sch

DÚNEDIN TERRACE

MOUNT TOWN ROAD UPPER

Castle Park

TIVOLI ROAD

TIVOLI TERRACE SOUTH

Turkish Consulate

Club House

DÚN LAOGHAIRE GOLF COURSE

ABBEY PARK

SPORTS GROUND

OLIVER PLUNKET

RORY O'CONNOR PARK

ROSE PARK

BIRCHGROVE

ASHGROVE

GLENAGEARY ROAD

Fire Station

ASHGROVE INDUSTRIAL ESTATE

GLENAGEARY WOODS

GLENAGEARY ROAD UPPER

SILCHESTER

SPORTS GROUND

GLENAGEARY

Kill O' The Grange

Garda SS

GRANGEWOOD

Blackrock Education Centre

DÚN LAOGHAIRE GOLF COURSE

59

Convent

GLENAGEARY

CARRIGLEA DOWNS

POTTERY RD

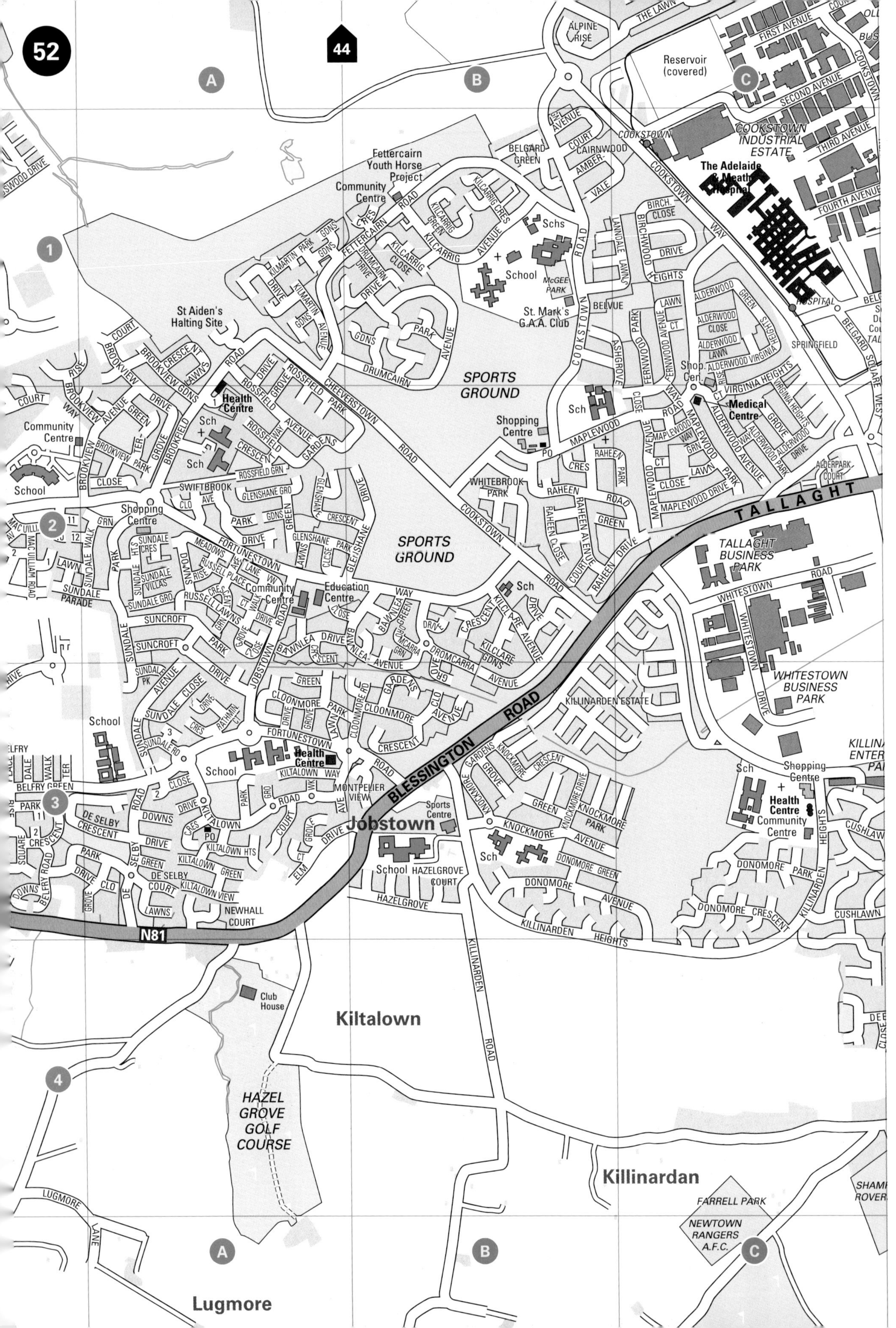

52
44
A
B
C
1
2
3
4
Reservoir (covered)
COOKSTOWN INDUSTRIAL ESTATE
The Adelaide & Meath Hospital
FIRST AVENUE
SECOND AVENUE
THIRD AVENUE
FOURTH AVENUE
COOKSTOWN WAY
COOKSTOWN ROAD
HOSPITAL
BELGARD SQUARE WEST
SPRINGFIELD
ALPINE RISE
THE LAWN
BELGARD GREEN
CAIRNWOOD
AMBERVALE
Fettercairn Youth Horse Project
Community Centre
FETTERCAIRN ROAD
KILCARRIG AVENUE
KILMARTIN PARK
DRUMCAIRN
Schs
School
McGEE PARK
St. Mark's G.A.A. Club
BELVUE
BIRCHWOOD HEIGHTS
ALDERWOOD
FERNWOOD AVENUE
Shop. Cen.
Medical Centre
VIRGINIA HEIGHTS
ALDERPARK COURT
St Aiden's Halting Site
SPORTS GROUND
CHEEVERSTOWN ROAD
ROSSFIELD AVENUE
Health Centre
Sch
BROOKFIELD
BROOKVIEW
Community Centre
School
Shopping Centre
MAPLEWOOD ROAD
Shopping Centre
PO
WHITEBROOK PARK
RAHEEN
TALLAGHT
TALLAGHT BUSINESS PARK
WHITESTOWN ROAD
WHITESTOWN DRIVE
WHITESTOWN BUSINESS PARK
SWIFTBROOK
GLENSHANE
FORTUNESTOWN LANE
Community Centre
Education Centre
BAWNLEA
KILCLARE
DROMCARRA
SPORTS GROUND
MACUILLIAM
SUNDALE
SUNCROFT
JOBSTOWN ROAD
CLOONMORE
KILLINARDEN ESTATE
BLESSINGTON ROAD
KNOCKMORE
School
Health Centre
KILTALOWN
MONTPELIER VIEW
Sports Centre
Jobstown
School
HAZELGROVE COURT
HAZELGROVE
DONOMORE
KILLINARDEN HEIGHTS
Sch
Shopping Centre
Health Centre
Community Centre
KILLINARDEN ENTERPRISE PARK
CUSHLAWN
BELFRY
DE SELBY
NEWHALL COURT
N81
Club House
Kiltalown
KILLINARDEN ROAD
HAZEL GROVE GOLF COURSE
Killinardan
FARRELL PARK
NEWTOWN RANGERS A.F.C.
LUGMORE LANE
Lugmore

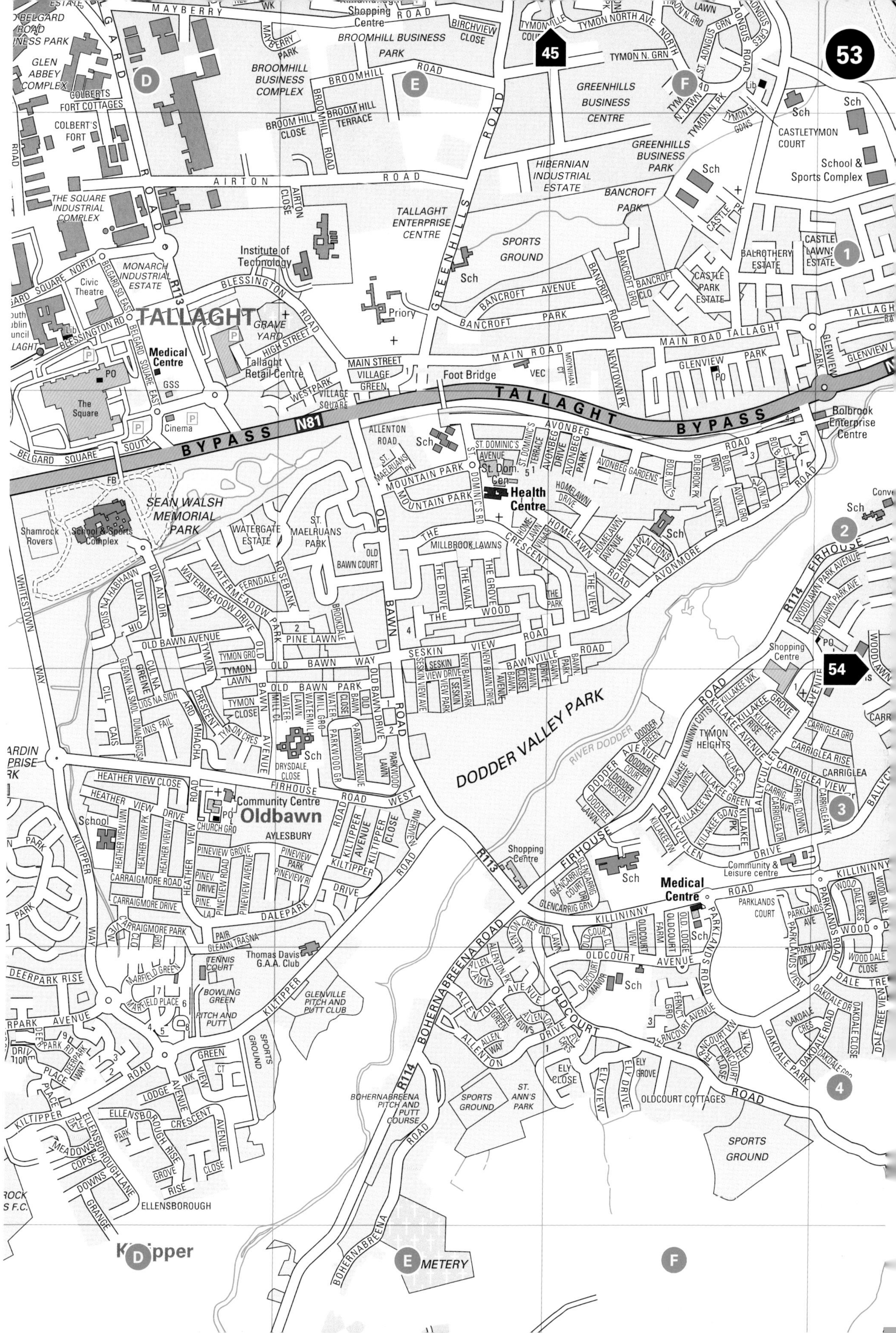
45
54
D
E
F
TALLAGHT
Oldbawn
Kiltipper
MAYBERRY
BROOMHILL BUSINESS PARK
BROOMHILL BUSINESS COMPLEX
BIRCHVIEW CLOSE
BROOMHILL ROAD
BROOM HILL CLOSE
BROOM HILL TERRACE
TYMON NORTH AVE
TYMON N. GRN
GREENHILLS BUSINESS CENTRE
GREENHILLS BUSINESS PARK
HIBERNIAN INDUSTRIAL ESTATE
BANCROFT PARK
CASTLETYMON COURT
School & Sports Complex
GLEN ABBEY COMPLEX
COLBERTS FORT COTTAGES
COLBERT'S FORT
AIRTON ROAD
AIRTON CLOSE
THE SQUARE INDUSTRIAL COMPLEX
MONARCH INDUSTRIAL ESTATE
TALLAGHT ENTERPRISE CENTRE
Institute of Technology
SPORTS GROUND
BALROTHERY ESTATE
CASTLE LAWNS ESTATE
CASTLE PARK ESTATE
GREENHILLS ROAD
BELGARD SQUARE NORTH
BLESSINGTON ROAD
Civic Theatre
GRAVE YARD
HIGH STREET
Priory
BANCROFT AVENUE
BANCROFT PARK
MAIN ROAD TALLAGHT
Medical Centre
Tallaght Retail Centre
MAIN STREET
VILLAGE GREEN
Foot Bridge
VEC
NEWTOWN PK
GLENVIEW PARK
The Square
Cinema
TALLAGHT BYPASS
N81
Bolbrook Enterprise Centre
BELGARD SQUARE SOUTH
ALLENTON ROAD
AVONBEG ROAD
MOUNTAIN PARK
St. Dom. Cen.
Health Centre
SEAN WALSH MEMORIAL PARK
Shamrock Rovers
School & Sports Complex
WATERGATE ESTATE
ST. MAELRUANS PARK
OLD BAWN COURT
THE MILLBROOK LAWNS
HOMELAWN
AVONMORE ROAD
FIRHOUSE ROAD
WHITESTOWN WAY
WATERMEADOW DRIVE
OLD BAWN ROAD
PINE LAWN
OLD BAWN AVENUE
SESKIN VIEW ROAD
OLD BAWN WAY
BAWNVILLE ROAD
DODDER VALLEY PARK
RIVER DODDER
Shopping Centre
TYMON HEIGHTS
KILLAKEE AVENUE
BALLYCULLEN DRIVE
CARRIGLEA
Sch
DRYSDALE CLOSE
FIRHOUSE ROAD WEST
HEATHER VIEW CLOSE
Community Centre
AYLESBURY
School
KILTIPPER ROAD
R113
R114
Community & Leisure centre
KILLININNY ROAD
PARKLANDS ROAD
OLDCOURT AVENUE
OLDCOURT ROAD
BOHERNABREENA ROAD
ALLENTON DRIVE
Thomas Davis G.A.A. Club
TENNIS COURT
BOWLING GREEN
PITCH AND PUTT
GLENVILLE PITCH AND PUTT CLUB
DEERPARK RISE
ELLENSBOROUGH
BOHERNABREENA PITCH AND PUTT COURSE
ST. ANN'S PARK
OLDCOURT COTTAGES
METERY

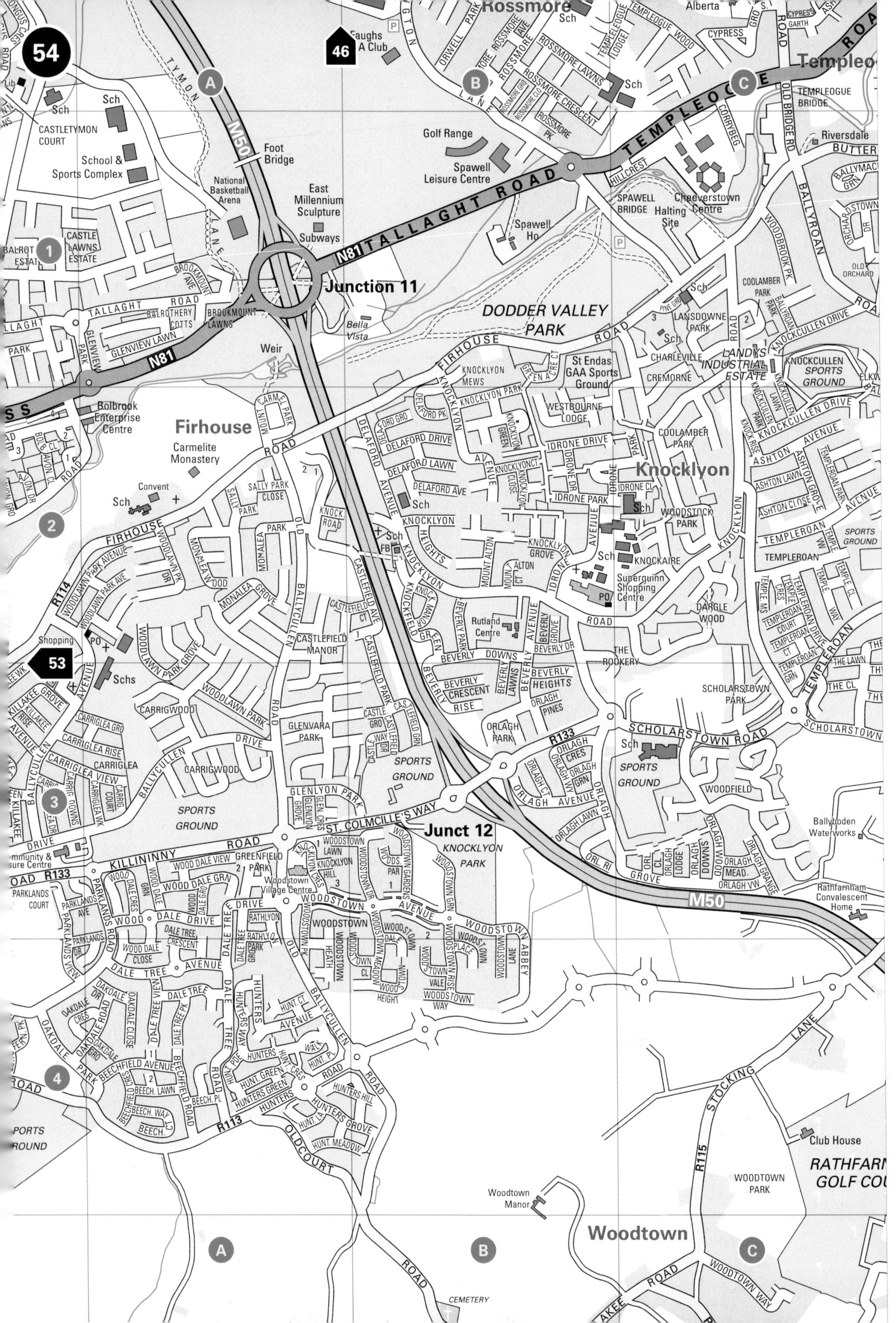

54
46
53
Rossmore
Templeogue
Alberta
Faughs GAA Club
Sch
Castletymon Court
School & Sports Complex
Tymon Lane
M50
Foot Bridge
National Basketball Arena
East Millennium Sculpture
Subways
Junction 11
Golf Range
Spawell Leisure Centre
Tallaght Road
N81
Templeogue Road
Orwell Park
Rossmore Lawns
Rossmore Crescent
Templeogue Wood
Cypress Grove
Templeogue Bridge
Old Bridge Rd
Riversdale
Corrybeg
Hillcrest
Spawell Bridge
Halting Site
Cheeverstown Centre
Spawell Ho
Balrothery Estate
Castle Lawns Estate
Brookmount Ave
Brookmount Lawns
Balrothery Cotts
Glenview Park
Glenview Lawn
Bella Vista
Weir
Dodder Valley Park
Firhouse Road
Knocklyon Mews
St Endas GAA Sports Ground
Charleville
Cremorne
Lansdowne Park
Landys Industrial Estate
Knockcullen Sports Ground
Knockcullen Drive
Ballyroan
Woodbrook Pk
Coolamber Park
Orchardstown Dr
Old Orchard
Bolbrook Enterprise Centre
Firhouse
Carmelite Monastery
Mount Carmel Park
Convent
Delaford Drive
Delaford Lawn
Delaford Ave
Delaford Avenue
Knocklyon Park
Knocklyon Green
Westbourne Lodge
Idrone Drive
Idrone Park
Idrone Avenue
Coolamber Park
Knocklyon
Ashton Avenue
Ashton Lawn
Ashton Grove
Ashton Close
Templeroan Park
Templeroan
Templeroan Avenue
Templeroan Drive
Sports Ground
Woodstock Park
Knockaire
Superquinn Shopping Centre
Knocklyon Heights
Knocklyon Grove
Mount Alton
Sally Park
Sally Park Close
Monalea Park
Monalea Grove
Monalea Wood
Woodlawn Park Avenue
Woodlawn Park Ave
Woodlawn Park Grove
Woodlawn Park
Ballycullen Road
Castlefield Manor
Castlefield Ave
Castlefield Park
Knockfield Manor
Beverly Park
Beverly Downs
Beverly Avenue
Beverly Crescent
Beverly Rise
Beverly Lawns
Beverly Heights
Rutland Centre
The Rookery
Dargle Wood
Scholarstown Park
Scholarstown Road
Orlagh Pines
Orlagh Park
Orlagh Crescent
Orlagh Avenue
Orlagh Grove
Orlagh Downs
Orlagh Lodge
Orlagh Grange
Woodfield
R133
R114
Shopping
Schs
Killakee Grove
Carriglea Rise
Carriglea View
Carriglea
Carrigwood
Carrigwood Drive
Ballycullen Drive
Glenvara Park
Glenlyon Park
St. Colmcille's Way
Junct 12
Knocklyon Park
Sports Ground
Killininny Road
Community & Leisure Centre
Greenfield Park
Woodstown Lawn
Knocklyon Hill
Woodstown Gardens
Woodstown Village Centre
Woodstown Avenue
Woodstown
Woodstown Heath
Woodstown Meadow
Woodstown Rise
Woodstown Place
Woodstown Abbey
Woodstown Vale
Woodstown Way
Parklands Court
Parklands Road
Parklands Ave
Parklands View
Wood Dale View
Wood Dale Grn
Wood Dale Drive
Wood Dale Close
Dale Tree Crescent
Dale Tree Avenue
Dale Tree Drive
Dale Tree Road
Rathlyon Park
Oakdale Road
Oakdale Close
Oakdale Drive
Beechfield Avenue
Beechfield Road
Beech. Lawn
Beech. Way
Beech. Pl
Hunters Way
Hunters Avenue
Hunters Green
Hunters Hill
Hunters Grove
Hunt. Meadow
Ballycullen Road
Oldcourt Road
R113
Sports Ground
Ballyboden Waterworks
Rathfarnham Convalescent Home
Stocking Lane
R115
Club House
Rathfarnham Golf Course
Woodtown Park
Woodtown Manor
Woodtown
Woodtown Way
Cemetery
M50

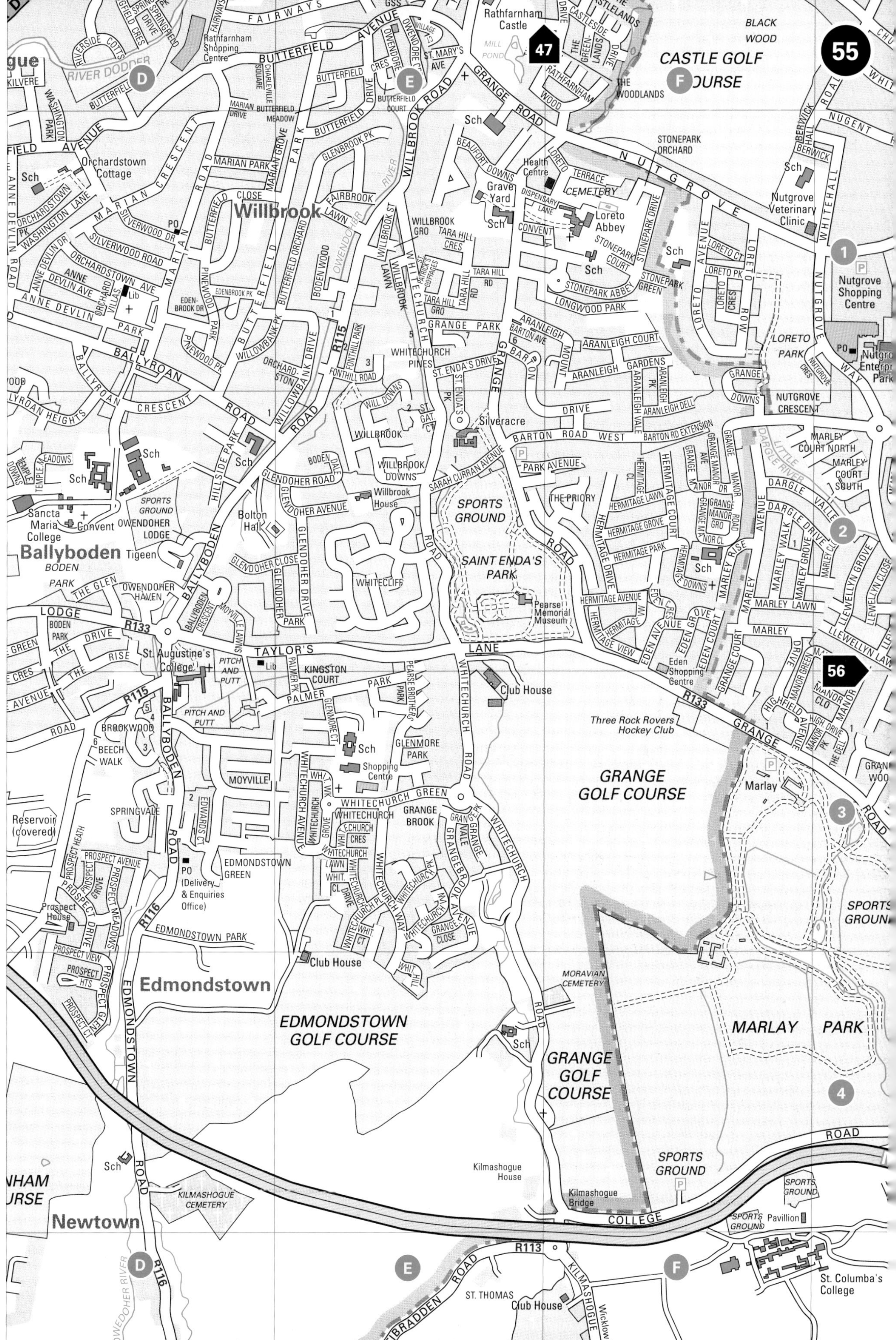

Willbrook
Ballyboden
Edmondstown
Newtown
Rathfarnham Castle
CASTLE GOLF COURSE
GRANGE GOLF COURSE
EDMONDSTOWN GOLF COURSE
MARLAY PARK
SAINT ENDA'S PARK
SPORTS GROUND
Nutgrove Shopping Centre
Loreto Abbey
Pearse Memorial Museum
St. Augustine's College
Sancta Maria College
St. Columba's College
Three Rock Rovers Hockey Club
Kilmashogue House
Kilmashogue Bridge
MORAVIAN CEMETERY
KILMASHOGUE CEMETERY
TAYLOR'S LANE
GRANGE ROAD
NUTGROVE AVENUE
BUTTERFIELD AVENUE
WILLBROOK ROAD
WHITECHURCH ROAD
BALLYBODEN ROAD
EDMONDSTOWN ROAD
COLLEGE ROAD
BALLYROAN ROAD
MARIAN CRESCENT
47
56

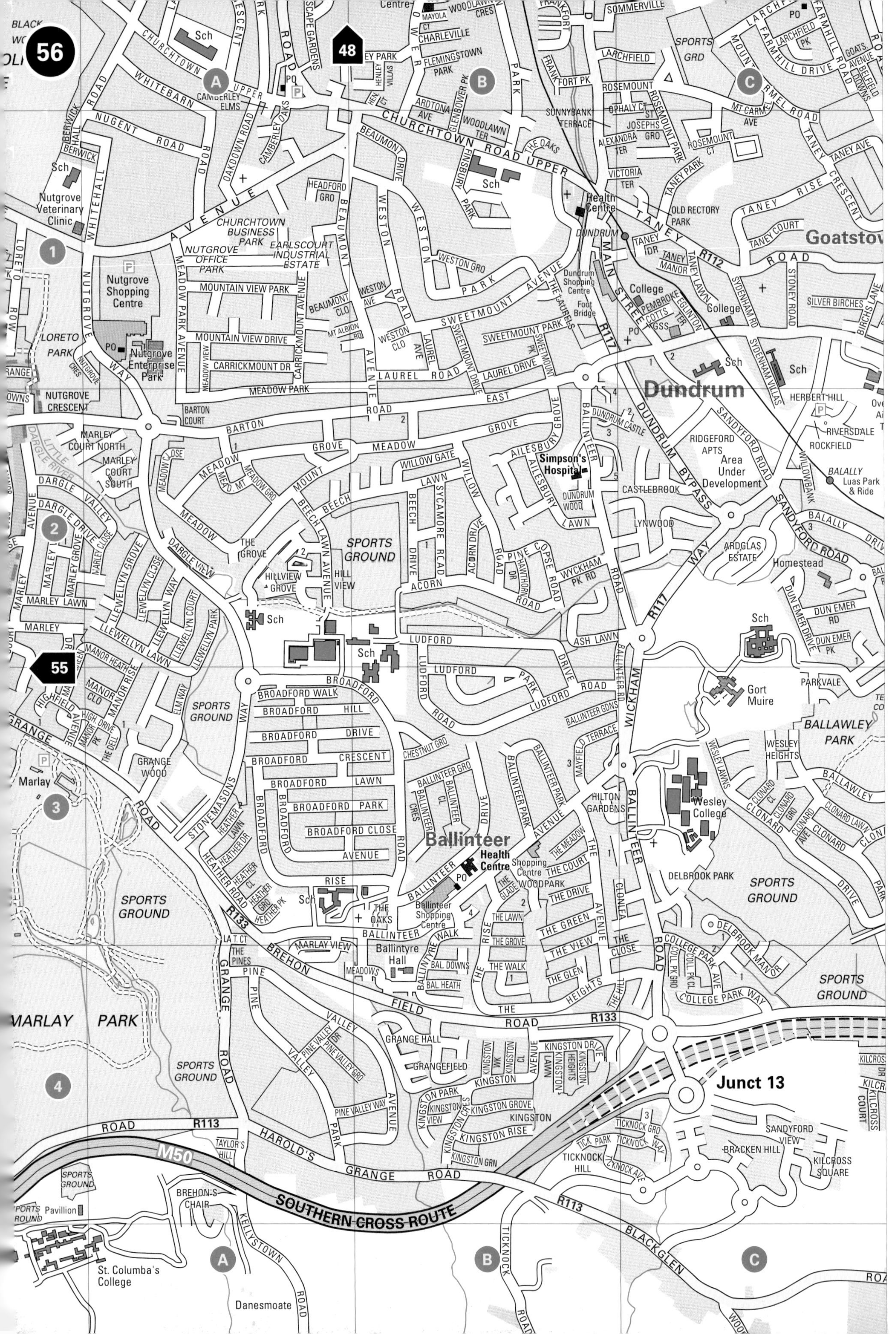
48
55
Churchtown Road Upper
Nutgrove Avenue
Nutgrove Shopping Centre
Nutgrove Enterprise Park
Churchtown Business Park
Nutgrove Office Park
Earlscourt Industrial Estate
Dundrum
Dundrum Shopping Centre
Main Street
Taney Road
Goatstown
Sandyford Road
Dundrum Bypass
Simpson's Hospital
Balally
Luas Park & Ride
Ballinteer
Ballinteer Shopping Centre
Health Centre
Wesley College
Gort Muire
Ballawley Park
Marlay Park
Loreto Park
Sports Ground
Grange Road
Brehon Field Road
Stonemasons Way
Wyckham Way
Ballinteer Road
Junct 13
M50
Southern Cross Route
Blackglen Road
Ticknock Road
Kellystown Road
Harold's Grange Road
St. Columba's College
Danesmoate
Pavillion
Brehon's Chair
Ticknock Hill
Kilcross Square
Sandyford View
Bracken Hill
Kingston
Grangefield
Grange Hall
Pine Valley
Ballintyre Hall
Marlay
Grange Wood
Sweetmount Avenue
Ludford Road
Broadford Road
Barton Road East
Meadow Grove
Area Under Development
Ridgeford Apts
Ardglas Estate
Homestead
Delbrook Park
College Park Way
R112
R117
R113
R133

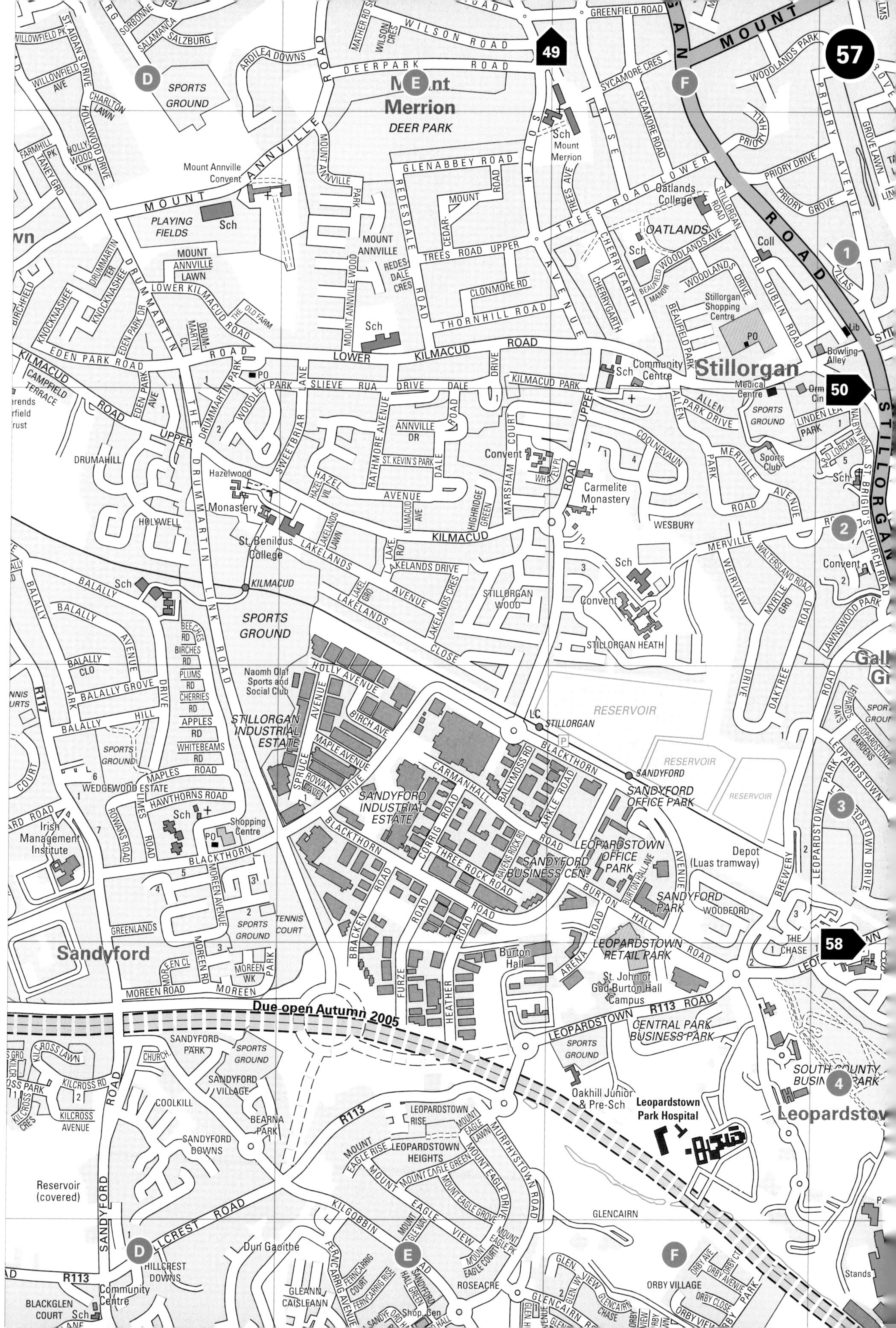
57
49
50
58
Mount Merrion
DEER PARK
Stillorgan
Sandyford
Leopardstown
OATLANDS
Mount Anville Convent
PLAYING FIELDS
SPORTS GROUND
STILLORGAN ROAD
MOUNT ANNVILLE ROAD
LOWER KILMACUD ROAD
UPPER KILMACUD ROAD
DRUMMARTIN LINK ROAD
DEERPARK ROAD
WILSON ROAD
GREENFIELD ROAD
SOUTH AVENUE
TREES ROAD UPPER
TREES ROAD LOWER
GLENABBEY ROAD
REDESDALE ROAD
THORNHILL ROAD
CLONMORE RD
SYCAMORE CRES
PRIORY AVENUE
PRIORY DRIVE
PRIORY GROVE
WOODLANDS PARK
WOODLANDS DRIVE
OLD DUBLIN ROAD
Stillorgan Shopping Centre
Oatlands College
Community Centre
Medical Centre
Bowling Alley
Carmelite Monastery
Hazelwood Monastery
St. Benildus College
KILMACUD
STILLORGAN
SANDYFORD
LC
RESERVOIR
STILLORGAN INDUSTRIAL ESTATE
SANDYFORD INDUSTRIAL ESTATE
SANDYFORD OFFICE PARK
LEOPARDSTOWN OFFICE PARK
SANDYFORD BUSINESS CEN.
SANDYFORD PARK
LEOPARDSTOWN RETAIL PARK
CENTRAL PARK BUSINESS PARK
SOUTH COUNTY BUSINESS PARK
Naomh Olaf Sports and Social Club
Irish Management Institute
Depot (Luas tramway)
St. John of God Burton Hall Campus
Burton Hall
Oakhill Junior & Pre-Sch
Leopardstown Park Hospital
Due open Autumn 2005
LEOPARDSTOWN R113 ROAD
BLACKTHORN ROAD
BALALLY DRIVE
BALALLY AVENUE
STILLORGAN HEATH
STILLORGAN WOOD
WESBURY
MERVILLE AVENUE
LAKELANDS AVENUE
HOLLY AVENUE
BIRCH AVE
MAPLE AVENUE
CARMANHALL ROAD
BALLYMOSS RD
ARKLE ROAD
THREE ROCK ROAD
BURTON HALL ROAD
MOREEN ROAD
SANDYFORD ROAD
HILLCREST ROAD
KILGOBBIN ROAD
MURPHYSTOWN ROAD
LEOPARDSTOWN HEIGHTS
LEOPARDSTOWN RISE
MOUNT EAGLE VIEW
GLENCAIRN
ORBY VILLAGE
ROSEACRE
Dun Gaoithe
Reservoir (covered)
COOLKILL
SANDYFORD VILLAGE
SANDYFORD DOWNS
HILLCREST DOWNS
BLACKGLEN COURT
DRUMAHILL
HOLYWELL
Stands

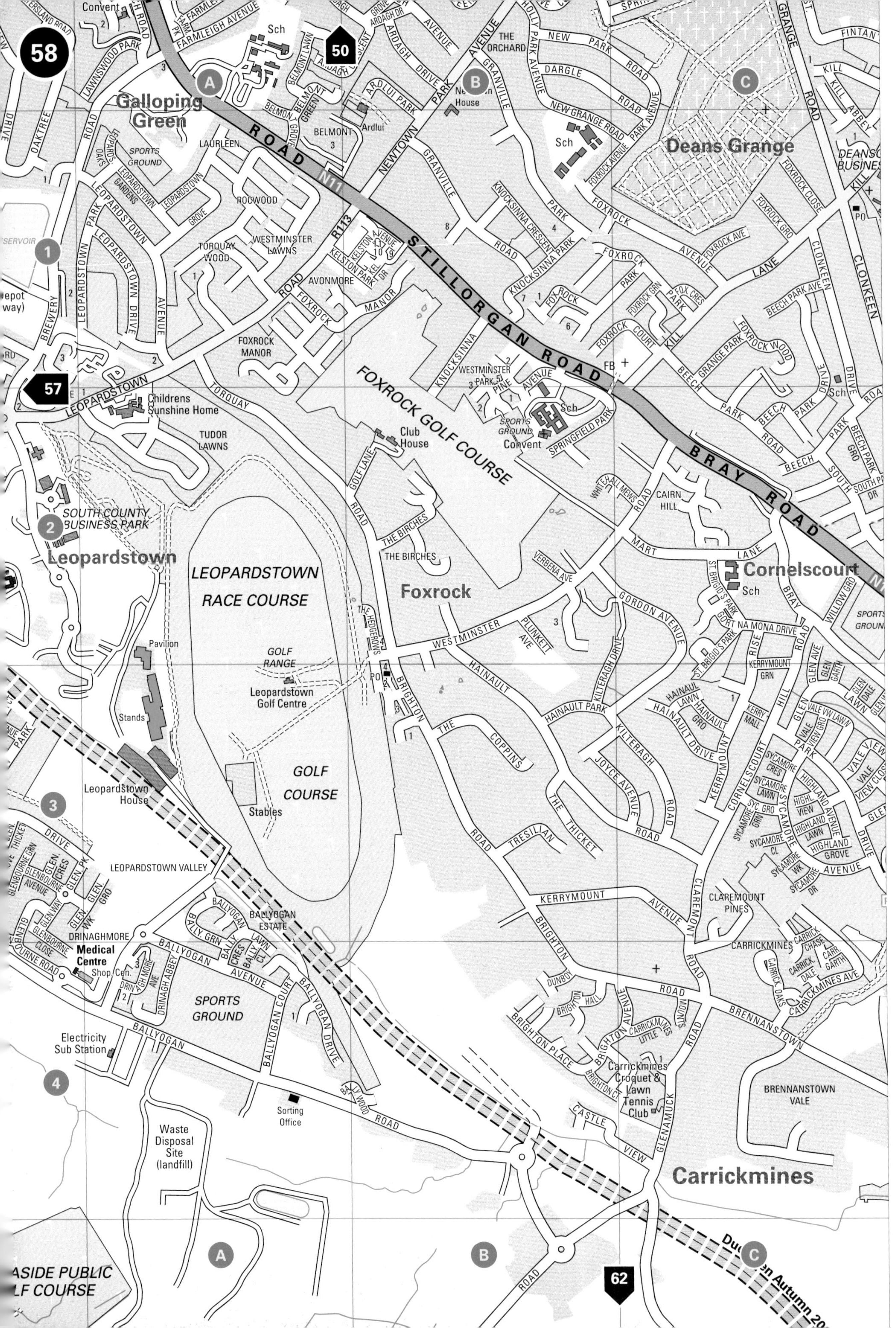

58
50
57
62
Galloping Green
Deans Grange
Leopardstown
Foxrock
Cornelscourt
Carrickmines
STILLORGAN ROAD
N11
BRAY ROAD
R113
FOXROCK GOLF COURSE
LEOPARDSTOWN RACE COURSE
GOLF RANGE
Leopardstown Golf Centre
GOLF COURSE
Stables
Pavilion
Stands
Leopardstown House
SOUTH COUNTY BUSINESS PARK
Childrens Sunshine Home
TUDOR LAWNS
FOXROCK MANOR
Club House
Convent
Sch
SPORTS GROUND
THE ORCHARD
Newtown House
Ardlui
BELMONT
LAURLEEN
ROCWOOD
WESTMINSTER LAWNS
TORQUAY WOOD
AVONMORE
THE BIRCHES
CAIRN HILL
LEOPARDSTOWN VALLEY
DRINAGHMORE
Medical Centre
Shop. Cen.
BALLYOGAN ESTATE
Electricity Sub Station
Sorting Office
Waste Disposal Site (landfill)
CLAREMOUNT PINES
BRENNANSTOWN VALE
Carrickmines Croquet & Lawn Tennis Club
KERRYMOUNT AVENUE
BRIGHTON ROAD
WESTMINSTER ROAD
HAINAULT ROAD
GORDON AVENUE
KILTERAGH ROAD
CLAREMOUNT ROAD
BRENNANSTOWN ROAD
BALLYOGAN ROAD
BALLYOGAN AVENUE
GLENAMUCK ROAD
TORQUAY ROAD
LEOPARDSTOWN AVENUE
CLONKEEN DRIVE
FOXROCK AVENUE
KILL LANE
SPORTS GROUND
A
B
C
1
2
3
4

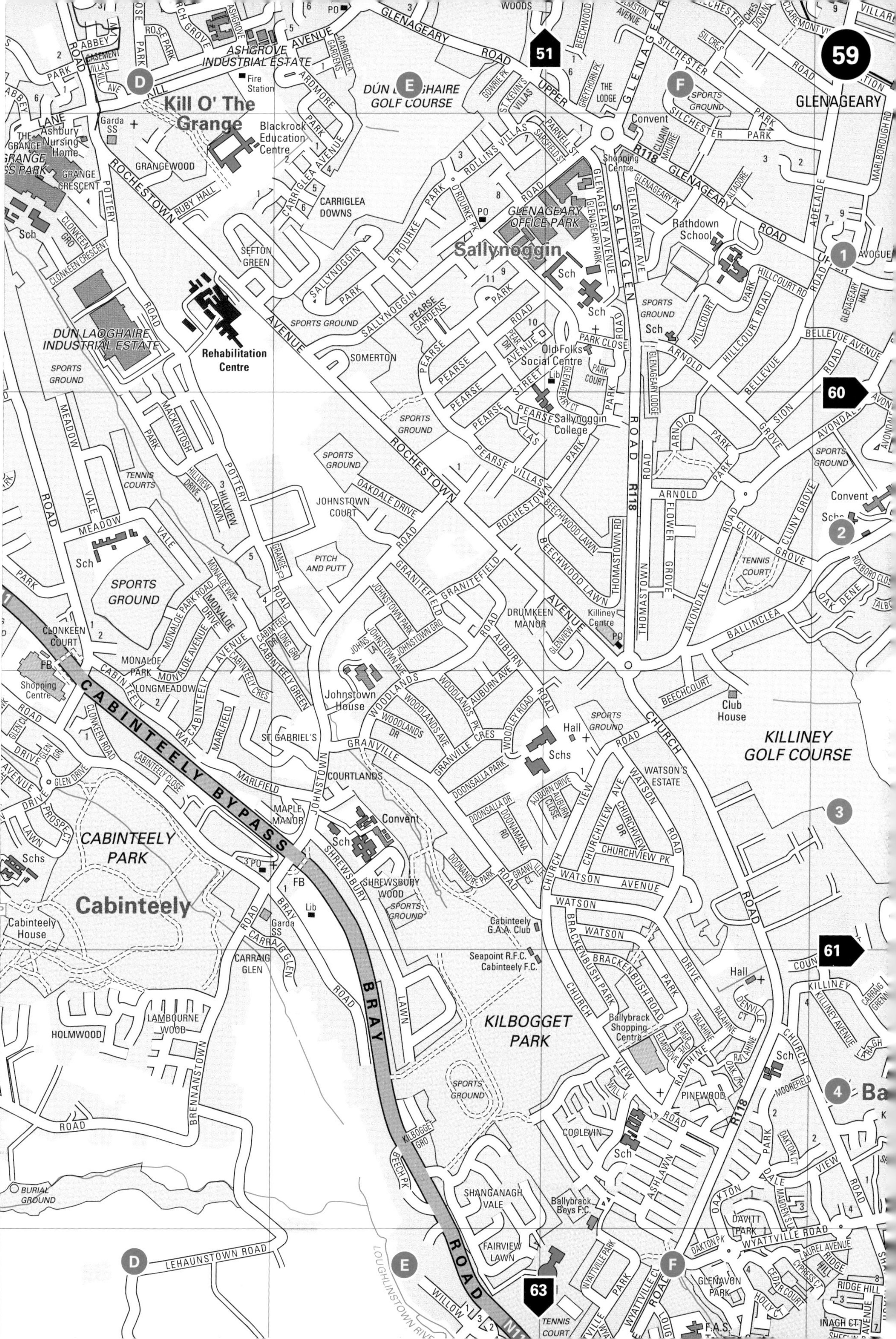

51
GLENAGEARY
Kill O' The Grange
ASHGROVE INDUSTRIAL ESTATE
DÚN LAOGHAIRE GOLF COURSE
Blackrock Education Centre
GRANGEWOOD
ROCHESTOWN AVENUE
CARRIGLEA DOWNS
GLENAGEARY OFFICE PARK
Sallynoggin
Rathdown School
SEFTON GREEN
Rehabilitation Centre
DÚN LAOGHAIRE INDUSTRIAL ESTATE
SOMERTON
Old Folks Social Centre
Sallynoggin College
60
JOHNSTOWN COURT
PITCH AND PUTT
DRUMKEEN MANOR
Killiney Centre
CABINTEELY BYPASS
Johnstown House
KILLINEY GOLF COURSE
Club House
WATSON'S ESTATE
COURTLANDS
MAPLE MANOR
CABINTEELY PARK
Cabinteely
Cabinteely House
SHREWSBURY WOOD
Cabinteely G.A.A. Club
Seapoint R.F.C. Cabinteely F.C.
CARRAIG GLEN
61
KILBOGGET PARK
Ballybrack Shopping Centre
LAMBOURNE WOOD
HOLMWOOD
BRAY ROAD
PINEWOOD
COOLEVIN
SHANGANAGH VALE
Ballybrack Boys F.C.
DAVITT PARK
BURIAL GROUND
LEHAUNSTOWN ROAD
FAIRVIEW LAWN
63
GLENAVON PARK
WYATTVILLE ROAD
LOUGHLINSTOWN RIVER
TENNIS COURT

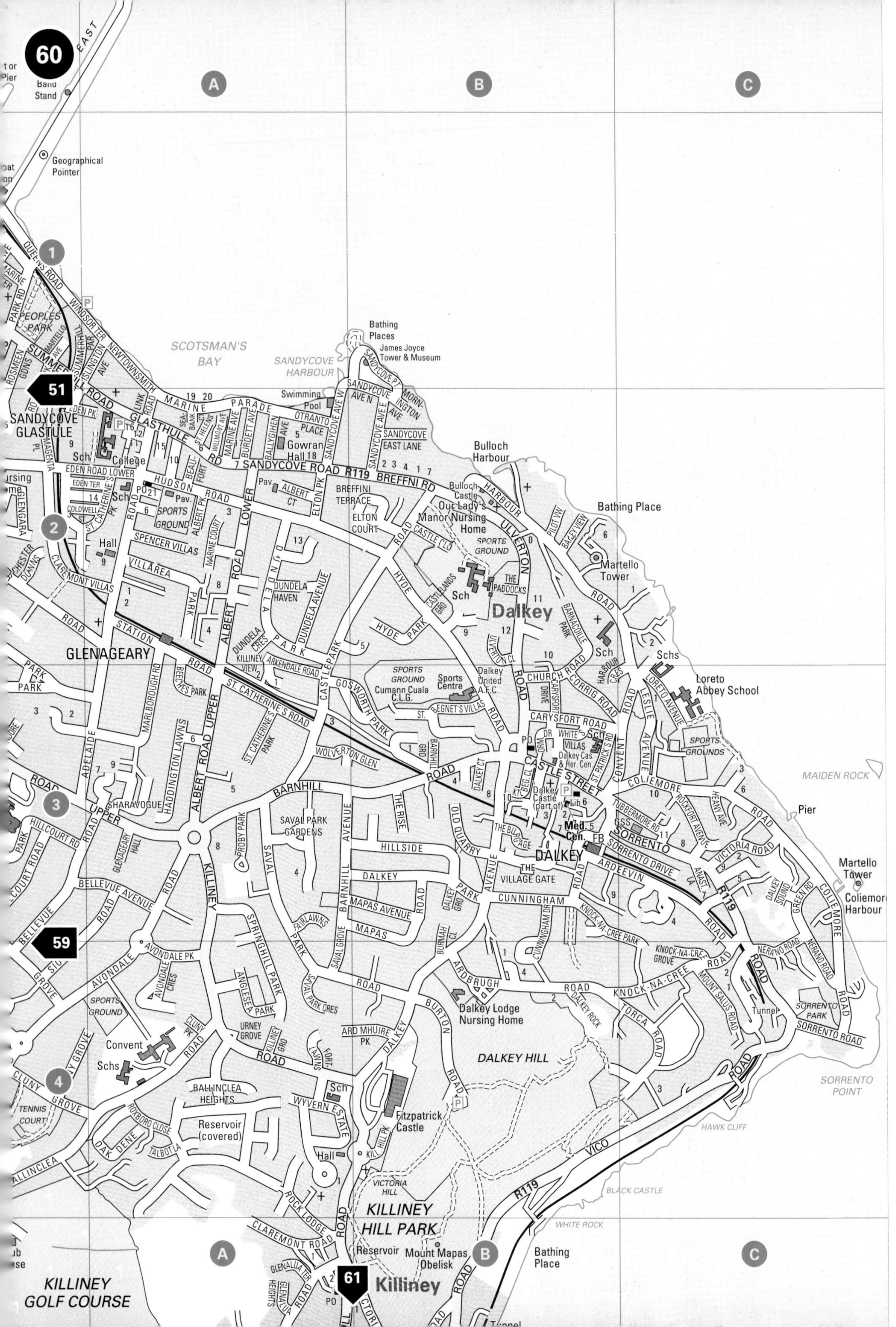

EAST

Ⓐ Ⓑ Ⓒ

Band Stand

Geographical Pointer

51

SCOTSMAN'S BAY

SANDYCOVE HARBOUR

Bathing Places

James Joyce Tower & Museum

Swimming Pool

PEOPLES PARK

SANDYCOVE GLASTULE

Bulloch Harbour

Bathing Place

SANDYCOVE ROAD R119 BREFFNI RD

Bulloch Castle

Our Lady's Manor Nursing Home

Martello Tower

Gowran Hall

Breffini Terrace

ELTON COURT

SPORTS GROUND

THE PADDOCKS

Dalkey

2

SPORTS GROUND

Sch

Schs

Loreto Abbey School

GLENAGEARY

DUNDELA HAVEN

HYDE PARK

SPORTS GROUND Cumann Cuala C.L.G.

Sports Centre

Dalkey United A.F.C.

Begnet's Villas

CARYSFORT ROAD

SPORTS GROUNDS

MAIDEN ROCK

3

SHARAVOGUE

WOLVERTON GLEN

BARNHILL

SAVAL PARK GARDENS

HILLSIDE

THE RISE

OLD QUARRY

CASTLE STREET

Dalkey Cas. & Her. Cen.

Dalkey Castle (part of)

Lib.

Med. Cen.

DALKEY

SORRENTO

Pier

Martello Tower

Coliemore Harbour

PROBY PARK

THE BURGAGE

THE VILLAGE GATE

SORRENTO DRIVE

ARDEEVIN

VICTORIA ROAD

59

SPORTS GROUND

AVONDALE PK

AVONDALE CRES

URNEY GROVE

FAIRLAWNS

MAPAS AVENUE

DALKEY

MAPAS ROAD

CUNNINGHAM ROAD

Dalkey Lodge Nursing Home

KNOCK-NA-CREE PARK

KNOCK-NA-CREE GROVE

KNOCK-NA-CREE ROAD

Tunnel

SORRENTO PARK

SORRENTO ROAD

4

Convent Schs

BALLINCLEA HEIGHTS

Reservoir (covered)

ARD MHUIRE PK

Sch

Hall

Fitzpatrick Castle

VICTORIA HILL

DALKEY HILL

VICO ROAD

SORRENTO POINT

TENNIS COURT

OAK DENE

TALBOT

ROCK LODGE ROAD

KILLINEY HILL PARK

Reservoir

Mount Mapas Obelisk

HAWK CLIFF

BLACK CASTLE

WHITE ROCK

Bathing Place

KILLINEY GOLF COURSE

Ⓐ Ⓑ Ⓒ

61 **Killiney**

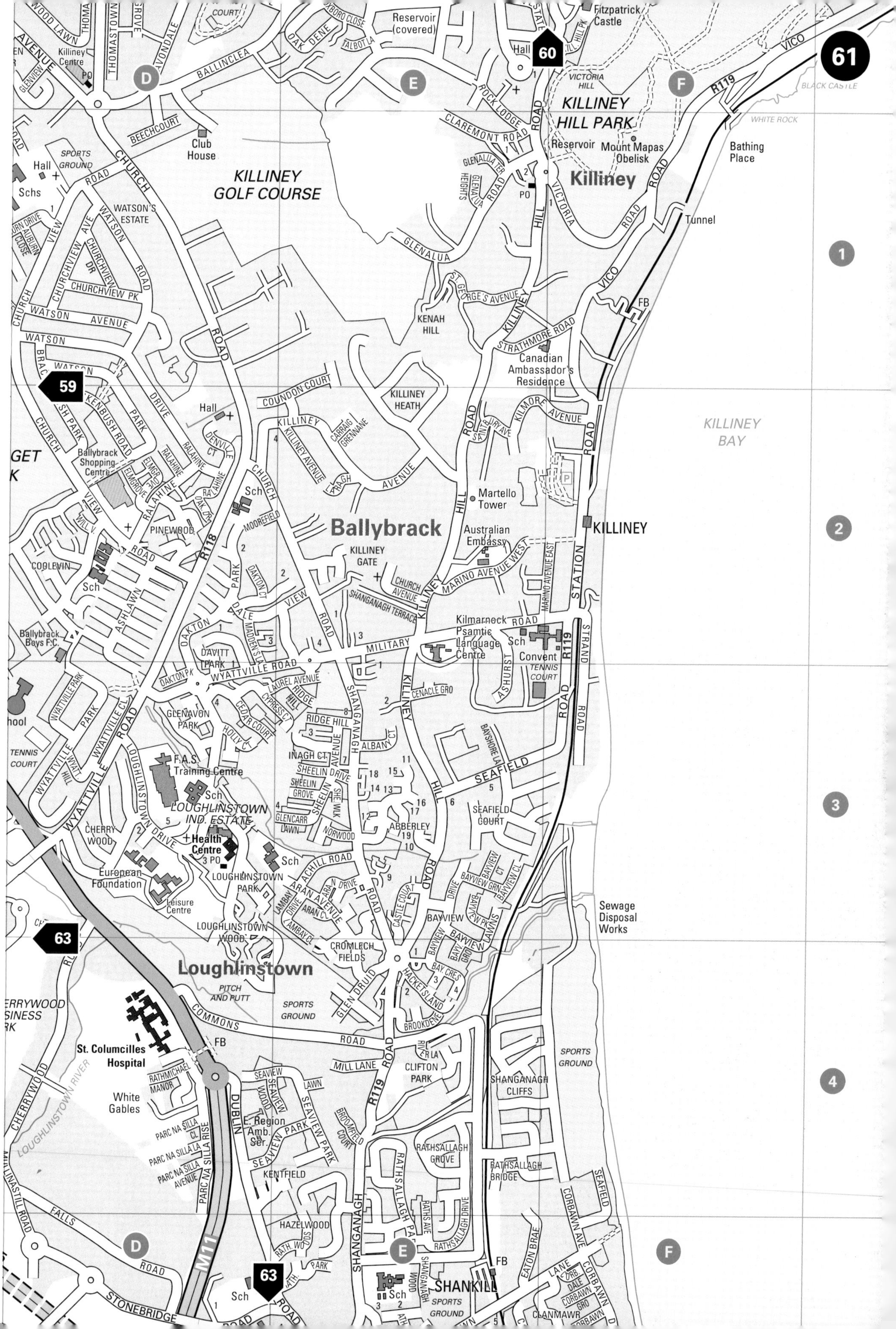
Killiney
Ballybrack
Loughlinstown
KILLINEY GOLF COURSE
KILLINEY HILL PARK
KILLINEY BAY
Fitzpatrick Castle
Reservoir (covered)
Mount Mapas Obelisk
Bathing Place
Tunnel
Canadian Ambassador's Residence
Martello Tower
Australian Embassy
KILLINEY
Kilmarnock Psamtic Language Centre
Convent
F.A.S. Training Centre
LOUGHLINSTOWN IND. ESTATE
Health Centre
European Foundation
Leisure Centre
Sewage Disposal Works
St. Columcilles Hospital
White Gables
E. Region Amb. Ser.
Ballybrack Shopping Centre
Ballybrack Boys F.C.
Club House
SHANKILL
SHANGANAGH CLIFFS
CLIFTON PARK
RATHSALLAGH BRIDGE
PITCH AND PUTT
SPORTS GROUND
R119
R118
M11
59
60
63

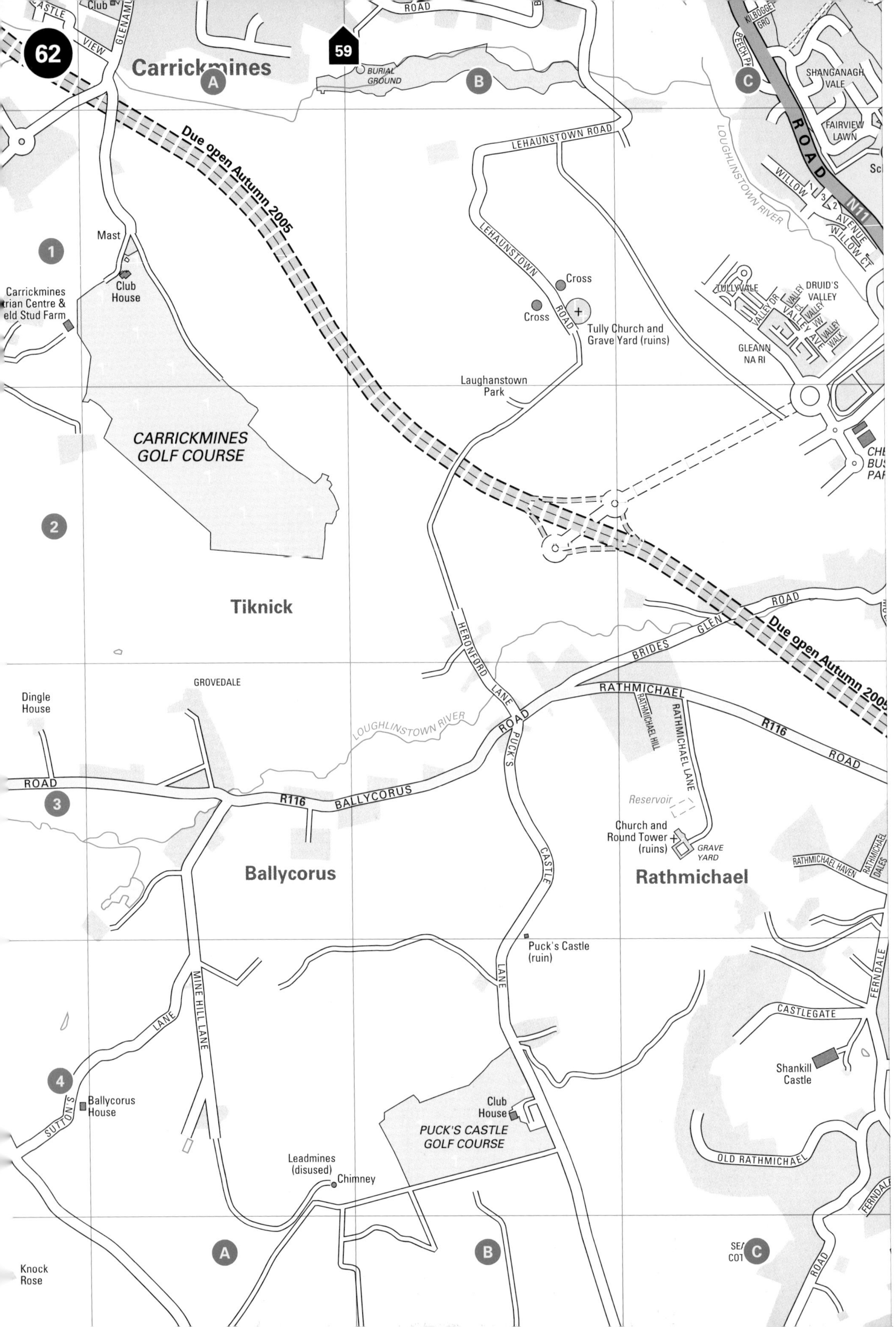

59
Carrickmines
A
B
C
BURIAL GROUND
LEHAUNSTOWN ROAD
Due open Autumn 2005
SHANGANAGH VALE
FAIRVIEW LAWN
LOUGHLINSTOWN RIVER
WILLOW
AVENUE
WILLOW CT
N11
Mast
Club House
1
Carrickmines
trian Centre &
eld Stud Farm
LEHAUNSTOWN ROAD
Cross
Cross
Tully Church and Grave Yard (ruins)
TULLYVALE
DRUID'S VALLEY
GLEANN NA RI
Laughanstown Park
CARRICKMINES GOLF COURSE
2
Tiknick
HERONFORD LANE
ROAD
GLEN
BRIDES
Due open Autumn 2005
RATHMICHAEL
RATHMICHAEL HILL
RATHMICHAEL LANE
R116
ROAD
GROVEDALE
Dingle House
LOUGHLINSTOWN RIVER
ROAD
PUCK'S
ROAD
3
R116
BALLYCORUS
Reservoir
Church and Round Tower (ruins)
GRAVE YARD
RATHMICHAEL HAVEN
Ballycorus
CASTLE
Rathmichael
Puck's Castle (ruin)
LANE
MINE HILL LANE
LANE
FERNDALE
CASTLEGATE
4
Shankill Castle
Ballycorus House
SUTTON'S
Club House
PUCK'S CASTLE GOLF COURSE
OLD RATHMICHAEL
Leadmines (disused)
Chimney
A
B
C
ROAD
Knock Rose

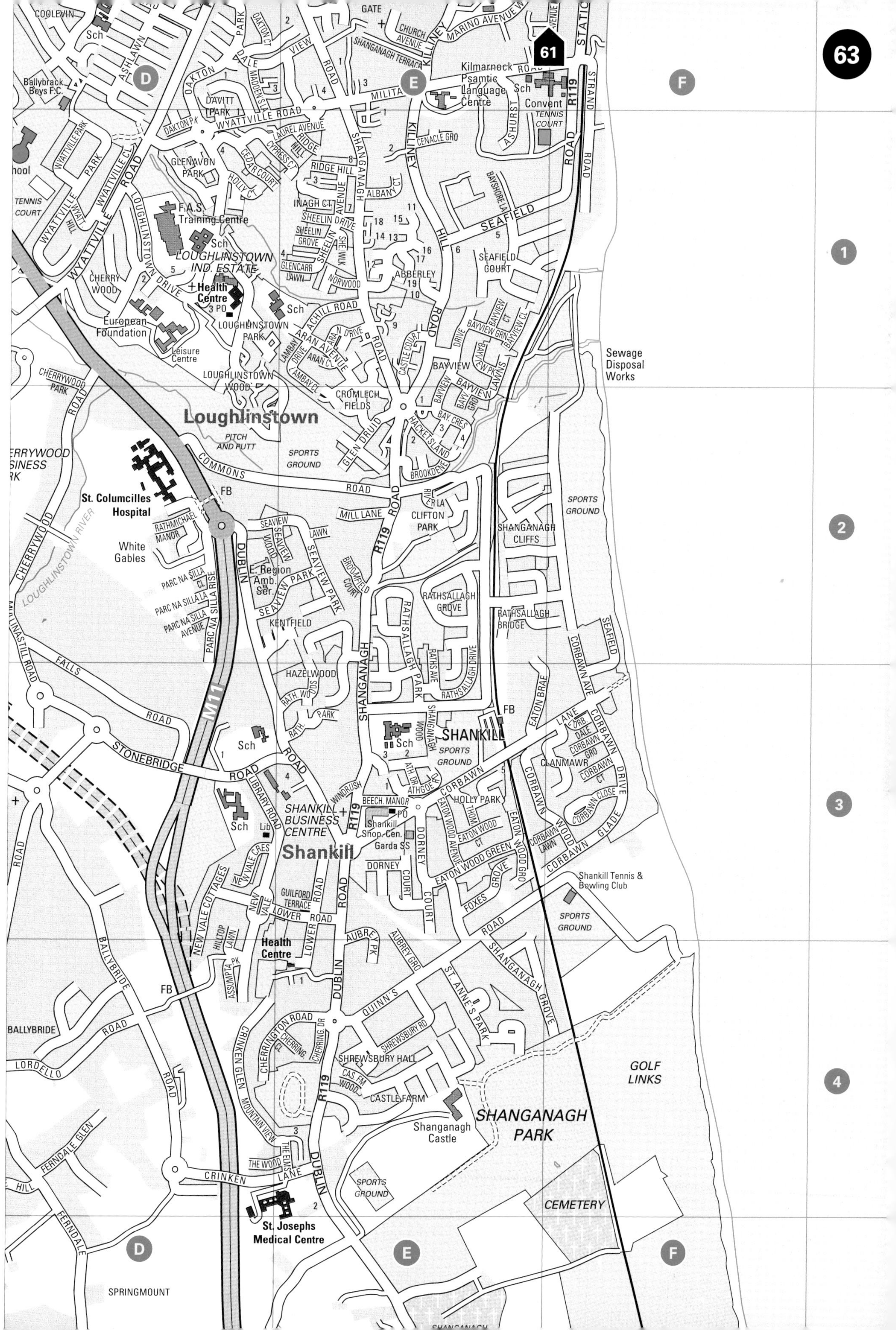

61
Loughlinstown
Shankill
SHANKILL
St. Columcilles Hospital
White Gables
E. Region Amb. Ser.
F.A.S. Training Centre
LOUGHLINSTOWN IND. ESTATE
Health Centre
European Foundation
Leisure Centre
Kilmarnock
Psamtic Language Centre
Convent
Sewage Disposal Works
SHANKILL BUSINESS CENTRE
Shankill Shop. Cen.
Garda SS
Shankill Tennis & Bowling Club
SHANGANAGH PARK
Shanganagh Castle
St. Josephs Medical Centre
GOLF LINKS
CEMETERY
SPORTS GROUND
PITCH AND PUTT
BALLYBRIDE
SPRINGMOUNT
M11
R119
D
E
F
1
2
3
4

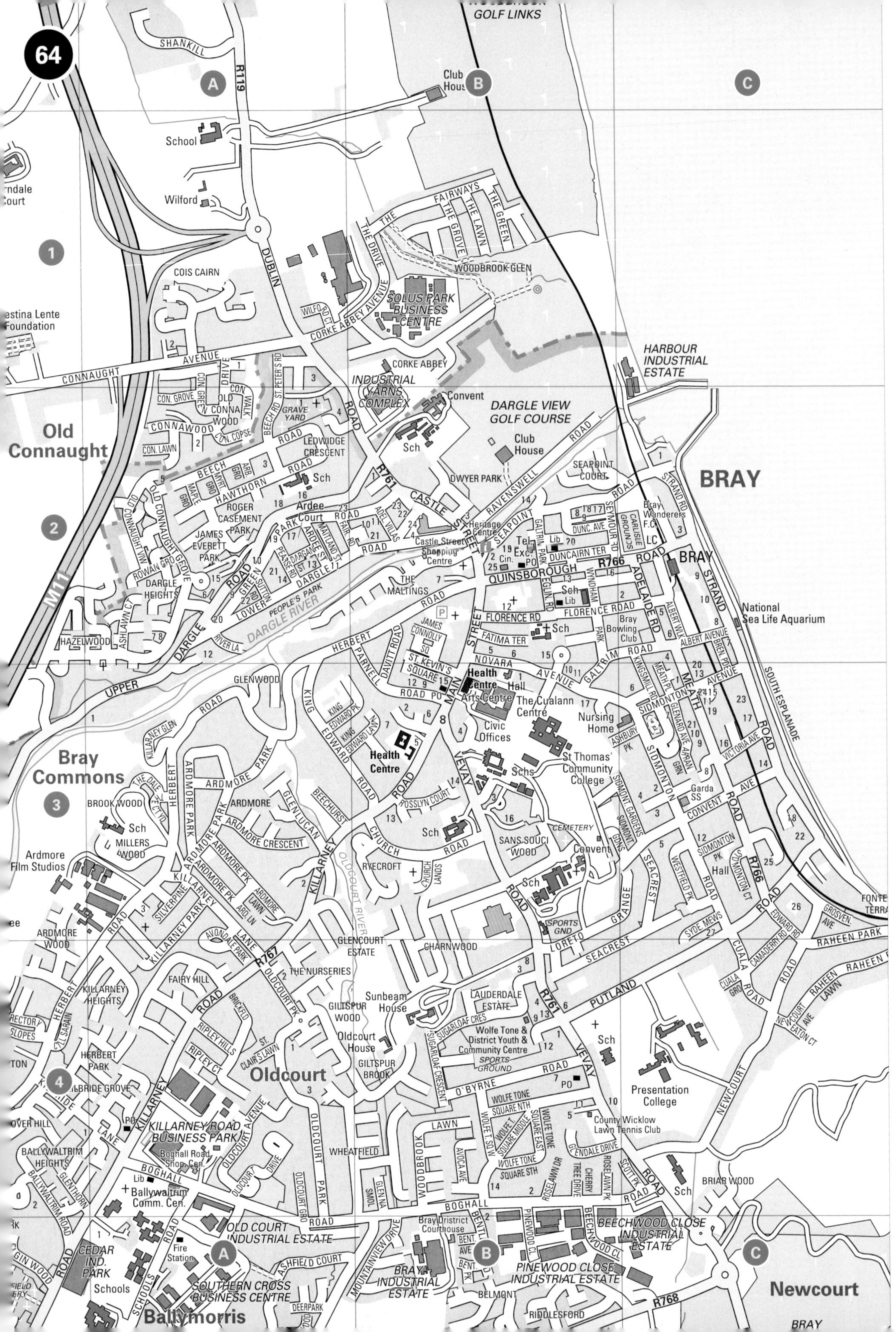
GOLF LINKS
SHANKILL
R119
Club House
School
Wilford
Old Connaught
COIS CAIRN
DUBLIN ROAD
CONNAUGHT AVENUE
THE FAIRWAYS
THE GROVE
THE LAWN
THE GREEN
THE DRIVE
WOODBROOK GLEN
SOLUS PARK BUSINESS CENTRE
CORKE ABBEY AVENUE
CORKE ABBEY
INDUSTRIAL YARNS COMPLEX
Convent
HARBOUR INDUSTRIAL ESTATE
DARGLE VIEW GOLF COURSE
Club House
BRAY
M11
Bray Commons
Ardmore Film Studios
ARDMORE WOOD
BROOK WOOD
MILLERS WOOD
KILLARNEY HEIGHTS
HERBERT PARK
BALLYWALTRIM HEIGHTS
Ballywaltrim Comm. Cen.
Oldcourt
OLD COURT INDUSTRIAL ESTATE
CEDAR IND. PARK
Schools
Ballymorris
SOUTHERN CROSS BUSINESS CENTRE
BRAY INDUSTRIAL ESTATE
PINEWOOD CLOSE INDUSTRIAL ESTATE
BEECHWOOD CLOSE INDUSTRIAL ESTATE
Newcourt
Presentation College
County Wicklow Lawn Tennis Club
Wolfe Tone & District Youth & Community Centre
Sunbeam House
Oldcourt House
GLENCOURT ESTATE
THE NURSERIES
CHARNWOOD
LAUDERDALE ESTATE
SANS SOUCI WOOD
CEMETERY
St Thomas' Community College
The Cualann Centre
Civic Offices
Health Centre
Arts Centre
Nursing Home
National Sea Life Aquarium
Bray Wanderers F.C.
Heritage Centre
Castle Street Shopping Centre
THE MALTINGS
DARGLE RIVER
PEOPLE'S PARK
QUINSBOROUGH ROAD
R766
R761
R767
R768
MAIN STREET
STRAND ROAD
SOUTH ESPLANADE
MEATH ROAD
SIDMONTON ROAD
NOVARA AVENUE
FLORENCE ROAD
ADELAIDE RD
SEAPOINT ROAD
RAVENSWELL ROAD
CASTLE STREET
DARGLE ROAD
UPPER DARGLE ROAD
HERBERT ROAD
KING EDWARD ROAD
VEVAY ROAD
CHURCH ROAD
KILLARNEY ROAD
BOGHALL ROAD
PUTLAND ROAD
SEACREST
NEWCOURT ROAD
RAHEEN PARK
CUALA ROAD
DWYER PARK
Garda SS
Bray Bowling Club
KILLARNEY ROAD BUSINESS PARK
Boghall Road Shop. Cen.
Bray District Courthouse
Fire Station
BRIAR WOOD
BELMONT
RIDDLESFORD
DEERPARK
WHEATFIELD
A
B
C
1
2
3
4

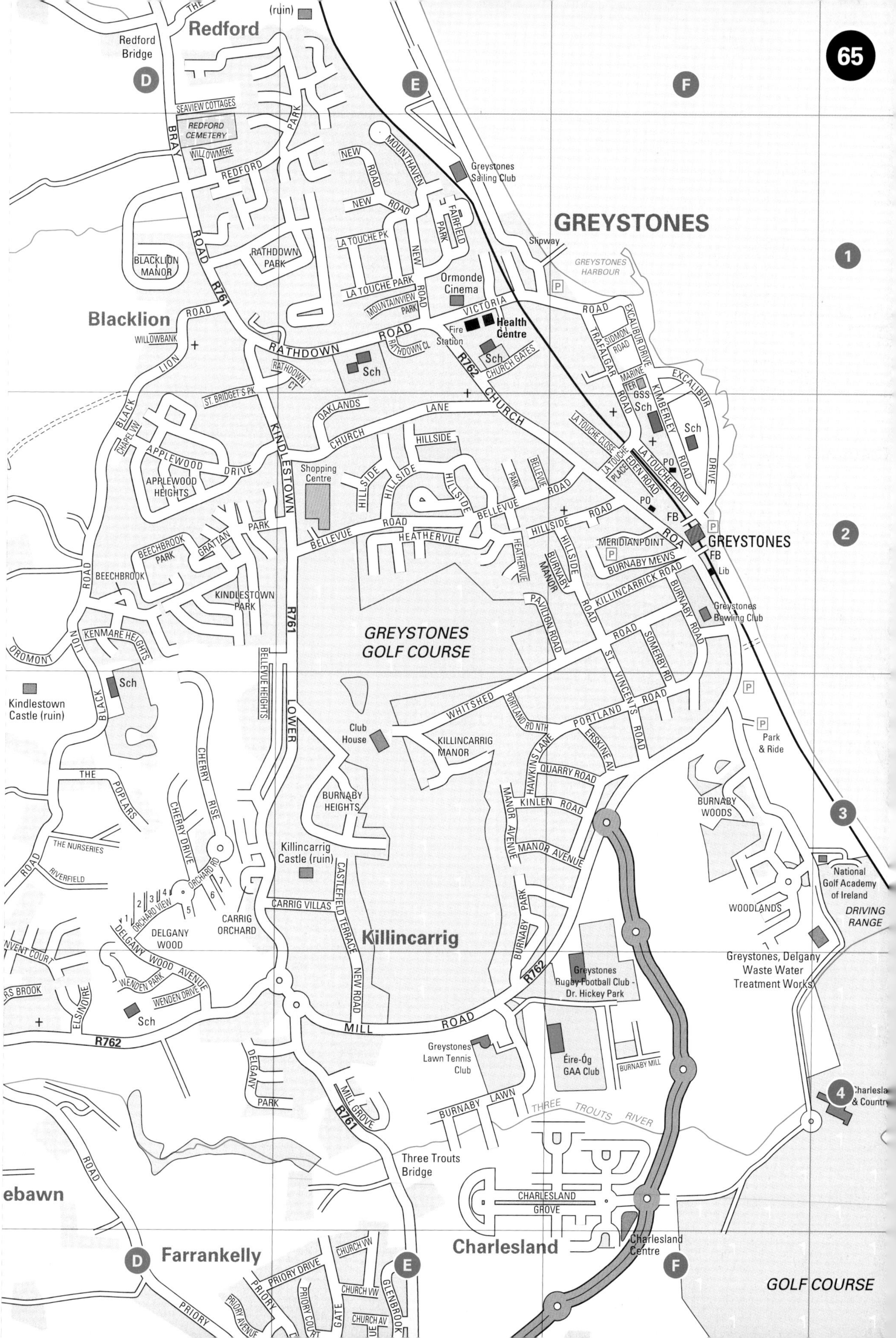

Redford
Redford Bridge
(ruin)
D
E
F
SEAVIEW COTTAGES
REDFORD CEMETERY
WILLOWMERE
BRAY ROAD
R761
REDFORD
PARK
MOUNTHAVEN
NEW ROAD
NEW ROAD
Greystones Sailing Club
FAIRFIELD PARK
GREYSTONES
Slipway
GREYSTONES HARBOUR
1
LA TOUCHE PK
RATHDOWN PARK
BLACKLION MANOR
LA TOUCHE PARK
Ormonde Cinema
MOUNTAINVIEW PARK
Blacklion
ROAD
WILLOWBANK
VICTORIA ROAD
Health Centre
Fire Station
RATHDOWN ROAD
RATHDOWN CL
Sch
R762
CHURCH GATES
TRAFALGAR ROAD
SIDMON ROAD
EXCALIBUR DRIVE
EXCALIBUR
MARINE TER
GSS
KIMBERLEY ROAD
RATHDOWN CT
ST. BRIDGET'S PK
OAKLANDS
LANE
CHURCH
BLACK LION
CHAPEL VW
APPLEWOOD DRIVE
APPLEWOOD HEIGHTS
KINDLESTOWN
CHURCH
HILLSIDE
Shopping Centre
HILLSIDE
HILLSIDE
HILLSIDE
LA TOUCHE CLOSE
LA TOUCHE PLACE
LA TOUCHE ROAD
EDEN ROAD
PO
BELLEVUE
PARK
BELLEVUE ROAD
BELLEVUE
ROAD
BELLEVUE ROAD
HEATHERVUE
HILLSIDE
HILLSIDE
ROAD
FB
GREYSTONES
2
PARK
GRATTAN
BEECHBROOK PARK
BEECHBROOK
ROAD
KINDLESTOWN PARK
R761
HEATHERVUE
BURNABY MANOR
MERIDIANPOINT
BURNABY MEWS
Lib
KILLINCARRICK ROAD
BURNABY ROAD
PAVILION ROAD
ROAD
Greystones Bowling Club
KENMARE HEIGHTS
LION
DROMONT
GREYSTONES GOLF COURSE
ROAD
SOMERBY RD
ST. VINCENTS ROAD
ROAD
Sch
Kindlestown Castle (ruin)
BLACK
BELLEVUE HEIGHTS
LOWER
WHITSHED
PORTLAND RD NTH
PORTLAND
ERSKINE AV
Park & Ride
Club House
KILLINCARRIG MANOR
HAWKINS LANE
QUARRY ROAD
CHERRY RISE
THE POPLARS
CHERRY DRIVE
BURNABY HEIGHTS
MANOR AVENUE
KINLEN ROAD
MANOR AVENUE
BURNABY WOODS
3
THE NURSERIES
ROAD
RIVERFIELD
Killincarrig Castle (ruin)
CASTLEFIELD TERRACE
ORCHARD RD
ORCHARD VIEW
1 2 3 4 5 6 7
CARRIG VILLAS
CARRIG ORCHARD
DELGANY WOOD
DELGANY WOOD AVENUE
Killincarrig
BURNABY PARK
R762
Greystones Rugby Football Club - Dr. Hickey Park
National Golf Academy of Ireland
WOODLANDS
DRIVING RANGE
Greystones, Delgany Waste Water Treatment Works
CONVENT COURT
RS BROOK
ELSINOIRE
WENDEN PARK
WENDEN DRIVE
Sch
NEW ROAD
MILL ROAD
R762
Greystones Lawn Tennis Club
Éire-Óg GAA Club
BURNABY MILL
DELGANY PARK
MILL GROVE
R761
BURNABY LAWN
THREE TROUTS RIVER
4
Charlesla
& Countr
ROAD
Three Trouts Bridge
ebawn
CHARLESLAND GROVE
Charlesland Centre
Charlesland
D
Farrankelly
E
F
CHURCH VW
PRIORY DRIVE
PRIORY COURT
CHURCH VW
CHURCH AV
GATE
GLENBROOK
PRIORY
PRIORY AVENUE
PRIORY
GOLF COURSE

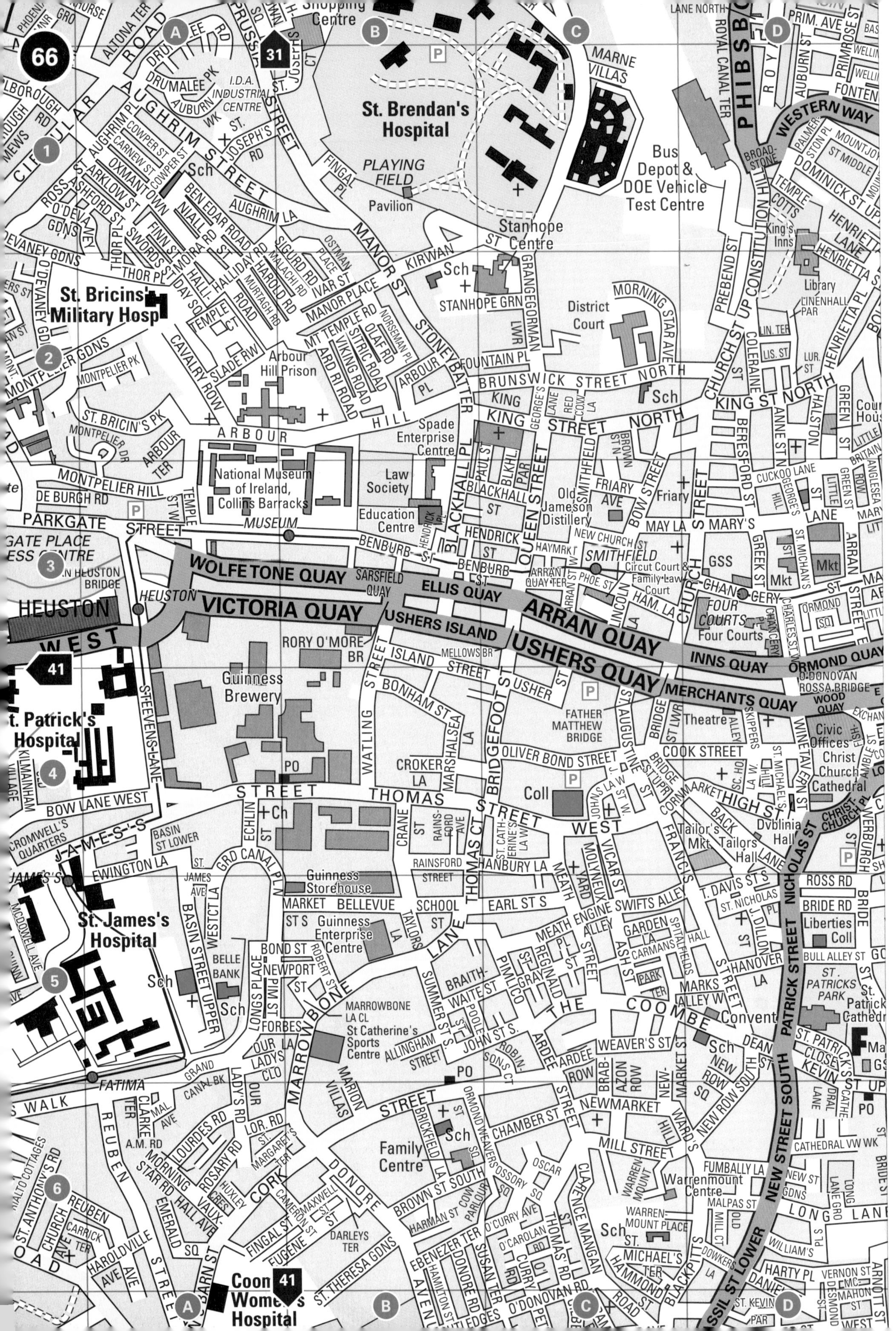
A
B
C
D
1
2
3
4
5
6
31
41
Shopping Centre
St. Brendan's Hospital
PLAYING FIELD
Pavilion
I.D.A. INDUSTRIAL CENTRE
MARNE VILLAS
Bus Depot & DOE Vehicle Test Centre
PHIBSBORO
ROYAL CANAL TER
WESTERN WAY
PRIM. AVE
PRIMROSE ST
AUBURN ST
FONTENOY
BROADSTONE
DOMINICK ST UPPER
HENRIETTA LANE
HENRIETTA ST
HENRIETTA PL
King's Inns
Library
LINENHALL PAR
CONSTITUTION HILL
PREBEND ST
CHURCH ST UPPER
COLERAINE ST
LIN. TER
LIS. ST
LUR. ST
Stanhope Centre
STANHOPE GRN
GRANGEGORMAN LWR
KIRWAN ST
MANOR ST
MANOR PLACE
District Court
MORNING STAR AVE
FOUNTAIN PL
BRUNSWICK STREET NORTH
KING ST NORTH
KING STREET NORTH
ANNE ST N
HALSTON ST
GREEN ST
Court House
LITTLE BRITAIN ST
ANGLESEA ROW
CUCKOO LANE
GEORGE'S HILL
LITTLE GREEN ST
MARY'S LANE
ST. MICHAN'S ST
ARRAN ST
Mkt
CIRCULAR ROAD
AUGHRIM STREET
AUGHRIM LA
ALTONA TER
DRUMALEE RD
DRUMALEE PK
AUBURN ST
ST. JOSEPH'S RD
PRUSSIA ST
ST. JOSEPH'S CT
FINGAL PL
OSTMAN PLACE
SIGURD RD
MALACHI RD
IVAR ST
HAROLD RD
MURTAGH RD
HALLIDAY RD
HALLIDAY SQ
NIALL ST
MORA RD
BEN EDAR ROAD
FINN ST
SWORDS ST
OXMANTOWN RD
ARKLOW ST
ASHFORD ST
ROSS ST
COWPER ST
CARNEW ST
O'DEVANEY GDNS
DEVANEY GDNS
THOR PL
St. Bricins Military Hosp
TEMPLE CT
CAVALRY ROW
SLADE RW
Arbour Hill Prison
MT TEMPLE RD
NORSEMAN PL
SITRIC ROAD
OLAF RD
VIKING ROAD
ARD RI ROAD
ARBOUR PL
ARBOUR HILL
STONEYBATTER
MONTPELIER GDNS
MONTPELIER PK
ST. BRICIN'S PK
MONTPELIER DR
ARBOUR TER
MONTPELIER HILL
DE BURGH RD
National Museum of Ireland, Collins Barracks
Spade Enterprise Centre
Law Society
Education Centre
BLACKHALL PL
PAUL ST
BLACKHALL ST
QUEEN STREET
SMITHFIELD
Old Jameson Distillery
FRIARY AVE
BOW STREET
Friary
CHURCH STREET
MAY LA
HENDRICK ST
BENBURB ST
NEW CHURCH ST
HAYMRKT
Circuit Court & Family Law Court
GSS
PARKGATE STREET
MUSEUM
HEUSTON
HEUSTON BRIDGE
WOLFE TONE QUAY
SARSFIELD QUAY
ELLIS QUAY
ARRAN QUAY
ARRAN QUAY TER
PHOE. ST
CHANCERY ST
HAM. LA
FOUR COURTS
Four Courts
ORMOND SQ
VICTORIA QUAY
USHERS ISLAND
USHERS QUAY
INNS QUAY
ORMOND QUAY
O'DONOVAN ROSSA BRIDGE
MERCHANTS QUAY
WOOD QUAY
ST. JOHN'S RD WEST
Guinness Brewery
RORY O'MORE BR
MELLOWS BR
ISLAND STREET
BONHAM ST
WATLING STREET
MARSHALSEA LA
BRIDGEFOOT ST
USHER ST
FATHER MATTHEW BRIDGE
ST. AUGUSTINE ST
BRIDGE ST LWR
Theatre
SKIPPERS ALLEY
WINETAVERN ST
Civic Offices
Christ Church Cathedral
St. Patrick's Hospital
STEEVENS LANE
KILMAINHAM
BOW LANE WEST
OLIVER BOND STREET
COOK STREET
CROKER LA
THOMAS STREET WEST
JAMES'S STREET
ECHLIN ST
Ch
CRANE ST
RAINSFORD AVE
Coll
HIGH ST
BACK LANE
Tailor's Mkt
Tailors Hall
Dvblinia Hall
CHRISTCHURCH PL
WERBURGH ST
CROMWELL'S QUARTERS
BASIN ST LOWER
EWINGTON LA
GRD CANAL PLN
JAMES'S
ST. JAMES AVE
THOMAS CT
RAINSFORD STREET
HANBURY LA
MEATH ST
VICAR ST
MOLYNEUX YARD
FRANCIS ST
ST. CATHERINE'S LA W
Guinness Storehouse
St. James's Hospital
MCDOWELL AVE
BASIN STREET UPPER
WESTCT LA
MARKET
BELLEVUE
SCHOOL ST
EARL ST S
ENGINE ALLEY
SWIFTS ALLEY
T. DAVIS ST S
ST. NICHOLAS PL
J. DILLON ST
ROSS RD
BRIDE RD
Liberties Coll
BULL ALLEY ST
Guinness Enterprise Centre
TAYLORS LA
MEATH PL
GARDEN LA
CARMANS HALL
SPITALFIELDS
BELLE BANK
Sch
BOND ST
NEWPORT ST
ROBERT ST
PIM ST
LONGS PLACE
MARROWBONE LANE
SUMMER ST S.
BRAITHWAITE ST
PIMLICO
GRAY ST
REGINALD ST
ASH ST
PARK TER
HANOVER LA
ST. PATRICKS PARK
St. Patrick's Cathedral
THE COOMBE
MARKS ALLEY W
Convent
NICHOLAS ST
PATRICK STREET
NEW STREET SOUTH
MARROWBONE LA CL
St Catherine's Sports Centre
ALLINGHAM STREET
JOHN ST S.
ROBINSON'S CT
FORBES LA
OUR LADY'S CLO
WEAVER'S ST
ARDEE ROW
ARDEE ST
BRABAZON ROW
NEWMARKET ST
NEW ROW SQ
NEW ROW SOUTH
DEAN ST
ST. PATRICK'S CLOSE
KEVIN ST UPPER
FATIMA
GRAND CANAL BK
MARION VILLAS
PO
STREET
BRICKFIELD LA
ORMOND ST
WEAVERS SQ
Family Centre
NEWMARKET
CHAMBER ST
HILL
CATHEDRAL VW WK
WALK
REUBEN STREET
CLARKE TER
MAL. AVE
LORDS RD
LOR. RD
OUR LADY'S RD
A.M. RD
MORNING STAR RD
ROSARY RD
HUXLEY CRES
ST. MARGARET'S TER
CORK ST
DONORE AVE
OSSORY SQ
OSCAR SQ
CLARENCE MANGAN RD
MILL STREET
WARRENMOUNT
Warrenmount Centre
FUMBALLY LA
MILL CT
MALPAS ST
NEW ST GDNS
LONG LANE
RIALTO COTTAGES
ST. ANTHONY'S RD
REUBEN AVE
CARRICK TER
CHURCH AVE
HAROLDVILLE AVE
EMERALD SQ
VAUX HALL AVE
CAMERON ST
MAXWELL ST
FINGAL ST
EUGENE ST
DARLEYS TER
BROWN ST SOUTH
HARMAN ST
COW PARLOUR
O'CURRY AVE
O'CAROLAN RD
CURRY RD
WARRENMOUNT PLACE
ST. MICHAEL'S TER
HAMMOND RD
BLACKPITTS
DOWKERS LA
WILLIAM'S PL
HARTY PL
VERNON ST
MCMAHON ST
ARNOTT ST
DANIEL ST
ST. KEVIN PAR
DESMOND ST
CLANBRASSIL ST LOWER
Coombe Women's Hospital
ST. THERESA GDNS
EBENEZER TER
HAMILTON ST
DONORE RD
SUSAN TER
ST. THOMAS' RD
O'DONOVAN RD
ROAD

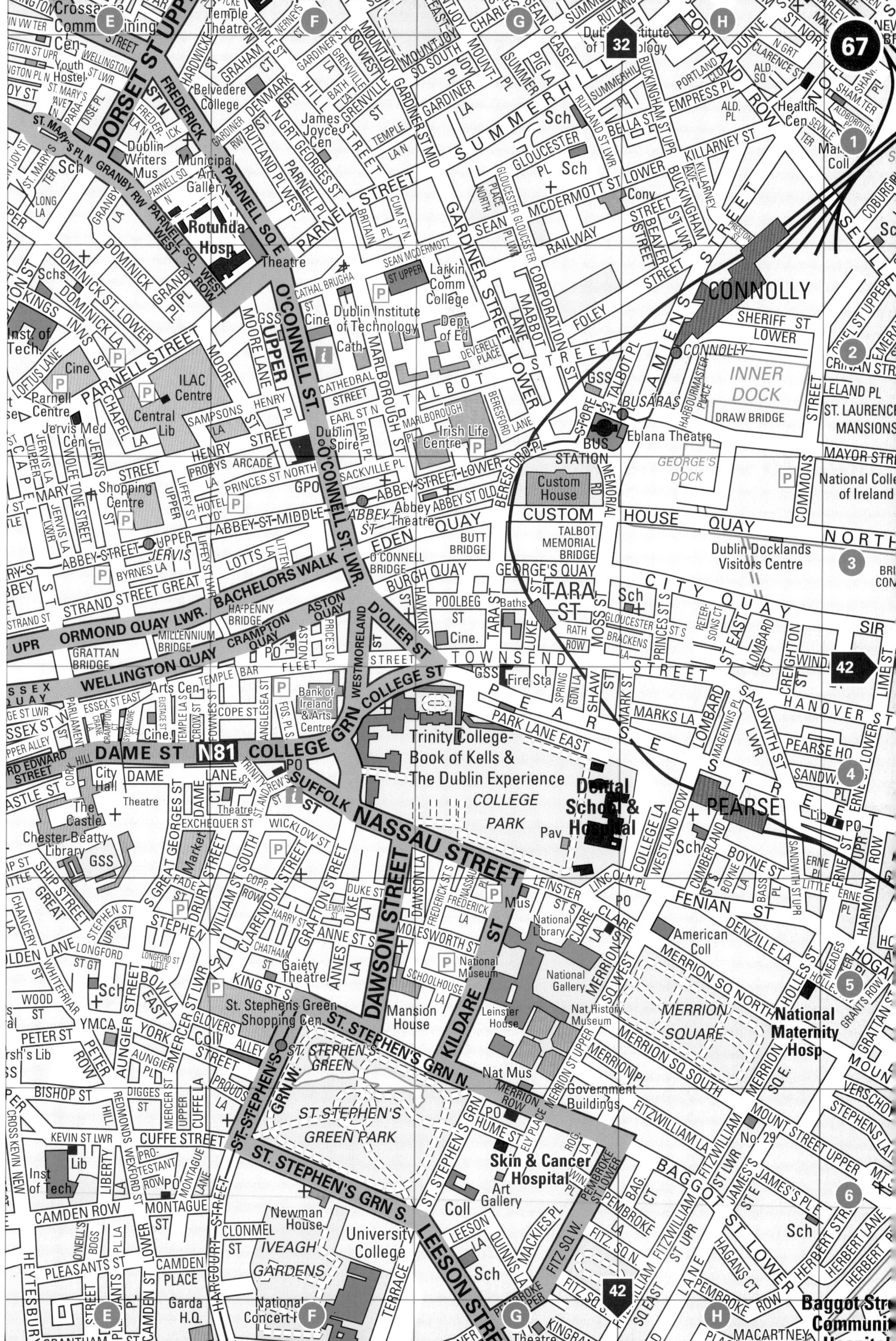
67
E
F
G
H
32
42
1
2
3
4
5
6
DORSET ST UPPER
FREDERICK ST N
Belvedere College
James Joyce Cen
Dublin Writers Mus
Municipal Art Gallery
Temple Theatre
Crossaig Comm Training Cen
Youth Hostel
Dublin Institute of Technology
SUMMERHILL
GARDINER ST MID
MOUNTJOY SQ SOUTH
PARNELL STREET
PARNELL SQ E
PARNELL SQ WEST
GRANBY RW
Rotunda Hosp
Gate Theatre
SEAN MCDERMOTT ST LOWER
GLOUCESTER PL
RAILWAY ST
FOLEY ST
Cony
CONNOLLY
SHERIFF ST LOWER
INNER DOCK
DRAW BRIDGE
GEORGE'S DOCK
BUSARAS
Eblana Theatre
BUS STATION
Custom House
National College of Ireland
MAYOR ST
ST. LAURENCE MANSIONS
Larkin Comm College
Dept of Ed
Dublin Institute of Technology
Cath.
O'CONNELL ST. UPPER
O'CONNELL ST. LWR.
TALBOT STREET
GARDINER STREET LOWER
MARLBOROUGH ST
CATHEDRAL STREET
Dublin Spire
Irish Life Centre
GPO
ABBEY STREET LOWER
ABBEY ST OLD
Abbey Theatre
ABBEY ST MIDDLE
ABBEY STREET UPPER
JERVIS
HENRY STREET
ILAC Centre
Central Lib
Jervis Med Cen
Parnell Centre
Inst. of Tech.
MARY STREET
Shopping Centre
CAPEL STREET
PRINCES ST NORTH
CUSTOM HOUSE QUAY
NORTH WALL QUAY
Dublin Docklands Visitors Centre
TALBOT MEMORIAL BRIDGE
MEMORIAL RD
EDEN QUAY
BUTT BRIDGE
O'CONNELL BRIDGE
BACHELORS WALK
GEORGE'S QUAY
BURGH QUAY
CITY QUAY
TARA ST
STRAND STREET GREAT
ORMOND QUAY LWR.
HA'PENNY BRIDGE
MILLENNIUM BRIDGE
GRATTAN BRIDGE
WELLINGTON QUAY
ASTON QUAY
CRAMPTON QUAY
D'OLIER ST
WESTMORELAND ST
POOLBEG ST
Cine.
TOWNSEND STREET
Fire Sta
PEARSE STREET
PARK LANE EAST
HANOVER
PEARSE HO
Arts Cen
TEMPLE BAR
FLEET STREET
Bank of Ireland & Arts Centre
COLLEGE ST
COLLEGE GRN
DAME ST
N81
DAME LANE
ESSEX QUAY
PARLIAMENT ST
City Hall
The Castle
Chester Beatty Library
Trinity College- Book of Kells & The Dublin Experience
COLLEGE PARK
Dental School & Hospital
PEARSE
SUFFOLK ST
NASSAU STREET
WICKLOW ST
EXCHEQUER ST
Market
S GREAT GEORGES ST
DRURY STREET
WILLIAM ST SOUTH
CLARENDON STREET
GRAFTON STREET
DAWSON STREET
DUKE ST
ANNE ST S
MOLESWORTH ST
KILDARE ST
National Library
National Museum
National Gallery
Leinster House
Nat History Museum
FENIAN ST
American Coll
MERRION SQUARE
MERRION SQ NORTH
MERRION SQ SOUTH
MERRION SQ WEST
National Maternity Hosp
HOLLES ST
Gaiety Theatre
Mansion House
KING ST S
St. Stephens Green Shopping Cen
ST. STEPHEN'S GRN N.
ST. STEPHEN'S GRN W.
ST. STEPHEN'S GREEN PARK
ST. STEPHEN'S GRN S.
Nat Mus
MERRION ROW
Government Buildings
MERRION STREET UPPER
Skin & Cancer Hospital
Art Gallery
HUME ST
BAGGOT ST LOWER
FITZWILLIAM ST LWR
MOUNT STREET UPPER
No. 29
YMCA
AUNGIER STREET
STEPHEN ST UPPER
PETER ST
BISHOP ST
CUFFE STREET
KEVIN ST LWR
Lib
Inst of Tech
CAMDEN ROW
MONTAGUE
HARCOURT STREET
Newman House
University College
IVEAGH GARDENS
National Concert Hall
LEESON STREET
Garda H.Q.
CAMDEN PLACE
PLEASANTS ST
HEYTESBURY
FITZ SQ W.
FITZ SQ N.
PEMBROKE ST LOWER
PEMBROKE ROW
Baggot Street Community Hospital
MACARTNEY
Theatre

Index to street names

General abbreviations

All	Alley	Cotts	Cottages	Gra	Grange	Ms	Mews	Sq	Square
Av	Avenue	Cres	Crescent	Grd	Ground	Mt	Mount	St.	Saint
Ave	Avenue	Ct	Court	Grn	Green	N	North	St	Street
Bk	Bank	Dr	Drive	Gro	Grove	No	Numbers	Sta	Station
Bldgs	Buildings	Dws	Dwellings	Ho	House	Par	Parade	Ter	Terrace
Boul	Boulevard	E	East	Hosp	Hospital	Pas	Passage	Vil	Villa, Villas
Br	Bridge	Ex	Exchange	Hts	Heights	Pk	Park	Vw	View
Bri	Bridge	Ext	Extension	Junct	Junction	Pl	Place	W	West
Cem	Cemetery	Fld	Field	La	Lane	Prom	Promenade	Wd	Wood
Cen	Central, Centre	Flds	Fields	Lo	Lodge	Rd	Road	Wds	Woods
Cl	Close	Fm	Farm	Lwr	Lower	Ri	Rise	Wk	Walk
Clo	Close	Gdn	Garden	Mans	Mansions	S	South	Yd	Yard
Coll	College	Gdns	Gardens	Mkt	Market	Sch	School		

District abbreviations

Abb.	Abberley	Carrick.	Carrickmines	Dunb.	Dunboyne	Leix.	Leixlip	Sally.	Sallynoggin
B'brack	Ballybrack	Castle.	Castleknock	Fox.	Foxrock	Leo.	Leopardstown	Sandy.	Sandyford
B'mun	Ballymun	Clond.	Clondalkin	G'geary	Glenageary	Lou.V.	Louisa Valley	Shank.	Shankill
Bald.	Baldoyle	Clons.	Clonsilla	Gra M.	Grange Manor	Lough.	Loughlinstown	Still.	Stillorgan
Balg.	Balgriffin	Collins.	Collinstown	Grey.	Greystones	Mala.	Malahide	Will.	Willbrook
Black.	Blackrock	Cool.	Coolmine	Jobs.	Jobstown	Manor.	Manorfields		
Boot.	Booterstown	Corn.	Cornelscourt	Kill.	Killiney	Mulh.	Mulhuddart		
Cabin.	Cabinteely	D.L.	Dún Laoghaire	Kilt.	Kiltipper	Palm.	Palmerston		
Carp.	Carpenterstown	Deans Gra	Deans Grange	Kins.	Kinsaley	Port.	Portmarnock		

Some streets are not named on the map due to insufficient space. In some of these cases the nearest street that does appear on the map is listed in *italics*. In other cases they are indicated on the map by a number which is listed here in **bold**.

A

Allied Ind Est 39 F3
Allingham St 66 B5
All Saints Dr 34 B2
All Saints Pk 34 B2
All Saints Rd 34 A2
Alma Pl 51 D3
Alma Rd 50 C2
Almeida Av
off Brookfield St 41 D2
Almeida Ter
off Brookfield St 41 D2
Alone Wk 33 F1
Alpine Hts 44 A1
Alpine Ri 44 B4
Altadore 59 F1
Altona Ter 66 A1
Alverno 33 E3
Amber Vale 52 B1
Amiens St 67 H2
Anastasia La 60 C3
Anfield Cl 28 A1
Anfield Ct 28 A2
Anfield Cres 28 A2
Anfield Dr 28 A2
Anfield Lawn **1** 28 A2
Anfield Vw **2** 28 A2
Anglesea Av 50 B2
Anglesea Br 49 D1
Anglesea Fruit Mkt
off Green St Little 66 D3
Anglesea La 51 F3
Anglesea Pk 60 A4
Anglesea Rd 49 D1
Anglesea Row 66 D3
Anglesea St 67 F4
Anley Ct 27 E2
Annabeg **1** 59 F4
Annadale Av 32 C3
Annadale Cres 32 C2
Annadale Dr 32 C2
Annagh Ct **1** 17 D3
Annaly 14 B3
Annaly Rd 31 E3
Annamoe Dr 31 E3
Annamoe Par 31 E4
Annamoe Pk 31 E4
Annamoe Rd 31 E3
Annamoe Ter 31 E4
Anna Vil 48 B1
Annaville Av 50 B4
Annaville Gro 48 C4
Annaville Ter
off Annaville Gro 48 C4
Anne Devlin Av 55 D1
Anne Devlin Dr 55 D1
Anne Devlin Pk 55 D1
Anne Devlin Rd 55 D1
Anner Rd 40 C2
Annes La 67 F5
Annesley Av 32 C4
Annesley Br 32 C3
Annesley Br Rd 32 C3
Annesley Pk 48 B1
Annesley Pl 32 C3
Anne St N 66 D2
Anne St S 67 F5
Annsbrook 48 C3
Annville Dr 57 E2
Appian Way, The 42 B4
Apples Rd 57 D3
Applewood Dr 65 D2
Applewood Hts 65 D2
Aran Av 63 E1
Aran Cl 63 E1
Aran Dr 63 E1
Aranleigh Ct 55 F1
Aranleigh Dell 55 F2
Aranleigh Gdns 55 F1
Aranleigh Mt 55 E1
Aranleigh Pk 55 F1
Aranleigh Vale 55 F1
Áras An Uachtaráin 30 B3
Aras Naclunne 38 C4
Aravon Ct **8** 64 C3
Arbour Hill 66 A2
Arbour Pl 66 B2
Arbour Ter 66 A2
Arbutus Av 41 E4
Arbutus Gro 64 A2
Arbutus Pl 41 F3
Arcade 67 F3
Archers Wd 16 A1
Arches, The **11** 63 E1
Ardagh Av 50 B4
Ardagh Cl **1** 50 B4
Ardagh Ct 50 A4
Ardagh Cres 50 A4
Ardagh Dr 50 B4
Ardagh Gro 50 A4
Ardagh Pk 50 B4
Ardagh Pk Rd 50 B4
Ardagh Rd 41 D4
Ardara Av 22 C3
Ardbeg Cres 21 F4
Ardbeg Dr 21 F4
Ardbeg Pk 21 F4
Ardbeg Rd 21 F4
Ardbrugh Cl **1** 60 B4
Ardbrugh Rd 60 B4
Ardbrugh Vil **2** 60 B4
Ardcian Pk 6 B1
Ardcollum Av 21 E4
Ardee Gro 42 A4
Ardeen 26 C2
Ardee Rd 42 A4
Ardee Row 66 C5
Ardee St *Dublin 8* 66 C5
Ardee St *Bray* 64 A2
Ardeevin Av 26 C2
Ardeevin Ct 26 C2
Ardeevin Dr 26 C2
Ardeevin Rd 60 B3
Ardenza Pk
off Seapoint Av 50 C2
Ardenza Ter 50 C2
Ardglas Est 56 C2
Ardilaun 11 F3
Ardilaun Rd 32 B4
Ardilea Downs 49 D4
Ardlea Rd 21 E4
Ard Lorcain 50 A4
Ard Lorcain Vil **1** 50 A4
Ardlui Pk 50 B4
Ardmeen Pk 50 B4
Ard Mhacha 53 D3
Ard Mhuire Pk 60 A4
Ardmore 64 A3
Ardmore Av 31 E4
Ardmore Cl 21 D4
Ardmore Cres *Dublin 5* 21 E4
Ardmore Cres *Bray* 64 A3
Ardmore Dr 21 D4
Ardmore Gro 21 D4
Ardmore Lawn 64 A3
Ardmore Pk *Dublin 5* 21 E4
Ardmore Pk *Bray* 64 A3
Ardmore Pk *D.L.* 51 E4
Ard Na Meala 20 A2
Ardpatrick Rd 30 C3
Ard Ri Pl
off Ard Ri Rd 66 B2
Ard Ri Rd 66 B2
Ardtona Av 48 B4
Arena Rd 57 F4
Argyle Rd 42 C4
Arkendale Ct **1** 60 A3
Arkendale Rd 60 A2
Arkendale Wds **2** 60 A3
Arkle Rd 57 E3
Arkle Sq **1** 57 F4
Arklow St 66 A1
Armagh Rd 46 C1
Armstrong St
off Harolds Cross Rd 41 F4
Arnold Gro 59 F1
Arnold Pk 59 F2
Arnott St 66 D6
Arran Ct **2** 17 D3
Arran Grn 64 C3
Arranmore Av 32 A3
Arranmore Rd 42 C4
Arran Quay 66 C3
Arran Quay Ter 66 C3
Arran Rd 32 B2
Arran St E 66 D3
Arran St W 66 C3
Arthur Griffith Pk 27 D3
Arundel 51 D3
Ascal An Charrain Chno
(Nutgrove Av) 55 F1
Ascal Bhaile An Abba
(Abbotstown Av) 18 B3
Ascal Bhaile Thuaidh
(Ballyhoy Av) 34 B2
Ascal Dun Eanna
(Ennafort Av) 34 A2
Ascal Measc (Mask Av) 21 F4
Ascal Phairc An Bhailtini
(Villa Park Av) 30 C3
Ascal Ratabhachta
(Ratoath Av) 18 B4
Asgard Pk 25 F3
Asgard Rd 25 F3
Ash, The 29 E1
Ashberry 26 C4
Ashbrook *Dublin 3* 33 E2
Ashbrook *Dublin 7* 30 A2
Ashbrook *Leix.* 15 D2
Ashbury Pk 64 B3
Ashcroft 34 B1
Ashcroft Gro **1** 16 A2
Ashdale Av 47 E2
Ashdale Cl 7 E3
Ashdale Gdns 47 E2
Ashdale Pk 47 E2
Ashdale Rd *Dublin 6W* 47 E2
Ashdale Rd *Swords* 10 A1
Ashfield (Templeogue) 46 C4
Ashfield Av *Dublin 6* 48 B1
Ashfield Av *Dublin 24* 45 D3
Ashfield Cl *Dublin 6W*
off Ashfield 46 C4
Ashfield Cl *Dublin 24* 45 D3
Ashfield Ct 16 A2
Ashfield Dr 45 D3
Ashfield Gdns 16 A2
Ashfield Grn 16 A1
Ashfield Gro 16 A1
Ashfield Lawn 16 A1
Ashfield Pk
(Templeogue)
Dublin 6W
off Ashfield 46 C4
Ashfield Pk (Terenure)
Dublin 6W 47 E2
Ashfield Pk *Dublin 24* 45 D3
Ashfield Pk *Boot.* 49 E3
Ashfield Pk **7** *Mulh.* 16 A2
Ashfield Rd (Ranelagh) 48 B1
Ashfield Way 16 A2
Ashford Cotts
off Ashford St 66 A1
Ashford Pl
off Ashford St 66 A1
Ashford St 66 A1
Ashgrove *Dublin 24* 52 C1
Ashgrove *D.L.* 51 D4
Ashgrove Ind Est 51 D4
Ashgrove Ter **1** 56 C1
Ashington Av 30 C2
Ashington Cl 30 B1
Ashington Ct 30 C2
Ashington Dale 30 C1
Ashington Gdns 30 C2
Ashington Grn 30 C2
Ashington Ms 30 C1
Ashington Pk 30 B2
Ashington Ri 30 B1
Ash Lawn *Dublin 16* 56 B2
Ashlawn *B'brack* 59 F4
Ashlawn Ct 64 A2
Ashleaf Shop Cen 46 B2
Ashleigh Grn 29 D1
Ashleigh Gro 17 D4
Ashleigh Lawn 11 D1
Ashley Av 7 D2
Ashley Dr **5** 7 D2
Ashley Gro **4** 7 D2
Ashley Hts **6** 64 A2
Ashley Ri 11 F2
Ashling Cl 41 D4
Ashling Hts 16 C3
Ash Pk Av 27 D4
Ash Pk Ct 27 E4
Ash Pk Gro 27 E3
Ash Pk Heath 27 E3
Ash St 66 C5
Ashton Av 54 C2
Ashton Cl 54 C2
Ashton Gro 54 C2
Ashton Lawn 54 C2
Ashton Pk 51 D3
Ashtown Gate Rd 30 A2
Ashtown Gro 30 B2
Ashtown Rd 30 A1
Ashtown Sta 30 A1
Ashurst 63 E1
Ashville Cl 27 E2
Ashwood Dr 38 A4
Ashwood Lawns 38 A4
Ashwood Pk 38 A4
Ashwood Rd 38 A4
Ashwood Way 38 A4
Aspen Dr 7 F3
Aspen Pk **1** *D.L.* 59 E1
Aspen Pk *Swords* 7 F3
Aspen Rd 7 E3
Aspen Wds 16 A4
Aspen Wds Av 16 A4
Aspen Wds Lawn 16 A4
Assumpta Pk 63 D4
Aston Pl 67 F3
Aston Quay 67 F3
Athgoe Dr 63 E3
Athgoe Rd 63 E3
Athlumney Vil 42 A4
Atmospheric Rd **3** 60 A3
Aubrey Gro 63 E3
Aubrey Pk 63 E3
Auburn Av *Dublin 4* 48 C1
Auburn Av *Dublin 15* 29 E2
Auburn Av *Cabin.* 59 E3
Auburn Cl *Dublin 15*
off Auburn Dr 29 E1
Auburn Cl *Cabin.* 59 F3
Auburn Dr *Dublin 15* 29 E1
Auburn Dr *Cabin.* 59 E3
Auburn Grn
off Auburn Dr 29 E1
Auburn Gro 10 B1
Auburn Rd *Dublin 4*
off Auburn Av 48 C1
Auburn Rd *Cabin.* 59 E2
Auburn St 66 D1
Auburn Vil *Dublin 6* 47 F2
Auburn Vil **14** *Bray* 64 A2
Auburn Wk 66 A1
Aughavanagh Rd 41 E4
Aughrim La 66 A1
Aughrim Pl 66 A1
Aughrim St 66 A1
Aughrim Vil
off Aughrim St 66 A1
Augustine Vil **1** 64 C3
Aulden Gra 21 D2
Aungier Pl 67 E5
Aungier St 67 E5
Austins Cotts
off Annesley Pl 32 C3
Avalon **1** 58 B3
Ave Maria Rd 66 A6
Avenue, The
Dublin 6W 46 C4
Avenue, The (Ballinteer)
Dublin 16 56 B3
Avenue, The
(Ballyboden)
Dublin 16 54 C3
Avenue, The
(Lutterell Hall) *Dunb.* 12 A1
Avenue, The *Gra M.* 27 D4
Avenue, The *Kins.* 7 E3
Avenue, The *Lou.V.* 15 E1
Avenue, The **4** *Mala.* 11 F1
Avenue, The *Manor.* 14 B2
Avenue, The *Mulh.* 16 A1
Avenue, The *Swords* 7 D1
Avenue Rd 41 F3
Avila Apartments **2** 50 B4
Avila Pk 18 B3
Avoca Av *Black.* 50 A2
Avoca Av *Bray* 64 B4
Avoca Pk 50 A3
Avoca Pl 50 B2
Avoca Rd 50 A3
Avonbeg Ct **1** 53 E2
Avonbeg Dr 53 F2
Avonbeg Gdns 53 F2
Avonbeg Ind Est 39 F4
Avonbeg Pk 53 F2
Avonbeg Rd 53 F2
Avondale 15 F1
Avondale Av 31 F4
Avondale Business Pk 50 B2
Avondale Ct **4** 60 A2
Avondale Cres 60 A4
Avondale Lawn 50 B3
Avondale Lawn
Extension 50 B3
Avondale Pk *Dublin 5* 34 C2
Avondale Pk *Bray* 64 A3
Avondale Pk *Dalkey* 60 A4
Avondale Rd *Dublin 7* 31 F4
Avondale Rd *Dalkey* 60 A4
Avondale Sq 12 A2
Avondale Ter 46 B2
Avonmore 58 A1
Avonmore Av **1** 53 F2
Avonmore Cl 53 F2
Avonmore Dr 53 F2
Avonmore Gro 53 F2
Avonmore Pk 53 F2
Avonmore Rd 53 F2
Aylesbury 53 E3
Ayrefield Av 22 A4
Ayrefield Ct 22 A4
Ayrefield Dr 22 A4
Ayrefield Gro 22 A4
Ayrefield Pl 22 A4

B

Bachelors Wk 67 F3
Back La *Dublin 8* 66 D4
Back La **3** *Dublin 13* 23 F3
Back Rd 10 C1
Baggot Cl
off Baggot St Lwr 67 G6
Baggot Ct 67 H6
Baggot La 42 C3
Baggot Rd 30 B3
Baggot St Lwr 42 B3
Baggot St Upr 42 C3
Baggot Ter
off Blackhorse Av 30 B3
Bailey Grn Rd 37 E3
Bailey Vw 60 B2
Balally Av 57 D2
Balally Cl 57 D2
Balally Dr 56 C2
Balally Gro 57 D3
Balally Hill 57 D3
Balally Pk 57 D2
Balally Rd 56 C2
Balally Ter **1** 57 D3
Balbutcher Dr 19 F1
Balbutcher La 19 F2
Balbutcher Way 19 F1
Balcurris Gdns 20 A2
Balcurris Rd 20 A2
Baldoyle Ind Est 23 E4
Baldoyle Rd 24 A2
Balfe Av 46 B1
Balfe Rd 46 B1
Balfe Rd E 46 B1
Balfe St
off Chatham St 67 F5
Balgaddy Rd 27 F4
Balglass Est 25 E3
Balglass Rd 25 F3
Balgriffin 22 B1
Balgriffin Cotts 22 B2
Balgriffin Rd 22 B2
Balkill Pk 25 E3
Balkill Rd 25 F4
Ballawley Ct 56 C3
Ballinclea Hts 60 A4
Ballinclea Rd 59 F2
Ballinteer 56 B3
Ballinteer Av 56 B3
Ballinteer Cl 56 B3
Ballinteer Ct **2** 56 B3
Ballinteer Cres 56 B3
Ballinteer Dr 56 B3
Ballinteer Gdns 56 B3
Ballinteer Gro 56 B3
Ballinteer Pk 56 B3
Ballinteer Rd 56 B2
Ballinteer Shop Cen 56 B3
Ballintrane Wd 6 C2
Ballintyre Downs 56 B4
Ballintyre Heath 56 B4
Ballintyre Meadows 56 A4
Ballintyre Wk 56 B4
Ballintyre Wds **4** 56 B3
Ball's Br 43 D4
Ballsbridge Av 43 D4
Ballsbridge Pk 43 D4
Ballsbridge Ter
off Ballsbridge Av 43 D4
Ballsbridge Wd 43 D3
Ballyboden Cres 55 D2
Ballyboden Rd
Dublin 14 55 D2
Ballyboden Rd
Dublin 16 55 D2
Ballyboggan Ind Est 30 C1
Ballyboggan Rd 31 D1
Ballybough Av
off Spring Gdn St 32 C4
Ballybough Br 32 C3
Ballybough Ct
off Spring Gdn St 32 C4
Ballybough Rd 32 B4
Ballybrack 61 E2
Ballybrack Shop Cen 59 F4
Ballybride 63 D4
Ballybride Rd 63 D3
Ballycoolin Business
& Tech Pk 17 E1
Ballycoolin Rd 17 E2
Ballycorus 62 A3
Ballycullen Av 53 F3
Ballycullen Dr 54 A3
Ballydowd Dr 27 E3
Ballydowd Gro 27 E2
Ballydowd Manor 27 E3
Ballyfermot Av 39 F2
Ballyfermot Cres 39 F2
Ballyfermot Dr 39 E2
Ballyfermot Par 39 E2
Ballyfermot Rd (Bothar
Baile Thormod) 39 E2
Ballygall Av 19 E3
Ballygall Cres 19 D4
Ballygall Par 19 D4
Ballygall Pl 19 E4
Ballygall Rd E 19 F4
Ballygall Rd W 19 D4
Ballygihen Av 60 A2
Ballygihen Vil **5** 60 A2
Ballyhoy Av (Ascal Bhaile
Thuaidh) 34 B2
Ballymace Grn 54 C1
Ballymanagin La **1** 38 B4
Ballymoss Par **2** 57 F4
Ballymoss Rd 57 E3
Ballymount Av
Dublin 12 45 F3
Ballymount Av
Dublin 24 45 F3
Ballymount Cross 45 E2
Ballymount Cross
Ind Est 45 D2
Ballymount Dr 45 F2
Ballymount Ind Est 45 F2
Ballymount Lwr Rd 45 E2
Ballymount Rd 45 D3
Ballymount Rd Ind Est 45 F1
Ballymount Rd Upr 45 E2
Ballymount Trd Est 46 A2
Ballymun Ind Est 19 F1
Ballymun Rd 32 A1
Ballymun Shop Cen 20 A2
Ballyneety Rd 40 A2
Ballyogan Av 58 A3
Ballyogan Cl 58 A4
Ballyogan Ct 58 A4
Ballyogan Cres 58 A4
Ballyogan Dr 58 A4
Ballyogan Est 58 A3
Ballyogan Grn 58 A3
Ballyogan Lawn 58 A3
Ballyogan Rd **1** 58 A4
Ballyogan Wd 58 A4
Ballyolaf Manor **1** 56 C2
Ballyowen Av 27 F2
Ballyowen Castle
Shop & Med Cen 27 E3
Ballyowen Ct 27 F2
Ballyowen Cres 27 F2
Ballyowen Dr 27 F2
Ballyowen Grn 27 F2
Ballyowen Gro 27 F2
Ballyowen La 27 F2
Ballyowen Lawn 27 F2
Ballyowen Rd 13 F1
Ballyowen Vw 27 F2
Ballyowen Way 27 F2
Ballyroan Ct **1** 54 C1
Ballyroan Cres 55 D1
Ballyroan Hts 54 C2
Ballyroan Pk 54 C1
Ballyroan Rd 54 C1
Ballyshannon Av 21 D3
Ballyshannon Rd 21 D3
Ballytore Rd 47 F3
Balnagowan 48 B2
Balrothery Cotts 54 A1
Balrothery Est 53 F1
Balscadden Rd 25 F3
Bancroft Av 53 E1
Bancroft Cl 53 F1
Bancroft Gro 53 F1
Bancroft Pk 53 E1
Bancroft Rd 53 F1
Bangor Dr 41 D4
Bangor Rd 41 D4
Bank of Ireland 67 F4

Bankside Cotts 48 B3
Bannow Rd 31 D2
Bann Rd 31 D1
Bantry Rd 32 A1
Bantry Sq **4** 17 D3
Banville Av 39 E3
Barclay Ct 50 B2
Bargy Rd 33 D4
Barnacoille Pk 60 B2
Barnamore Cres *off Barnamore Gro* 31 D1
Barnamore Gro 31 D1
Barnamore Pk 31 D1
Barnewall Dr 19 F2
Barnhall Dr 15 D2
Barnhill Av 60 A3
Barnhill Cross Rd 26 C2
Barnhill Gro 60 B3
Barnhill Lawn **1** 60 B3
Barnhill Pk **4** 60 A3
Barnhill Rd 60 A3
Barnville Pk 38 C3
Barrett St 51 E3
Barrow Rd 31 E2
Barrow Sta 42 C2
Barrow St 42 C2
Barry Av 18 C2
Barry Dr 18 C2
Barry Grn 18 C3
Barry Pk 18 C3
Barry Rd 18 C3
Barryscourt Rd 21 E3
Barton Av 55 E1
Barton Ct 56 A2
Barton Dr 55 E1
Barton Rd E 56 A2
Barton Rd Extension 55 F2
Barton Rd W (Willbrook) 55 E2
Bartra Rock **6** 60 B2
Basin St Lwr 66 A4
Basin St Upr 66 A5
Basin Vw Ter 31 F4
Baskin Cotts 10 A3
Baskin La 9 E2
Bass Pl 67 H5
Bath Av 43 D3
Bath Av Gdns 43 D3
Bath Av Pl 43 D3
Bath La 67 F1
Bath Pl 50 B2
Bath St 43 D2
Bawn, The 11 D1
Bawn Gro, The 11 D1
Bawnlea Av 52 B2
Bawnlea Cl 52 A2
Bawnlea Cres 52 A2
Bawnlea Dr 52 A2
Bawnlea Grn 52 B2
Bawnville Av 53 E3
Bawnville Cl 53 E3
Bawnville Dr 53 F2
Bawnville Pk 53 F2
Bawnville Rd 53 E2
Baymount Pk 34 B3
Bayshore La 63 E1
Bayside Boul N 23 E4
Bayside Boul S 23 E4
Bayside Pk 23 E4
Bayside Sq E 23 E4
Bayside Sq N 23 E4
Bayside Sq S 23 E4
Bayside Sq W 23 E4
Bayside Sta 23 F4
Bayside Wk 23 E4
Bayswater Ter **7** 60 B2
Bayview *Dublin 4 off Pembroke St* 43 D2
Bayview **2** *Bray* 64 B2
Bayview *Lough.* 63 E1
Bayview Av 32 C4
Bayview Cl 63 E1
Bayview Ct 63 E1
Bayview Cres 63 E2
Bayview Dr 63 E2
Bayview Glade **1** 63 E2
Bayview Glen **4** 63 E2
Bayview Grn 63 E1
Bayview Gro 63 E2
Bayview Lawn 63 E1
Bayview Pk 63 E1
Bayview Ri **3** 63 E2
Beach Av 43 E3
Beach Dr 43 E3
Beach Pk 11 F3
Beach Rd 43 E3
Beach Vw 35 E1
Beaconsfield Ct *off The Belfry* 40 C2
Bearna Pk 57 D4
Beattys Av 43 D4
Beaufield Manor 57 F1
Beaufield Pk 57 F1
Beaufort 60 A2
Beaufort Downs 55 E1
Beaumont Av 56 A1
Beaumont Cl 56 A1
Beaumont Cres 21 D4
Beaumont Dr 56 B1
Beaumont Gdns 50 A2
Beaumont Gro 20 C4
Beaumont Rd 20 C4
Beau Pk Av 23 D3
Beau Pk Cres 23 D3
Beau Pk Rd 23 D3
Beau Pk Row 23 D3
Beau Pk Sq 23 D3
Beau Pk St 23 D2
Beau Pk Ter 23 D3
Beauvale Pk 21 E4
Beaver Row 48 C2
Beaver St 67 H1
Beckett Way 38 C4
Bedford Row *off Temple Bar* 67 F4
Beechbrook 65 D2
Beechbrook Gro **7** 22 C3
Beechbrook Pk 65 D2
Beechcourt 59 F3
Beechdale 12 B3
Beechdale Ms 48 A1
Beech Dr 56 B2
Beeches, The *Dublin 13* 22 C4
Beeches, The **6** *Dublin 14* 55 E1
Beeches, The **12** *Abb.* 63 E1
Beeches, The *Black.* 51 D3
Beeches Pk 60 A3
Beeches Rd 57 D2
Beechfield 14 A1
Beechfield Av *Dublin 12* 46 B2
Beechfield Av *Dublin 24* 54 A4
Beechfield Cl *Dublin 12* 46 B2
Beechfield Cl **1** *Dublin 24* 54 A4
Beechfield Cl **1** *Dunb.* 14 A1
Beechfield Ct *Dublin 24* 54 A4
Beechfield Ct **1** *Clons.* 14 A2
Beechfield Cres 54 A4
Beechfield Dr 14 A1
Beechfield Grn **2** 14 A1
Beechfield Haven **1** 63 E3
Beechfield Hts **2** 14 A2
Beechfield Lawn *Dublin 24* 54 A4
Beechfield Lawn **1** *Clons.* 14 B1
Beechfield Manor 63 E3
Beechfield Meadows 14 A1
Beechfield Pk **2** 54 A4
Beechfield Pl *Dublin 24* 54 A4
Beechfield Pl *Clons.* 14 B1
Beechfield Ri 14 B1
Beechfield Rd *Dublin 12* 46 B2
Beechfield Rd *Dublin 24* 54 A4
Beechfield Rd (Hartstown) *Clons.* 14 A2
Beechfield Vw 14 A1
Beechfield Way *Dublin 24* 54 A4
Beechfield Way *Clons.* 14 A1
Beech Gro *Boot.* 49 F3
Beech Gro *Lucan* 27 D2
Beech Hill *off Beech Hill Rd* 48 C2
Beech Hill Av 49 D1
Beech Hill Cres 49 D2
Beech Hill Dr 49 D1
Beech Hill Rd 48 C2
Beech Hill Ter 49 D2
Beech Hill Vil *off Beech Hill Ter* 49 D2
Beech Lawn *Dublin 16* 56 A2
Beechlawn *Boot.* 49 F4
Beech Lawn Av 56 A2
Beechlawn Ind Complex 46 A2
Beechmount Dr 48 C3
Beech Pk *Dublin 15* 29 E1
Beech Pk *Cabin.* 59 E4
Beech Pk *Lucan* 27 D2
Beech Pk Av *Dublin 5* 21 F3
Beech Pk Av *Dublin 15* 29 E1
Beech Pk Av *Deans Gra* 58 C1
Beechpark Ct 21 F3
Beech Pk Cres 29 E1
Beech Pk Dr 58 C2
Beech Pk Gro 58 C2
Beech Pk Lawn 29 E1
Beech Pk Rd 58 C1
Beech Rd *Dublin 12* 45 E1
Beech Rd *Bray* 64 A2
Beech Rd **3** *Shank.* 63 E4
Beech Row **3** *Clond.* 44 B1
Beech Row (Ronanstown) *Clond.* 38 A3
Beechurst 64 A3
Beechview **1** 55 D3
Beech Wk 55 D3
Beechwood Av Lwr 48 B1
Beechwood Av Upr 48 B1
Beechwood Cl *Bray* 64 B4
Beechwood Cl *Manor.* 14 C2
Beechwood Downs 14 C2
Beechwood Gro **1** 51 F4
Beechwood Lawn 59 F2
Beechwood Pk *Dublin 6* 48 A1
Beechwood Pk *D.L.* 51 F4
Beechwood Rd 48 B1
Belcamp Av 22 A3
Belcamp Cres 21 F1
Belcamp Gdns 21 F1
Belcamp Grn 22 A3
Belcamp Gro 22 A3
Belcamp La 22 A3
Belclare Av 19 F2
Belclare Cres 19 F2
Belclare Dr 19 F2
Belclare Grn 19 F2
Belclare Gro 19 F2
Belclare Lawns 19 F2
Belclare Pk 19 E2
Belclare Ter 19 E2
Belclare Way 19 F2
Belfield Cl 48 C3
Belfield Ct 49 D2
Belfield Downs 48 C4
Belfield Office Pk 48 C2
Belfry, The 40 C2
Belfry Gro 52 A3
Belgard Cl **1** 45 D4
Belgard Grn 52 B1
Belgard Hts 44 C4
Belgard Ind Est 45 D4
Belgard Rd 45 D4
Belgard Sq E 53 D1
Belgard Sq N 52 C1
Belgard Sq S 53 D2
Belgard Sq W 52 C1
Belgrave Av 48 A1
Belgrave Pl 48 A1
Belgrave Rd *Dublin 6* 48 A1
Belgrave Rd *Black.* 50 C2
Belgrave Sq E *Dublin 6* 48 A1
Belgrave Sq E *Black.* 51 D3
Belgrave Sq N *Dublin 6* 48 A1
Belgrave Sq N *Black.* 50 C2
Belgrave Sq S *Dublin 6* 48 A1
Belgrave Sq S *Black.* 50 C2
Belgrave Sq W *Dublin 6* 48 A1
Belgrave Sq W *Black.* 50 C2
Belgrave Ter *Black. off Belgrave Rd* 50 C2
Belgrave Ter **9** *Bray* 64 C3
Belgrave Vil **10** 64 C3
Belgrove Lawn 29 F4
Belgrove Pk 39 F1
Belgrove Rd 33 F3
Bella Av *off Bella St* 67 G1
Bella St 67 G1
Belle Bk 66 A5
Belleville Av 47 F2
Bellevue 66 B5
Bellevue Av *Boot.* 49 F2
Bellevue Av *Dalkey* 59 F1
Bellevue Copse 49 F2
Bellevue Ct 49 F2
Bellevue Hts 65 D2
Bellevue Pk *Boot.* 49 E2
Bellevue Pk *Grey.* 65 E2
Bellevue Pk Av 49 F2
Bellevue Rd *Dalkey* 59 F2
Bellevue Rd *Grey.* 65 E2
Bellmans Wk *off Ferrymans Crossing* 42 C1
Belmont 58 A1
Belmont Av 48 C1
Belmont Ct *off Belmont Av* 48 C1
Belmont Gdns 48 C1
Belmont Grn 50 A4
Belmont Gro 50 A4
Belmont Lawn 50 A4
Belmont Pk *Dublin 4* 48 C1
Belmont Pk *Dublin 5* 34 C1
Belmont Vil 48 C1
Belton Pk Av 33 D1
Belton Pk Gdns 33 D1
Belton Pk Rd 33 D1
Belton Pk Vil 33 D1
Belton Ter **3** 64 B2
Belvidere Av 32 A4
Belvidere Ct 32 A4
Belvidere Pl 32 A4
Belvidere Rd 32 A3
Belview Bldgs *off School St* 66 B5
Belvue 52 B1
Benbulbin Av 40 C4
Benbulbin Rd 40 C3
Benburb St 66 B3
Beneavin Ct 19 E4
Beneavin Dr 19 F4
Beneavin Pk 19 E3
Beneavin Rd 19 E3
Ben Edar Rd 66 A1
Bengal Ter 31 F2
Ben Inagh Pk 50 B1
Benmadigan Rd 40 C3
Benson St 43 D2
Benson St Enterprise Cen 42 C2
Bentley Rd 64 B4
Beresford 32 B2
Beresford Av 32 B2
Beresford La *Dublin 1* 67 G2
Beresford La *Dublin 9* 32 B2
Beresford Pl 67 G3
Beresford St 66 D2
Berkeley Rd 31 F3
Berkeley St 32 A4
Berkeley Ter 42 C3
Berryfield 26 C4
Berryfield Cres 18 C4
Berryfield Dr 18 C4
Berryfield Rd 18 C4
Berwick 55 F1
Berwick Av 6 A1
Berwick Ct 6 A1
Berwick Cres 6 A1
Berwick Dr 6 A1
Berwick Gro 6 A1
Berwick Hall 55 F1
Berwick Lawn 6 A1
Berwick Pl 6 A1
Berwick Ri 6 A1
Berwick Vw 6 A1
Berwick Wk **2** 6 A1
Berwick Way 6 A1
Berystede *off Leeson Pk* 42 B4
Bessborough Av 32 C4
Bessborough Par 42 A4
Besser Dr 38 B3
Bethesda Pl *off Dorset St Upr* 67 E1
Bettyglen 35 D2
Bettysford **7** 44 B1
Bettystown Av 34 B2
Beverly Av 54 B3
Beverly Cres 54 B3
Beverly Downs 54 B2
Beverly Dr 54 B2
Beverly Gro 54 B2
Beverly Hts 54 B3
Beverly Lawns 54 B3
Beverly Pk 54 B2
Beverly Ri 54 B3
Bewley 27 E2
Bewley Av 27 E3
Bewley Dr 27 E2
Bewley Gro 27 E3
Bewley Lawn 27 E2
Big Br 47 E3
Bigger Rd 46 B1
Binn Eadair Vw 24 A2
Binns Br 32 A3
Birch Av 57 E3
Birch Dale **2** *D.L.* 59 E1
Birch Dale **1** *Fox.* 58 B2
Birchdale Cl 7 F3
Birchdale Dr 7 F3
Birchdale Pk 7 F3
Birchdale Rd 7 F3
Birches, The 58 B2
Birches Rd 57 D2
Birchfield 57 D1
Birchgrove 51 D4
Birchs La 56 C1
Birchview Av 45 E4
Birchview Cl 45 E4
Birchview Ct *off Treepark Rd* 45 E4
Birchview Dr 45 E4
Birchview Hts *off Birchview Dr* 45 E4
Birchview Lawn *off Birchview Av* 45 E4
Birchview Ri *off Birchview Dr* 45 E4
Birchwood Cl 52 C1
Birchwood Dr 52 C1
Birchwood Hts 52 C1
Bird Av 48 C3
Bishop St 67 E6
Black Av, The 26 A1
Blackberry La *Dublin 6* 42 A4
Blackberry La *Port.* 11 F3
Blackberry Ri 11 F3
Blackcourt Rd 16 C2
Blackditch Dr 39 D2
Blackditch Rd 39 E2
Blackhall Par 66 C3
Blackhall Pl 66 B3
Blackhall St 66 B3
Blackheath Av 33 F3
Blackheath Ct 34 A4
Blackheath Dr 33 F3
Blackheath Gdns 33 F3
Blackheath Gro 33 F3
Blackheath Pk 33 F3
Blackhorse Av 30 C3
Blackhorse Br 40 B3
Blackhorse Gro 31 D4
Blackhorse Ind Est 31 D4
Blacklion Manor 65 D1
Black Lion Rd 65 D2
Blackpitts 41 F3
Blackrock Business Pk 50 B2
Blackrock Coll 50 A1
Blackrock Shop Cen 50 B1
Blackrock Sta 50 B1
Black St 41 D1
Blackthorn Av 57 E3
Blackthorn Cl *Port.* 11 F2
Blackthorn Cl **1** *Still.* 57 E3
Blackthorn Ct **3** 57 D3
Blackthorn Dr 57 D3
Blackthorn Grn **4** 57 D3
Blackthorn Gro **2** 57 D3
Blackthorn Rd 57 E3
Blackwater Rd 31 E2
Blackwood 14 A2
Blackwood Cl 14 A3
Blackwood Cres 14 A2
Blackwood Dr 14 A2
Blackwood La 11 E2
Blackwood Lawn 14 A2
Blackwood Ms 14 A2
Blackwood Pk 14 A3
Blackwood Pl 14 A3
Blakesfield 14 C2
Blakestown Cotts 16 A3
Blakestown Dr 16 A2
Blakestown Rd 16 A3
Blakestown Way 16 B2
Blanchardstown Business & Tech Park 17 D2
Blanchardstown Bypass 16 C3
Blanchardstown Cen 16 B3
Blanchardstown Ind Pk 17 D1
Blanchardstown Rd N 16 C2
Blanchardstown Rd S 16 A4
Blarney Pk 47 D1
Blasket Sq 17 D3
Blessington Ct *off Blessington St* 32 A4
Blessington Rd *Dublin 24* 53 D1
Blessington Rd *Jobs.* 52 B3
Blessington St 31 F4
Bloom Cotts 41 F3
Bloomfield Av (Donnybrook) *Dublin 4* 42 B4
Bloomfield Av *Dublin 8* 41 F3
Bloomfield Pk 41 F4
Bluebell Av 39 F3
Bluebell Ind Est 39 E4
Bluebell Rd 40 A4
Blunden Dr 22 B3
Blythe Av *off Church Rd* 42 C1
Boden Dale 55 E2
Boden Mill **2** 55 D3
Boden Pk 55 D2
Boden Wd 55 E1
Boeing Rd 20 C1
Boghall Rd 64 B4
Bohernabreena Rd 53 E4
Bolbrook Av **2** 53 F2
Bolbrook Cl 53 F2
Bolbrook Dr **3** 53 F2
Bolbrook Enterprise Cen 54 A2
Bolbrook Gro 53 F2
Bolbrook Pk 53 F2
Bolbrook Vil 53 F2
Bolton St 66 D2
Bond Dr 43 E1
Bond Rd 33 D4
Bond St 66 A5
Bonham St 66 B4
Boolavogue Rd 43 D1
Booterstown Av 49 F3
Booterstown Pk 49 F4
Boot Rd 44 B2
Boroimhe Alder 6 B4
Boroimhe Ash 6 B4
Boroimhe Aspen 6 B3
Boroimhe Beech 6 B4
Boroimhe Birches 6 B3
Boroimhe Blackthorn 6 B3
Boroimhe Cedars 6 B3
Boroimhe Cherry 6 B3
Boroimhe Elms 6 C4
Boroimhe Hawthorns 6 B3
Boroimhe Laurels 6 B3
Boroimhe Maples 6 C4
Boroimhe Oaks 6 C4
Boroimhe Pines 6 C3
Boroimhe Poplars 6 C3
Boroimhe Willows 6 C3
Botanic Av 32 A2
Botanic Gdns 31 F2
Botanic Ms 31 F2
Botanic Pk 32 A2
Botanic Rd 31 F3
Botanic Vil *off Botanic Rd* 32 A2
Bothar An Easa (Watermill Rd) 34 B2
Bothar Baile Thormod (Ballyfermot Rd) 39 E2
Bothar Chille Na Manac (Walkinstown Rd) 46 A1
Bothar Cloiginn (Cleggan Rd) 39 D2
Bothar Coilbeard (Con Colbert Rd) *Dublin 8* 40 C2
Bothar Coilbeard (Con Colbert Rd) *Dublin 10* 40 B2
Bothar Dhroichead Chiarduibh (Cardiffsbridge Rd) 18 C3
Bothar Drom Finn (Drumfinn Rd) 39 E2

Bothar Loch Con (Lough Conn Rd) 39 E1
Bothar Phairc An Bhailtini (Villa Park Rd) 30 C3
Bothar Raitleann (Rathland Rd) 47 D2
Boundary Rd 33 E4
Bow Br 41 D2
Bow La E 67 E5
Bow La W 41 D2
Bow St 66 C3
Boyne La 67 H5
Boyne Rd 31 D1
Boyne St 67 H4
Brabazon Cotts **4** 64 B2
Brabazon Row 66 C6
Brabazon Sq *off Gray St* 66 C5
Brabazon St *off The Coombe* 66 C5
Bracetown Business Pk 12 C1
Brackenbush Pk 59 F3
Brackenbush Rd 59 F4
Bracken Dr 11 F2
Bracken Hill 56 C4
Bracken Rd 57 E4
Brackens La 67 G3
Brackenstown Av 6 C2
Braemor Av 48 A4
Braemor Dr 48 A4
Braemor Gro 48 A4
Braemor Pk 48 A3
Braemor Rd 48 A4
Brainborough Ter *off South Circular Rd* 41 E3
Braithwaite St 66 B5
Bramblefield 14 C1
Bramblefield Ct 14 C1
Bramblefield Cres 14 C1
Bramblefield Dr 14 C1
Bramblefield Pk 14 C1
Bramblefield Vw 16 A1
Bramblefield Wk 14 C1
Bramley Av 28 C2
Bramley Ct 28 C2
Bramley Cres 28 C2
Bramley Garth 28 C2
Bramley Grn 28 C1
Bramley Gro 28 C1
Bramley Heath 28 C2
Bramley Pk 28 B2
Bramley Rd 28 C1
Bramley Vw 28 C1
Bramley Wk 28 B1
Bramley Way 28 C2
Branch Rd N 43 F1
Branch Rd N Extension 43 F1
Branch Rd S 43 F1
Brandon Rd 40 B4
Bray 64 C2
Bray Head Ter **1** 64 B4
Bray Rd *Cabin.* 59 E4
Bray Rd *Corn.* 58 C2
Bray Sta 64 C2
Breakwater Rd S 43 F1
Breffini Ter 60 B2
Breffni Gdns **1** 24 A1
Breffni Rd 60 B2
Breffni Ter 60 A2
Bregia Rd 31 E3
Brehon Fld Rd 56 A3
Brehon's Chair 56 A4
Bremen Av 43 E2
Bremen Gro 43 E2
Bremen Rd 43 E2
Brendan Behan Ct *off Russell St* 32 B4
Brendan Rd 48 C1
Brennans Par 64 C2
Brennans Ter **7** 64 C2
Brennanstown Rd 59 D4
Brennanstown Vale 58 C4
Brewery Rd 57 F3
Brian Av 32 C2
Brian Boru St 34 A4
Brian Rd 32 C3
Brian Ter 32 C3
Briarfield Gro 35 D1
Briarfield Rd 34 C1
Briarfield Vil 35 D1
Briars, The 28 C4
Briar Wk 11 F2
Briar Wd 64 C4
Briarwood Av 16 A2
Briarwood Cl 16 A2
Briarwood Gdns 16 A2
Briarwood Grn 16 A2
Briarwood Lawn 16 A2
Briarwood Pk **2** 16 A2
Briarwood Rd **3** 16 A2
Brickfield 64 A4
Brickfield Dr 41 D3
Brickfield La 66 B6
Bride Rd 66 D5
Brides Glen Rd 62 C2
Bride St 66 D5
Bridgecourt Office Pk 45 F1
Bridgefoot St 66 C4
Bridge St *Dublin 4* 43 D2
Bridge St *Swords* 6 C1
Bridge St Lwr 66 C4
Bridge St Upr 66 C4
Bridgeview **1** 38 C2
Bridgewater Quay 40 C1
Brighton Av *Dublin 3* 33 D3
Brighton Av *Dublin 6* 47 F2
Brighton Av *Black.* 51 D3
Brighton Av *Carrick.* 58 B4
Brighton Cotts **2** 58 B3
Brighton Ct 58 B4
Brighton Gdns 47 F2
Brighton Grn 47 E2
Brighton Hall 58 B4
Brighton Lo **3** 58 B3
Brighton Pl 58 B4
Brighton Rd *Dublin 6* 47 F2
Brighton Rd *Fox.* 58 B3
Brighton Sq 47 F2
Brighton Ter **7** 60 A2
Brighton Vale 50 C2
Britain Pl 67 F1
Britain Quay 43 D2
Broadford Av 56 A3
Broadford Cl 56 A3
Broadford Cres 56 A3
Broadford Dr 56 A3
Broadford Hill 56 A3
Broadford Lawn 56 A3
Broadford Pk 56 A3
Broadford Ri 56 A3
Broadford Rd 56 A3
Broadford Wk 56 A3
Broadmeadow 6 C1
Broadmeadow Rd 6 C1
Broadstone 66 D1
Broadstone Av *off Phibsborough Rd* 66 D1
Broadway Dr 16 B4
Broadway Gro 16 B4
Broadway Pk 16 B4
Broadway Rd 16 B4
Brompton Ct 16 C4
Brompton Grn 16 C4
Brompton Gro 16 C4
Brompton Lawn 16 C4
Brookdale 53 E2
Brookdale Av 6 A3
Brookdale Cl 6 A2
Brookdale Ct 6 A3
Brookdale Dr 6 A2
Brookdale Grn 6 A2
Brookdale Gro 6 A2
Brookdale Lawns 6 A2
Brookdale Pk 6 A2
Brookdale Rd 6 A3
Brookdale Wk 6 A2
Brookdale Way 6 A2
Brookdene 63 E2
Brookfield *Dublin 5* 34 A1
Brookfield *Dublin 6* 48 B2
Brookfield *Black.* 50 A2
Brookfield *Lucan* 26 C4
Brookfield Av *Black.* 50 B2
Brookfield Av **25** *Bray* 64 C3
Brookfield Ct **1** 52 A2
Brookfield Est 47 D2
Brookfield Pl 50 B2
Brookfield Rd *Dublin 8* 41 D2
Brookfield Rd *Dublin 24* 52 A2
Brookfield St 41 D2
Brookfield Ter 50 B2
Brookhaven Dr 16 C2
Brookhaven Gro 16 C2
Brookhaven Lawn 16 C2
Brookhaven Pk 16 C2
Brookhaven Ri 16 C2
Brooklands 49 E1
Brooklawn *Dublin 3* 33 E3
Brooklawn *Black.* 50 A2
Brooklawn *Lucan* 26 C4
Brooklawn Av 50 C3
Brooklawn Wd 50 C3
Brookmount Av 54 A1
Brookmount Lawns *off Tallaght Rd* 54 A1
Brookpark 26 C4
Brook Pk Ct 51 D3
Brookstone La **4** 23 F3
Brookstone Rd 23 F3
Brookvale 27 D2
Brookvale Downs 47 E3
Brookvale Rd *Dublin 4* 48 C1
Brookvale Rd *Dublin 14* 47 E4
Brookview Av 52 A2
Brookview Cl 52 A2
Brookview Ct 52 A1
Brookview Cres 52 A1
Brookview Dr 52 A1
Brookview Gdns 52 A1
Brookview Grn 52 A2
Brookview Gro 52 A2
Brookview Lawns 52 A1
Brookview Pk 52 A2
Brookview Ter 52 A2
Brookville 19 D3
Brookville Cres 21 F3
Brookville Pk (Artane) *Dublin 5* 21 F4
Brookville Pk (Coolock) *Dublin 5* 22 A4
Brookville Pk *D.L.* 50 C4
Brookwood *Dublin 16* 55 D3
Brook Wd *Bray* 64 A3
Brookwood Av 33 F1
Brookwood Cres 34 A2
Brookwood Dr 33 F1
Brookwood Glen 34 A2
Brookwood Gro 33 F1
Brookwood Hts 33 F1
Brookwood Lawn 34 A2
Brookwood Meadow 33 F1
Brookwood Pk 33 F1
Brookwood Ri 34 A2
Brookwood Rd 33 F1
Broombridge Rd 31 D2
Broombridge Sta 31 D2
Broomfield 11 D1
Broomfield Ct 63 E2
Broomhill Business Complex 45 D4
Broomhill Business Pk 45 E4
Broom Hill Cl 53 D1
Broomhill Rd 45 E4
Broom Hill Ter 45 E4
Brown St N 66 C2
Brown St S 66 B6
Brunswick Pl *off Pearse St* 42 C2
Brunswick St N 66 C2
Brusna Cotts 50 B2
Buckingham St Lwr 67 H1
Buckingham St Upr 67 H1
Buckleys La 15 F2
Buirg An Ri Glen 27 F4
Buirg An Ri Ter 27 F4
Bulfin Gdns 40 C2
Bulfin Rd 40 C2
Bulfin St 40 C3
Bull All St 66 D5
Bullock Steps **8** 60 B2
Bunratty Av 21 F3
Bunratty Dr 21 F3
Bunratty Rd 21 E3
Bunting Rd 46 A1
Burdett Av 60 A2
Burgage, The 60 B3
Burgess La *off Haymarket* 66 C3
Burgh Quay 67 F3
Burke Pl 41 D2
Burleigh Ct 42 B3
Burlington Gdns 42 B3
Burlington Rd 42 B4
Burmah Cl 60 B4
Burnaby Hts 65 E3
Burnaby Lawn 65 E4
Burnaby Manor 65 F2
Burnaby Ms 65 F2
Burnaby Mill 65 F4
Burnaby Pk 65 E4
Burnaby Rd 65 F2
Burnaby Wds 65 F3
Burnell Pk Av 28 C2
Burnell Pk Grn 28 C2
Burren Ct 19 F2
Burris Ct *off School Ho La W* 66 D4
Burrow Ct 11 F3
Burrowfield Rd 24 A2
Burrow Rd 24 B2
Burton Hall Av 57 F3
Burton Hall Rd 57 F3
Burton Rd 60 B4
Bushfield 44 A2
Bushfield Av 48 C1
Bushfield Dr 44 A2
Bushfield Grn 44 A2
Bushfield Gro 44 A3
Bushfield Lawns 44 A3
Bushfield Pl 42 B4
Bushfield Ter 48 B1
Bushy Pk Gdns 47 E3
Bushy Pk Rd 47 E3
Buterly Business Pk 21 E4
Butt Br 67 G3
Buttercup Cl **1** 22 A3
Buttercup Dr 22 A3
Buttercup Pk **2** 22 A3
Buttercup Sq **3** 22 A3
Butterfield Av 47 D4
Butterfield Cl 55 D1
Butterfield Ct 47 E4
Butterfield Cres 47 E4
Butterfield Dr 55 E1
Butterfield Gro 47 D4
Butterfield Meadow 47 D4
Butterfield Orchard 55 E1
Butterfield Pk 55 D1
Byrnes La 67 E3

C

Cabinteely 59 D3
Cabinteely Av 59 D3
Cabinteely Bypass 59 D3
Cabinteely Cl 59 D3
Cabinteely Ct **4** 59 D2
Cabinteely Cres 59 D2
Cabinteely Dr 59 D2
Cabinteely Grn 59 D2
Cabinteely Pk **2** 59 D3
Cabinteely Way 59 D2
Cabra Dr 31 E3
Cabra Gro 31 E3
Cabra Pk 31 F3
Cabra Rd 31 D3
Cadogan Rd 32 C3
Cairn Ct 19 F2
Cairn Hill 58 C2
Cairnwood 52 B1
Cairnwood Av 52 B1
Cairnwood Ct 52 B1
Cairnwood Grn 52 B1
Calderwood Av 32 C1
Calderwood Gro 32 C1
Calderwood Rd 32 C2
Caledon Rd 32 C4
Callaghan Br 14 C4
Callary Rd 49 E4
Calmount Rd 45 F2
Camac Pk 39 F4
Camac Ter *off Bow Br* 41 D2
Camaderry Rd 64 C4
Camberley Elms 48 A4
Camberley Oaks 56 A1
Cambridge Av 43 E2
Cambridge La 47 F1
Cambridge Rd *Dublin 4* 43 D2
Cambridge Rd (Rathmines) *Dublin 6* 48 A1
Cambridge Sq 43 D2
Cambridge Ter 42 B4
Cambridge Vil *off Belgrave Rd* 48 A1
Camden Lock *off South Docks Rd* 43 D2
Camden Mkt *off Camden St Lwr* 42 A3
Camden Pl 67 E6
Camden Row 67 E6
Camden St Lwr 42 A3
Camden St Upr 42 A3
Cameron Sq 41 D2
Cameron St 66 A6
Campbell's Ct *off Little Britain St* 66 D2
Campbells Row *off Portland St N* 32 B4
Campfield Ter 57 D2
Canal Bk 39 D4
Canal Rd 42 A4
Canal Ter 40 A3
Canal Turn 38 B4
Canal Wk 39 E3
Cannonbrook 27 D3
Cannonbrook Lawn 27 D3
Cannonbrook Pk 27 D3
Cannon Rock Vw 25 F3
Canonbrook Av 26 C3
Canonbrook Ct 26 C3
Canon Lillis Av 32 C4
Canon Mooney Gdns *off Cambridge Rd* 43 D2
Canon Troy Ct 39 F1
Capel St 67 E2
Cappagh Av 18 C3
Cappagh Dr 18 C3
Cappaghmore 38 A4
Cappagh Rd 18 C3
Cappoge Cotts 18 A2
Captains Av 46 C1
Captains Dr 46 C1
Captain's Hill 15 F2
Captains Rd 46 C1
Caragh Rd 31 D4
Cara Pk 21 F1
Carberry Rd 32 C1
Cardiff Br *off Phibsborough Rd* 31 F4
Cardiff Castle Rd 18 C3
Cardiffsbridge Av 18 B4
Cardiffsbridge Gro *off Cappagh Rd* 18 C3
Cardiffsbridge Rd (Bothar Dhroichead Chiarduibh) 18 C3
Cardiffs La 42 C2
Cards La *off Townsend St* 67 G4
Caritas Convalescent Cen & St. Mary's Cen 49 F2
Carleton Rd 33 D3
Carlingford Par 42 C2
Carlingford Pl *off Carlingford Par* 42 C2
Carlingford Rd 32 A3
Carlisle Av 42 C4
Carlisle St 41 F3
Carlisle Ter **2** 51 F4
Carlton Ct *Dublin 3* 33 E3
Carlton Ct *Swords* 6 C3
Carlton Ms *off Shelbourne Av* 43 D3
Carlton Ter **5** 64 B2
Carlton Vil **6** 64 B2
Carmanhall Rd 57 E3
Carmans Hall 66 C5
Carmelite Cen 42 C4
Carmelite Monastery *Dublin 14* 49 D3
Carmelite Monastery *Still.* 57 F2
Carna Rd 39 D2
Carndonagh Dr 23 D4
Carndonagh Lawn 23 D4
Carndonagh Pk 23 D4
Carndonagh Rd 23 D4
Carne Ct 14 C2
Carnew St 66 A1
Carnlough Rd 31 D3
Caroline Row *off Bridge St* 43 D2
Carpenterstown Av 28 C1
Carpenterstown Pk E 28 B1
Carpenterstown Rd 28 C2
Carraig Glen 59 D3
Carraig Grennane 61 E2
Carraigmore Cl 53 D3
Carraigmore Dr 53 D3
Carraigmore Gro 53 D3
Carraigmore Pk 53 D3
Carraigmore Rd 53 D3
Carraigmore Vw 53 D3
Carraroe Av 22 C4
Carrickbrack Heath 24 C3
Carrickbrack Hill 24 C4
Carrickbrack Lawn 24 C4
Carrickbrack Pk 24 C4
Carrickbrack Rd 24 C4
Carrick Brennan Lawn 51 D3
Carrickbrennan Rd 51 D3
Carrick Ct 11 F3
Carrickhill Cl 11 F2
Carrickhill Dr 11 F3
Carrickhill Hts 11 F3
Carrickhill Ri 11 F2
Carrickhill Rd 11 F4
Carrickhill Rd Mid 11 F3
Carrickhill Rd Upr 11 F2
Carrickhill Wk 11 F2
Carrick Lawn **1** 57 D2
Carrickmines 58 C4
Carrickmines Av 58 C4
Carrickmines Chase 58 C3
Carrickmines Dale 58 C4
Carrickmines Garth 58 C4
Carrickmines Little 58 C4
Carrickmines Oaks 58 C4
Carrickmount Av 56 A1
Carrickmount Dr 56 A1
Carrick Ter 41 D3
Carrigallen Dr *off Carrigallen Rd* 31 D1
Carrigallen Pk *off Carrigallen Rd* 31 D1
Carrigallen Rd 31 D1
Carriglea 54 A3
Carriglea Av *Dublin 24* 53 F3
Carriglea Av *D.L.* 59 E1
Carriglea Ct *Dublin 24* 54 A3
Carriglea Ct **1** *D.L.* 51 E4
Carriglea Downs *Dublin 24* 53 F3
Carriglea Downs *D.L.* 59 E1
Carriglea Dr 53 F3
Carriglea Gdns 51 E4
Carriglea Gro 53 F3
Carriglea Ind Est 40 A4
Carriglea Ri 53 F3
Carriglea Vw 53 F3
Carriglea Wk 54 A3
Carrig Orchard 65 D3
Carrig Rd 19 F2
Carrig Vil 65 D3
Carrigwood 54 A3
Carrow Rd 40 B3
Carysfort Av 50 B2
Carysfort Downs 50 A4
Carysfort Dr 60 B3
Carysfort Gro 50 B4
Carysfort Hall 50 B3
Carysfort Pk 50 B3
Carysfort Rd 60 B3
Carysfort Wd 50 B4
Casana Vw 25 F4
Casement Cl 18 C3
Casement Dr 18 C3
Casement Grn 18 C3
Casement Gro 18 C3
Casement Pk 18 C3
Casement Rd (Finglas S) *Dublin 11* 19 D4
Casement Rd (Finglas W) *Dublin 11* 18 C3
Casement Vil 51 D4
Cashel Av 47 D1
Cashel Business Cen 47 D2
Cashel Rd 46 C1
Casimir Av 47 E1
Casimir Ct 47 F1
Casimir Rd 47 E1
Casino Pk 33 D2
Casino Rd 32 C2
Castaheany 14 B2
Castilla Pk 34 A4
Castle Av *Dublin 3* 33 F3
Castle Av *Clond.* 44 B1
Castle Av *Swords* 7 D2
Castlebrook 56 C2
Castlebyrne Pk 50 B3
Castle Cl *Clond.* 38 B4
Castle Cl *D.L.* 60 B2
Castle Ct *Dublin 3* 33 E2
Castle Ct **2** *Dublin 16* 56 C2
Castle Ct *Boot.* 49 F3
Castle Ct *Lough.* 63 E1
Castle Cove **2** 60 B3
Castle Cres **6** 44 B1

Castlecurragh Heath 16 B1
Castlecurragh Pk 16 B1
Castlecurragh Vale 16 B1
Castledawson Av 50 A1
Castle Dr *Clond.* 44 B1
Castle Dr *Swords* 7 D2
Castle Elms 21 F3
Castle Fm *Shank.* 63 E4
Castlefarm *Swords* 6 C1
Castlefarm Wd 63 E4
Castlefield Av 54 B2
Castlefield Ct *Dublin 16* 54 A2
Castlefield Ct *Clons.* 14 C4
Castlefield Dr 54 B3
Castlefield Grn 54 B3
Castlefield Gro 54 B3
Castlefield Lawn **1** 54 B2
Castlefield Manor *Dublin 24* 54 A2
Castlefield Manor *Mala.* 11 D1
Castlefield Pk *Dublin 16* 54 B2
Castlefield Pk *Clons.* 14 C4
Castlefield Ter 65 E3
Castlefield Way 54 B3
Castlefield Wds 14 C4
Castleforbes Ind Est 43 D1
Castleforbes Rd 43 D1
Castle Gate *Dublin 15* 29 F2
Castlegate *Shank.* 62 C4
Castle Golf Course 47 F4
Castlegrange Av 6 C1
Castlegrange Cl **1** 7 D1
Castlegrange Hts **5** 6 C1
Castlegrange Hill **2** 7 D1
Castlegrange Rd 7 D1
Castlegrange Way 6 C1
Castle Gro *Dublin 3* 33 F2
Castle Gro *Clond.* 44 B1
Castle Gro *Swords* 7 D2
Castlekevin Rd 21 E3
Castleknock Av 29 D1
Castleknock Brook 29 D1
Castleknock Cl 28 C1
Castleknock Coll 29 D2
Castleknock Cres 29 D1
Castleknock Dale 29 D1
Castleknock Downs 28 C1
Castleknock Dr 29 D1
Castleknock Elms 29 D1
Castleknock Glade 29 D1
Castleknock Gra 28 C1
Castleknock Grn 29 E2
Castleknock Gro 29 D1
Castleknock Laurels 29 D1
Castleknock Lo 29 E2
Castleknock Meadows 28 C1
Castleknock Oaks 29 D1
Castleknock Pk 29 E2
Castleknock Parklands 29 D1
Castleknock Pines Lwr 29 E1
Castleknock Pines Upr 29 E1
Castleknock Ri 28 C1
Castleknock Rd 29 F2
Castleknock Sta 17 D4
Castleknock Vale 28 C1
Castleknock Vw 29 D1
Castleknock Village Cen 29 E2
Castleknock Wk 28 C1
Castleknock Way 28 C1
Castleknock Wd 29 D1
Castlelands **9** 60 B2
Castlelands, The 47 F4
Castlelands Gro 60 B2
Castle Lawns Est 53 F1
Castle Mkt *off Drury St* 67 E5
Castle Pk *Dublin 24* 53 F1
Castle Pk *Black.* 51 D3
Castle Pk *Clond.* 44 B1
Castle Pk *Leix.* 15 F2
Castle Pk *Swords* 7 D2
Castle Pk Est 53 F1
Castlepark Rd 60 A3
Castle Riada 27 E3
Castle Riada Av 27 E3
Castle Riada Cres 27 E3
Castle Riada Dr 27 E4
Castle Riada Gro 27 E3
Castle Rd *Dublin 3* 33 F3
Castle Rd *Lucan* 27 E3
Castle Rosse 23 E3
Castlerosse Cres 23 E3
Castlerosse Dr 23 E3
Castlerosse Vw 23 E3
Castle Shop Cen 7 D2
Castleside Dr 47 F4
Castle St *Dublin 2* 66 D4
Castle St *Bray* 64 B2
Castle St *Dalkey* 60 B3
Castle St Shop Cen 64 B2
Castletimon Av 21 D3
Castletimon Dr 21 D3
Castletimon Gdns 21 D3
Castletimon Grn 21 D3
Castletimon Pk 21 D3
Castletimon Rd 21 D3
Castletown 15 D2
Castletymon Ct 53 F1
Castleview *Dublin 5* 21 E4
Castleview **3** *Dublin 16* 56 B2
Castle Vw *Carrick.* 58 B4
Castleview Est 12 A2
Castle Vw Rd 44 B1
Castle Vil **3** 60 B3
Castlewood 14 C2
Castlewood Av 48 A1
Castlewood Cl *off Castlewood Av* 48 A1
Castlewood La 48 A1
Castlewood Pk 48 A1
Castlewood Pl 48 A1
Castlewood Ter 48 A1
Cathal Brugha St 67 F2
Cathedral La 66 D6
Cathedral St 67 F2
Cathedral Vw Ct *off Cathedral Vw Wk* 66 D6
Cathedral Vw Wk 66 D6
Catherines La *off Church St Upr* 66 D2
Catherine St *off Ash St* 66 C5
Cats Ladder **3** 60 C4
Cavalry Row 66 A2
Cavendish Row *off Parnell St* 67 F1
Ceannchor Rd 37 D4
Ceannt Fort 41 D2
Cecil Av 33 D3
Cecilia St *off Temple La S* 67 E4
Cedar Av 45 D3
Cedar Brook Av 38 C3
Cedar Brook Pl 38 C3
Cedar Brook Wk 38 C3
Cedar Brook Way 38 C3
Cedar Ct *Dublin 6W* 47 E2
Cedar Ct *Dunb.* 12 B2
Cedar Ct *Lough.* 63 D1
Cedar Dr *Dunb.* 12 B2
Cedar Dr *Palm.* 28 C4
Cedar Gro **1** 16 A3
Cedar Hall *off Prospect La* 48 C2
Cedar Lo **6** 55 D3
Cedarmount Rd 57 E1
Cedar Pk *Dublin 13* 22 C4
Cedar Pk *Leix.* 15 E2
Cedars, The **13** *Abb.* 63 E1
Cedars, The *D.L.* 50 C3
Cedar Sq 50 A3
Cedar Wk 34 C1
Cedarwood Av 19 E3
Cedarwood Cl 19 E3
Cedarwood Grn 19 E2
Cedarwood Gro 19 E3
Cedarwood Pk 19 E3
Cedarwood Ri 19 E3
Cedarwood Rd 19 E2
Ceide Dun Eanna (Ennafort Dr) 34 A2
Ceide Gleannaluinn (Glenaulin Dr) 39 E1
Ceide Phairc An Bhailtini (Villa Park Dr) 30 C3
Celbridge Rd *Leix.* 15 E2
Celbridge Rd *Lucan* 26 B2
Celestine Av 43 D2
Celtic Pk Av 33 D1
Celtic Pk Rd 33 D1
Cenacle Gro 63 E1
Central Pk Business Pk 57 F4
Centre Pt Business Pk 45 D1
Century Business Pk 19 D2
Chalet Gdns 27 E2
Chamber St 66 C6
Chancery La 67 E5
Chancery Pl 66 D3
Chancery St 66 D3
Chanel Av 21 F4
Chanel Gro 21 F3
Chanel Rd 21 E4
Chapel Av 43 D2
Chapelizod Bypass 39 E1
Chapelizod Ct 39 E1
Chapelizod Hill Rd 39 E1
Chapelizod Ind Est 39 F1
Chapelizod Rd *Dublin 8* 40 A1
Chapelizod Rd *Dublin 20* 40 A1
Chapel La *Dublin 1* 67 E2
Chapel La **1** *Bray* 64 A2
Chapel La *Swords* 7 D2
Chapel Rd 10 B3
Chapel Vw 65 D2
Charlemont 33 D1
Charlemont Av 51 F3
Charlemont Ct 42 A4
Charlemont Gdns *off Charlemont St* 42 A3
Charlemont Mall 42 A4
Charlemont Par 32 C4
Charlemont Pl 42 A4
Charlemont Rd 33 D3
Charlemont Sq *off Charlemont St* 42 A3
Charlemont St 42 A3
Charlesland Gro 65 E4
Charles La 32 B4
Charles St Gt 32 B4
Charles St W 66 D3
Charleston Av 48 A1
Charleston Rd 48 A1
Charlestown 19 D1
Charlestown Av 19 D2
Charlestown Ct 19 D1
Charlestown Dr 19 D1
Charlestown Grn 19 D1
Charlestown Pk 19 D1
Charlestown Way 19 D1
Charleville *Dublin 14* 48 B4
Charleville *Dublin 16* 54 C1
Charleville Av 32 C4
Charleville Mall 32 B4
Charleville Rd *Dublin 6* 47 F1
Charleville Rd *Dublin 7* 31 E3
Charleville Sq 47 D4
Charlotte Quay 42 C2
Charlotte Ter **2** 60 C3
Charlotte Way 42 A3
Charlton Lawn 49 D4
Charnwood *Bray* 64 B4
Charnwood *Clons.* 14 C4
Charnwood Av 14 C4
Charnwood Cts 14 C4
Charnwood Dale 14 C4
Charnwood Gdns 14 C4
Charnwood Grn 16 A4
Charnwood Gro 14 C4
Charnwood Heath 14 C4
Charnwood Meadows 14 C4
Charnwood Pk 14 C4
Chase, The 57 F3
Chatham Row *off William St S* 67 F5
Chatham St 67 F5
Chaworth Ter *off Hanbury La* 66 C4
Cheaters La *off Redmonds Hill* 67 E6
Cheeverstown Cen 54 C1
Cheeverstown Rd 52 A1
Chelmsford La 42 B4
Chelmsford Rd 42 B4
Chelsea Gdns 34 A4
Cheltenham Pl *off Portobello Br* 42 A4
Cherbury Ct 49 F4
Cherbury Gdns 49 F4
Cherbury Ms 49 F4
Cherbury Pk Av 27 D3
Cherbury Pk Rd 27 D3
Cherries, The **1** 56 A3
Cherries Rd 57 D3
Cherrington Cl 63 E4
Cherrington Dr 63 E4
Cherrington Rd 63 D4
Cherry Av *Carp.* 28 B1
Cherry Av *Swords* 6 B3
Cherry Ct *Dublin 6W* 47 E2
Cherry Ct **6** *Grey.* 65 D3
Cherry Ct **2** *Lough.* 63 D1
Cherry Dr *Carp.* 28 B1
Cherry Dr *Grey.* 65 D3
Cherryfield Av *Dublin 6* 48 B1
Cherryfield Av *Dublin 12* 46 B2
Cherryfield Cl 14 C3
Cherryfield Ct 14 B3
Cherryfield Dr 46 B2
Cherryfield Lawn 14 C3
Cherryfield Pk 14 C3
Cherryfield Rd 46 A2
Cherryfield Vw 14 B3
Cherryfield Wk 14 C2
Cherry Gdns **7** 65 D3
Cherrygarth *Still.* 57 F1
Cherry Garth *Swords* 6 B3
Cherry Gro *Dublin 12* 46 B2
Cherry Gro **5** *Grey.* 65 D3
Cherry Gro *Swords* 6 B3
Cherry Lawn 28 C1
Cherry Lawns 26 C3
Cherrymount Cres 33 D2
Cherrymount Gro 33 D2
Cherrymount Pk 31 F3
Cherry Orchard Av 39 D3
Cherry Orchard Ct 39 D3
Cherry Orchard Cres 39 D3
Cherry Orchard Dr 39 D3
Cherry Orchard Grn 38 C2
Cherry Orchard Gro 39 D3
Cherry Orchard Ind Est 39 D1
Cherry Orchard Par **1** 39 D3
Cherry Orchard Pk 39 D3
Cherry Orchard Sta 39 D3
Cherry Orchard Way *off Cherry Orchard Av* 39 D3
Cherry Pk *Carp.* 28 B1
Cherry Pk *Swords* 6 B3
Cherry Ri 65 D3
Cherry Tree Dr 64 B4
Cherry Wd 63 D1
Cherrywood Av 44 A1
Cherrywood Business Pk 62 C2
Cherrywood Pk 63 D1
Cherrywood Rd 63 D2
Chester Downs 51 F4
Chesterfield Av *Dublin 8* 30 B4
Chesterfield Av *Dublin 15* 29 F2
Chesterfield Cl 29 F2
Chesterfield Copse 29 F2
Chesterfield Gro 29 F2
Chesterfield Pk 29 F2
Chesterfield Vw 29 F2
Chester Rd 42 A4
Chester Sq **8** 60 A2
Chestnut Ct 21 D4
Chestnut Gro *Dublin 16* 56 B3
Chestnut Gro *Dublin 24* 45 D3
Chestnut Gro *Dunb.* 12 B3
Chestnut Pk **2** 58 B1
Chestnut Rd *Dublin 12* 45 E1
Chestnut Rd *Still.* 49 E4
Christ Ch Cath 66 D4
Christchurch Pl 66 D4
Church Av (Irishtown) *Dublin 4* 43 D3
Church Av (Rathmines) *Dublin 6* 48 A1
Church Av *Dublin 8* 41 D3
Church Av (Glasnevin) *Dublin 9* 32 A1
Church Av (Blanchardstown) *Dublin 15* 16 C4
Church Av *Kill.* 61 E2
Church Av **2** *Port.* 11 E4
Church Av N (Drumcondra) 32 B2
Church Ct 29 E2
Churchfields 48 B3
Church Gdns 48 A1
Church Gates 65 E1
Church Gro 53 D3
Churchill Ms **10** 60 B2
Churchill Ter 43 D4
Church Lands *Bray* 64 B3
Churchlands *Sandy.* 57 D4
Church La *Dublin 2* *off College Grn* 67 F4
Church La (Rathfarnham) *Dublin 14* 47 E4
Church La *Grey.* 65 E2
Church La S *off Kevin St Lwr* 67 E6
Church Pk Av 47 E1
Church Pk Ct 47 E1
Church Pk Dr 47 E1
Church Pk Lawn 47 E1
Church Pk Vw 47 E1
Church Pk Way 47 E1
Church Rd *Dublin 3* 42 C1
Church Rd (Finglas) *Dublin 11* 19 D4
Church Rd *Dublin 13* 24 B3
Church Rd *Bray* 64 B3
Church Rd *Dalkey* 60 B3
Church Rd *Grey.* 65 E1
Church Rd *Kill.* 59 F3
Church Rd *Mulh.* 16 B1
Church Rd *Swords* 6 C2
Church St *Dublin 7* 66 D3
Church St (Finglas) *Dublin 11* 19 D4
Church St (Howth) *Dublin 13* 25 E3
Church St E 42 C1
Church St Upr 66 D2
Church Ter *Dublin 7* *off Church St* 66 D3
Church Ter **7** *Bray* 64 B2
Churchtown Av 48 B3
Churchtown Business Pk 56 A1
Churchtown Cl 48 B3
Churchtown Dr 48 B3
Churchtown Rd Lwr 48 B3
Churchtown Rd Upr 56 B1
Church Vw **1** 44 A2
Churchview Av 59 F3
Churchview Dr 59 F3
Churchview Pk 59 F3
Church Vw Rd 59 F4
Cianlea 6 B1
Cian Pk 32 B2
Cill Cais 53 D3
Cill Eanna 34 B2
Cill Manntan Pk **2** 64 B3
City Junct Business Pk 22 B2
Citylink Business Pk 39 F4
City Quay 67 H3
Claddagh Grn 39 D2
Claddagh Rd 39 D2
Claddagh Ter **8** 64 C2
Clanawley Rd 33 F2
Clanboy Rd 33 E1
Clanbrassil Cl 41 F4
Clanbrassil St Lwr 41 F3
Clanbrassil St Upr 41 F4
Clancarthy Rd 33 E2
Clancy Av 19 D3
Clancy Rd 19 E3
Clandonagh Rd 33 E1
Clanhugh Rd 33 E2
Clanmahon Rd 33 E1
Clanmaurice Rd 33 E1
Clanmawr 63 F3
Clanmoyle Rd 33 E2
Clanranald Rd 33 E1
Clanree Rd 33 E1
Clanwilliam Pl 42 C3
Clarehall Shop Cen 22 B3
Clare La 67 G5
Claremont Av 31 F1
Claremont Ct 31 E2
Claremont Dr 19 F4
Claremont Gro **1** 61 E1
Claremont Pk (Pairc Clearmont) 43 E3
Claremont Rd *Dublin 4* 43 E3
Claremont Rd *Dublin 13* 24 C2
Claremont Rd *Cabin.* 58 C3
Claremont Rd *Kill.* 61 E1
Claremont Vil 51 F4
Claremont Pines 58 C3
Claremount Ter **11** 64 C3
Clarence Mangan Rd 66 C6
Clarence St 51 E3
Clarendon Mkt *off Chatham St* 67 F5
Clarendon Row *off Clarendon St* 67 F5
Clarendon St 67 F5
Clare Rd 32 B1
Clare St 67 G5
Clareville Ct 31 F2
Clareville Gro 31 F2
Clareville Pk 31 F2
Clareville Rd 47 E1
Clarinda Manor 51 F4
Clarinda Pk E 51 F4
Clarinda Pk N 51 F3
Clarinda Pk W 51 F4
Clarke Ter 66 A6
Clarkeville Ter **1** 29 D4
Classons Br 48 B3
Claude Rd 32 A3
Cleggan Av 39 D2
Cleggan Pk 39 D2
Cleggan Rd (Bothar Cloiginn) 39 D2
Clifden Dr 39 D2
Clifden Rd 39 E2
Cliffords La 7 E2
Cliff Ter **1** 60 B2
Cliff Wk (Fingal Way) 37 F1
Clifton Av 51 D3
Clifton La 51 D3
Clifton Ms 42 A4
Clifton Pk 63 E2
Clifton Ter 51 D3
Cliftonville Rd 32 A2
Clinches Ct 32 C4
Clogher Rd 41 D4
Cloghran 8 C1
Cloister Av 50 B3
Cloister Gate 50 B3
Cloister Grn 50 B3
Cloister Gro 50 B3
Cloister Pk 50 A3
Cloisters, The *Dublin 6W* 47 E2
Cloisters, The *Dublin 9* 32 C1
Cloister Sq 50 B3
Cloister Way 50 B3
Clonard Av 56 C3
Clonard Cl 56 C3
Clonard Dr 56 C3
Clonard Gro 56 C3
Clonard Lawn 56 C3
Clonard Pk 56 C3
Clonard Rd *Dublin 12* 40 C4
Clonard Rd *Dublin 16* 56 C3
Clonasleigh **2** 63 E3
Clondalkin 44 A1
Clondalkin Commercial Pk 38 B3
Clondalkin Enterprise Cen 38 A3
Clondalkin Sta 38 B3
Clonee Br 13 D3
Clonee Bypass 13 D3
Clonfadda Wd 49 F4
Clonfert Rd 47 D1
Clonkeen Ct 59 D2
Clonkeen Cres 59 D1
Clonkeen Dr 58 C1
Clonkeen Gro 59 D1
Clonkeen Lawn **1** 59 D2
Clonkeen Rd 58 C1
Clonlara Rd 43 E2
Clonlea 56 B3
Clonlea Wd **1** 56 B3
Clonliffe Av 32 B3
Clonliffe Gdns 32 B3
Clonliffe Rd 32 B3
Clonmacnoise Gro 47 D1
Clonmacnoise Rd 47 D1
Clonmellon Gro **6** 22 C3
Clonmel Rd 19 F3
Clonmel St 67 F6
Clonmore Rd *Dublin 3* 32 B4
Clonmore Rd *Still.* 57 E1
Clonmore Ter 32 B4
Clonrosse Ct *off Elton Dr* 22 B4
Clonrosse Dr 22 B4
Clonrosse Pk *off Elton Dr* 22 B4

Eden Rd 65 F2
Eden Rd Lwr 51 F4
Eden Rd Upr 51 F4
Eden Ter 51 F4
Edenvale Rd 48 B1
Eden Vil **3** 51 F4
Edgewood Lawns 16 C2
Edmondsbury Ct **1** 27 E2
Edmondstown 55 D4
Edmondstown Grn 55 D3
Edmondstown Pk 55 D3
Edmondstown Rd 55 D4
Edward Rd 64 C3
Edwards Ct 55 D3
Edwin Ct **5** 60 A3
Effra Rd 47 F1
Eglington Rd 64 B2
Eglinton Ct 48 C1
Eglinton Pk *Dublin 4* 48 C1
Eglinton Pk *D.L.* 51 E4
Eglinton Rd 48 C1
Eglinton Sq 48 C1
Eglinton Ter *Dublin 4* 48 C1
Eglinton Ter *Dublin 14* 56 C1
Elderberry 26 C4
Elderwood Rd 28 C4
Eldon Ter
off South Circular Rd 41 E3
Elgin Rd 42 C4
Elizabeth St 32 B3
Elkwood 54 C1
Ellenfield Rd 20 C4
Ellensborough 53 D4
Ellensborough Av 53 D4
Ellensborough Cl 53 D4
Ellensborough Copse 53 D4
Ellensborough Ct 53 D4
Ellensborough Cres 53 D4
Ellensborough Dale 53 D4
Ellensborough Downs 53 D4
Ellensborough Gra 53 D4
Ellensborough Grn 53 D4
Ellensborough Gro 53 D4
Ellensborough La 53 D4
Ellensborough Lo 53 D4
Ellensborough
Meadows 53 D4
Ellensborough Pk 53 D4
Ellensborough Ri 53 D4
Ellensborough Vw 53 D4
Ellensborough Wk 53 D4
Ellesmere **1** 57 F3
Ellesmere Av 31 E4
Ellis Quay 66 B3
Ellis St
off Benburb St 66 B3
Elmbrook 27 E3
Elmbrook Cres 27 E3
Elmbrook Lawn 27 E3
Elmbrook Wk 27 E3
Elmcastle Cl 45 E4
Elmcastle Ct 45 E4
Elmcastle Dr 45 E4
Elmcastle Grn 45 E4
Elmcastle Pk 45 E4
Elmcastle Wk 45 E4
Elm Cl 27 E4
Elm Ct *Jobs.* 52 A3
Elm Ct *Lucan* 27 E4
Elmdale Cl 39 D2
Elmdale Cres 39 D2
Elmdale Dr 39 D2
Elmdale Pk 38 C2
Elm Dene 27 E4
Elm Dr *Jobs.* 52 A3
Elm Dr *Lucan* 27 E4
Elmfield Av 22 C3
Elmfield Cl **1** 22 C3
Elmfield Ct **4** 22 C3
Elmfield Cres 22 C3
Elmfield Dr **2** 22 C3
Elmfield Grn 22 C3
Elmfield Gro 22 C3
Elmfield Ind Est 38 B4
Elmfield Lawn 22 C3
Elmfield Pk
off Elmfield Av 22 C3
Elmfield Ri 22 C3
Elmfield Vale **3** 22 C3
Elmfield Wk 22 C3
Elmfield Way 22 C3
Elm Grn 27 D4
Elmgrove *B'brack* 59 F4
Elm Gro *Black.* 50 B3
Elm Gro *Jobs.* 52 A3
Elm Gro *Lucan* 27 E4
Elm Gro Cotts
off Blackhorse Av 30 C3
Elmgrove Ter **9** 64 B2
Elm Mt Av 33 D1
Elm Mt Cl 33 D1
Elm Mt Ct 33 E1
Elm Mt Cres 21 D4
Elm Mt Dr 33 D1
Elm Mt Gro 21 D4
Elm Mt Hts 21 D4
Elm Mt Lawn 21 D4
Elm Mt Pk 21 D4
Elm Mt Ri 21 D4
Elm Mt Rd 33 D1
Elm Mt Vw 21 D4
Elm Pk 49 E1
Elmpark Av 42 B4
Elmpark Ter 47 E2
Elm Rd *Dublin 9* 33 D1
Elm Rd *Dublin 12* 45 E1
Elms, The *Dublin 4* 49 E2
Elms, The **14** *Abb.* 63 E1
Elms, The *Black.* 50 A2
Elms, The *Dunb.* 12 B2
Elms, The *Shank.* 63 E4
Elm Vale 27 E4
Elm Way *Dublin 16* 56 A3
Elm Way *Lucan* 27 E4
Elm Wd 27 E4
Elmwood Av Lwr 42 B4
Elmwood Av Upr
off Elmwood Av Lwr 48 B1
Elmwood Cl 14 B3
Elmwood Ct **8** 6 B1
Elmwood Dr 6 B1
Elmwood Pk 6 B1
Elmwood Rd 6 B1
Elner Ct 11 F2
Elsinoire 65 D4
Elton Ct *Dublin 13*
off Elton Dr 22 B4
Elton Ct *Dunb.* 12 B2
Elton Ct *D.L.* 60 B2
Elton Ct *Leix.* 15 E2
Elton Dr *Dublin 13* 22 B4
Elton Dr *Dunb.* 12 B2
Elton Gro 12 B2
Elton Pk *Dublin 13* 22 B4
Elton Pk *D.L.* 60 A2
Elton Wk
off Elton Dr 22 B4
Ely Cres 53 F4
Ely Dr 53 F4
Ely Grn **1** 53 F4
Ely Gro 53 F4
Ely Manor 53 F4
Ely Pl 67 G6
Ely Pl Upr
off Ely Pl 67 G6
Ely Vw 53 F4
Embassy Lawn 48 C2
Emerald Cotts 42 C3
Emerald Pl
off Sheriff St Lwr 42 C1
Emerald Sq 66 A6
Emerald St 42 C1
Emily Pl
off Sheriff St Lwr 67 H2
Emmet Ct 40 B3
Emmet Rd 40 B2
Emmet Sq 50 A1
Emmet St *Dublin 1* 32 B4
Emmet St
(Haroldscross)
Dublin 6 41 F4
Emmet St **1** *Sally.* 59 F1
Emor St 41 F3
Emorville Av 41 F3
Emorville Sq
off South Circular Rd 41 E3
Empress Pl 67 H1
Enaville Rd 32 C3
Engine All 66 C5
Ennafort Av
(Ascal Dun Eanna) 34 A2
Ennafort Ct 34 A2
Ennafort Dr
(Ceide Dun Eanna) 34 A2
Ennafort Gro 34 A2
Ennafort Pk 34 A2
Ennafort Rd 34 A2
Ennel Av 34 A1
Ennel Ct **3** 63 E1
Ennel Dr 34 A1
Ennel Pk 34 A1
Ennis Gro 43 D3
Enniskerry Rd 31 F3
Erne Pl 42 C2
Erne Pl Little 67 H4
Erne St Lwr 42 C2
Erne St Upr 42 C2
Erne Ter Front
off Erne St Upr 42 C2
Erne Ter Rere
off Erne St Upr 42 C2
Errigal Gdns 40 B4
Errigal Rd 40 B4
Erris Rd 31 E3
Erskine Av 65 F3
Esker Dr 26 C3
Esker La (north) *Lucan* 27 E2
Esker La (south) *Lucan* 27 E3
Esker Lawns 27 D2
Esker Lo 27 E3
Esker Lo Av 27 E3
Esker Lo Cl 27 E3
Esker Lo Vw 27 E3
Esker Manor 27 D3
Esker Meadow 27 E3
Esker Meadow Cl 27 E3
Esker Meadow Ct 27 E3
Esker Meadow Grn 27 E3
Esker Meadow Gro 27 E3
Esker Meadow Lawn 27 E3
Esker Meadow Ri 27 E3
Esker Meadow Vw 27 E3
Esker Pk 27 E3
Esker Pines 27 E2
Esker Rd 27 D3
Esker S 27 D4
Esker Wds Ct 27 E3
Esker Wds Dr 27 E3
Esker Wds Gro 27 E3
Esker Wds Ri 27 E3
Esker Wds Vw 27 E3
Esker Wds Wk 27 E3
Esmond Av 32 C3
Esmonde Ter **10** 64 A2
Esplanade Ter **14** 64 C3
Esposito Rd 46 B1
Essex Quay 66 D4
Essex St E 67 E4
Essex St W 67 E4
Estate Av 49 F2
Estate Cotts 42 C3
Estuary Ct 7 D1
Estuary Roundabout 7 D1
Eugene St 66 A6
Eustace St 67 E4
Everton Av 31 E4
Evora Cres 25 E3
Evora Pk 25 E3
Evora Ter
off St. Lawrence Rd 25 E3
Ewington La 66 A4
Excalibur Dr 65 F1
Exchange Ct
off Dame St 67 E4
Exchange St Lwr 66 D4
Exchange St Upr
off Lord Edward St 67 E4
Exchequer St 67 E4

F

Faber Gro **3** 51 D4
Fade St 67 E5
Fairbrook Lawn 55 E1
Fairfield Av 32 C4
Fairfield Pk *Dublin 6* 47 F2
Fairfield Pk *Grey.* 65 E1
Fairfield Rd
(Glasnevin) 32 A2
Fairgreen Ct **10** 64 B2
Fairgreen Rd 64 A2
Fairgreen Ter **11** 64 B2
Fairlawn Pk
off Fairlawn Rd 19 D4
Fairlawn Rd 19 D4
Fairlawns 60 A3
Fairview 32 C3
Fairview Av
(Irishtown) 43 D2
Fairview Av Lwr 32 C3
Fairview Av Upr 32 C3
Fairview Grn 32 C3
Fairview Lawn 62 C1
Fairview Pas
off Fairview Strand 32 C3
Fairview Strand 32 C3
Fairview Ter 32 C3
Fairways 47 D4
Fairways, The 64 B1
Fairways Av 19 E4
Fairways Grn 19 E4
Fairways Gro 19 E4
Fairways Pk 19 E4
Fairy Hill *Black.* 50 B4
Fairyhill *Bray* 64 A4
Faith Av 32 C4
Falcarragh Rd 20 B4
Falls Rd 63 D2
Farmhill Dr 48 C4
Farmhill Pk 57 D1
Farmhill Rd 48 C4
Farmleigh Av 50 A4
Farmleigh Cl 50 A4
Farmleigh Pk 50 A4
Farney Pk 43 E3
Farnham Cres 19 D4
Farnham Dr 19 D4
Farrenboley Cotts 48 B3
Farrenboley Pk 48 B3
Father Colohan Ter **4** 64 B3
Father Kitt Ct 46 C1
Father Matthew Br 66 C4
Fatima Mans 41 D3
Fatima Ter 64 B2
Faughart Rd 47 D1
Faussagh Av 31 D2
Faussagh Rd 31 E3
Feltrim 10 B2
Feltrim Hall 7 D3
Feltrim Ind Pk 7 E3
Feltrim Rd 10 A1
Fenian St 67 H5
Ferguson Rd 32 A2
Fergus Rd 47 E3
Fernbrook **2** 64 A1
Ferncourt Av 53 F4
Ferncourt Cl 53 F4
Ferncourt Cres **2** 53 F4
Ferncourt Dr **3** 53 F4
Ferncourt Grn 53 F4
Ferncourt Pk 53 F4
Ferncourt Vw 53 F4
Ferndale *Dublin 24* 53 D2
Ferndale *Manor.* 14 C2
Ferndale Av 19 E4
Ferndale Glen 63 D4
Ferndale Hill 62 C4
Ferndale Rd *Dublin 11* 19 E4
Ferndale Rd *Shank.* 63 D4
Fernhill Av 46 B3
Fernhill Pk 46 B3
Fernhill Rd 46 B3
Fernleigh 28 A2
Fernleigh Cl 28 A1
Fernleigh Ct 28 A2
Fernleigh Dale 28 A2
Fernleigh Dr 28 A1
Fernleigh Grn 28 A2
Fernleigh Gro 28 A2
Fernleigh Pk 28 A2
Fernleigh Pl **3** 28 A2
Fernleigh Vw 28 A2
Ferns Rd 47 D1
Fernvale Dr 40 B4
Fernwood Av 52 C1
Fernwood Cl 52 C2
Fernwood Ct 52 C1
Fernwood Lawn 52 C1
Fernwood Pk 52 C1
Fernwood Way 52 C2
Ferrard Rd 47 F2
Ferrycarrig Av 21 F2
Ferrycarrig Dr 21 F2
Ferrycarrig Grn **2** 21 F2
Ferrycarrig Pk 21 F2
Ferrycarrig Rd 21 F2
Ferrymans Crossing 42 C1
Fertullagh Rd 31 E3
Fettercairn Rd 52 A1
Fey Yerra **1** 58 A1
Fforester 27 E3
Fforester Cl 27 E3
Fforester Ct 27 E3
Fforester Lawn 27 E3
Fforester Pk 27 E3
Fforester Wk 27 E3
Fforester Way 27 E3
Field Av 46 B1
Fields Ter
off Ranelagh Rd 42 B4
Finches Ind Pk 40 A4
Findlater Pl
off Parnell St 67 F1
Findlaters St 41 D1
Findlater St **14** 60 A2
Fingal Pl 66 B1
Fingal St 66 A6
Finglas Business Cen 19 D2
Finglas Business Pk 31 E1
Finglas Pk 19 E3
Finglas Pl 19 D4
Finglas Rd 31 E1
Finglas Rd Old 31 F1
Finglas Shop Cen 19 D3
Finglaswood Rd 18 C3
Finlay Sq 49 E4
Finnsgreen 26 C4
Finnsgrove 26 C4
Finnstown Fairways 26 C4
Finn St 66 A1
Finnsvale 26 C4
Finnsview 26 C4
Finsbury Pk 56 B1
Firgrove **1** 63 E1
Firhouse Rd *Dublin 16* 54 B1
Firhouse Rd *Dublin 24* 54 B1
Firhouse Rd W 53 D3
First Av *Dublin 1* 42 C1
First Av (Inchicore)
Dublin 10 40 A2
First Av *Dublin 24* 44 C4
Fishamble St 66 D4
Fitzgerald Pk **2** 51 E4
Fitzgerald St 41 F4
Fitzgibbon La 32 B4
Fitzgibbon St 32 B4
Fitzmaurice Rd 19 F4
Fitzroy Av 32 A3
Fitzwilliam Ct
off Pembroke St Upr 67 G6
Fitzwilliam La 67 H6
Fitzwilliam Pl 42 B3
Fitzwilliam Quay 43 D2
Fitzwilliam Sq E 42 B3
Fitzwilliam Sq N 67 G6
Fitzwilliam Sq S 67 G6
Fitzwilliam Sq W 67 G6
Fitzwilliam St
(Ringsend) 43 D2
Fitzwilliam St Lwr 67 H6
Fitzwilliam St Upr 67 H6
Fleet St 67 F3
Fleming Pl 42 C3
Fleming Rd 32 A2
Flemings La
off Haddington Rd 42 C3
Flemingstown Pk 48 B4
Fleurville 50 B3
Floraville Av 44 B1
Floraville Dr 44 C2
Floraville Est 44 C1
Floraville Lawn 44 C1
Florence Rd 64 B2
Florence St
off Lennox St 42 A3
Florence Ter **2** 64 C2
Florence Vil **12** 64 B2
Flower Gro 59 F2
Foley St 67 G2
Fontenoy St 66 D1
Fontenoy Ter 64 C3
Fonthill Abbey **2** 55 E1
Fonthill Ct **3** 55 E1
Fonthill Pk 55 E1
Fonthill Retail Pk 38 A1
Fonthill Rd *Dublin 14* 55 E1
Fonthill Rd *Clond.* 38 A1
Fonthill Rd S 44 B2
Forbes La 66 A5
Forbes St 42 C2
Forest Av *Dublin 24* 45 E3
Forest Av *Swords* 6 B3
Forest Boul 6 A3
Forest Cl 45 E3
Forest Ct 6 A3
Forest Cres 6 B3
Forest Dale 6 B3
Forest Dr *Dublin 24* 45 E3
Forest Dr *Swords* 6 B3
Forest Flds Rd 6 B3
Forest Grn *Dublin 24* 45 E3
Forest Grn *Swords* 6 B3
Forest Gro 6 A3
Forest Lawn 45 E3
Forest Pk *Dublin 24* 45 E3
Forest Pk *Leix.* 15 E2
Forest Pk *Swords* 6 B3
Forest Rd 6 A4
Forest Vw **1** 6 B3
Forest Wk 6 B3
Forest Way **2** 6 B3
Forestwood Av 20 A2
Forestwood Cl 20 B2
Fortfield Av 47 D3
Fortfield Ct 47 D3
Fortfield Dr 47 D4
Fortfield Gdns 48 A2
Fortfield Gro 47 D3
Fortfield Pk 47 D4
Fortfield Rd 47 D3
Fortfield Ter 48 A2
Forth Rd 33 D4
Fortlawn 16 A3
Fortlawn Av 16 A3
Fortlawn Pk 16 A3
Fortlawns 60 A4
Fortunestown Rd 52 B3
Fosterbrook 49 F3
Foster Cotts
off Phibsborough Rd 31 F4
Foster Pl S 67 F4
Fosters, The 49 E4
Fosters Av 49 E4
Foster Ter 32 B4
Fountain Pl 66 B2
Fountain Rd 41 D1
Four Cts
(Courts of Justice) 66 D3
Fourth Av *Dublin 1* 42 C1
Fourth Av *Dublin 24* 52 C1
Fownes St 67 F4
Foxborough Av 27 E4
Foxborough Cl 27 F4
Foxborough Cres **1** 27 E4
Foxborough Downes 27 E4
Foxborough Dr 27 E4
Foxborough Gdns 27 F4
Foxborough Glen 27 F4
Foxborough Grn 27 F4
Foxborough Gro 27 F4
Foxborough Hts 27 F4
Foxborough Hill 27 E4
Foxborough La 27 F4
Foxborough Meadows 27 E4
Foxborough Pk 27 E4
Foxborough Pl 27 E4
Foxborough Ri 27 E4
Foxborough Row 27 F4
Foxborough Wk 27 F4
Foxborough Way 27 E4
Foxdene Dr 38 A3
Foxdene Gdns 38 A2
Foxdene Grn 27 F4
Foxdene Gro 38 A2
Foxdene Pk 38 A2
Foxes Gro 63 E3
Foxfield 26 C4
Foxfield Av 34 C1
Foxfield Cres 35 D1
Foxfield Dr 35 D1
Foxfield Grn 35 D1
Foxfield Gro 34 C1
Foxfield Hts 34 C1
Foxfield Lawn 35 D1
Foxfield Pk 35 D1
Foxfield Rd 34 C1
Foxfield St. John 35 D1
Foxford 27 F3
Foxhill Av 22 B4
Foxhill Cl 22 B3
Foxhill Ct 22 B4
Foxhill Cres 22 B4
Foxhill Dr 22 B4
Foxhill Grn 22 B3
Foxhill Gro 22 B3
Foxhill Lawn 22 B4
Foxhill Pk 22 B4
Foxhill Way 22 B4
Foxpark 26 C4
Foxrock 58 B2
Foxrock Av 58 B1
Foxrock Cl 58 C1
Foxrock Ct 58 B1
Foxrock Cres 58 C1
Foxrock Grn 58 C1
Foxrock Gro 58 C1
Foxrock Manor 58 A1
Foxrock Mt **1** 58 B1
Foxrock Pk 58 B1

Knocksinna Pk 58 B1
Knowth Ct 19 F2
Kor Dev Pk 39 F4
Kyber Rd 30 B4
Kyle-Clare Rd 43 E2
Kylemore Av 39 E3
Kylemore Dr 39 F3
Kylemore Pk Ind Est 39 F3
Kylemore Pk N 39 E3
Kylemore Pk S 39 F3
Kylemore Pk W 39 F3
Kylemore Rd *Dublin 10* 39 F2
Kylemore Rd *Dublin 12* 39 F2
Kylemore Rd *Dublin 20* 39 E1

L

Laburnum Rd 48 C2
Laburnum Wk 28 C4
Lad La 42 B3
Lady's Well Rd 16 B1
Lagan Rd 31 D1
Lakelands, The 47 E4
Lakelands Av 57 E2
Lakelands Cl 57 E2
Lakelands Cres 57 E2
Lakelands Dr 57 E2
Lakelands Gro 57 E2
Lakelands Lawn 57 E2
Lakelands Pk 47 E3
Lakelands Rd 57 E2
Lakeshore Dr 7 D3
Lakeview Dr 7 D3
Lally Rd 40 A2
Lambay Cl 63 E1
Lambay Dr 63 E1
Lambay Rd 32 A1
Lambourne Av 14 C4
Lambourne Ct 14 C4
Lambourne Dr 14 C4
Lambourne Pk 14 C4
Lambourne Rd 14 C4
Lambourne Village 33 F3
Lambourne Wd 59 D4
Lambs Ct *off James's St* 41 D2
Landen Rd 39 F3
Landscape Av 48 A4
Landscape Cres 48 A4
Landscape Gdns 48 A4
Landscape Pk 48 A4
Landscape Rd 48 A4
Landys Ind Est 54 C1
Lanesborough Av 19 D1
Lanesborough Dr 19 E1
Lanesborough Gdns 19 D1
Lanesborough Gro 19 E1
Lanesborough Rd 19 D1
Lanesborough Ter 19 D1
Lanesborough Vw 19 D2
Lanesville 51 D4
Langrishe Pl *off Summerhill* 67 G1
Lanndale Lawns 52 C1
Lansdowne Gdns *off Shelbourne Rd* 43 D3
Lansdowne Hall *off Tritonville Rd* 43 D3
Lansdowne La 43 D3
Lansdowne Pk *Dublin 4* 42 C3
Lansdowne Pk *Dublin 16* 54 C1
Lansdowne Rd 42 C3
Lansdowne Rd Stadium 43 D3
Lansdowne Rd Sta 43 D3
Lansdowne Ter *off Serpentine Av* 43 D4
Lansdowne Valley Cres *off Kilworth Rd* 40 B4
Lansdowne Valley Rd 40 A4
Lansdowne Village 43 D3
Lansdown Valley Pk 40 B3
Laracor Gdns 22 C4
Laragh 61 E2
Laragh Cl 22 C4
Laraghcon 26 C1
Laragh Gro *off Laragh Cl* 22 C4
Larch Dr **4** 55 D3
Larchfield *Dublin 14* 48 B4
Larchfield *Dunb.* 12 B3
Larchfield Pk 48 C4
Larchfield Rd 48 C4
Larch Gro 48 B1
Larkfield 27 F2
Larkfield Av *Dublin 6W* 47 E1
Larkfield Av *Lucan* 27 F3
Larkfield Cl 27 F2
Larkfield Ct 27 F3
Larkfield Gdns 47 E1
Larkfield Grn 27 F2
Larkfield Gro *Dublin 6W* 47 E2
Larkfield Gro (Ballyowen) *Lucan* 27 F2
Larkfield Pk 47 E1
Larkfield Pl 27 F3
Larkfield Ri 27 F2
Larkfield Vw 27 F3
Larkfield Way 27 F2
Larkhill Rd 20 A4
Latchford Cl 14 A2
Latchford Grn 14 B2
Latchford Pk 14 B2
Latchford Sq 14 B2
Latchford Ter 14 B2
La Touche Cl 65 F2
La Touche Ct 56 A3
La Touche Dr 40 A3
La Touche Pk 65 E1
La Touche Pl 65 F2
La Touche Rd *Dublin 12* 40 A4
La Touche Rd *Grey.* 65 F2
Lauderdale Est 64 B4
Lauderdale Ter **3** 64 B4
Lauders La 24 B2
Laundry La 47 F1
Laurel Av *Dublin 14* 56 B1
Laurel Av *Lough.* 63 D1
Laurel Ct 28 C1
Laurel Dr 56 B1
Laurel Hill **6** 51 F4
Laurel Lo Rd 29 D1
Laurel Pk 44 B1
Laurel Rd 56 B1
Laurels, The *Dublin 6W* 47 E2
Laurels, The *Dublin 14* 56 B1
Laurelton 47 F3
Laurence Brook 39 F1
Laurleen 58 A1
Lavarna Gro 47 D3
Lavarna Rd 47 D2
Laverna Av 28 C1
Laverna Dale 28 C1
Laverna Gro 28 C1
Laverna Way 28 C2
Lavery Av 39 D3
Lavista Av (Killester) *Dublin 5* 33 F2
La Vista Av *Dublin 13* 24 C4
Lawn, The *Dublin 11* 19 D3
Lawn, The (Ballinteer) *Dublin 16* 56 B3
Lawn, The (Ballyboden) *Dublin 16* 54 C2
Lawn, The (Cookstown) *Dublin 24* 44 C4
Lawn, The *Bray* 64 B1
Lawn, The *Kins.* 7 E3
Lawnswood Pk 50 A4
Lawson Ter **18** 60 A2
Lea Cres 43 E4
Leahys Ter 43 E3
Lea Rd 43 E4
Le Bas Ter *off Leinster Rd W* 47 F1
Le Broquay Av 39 E3
Ledwidge Cres 64 A2
Lee Rd 31 E2
Leeson Cl 42 B3
Leeson La 67 G6
Leeson Pk 42 B4
Leeson Pk Av 42 B4
Leeson Pl 42 B3
Leeson St Br 42 B3
Leeson St Lwr 67 G6
Leeson St Upr 42 B4
Leeson Village 42 B4
Le Fanu Dr 39 E3
Le Fanu Rd 39 E2
Lehaunstown Rd 62 B1
Leicester Av 47 F1
Leighlin Rd 47 D1
Lein Gdns (Gardini Lein) 34 B2
Lein Pk 34 A1
Lein Rd 34 A1
Leinster Av 32 C4
Leinster La *off Leinster St S* 67 G5
Leinster Lawn 48 C3
Leinster Mkt *off D'Olier St* 67 F3
Leinster Pl 47 F1
Leinster Rd 47 F1
Leinster Rd W 47 F1
Leinster Sq 48 A1
Leinster St E 32 C4
Leinster St N 31 F3
Leinster St S 67 G5
Leinster Ter **2** 44 B1
Leitrim Pl *off Grand Canal St Upr* 42 C3
Leixlip Br 15 D2
Leixlip Pk 15 E2
Leixlip Rd 26 B2
Leixlip Sta 15 D1
Leix Rd 31 E3
Leland Pl 42 C1
Lemon St 67 F5
Lennox Pl 42 A4
Lennox St 42 A3
Lentisk Lawn 22 C4
Leo Av *off Leo St* 32 A4
Leopardstown 58 A2
Leopardstown Av 58 A1
Leopardstown Ct **2** 57 F3
Leopardstown Dr 58 A1
Leopardstown Gdns 58 A1
Leopardstown Gro 58 A1
Leopardstown Hts 57 E4
Leopardstown Lawn **2** 58 A1
Leopardstown Oaks 58 A1
Leopardstown Office Pk 57 F3
Leopardstown Pk 58 A1
Leopardstown Retail Pk 57 F4
Leopardstown Ri 57 E4
Leopardstown Rd 57 F4
Leopardstown Valley 58 A3
Leo St 32 A4
Leslie Av 60 C3
Leslies Bldgs 31 F4
Leukos Rd 43 E2
Le Vere Ter 41 F4
Liberty La 67 E6
Library Rd *D.L.* 51 E3
Library Rd *Shank.* 63 D3
Liffey Cl 27 F3
Liffey Ct 27 F3
Liffey Cres 27 F3
Liffey Dale 27 F3
Liffey Dockyard 43 D1
Liffey Downs **1** 27 F2
Liffey Dr 27 F3
Liffey Gdns 27 F3
Liffey Glen **2** 27 F3
Liffey Grn 27 F3
Liffey Hall 27 F3
Liffey Lawn 38 A1
Liffey Pk 27 F3
Liffey Pl **3** 27 F3
Liffey Ri 27 F3
Liffey Rd 27 F3
Liffey Row 27 F2
Liffey St 40 A2
Liffey St Lwr 67 E3
Liffey St Upr 67 E3
Liffey St W *off Benburb St* 66 B3
Liffey Vale 27 F3
Liffey Valley Ave 27 F3
Liffey Valley Pk 27 F3
Liffey Vw 27 F3
Liffey Vw Apts **2** 15 F2
Liffey Wk 38 A1
Liffey Way 27 F3
Liffey Wd 27 F3
Limekiln Av 46 A3
Limekiln Cl 46 B3
Limekiln Dr 46 B3
Limekiln Gro 46 B2
Limekiln La 46 B3
Limekiln Pk 46 B3
Limekiln Rd 46 A3
Limelawn Pk 16 A4
Limelawn Pk Ct 16 A4
Limelawn Pk Glade 16 A4
Limelawn Pk Grn 16 A4
Limelawn Pk Hill 16 A4
Limelawn Pk Ri 16 A4
Limelawn Pk Wd 16 A4
Limes Rd 57 D3
Lime St 42 C2
Limetree Av 11 F2
Limewood Av 22 B4
Limewood Pk 22 B4
Limewood Rd 22 B4
Lincoln La 66 C3
Lincoln Pl 67 G5
Linden 50 A3
Linden Gro 50 A3
Linden Lea Pk 57 F2
Linden Vale 50 B3
Lindsay Rd 31 F3
Linenhall Par 66 D2
Linenhall Ter 66 D2
Link Rd 60 A2
Links, The 11 E4
Linnetfields 14 A2
Linnetfields Av 14 A2
Linnetfields Cl 14 A2
Linnetfields Ct 14 A2
Linnetfields Dr 14 A2
Linnetfields Pk 14 A2
Linnetfields Ri 14 A2
Linnetfields Sq 14 A2
Linnetfields Vw 14 A2
Linnetfields Wk 14 A2
Lios Cian 6 B1
Lios Na Sidhe 53 D3
Lisburn St 66 D2
Liscannor Rd 31 D2
Liscanor **1** 60 C2
Liscarne Ct 38 B2
Liscarne Gdns 38 B2
Lisle Rd 46 B1
Lismore Rd 47 D1
Lissadel Av 40 C3
Lissadel Ct 40 C4
Lissadel Cres 7 F2
Lissadel Dr 40 C4
Lissadel Gro 7 F3
Lissadel Pk 7 F3
Lissadel Rd 40 C4
Lissadel Wd 7 F3
Lissenfield 42 A4
Lissen Hall Av **4** 7 D1
Lissen Hall Ct **5** 7 D1
Lissen Hall Dr 7 E1
Lissen Hall Pk **1** 7 E1
Litten La 67 F3
Little Britain St 66 D2
Little Meadow **5** 59 D2
Littlepace 14 B1
Littlepace Cl 14 B1
Littlepace Ct 14 B1
Littlepace Cres 14 B1
Littlepace Dr 14 B1
Littlepace Gallops 14 B1
Littlepace Meadow 14 B1
Littlepace Pk 14 B1
Littlepace Rd 14 B1
Littlepace Vw 14 B1
Littlepace Wk 14 B1
Littlepace Way 14 B1
Littlepace Wds 14 B1
Little Strand St 66 D3
Llewellyn Cl 56 A2
Llewellyn Ct 56 A2
Llewellyn Gro 56 A2
Llewellyn Lawn 56 A2
Llewellyn Pk 56 A2
Llewellyn Way 56 A2
Lock Rd 26 C4
Lodge, The 51 F4
Loftus La 67 E2
Lohunda Cres 16 A4
Lohunda Dale 16 A4
Lohunda Downs 16 A4
Lohunda Dr 16 A4
Lohunda Gro 16 A4
Lohunda Pk 14 C3
Lohunda Rd 16 A4
Lombard Ct 67 H3
Lombard St E 67 H4
Lombard St W 41 F3
Lomond Av 32 C3
London Br 43 D3
Londonbridge Dr *off Londonbridge Rd* 43 D3
Londonbridge Rd 43 D3
Longdale Ter 20 A3
Longford La *off Longford St Gt* 67 E5
Longford Pl 51 E3
Longford St Gt 67 E5
Longford St Little 67 E5
Longford Ter 51 D3
Longlands 7 D2
Long La *Dublin 7* 67 E1
Long La (Tenter Flds) *Dublin 8* 66 D6
Long La Gro 66 D6
Longmeadow 59 D3
Longmeadow Gro 59 E2
Long Mile Rd 45 F1
Longs Pl 66 A5
Longwood Av 41 F3
Longwood Pk 55 F1
Lorcan Av 20 C3
Lorcan Cres 20 C3
Lorcan Dr 20 C3
Lorcan Grn 21 D3
Lorcan Gro 20 C3
Lorcan O'Toole Pk 46 C2
Lorcan Pk 20 C3
Lorcan Rd 20 C3
Lorcan Vil 21 D3
Lord Edward St 66 D4
Lordello Rd 63 D4
Lord's Wk 30 C4
Loreto Av *Dublin 14* 55 F1
Loreto Av *Dalkey* 60 C3
Loreto Ct 55 F1
Loreto Cres 55 F1
Loreto Gra 64 B4
Loreto Pk 55 F1
Loreto Rd 66 A6
Loreto Row 55 F1
Loreto Ter 55 F1
Loretto Av **2** 64 C3
Loretto Ter **3** 64 C3
Loretto Vil **4** 64 C3
Lorne Ter *off Brookfield Rd* 41 D2
Lotts 67 F3
Lough Conn Av 39 E1
Lough Conn Dr 39 E1
Lough Conn Rd (Bothar Loch Con) 39 E1
Lough Conn Ter 39 E1
Lough Derg Rd 34 B1
Loughlinstown 63 D2
Loughlinstown Dr 63 D1
Loughlinstown Ind Est 63 D1
Loughlinstown Pk 63 D1
Loughlinstown Wd 63 D1
Lough-na-mona 15 D2
Lough-Na-Mona Cl 15 D2
Lough-Na-Mona Cres 15 D2
Lough-Na-Mona Dr 15 D2
Lough-Na-Mona Pk 15 D1
Loughsallagh Br 12 C3
Lourdes Rd 66 A6
Louvain 49 D4
Louvain Glade 49 D4
Love La E 42 C3
Lower Dargle Rd 64 A2
Lower Dodder Rd 47 F3
Lower Glen Rd 29 E4
Lower Kilmacud Rd *Dublin 14* 57 D1
Lower Kilmacud Rd *Still.* 57 E1
Lower Rd *Dublin 20* 29 D3
Lower Rd *Shank.* 63 E4
Luby Rd 40 C2
Lucan 27 D2
Lucan Br 27 D2
Lucan Bypass 27 D3
Lucan Hts 27 D2
Lucan Rd *Dublin 20* 29 E4
Lucan Rd *Lucan* 27 F2
Lucan Rd *Palm.* 28 C4
Lucan Shop Cen 26 C3
Ludford Dr 56 B2
Ludford Pk 56 B3
Ludford Rd 56 B2
Lugaquilla Av 45 F3
Luke St 67 G3
Lullymore Ter 41 E3
Lurgan St 66 D2
Lutterell Hall 12 A1
Luttrell Pk 28 B1
Luttrell Pk Cl 28 B1
Luttrell Pk Ct 28 B1
Luttrell Pk Cres 28 B2
Luttrell Pk Dr 28 B1
Luttrell Pk Grn 28 B1
Luttrell Pk Gro 28 B1
Luttrell Pk La 28 B1
Luttrell Pk Vw 28 B1
Luttrellstown Av 28 B2
Luttrellstown Beeches 28 B2
Luttrellstown Chase 28 A2
Luttrellstown Cl 28 B2
Luttrellstown Ct 28 A2
Luttrellstown Dale 28 A2
Luttrellstown Dr 28 B2
Luttrellstown Glade 28 B2
Luttrellstown Grn 28 B2
Luttrellstown Gro 28 B2
Luttrellstown Heath 28 B2
Luttrellstown Hts 28 B2
Luttrellstown Lawn 28 B2
Luttrellstown Oaks 28 B2
Luttrellstown Pk 28 B2
Luttrellstown Pl 28 B2
Luttrellstown Ri 28 B2
Luttrellstown Thicket 28 B2
Luttrellstown Vw 28 B2
Luttrellstown Wk 28 B2
Luttrellstown Way 28 B2
Luttrellstown Wd 28 C2
Lynchs La 39 F2
Lynchs Pl 31 F4
Lyndon Gate 30 C3
Lynwood 56 C2

M

M50 Business Pk 45 E3
Mabbot La 67 G2
Mabel St 32 B3
Macartney Br 42 B3
McAuley Av 34 A1
McAuley Dr 34 A1
McAuley Pk 34 A1
McAuley Rd 34 A1
McCabe Vil 49 F3
McCarthy's Bldgs *off Cabra Rd* 31 F3
McDowell Av 41 D2
McGrane Ct **3** 56 C2
McKee Av 19 D2
McKee Barracks 31 D4
McKee Dr 31 D4
McKee Pk 31 D4
McKee Rd 19 D3
McKelvey Av 18 C2
McKelvey Rd 19 D2
Macken St 42 C2
Macken Vil 42 C2
Mackies Pl 67 G6
Mackintosh Pk 59 D2
McMahon St 66 D6
McMorrough Rd 47 E2
Macroom Av 21 F2
Macroom Rd 21 F2
Madden's La 59 F4
Madeleine Ter 40 B2
Madison Rd 41 D3
Magennis Pl 67 H4
Magennis Sq *off Pearse St* 67 H4
Magenta Cres 20 C2
Magenta Hall 20 C3
Magenta Pl 51 F4
Mageough Home 48 A2
Mahers Pl *off Macken St* 42 C2
Maiden Row 39 F1
Main Rd 53 E1
Main Rd Tallaght 53 F1
Main St (Raheny) *Dublin 5* 34 B2
Main St (Finglas) *Dublin 11* 19 D3
Main St (Baldoyle) *Dublin 13* 23 F3
Main St (Howth) *Dublin 13* 25 F3
Main St (Dundrum) *Dublin 14* 56 B1
Main St (Rathfarnham) *Dublin 14* 47 E4
Main St *Dublin 20* 39 F1
Main St *Dublin 24* 53 E1

Main St *Black.* 50 B2
Main St *Bray* 64 B3
Main St *Clond.* 44 B1
Main St *Dunb.* 12 A2
Main St *Leix.* 15 F2
Main St *Lucan* 26 C2
Main St *Swords* 6 C2
Maitland St 64 A2
Malachi Rd 66 B2
Malahide Rd *Dublin 3* 33 D3
Malahide Rd *Dublin 5* 33 E1
Malahide Rd *Dublin 17* 22 A4
Malahide Rd *Balg.* 22 B1
Malahide Rd *Swords* 7 D2
Malahide Roundabout 7 D2
Malborough Ct **9** 60 A3
Mall, The **2** *Dublin 13* 24 A1
Mall, The *Dublin 15* 16 B4
Mall, The *Leix.* 15 F2
Mall, The *Lucan* 26 C2
Mallin Av 66 A6
Malone Gdns 43 D2
Malpas Pl *off Malpas St* 66 D6
Malpas St 66 D6
Malpas Ter *off Malpas St* 66 D6
Maltings, The 64 B2
Mander's Ter *off Ranelagh Rd* 42 B4
Mangerton Rd 40 A4
Mannix Rd 32 A2
Manor Av *Dublin 6W* 47 D3
Manor Av *Grey.* 65 E3
Manor Cl 56 A3
Manor Cres 14 B2
Manor Dr 22 C3
Manorfields 14 B2
Manor Grn 55 F3
Manor Heath 56 A2
Manor Pk (Ballinteer) *Dublin 10* 55 F3
Manor Pk *Dublin 20* 39 D1
Manor Pl 66 B2
Manor Ri 56 A3
Manor Rd 39 D1
Manor St 66 B1
Mansion Ho 67 F5
Mantua Pk 7 D1
Maolbuille Rd 20 A4
Mapas Av 60 A3
Mapas Rd 60 B3
Maple Av *Castle.* 28 C1
Maple Av *Still.* 57 E3
Maple Cl 28 C1
Maple Dr *Dublin 6W* 47 E2
Maple Dr *Castle.* 28 C1
Maple Dr *Dunb.* 12 B2
Maple Glen 28 C1
Maple Grn 28 C1
Maple Gro *Bray* 64 A2
Maple Gro *Castle.* 28 C1
Maple Lawn 28 C1
Maple Manor 59 E3
Maple Rd 48 C2
Maples, The *Dublin 14* 48 C3
Maples, The *D.L.* 50 C3
Maples Rd 57 D3
Maplewood Av 52 C2
Maplewood Cl 52 C2
Maplewood Ct 52 C2
Maplewood Dr 52 C2
Maplewood Grn 52 C2
Maplewood Lawn 52 C2
Maplewood Pk 52 C2
Maplewood Rd 52 B2
Maplewood Way 52 C2
Maquay Br 42 C3
Maretimo Gdns E 50 C2
Maretimo Gdns W *off Newtown Av* 50 C2
Maretimo Pl *off Newtown Av* 50 C2
Maretimo Rd *off Newtown Av* 50 C2
Maretimo Vil *off Newtown Av* 50 B2
Marewood Cres 19 F2
Marewood Dr 19 F2
Marewood Gro 19 F2
Marfield Cl **5** 53 D4
Marfield Ct **6** 53 D4
Marfield Cres **8** 53 D4
Marfield Grn 53 D4
Marfield Gro **7** 53 D4
Marfield Lawn **4** 53 D4
Marfield Pl 53 D4
Margaret Pl 43 D2
Marguerite Rd 32 A2
Marian Cres 55 D1
Marian Dr 47 D4
Marian Gro 55 D1
Marian Pk *Dublin 13* 23 E4
Marian Pk (Rathfarnham) *Dublin 14* 55 D1
Marian Pk *Black.* 50 B4
Marian Rd 55 D1
Marie Vil **5** 64 C3
Marigold Av 22 A3
Marigold Ct **4** 22 A3
Marigold Cres **5** 22 A3
Marigold Gro **6** 22 A3
Marigold Pk **7** 22 A3
Marine Av 60 A2
Marine Ct 60 A2
Marine Dr 43 E3
Marine Par 60 A2
Marine Rd 51 F3
Mariners Cove 25 F4
Mariner's Port 42 C1
Marine Ter **9** *Bray* 64 C2
Marine Ter *D.L.* 51 F3
Marine Ter *Grey.* 65 F1
Marino Av 33 D2
Marino Av E 61 F2
Marino Av W 61 E2
Marino Grn 33 D2
Marino Inst of Ed 32 C2
Marino Mart 33 D3
Marino Pk 32 C3
Marino Pk Av 32 C3
Marion Vil 66 B5
Market Sq **8** 64 B3
Market St S 66 B5
Marks All W 66 D5
Marks La 67 H4
Mark St 67 H4
Marlay Vw 56 A4
Marlborough Ms 31 D4
Marlborough Pk **2** 59 F1
Marlborough Pl 67 F2
Marlborough Rd (Donnybrook) *Dublin 4* 48 B1
Marlborough Rd *Dublin 7* 31 D4
Marlborough Rd *G'geary* 60 A3
Marlborough St 67 F2
Marlborough Ter **10** 64 C2
Marley Av 55 F2
Marley Cl 56 A2
Marley Ct N 56 A2
Marley Ct S 56 A2
Marley Dr 55 F2
Marley Gro 55 F2
Marley Lawn 55 F2
Marley Ri 55 F2
Marley Vil **1** 55 F2
Marley Wk 55 F2
Marlfield 59 D3
Marne Vil 66 C1
Marrowbone La 66 B6
Marrowbone La Cl 66 B5
Marshalsea La 66 B4
Marsham Ct 57 E2
Martello Av 51 F3
Martello Ct 11 F2
Martello Ms 49 F1
Martello Ter *Boot.* 50 A1
Martello Ter **1** *Bray* 64 C2
Martello Vw 43 E3
Martello Wd 43 F4
Martin Savage Pk 30 A1
Martin Savage Rd 30 B3
Martins Row 29 F4
Martin St 42 A4
Mart La 58 C2
Maryfield Av 21 E4
Maryfield Coll 32 C1
Maryfield Cres 21 E4
Maryfield Dr 21 E4
Maryland **3** 63 E3
Mary's Abbey 66 D3
Mary's La 66 D3
Mary St 67 E3
Mary St Little 66 D3
Maryville Rd 34 A2
Mask Av (Ascal Measc) 21 F4
Mask Cres 21 F4
Mask Dr 21 F4
Mask Grn 21 F4
Mask Rd 21 F4
Mastersons La *off Charlemont St* 42 A3
Mather Rd N 49 E4
Mather Rd S 49 E4
Maunsell Pl *off Mountjoy St* 67 E1
Maxwell Rd 48 A1
Maxwell St 66 B6
Mayberry Pk 45 D4
Mayberry Rd 45 D4
Mayfield 47 F3
Mayfield Rd (Terenure) *Dublin 6W* 47 E2
Mayfield Rd (Kilmainham) *Dublin 8* 41 D3
Mayfield Ter *Dublin 16* 56 B3
Mayfield Ter **4** *Bray* 64 B4
May La 66 C3
Mayne, The 13 E2
Mayne Br 23 F2
Mayne Rd 23 D1
Mayola Ct 48 B4
Mayor St Lwr 42 C1
Mayor St Upr 43 D1
May St 32 B3
Mayville Ter **1** 60 C3
Maywood Av 34 C2
Maywood Cl 34 C2
Maywood Cres 34 C2
Maywood Dr 34 C2
Maywood Gro 34 C2
Maywood La 34 C2
Maywood Pk 34 C2
Maywood Rd 34 C2
Meades Ter 42 C2
Meadow, The *Dublin 16* 56 B3
Meadow, The *Mala.* 11 F1
Meadow Av **2** 56 B2
Meadowbank 47 F3
Meadowbrook Av 23 F4
Meadowbrook Lawn 23 F4
Meadowbrook Pk 23 F4
Meadow Cl *Dublin 16* 56 A2
Meadow Cl *Black.* 50 B4
Meadow Copse 14 C2
Meadow Ct **1** *Grey.* 65 D3
Meadow Ct **1** *Lough.* 63 D1
Meadow Dale **1** 14 C2
Meadow Downs 14 C3
Meadow Dr 14 C2
Meadow Grn 14 C3
Meadow Gro 56 A2
Meadow Mt 56 A2
Meadow Pk 56 A2
Meadow Pk Av 56 A1
Meadows, The *Dublin 5* 34 A2
Meadows, The *Dunb.* 12 A2
Meadows E, The 44 C4
Meadows W, The 44 C4
Meadow Vale 59 D2
Meadow Vw *Dublin 14* 56 A2
Meadow Vw *Dunb.* 12 A2
Meadowview Gro 26 B3
Meadow Vil **1** 56 A2
Meadow Way 14 C2
Meakstown Cotts 19 D1
Meath Pl *Dublin 8* 66 C5
Meath Pl *Bray* 64 C2
Meath Rd 64 C3
Meath Sq *off Gray St* 66 C5
Meath St 66 C4
Meehan Sq 49 E3
Meetinghouse La *off Mary's Abbey* 67 E3
Mellifont Av 51 F3
Mellowes Av 18 C3
Mellowes Ct 19 D3
Mellowes Cres 19 D3
Mellowes Pk 18 C3
Mellowes Rd 18 C3
Mellows Br 66 B3
Melrose Av 32 C3
Melrose Pk 7 E4
Melville Cl 19 E2
Melville Ct 19 D2
Melville Cres 19 D2
Melville Dr 19 D2
Melville Grn 19 D2
Melville Gro 19 E2
Melville Pk 19 D2
Melville Ter 19 D2
Melville Vw 19 D2
Melville Way 19 D2
Melvin Rd 47 E2
Memorial Rd 67 G3
Mercer St Lwr 67 E5
Mercer St Upr 67 E6
Merchamp 34 A4
Merchants Quay 66 C4
Merchants Rd 43 D1
Meretimo Vil **26** 64 C3
Meridianpoint 65 F2
Merlyn Dr 49 E1
Merlyn Pk 49 E1
Merlyn Rd 49 E1
Merrion Cres 49 F2
Merrion Gro 49 F3
Merrion Pk 49 F4
Merrion Pl 67 G5
Merrion Rd 43 D4
Merrion Row 67 G6
Merrion Shop Cen 49 E1
Merrion Sq E 67 H5
Merrion Sq N 67 H5
Merrion Sq S 67 H5
Merrion Sq W 67 G5
Merrion Strand 49 F1
Merrion St Lwr *off Clare St* 67 H5
Merrion St Upr 67 G6
Merrion Vw Av 49 E1
Merrion Village 49 E1
Merrywell Ind Est 45 E2
Merton Av 41 E3
Merton Cres 48 B2
Merton Dr 48 B1
Merton Rd 48 B2
Merton Wk 48 B2
Merville Av *Dublin 3* 32 C3
Merville Av *Still.* 57 F2
Merville Rd 57 F2
Mespil Rd 42 B3
Mews, The *Dublin 3* 33 F3
Mews, The (Dollymount) *Dublin 3* 34 B4
Mews, The **6** *Mala.* 11 F1
Michael Collins Pk 38 A4
Middle III 33 F2
Milesian Av 7 E3
Milesian Ct 7 E3
Milesian Gro 7 E3
Milesian Lawn 7 E3
Military Cem 30 C3
Military Rd (Rathmines) *Dublin 6* 42 A4
Military Rd (Kilmainham) *Dublin 8* 41 D2
Military Rd (Phoenix Pk) *Dublin 8* 40 A1
Military Rd *Kill.* 61 E2
Millbourne Av 32 A2
Millbrook Av 22 B4
Millbrook Ct 41 D2
Millbrook Dr 22 C4
Millbrook Gro 22 B4
Millbrook Lawns 53 E2
Millbrook Rd 22 B4
Millbrook Village *off Prospect La* 48 C2
Mill Cen 38 B4
Millennium Br 67 E3
Millennium Business Pk 17 F1
Millers Wd 64 A3
Millfarm 12 B2
Millgate Dr 46 B3
Mill Gro 65 E4
Mill La *Dublin 8 off Newmarket* 66 C6
Mill La *Dublin 15* 30 A1
Mill La *Dublin 20* 29 D4
Mill La *Leix.* 15 F2
Mill La *Lough.* 63 E2
Mill La Business Pk 26 A1
Millmount Av 32 A2
Millmount Gro 48 B3
Millmount Pl 32 B2
Millmount Ter (Drumcondra) *Dublin 9 off Millmount Av* 32 B2
Millmount Ter (Dundrum) *Dublin 14 off Millmount Gro* 48 B3
Millmount Vil 32 A2
Mill Pk 44 A1
Mill Pond Apartments, The **4** 44 B1
Mill Rd *Dublin 15* 17 D4
Mill Rd *Grey.* 65 E4
Millstead 17 D4
Millstream Rd 26 B2
Mill St 66 C6
Milltown Av 48 B2
Milltown Br Rd 48 B2
Milltown Dr 48 A4
Milltown Gro 48 A4
Milltown Hill *off Milltown Rd* 48 B2
Milltown Path 48 B2
Milltown Rd 48 B2
Millwood Pk 22 B4
Millwood Vil 22 B4
Milton Ter **14** 64 B2
Milward Ter **16** 64 C3
Mine Hill La 62 A4
Misery Hill 42 C2
Moatfield Av 22 A4
Moatfield Pk 22 A4
Moatfield Rd 22 A4
Moatview Av 21 F2
Moatview Ct 21 F1
Moatview Dr 21 F1
Moatview Gdns 21 F2
Moeran Rd 46 B1
Moira Rd 66 A2
Moland Pl *off Talbot St* 67 G2
Molesworth Pl *off Molesworth St* 67 G5
Molesworth St 67 F5
Molyneux Yd 66 C4
Monalea Dr 54 A2
Monalea Gro 54 A2
Monalea Pk 54 A2
Monalea Wd 54 A2
Monaloe Av 59 D3
Monaloe Ct **1** 59 D3
Monaloe Cres **2** 59 D2
Monaloe Dr 59 D2
Monaloe Pk 59 D2
Monaloe Pk Rd 59 D2
Monaloe Way 59 D2
Monarch Ind Est 53 D1
Monasterboice Rd 40 C4
Monastery Cres 44 C1
Monastery Dr 44 C1
Monastery Gate 45 D1
Monastery Gate Av 44 C1
Monastery Gate Cl 45 D1
Monastery Gate Copse 44 C1
Monastery Gate Grn 44 C1
Monastery Gate Lawns 45 D1
Monastery Gate Vil 44 C1
Monastery Heath 44 C1
Monastery Heath Av 44 C1
Monastery Heath Ct 44 C1
Monastery Heath Grn 44 C1
Monastery Heath Sq 44 C1
Monastery Hts **1** 44 C1
Monastery Pk 44 B1
Monastery Ri 44 B1
Monastery Rd 44 B1
Monastery Shop Cen 44 B1
Monastery Wk 44 C1
Monck Pl 31 F4
Monksfield 44 C1
Monksfield Ct 44 C1
Monksfield Downs 38 C4
Monksfield Gro 44 C1
Monksfield Hts 44 C1
Monksfield Lawn 38 C4
Monksfield Meadows 44 C1
Monksfield Wk 44 C1
Monkstown Av 51 D4
Monkstown Cres 51 D3
Monkstown Fm 51 D4
Monkstown Gate 51 E3
Monkstown Gro 51 D4
Monkstown Rd 50 C2
Monkstown Sq **4** 51 D4
Monkstown Valley 51 D3
Montague Ct *off Protestant Row* 67 E6
Montague La 67 E6
Montague Pl *off Montague La* 42 A3
Montague St 67 E6
Montebello Ter **17** 64 C3
Monte Vella **4** 60 B3
Montgommery Vw 7 E2
Montone Business Pk 39 D4
Montpelier Dr 41 D1
Montpelier Gdns 41 D1
Montpelier Hill 41 D1
Montpelier Par 50 C3
Montpelier Pk 66 A2
Montpelier Pl 41 E1
Montpelier Vw 52 B3
Montrose Av 21 D4
Montrose Cl 21 D4
Montrose Ct 21 D4
Montrose Cres 21 E3
Montrose Dr 21 D3
Montrose Gro 21 D4
Montrose Pk 21 D4
Moorefield 59 F4
Moore La 67 F2
Moore's Cotts **4** 50 B4
Moore St 67 F2
Mooretown 6 A1
Mooretown Av 6 C1
Mooretown Gro **3** 6 C1
Mooretown Pk **4** 6 C1
Mooretown Rd 6 C1
Moorfield 38 A3
Moorfield Av 38 B3
Moorfield Cl **2** 38 B3
Moorfield Dr 38 B3
Moorfield Grn 38 B3
Moorfield Lawns 38 B3
Moreen Av 57 D3
Moreen Cl 57 D4
Moreen Lawn **3** 57 D4
Moreen Pk 57 D4
Moreen Rd 57 D4
Moreen Wk 57 D4
Morehampton La 42 C4
Morehampton Rd 42 C4
Morehampton Sq 42 B4
Morehampton Ter 42 C4
Morgan Pl *off Inns Quay* 66 D3
Morning Star Av 66 C2
Morning Star Rd 66 A6
Mornington Av 60 B2
Mornington Gro 21 F4
Mornington Rd 48 B1
Morrogh Ter 32 C2
Moss St 67 G3
Mountain Pk 53 E2
Mountain Vw 63 D4
Mountain Vw Apartments **5** 64 B4
Mountain Vw Av *off Harolds Cross Rd* 47 F1
Mountain Vw Cotts *Dublin 6* 48 B1
Mountain Vw Cotts *Castle.* 28 B2
Mountain Vw Dr 56 A1
Mountain Vw Pk *Dublin 14* 56 A1
Mountainview Pk *Grey.* 65 E1
Mountain Vw Rd *Dublin 6* 48 B1
Mountain Vw Rd **1** *Kill.* 61 E2
Mountain Vil **2** 61 E2
Mount Albany 50 B4
Mount Albion Rd 56 A1
Mount Albion Ter **1** 56 A1
Mount Alton 54 B2
Mount Alton Ct 54 B2
Mount Andrew 27 F2
Mount Andrew Av 28 A4
Mount Andrew Cl 28 A4
Mount Andrew Ct 27 F2
Mount Andrew Dale 28 A4
Mount Andrew Gro 28 A4
Mount Andrew Ri 28 A4
Mount Annville 57 E1
Mount Annville Conv 57 D1

Mount Annville Lawn 57 D1
Mount Annville Pk 57 E1
Mount Annville Rd 57 D1
Mount Annville Wd 57 E1
Mount Argus Cl 47 E1
Mount Argus Ct 47 E1
Mount Argus Cres 47 E1
Mount Argus Grn 47 E1
Mount Argus Gro 47 E1
Mount Argus Pk 47 E1
Mount Argus Rd 47 E1
Mount Argus Ter 47 E1
Mount Argus Vw 47 E1
Mount Argus Way 47 E1
Mount Auburn **1** 60 A4
Mount Bellew Cres **1** 27 F3
Mount Bellew Grn **2** 27 E3
Mount Bellew Ri **1** 27 E3
Mount Bellew Way 27 E3
Mount Brown 41 D2
Mount Carmel Av 48 C4
Mount Carmel Pk 54 A2
Mount Carmel Rd 48 C4
Mount Dillon Ct 21 F4
Mountdown Dr 46 B3
Mountdown Pk 46 B3
Mountdown Rd 46 B3
Mount Drinan Av 7 E4
Mount Drinan Cres 7 E4
Mount Drinan Gro **5** 7 E4
Mount Drinan Lawn **1** 10 A1
Mount Drinan Pk 7 E4
Mount Drinan Wk 7 E4
Mount Drummond Av 41 F4
Mount Drummond Sq 41 F4
Mount Eagle Dr 57 E4
Mount Eagle Grn 57 E4
Mount Eagle Gro 57 E4
Mount Eagle Lawn 57 E4
Mount Eagle Pk 57 E4
Mount Eagle Ri 57 E4
Mount Eagle Vw 57 E4
Mount Eagle Way 57 E4
Mount Eden Rd 48 C1
Mountfield 11 D1
Mount Gandon 26 C2
Mount Harold Ter 47 F1
Mounthaven 65 E1
Mount Jerome Cem 41 E4
Mountjoy Cotts 32 A3
Mountjoy Par
off North Circular Rd 32 B4
Mountjoy Pl 67 G1
Mountjoy Prison 32 A3
Mountjoy Prison Cotts
off Cowley Pl 32 A3
Mountjoy Sq E 32 B4
Mountjoy Sq N 32 A4
Mountjoy Sq S 67 F1
Mountjoy Sq W 32 A4
Mountjoy St 66 D1
Mountjoy St Mid 66 D1
Mount Merrion Av 49 F4
Mount Norris Vil **18** 64 C3
Mount Olive Gro 22 C4
Mount Olive Pk 22 C4
Mount Olive Rd 22 C4
Mountpleasant Av Lwr 42 A4
Mountpleasant Av Upr 42 A4
Mountpleasant Bldgs 42 A4
Mountpleasant Par
off Mountpleasant Pl 42 A4
Mountpleasant Pl 42 A4
Mountpleasant Sq 42 A4
Mountpleasant Vil **15** 64 A2
Mount Prospect Av 34 A4
Mount Prospect Dr 34 A3
Mount Prospect Gro 34 B3
Mount Prospect Lawns 34 A4
Mount Prospect Pk 34 A4
Mount Sackville Conv 29 E3
Mount Salus Rd 60 C4
Mountsandel 58 C4
Mount Sandford 48 C1
Mount Shannon Rd 41 D3
Mount St Cres 42 C3
Mount St Lwr 42 C2
Mount St Upr 67 H6
Mount Symon 14 B3
Mount Symon Av 14 C4
Mount Symon Cl 14 C3
Mount Symon Cres 14 B3
Mount Symon Dale 14 B3
Mount Symon Dr 14 C3
Mount Symon Grn 14 B3
Mount Symon Lawn 14 C4
Mount Symon Pk 14 C4
Mount Symon Ri 14 C3
Mount Tallant Av 47 E2
Mount Tallant Ter
off Harolds Cross Rd 41 F4
Mount Temple Rd 66 B2
Mount Town Lwr 51 E4
Mounttown Pk **4** 51 E4
Mount Town Rd Upr 51 E3
Mount Vw Rd 16 A3
Mount Wd 51 E4
Mourne Rd 41 D3
Moyclare Av 23 F4
Moyclare Cl 23 F4
Moyclare Dr 23 F4
Moyclare Gdns 24 A2
Moyclare Pk 23 F4
Moyclare Rd 23 F4
Moycullen Rd 39 D2
Moy Elta Rd 32 C4
Moy Glas Av 27 E4
Moy Glas Chase 27 E4
Moy Glas Cl 27 E4
Moy Glas Ct 27 E4
Moy Glas Dale 27 E4
Moy Glas Dene 27 E4
Moy Glas Dr 27 E4
Moy Glas Glen 27 E4
Moy Glas Grn 27 E4
Moy Glas Gro 27 E4
Moy Glas Lawn 27 E4
Moy Glas Pk 27 E4
Moy Glas Rd 27 E4
Moy Glas Vale 27 E4
Moy Glas Vw 27 E4
Moy Glas Way 27 E4
Moy Glas Wd 27 E4
Moyle Cres 44 B1
Moyle Rd 31 D2
Moyne Rd 48 B1
Moynihan Ct 53 F1
Moyville 55 D3
Moyville Lawns 55 D2
Muckross Av 46 B2
Muckross Cres 46 B2
Muckross Dr 46 C2
Muckross Grn 46 C2
Muckross Gro 46 B2
Muckross Par
off Killarney Par 32 A3
Muckross Pk 46 B2
Muirfield Dr 40 A4
Mulberry Cres 28 C2
Mulberry Dr 28 C2
Mulberry Pk 28 C2
Mulcahy Keane Est 46 A2
Mulgrave St 51 F3
Mulgrave Ter 51 F4
Mulhuddart Wd 16 A1
Mullinastill Rd 63 D2
Mulroy Rd 31 E2
Mulvey Pk 48 C4
Munster St 31 F3
Munster Ter **3** 60 B2
Murphystown Rd 57 E4
Murrays Cotts
off Sarsfield Rd 40 B2
Murtagh Rd 66 A2
Muskerry Rd 39 F2
Mygan Business Pk 19 D2
Mygan Pk Ind Est 19 D2
Myra Cotts 40 C2
Myra Manor 10 C2
Myrtle Av **16** 51 F4
Myrtle Gro *Bray* 64 A2
Myrtle Gro *Still.* 57 F2
Myrtle Pk 51 F4

N

Naas Rd *Dublin 12* 45 E1
Naas Rd *Dublin 22* 45 D1
Naas Rd Business Pk 40 A4
Naas Rd Ind Pk 40 A4
Nangor Cres **1** 44 A1
Nangor Rd *Dublin 12* 38 C4
Nangor Rd *Clond.* 44 A1
Nangor Rd Business Cen 39 D4
Nanikin Av 34 B2
Nash St 40 A3
Nashville Pk 25 F3
Nashville Rd 25 F3
Nassau Pl 67 G5
Nassau St 67 F4
National Mus 67 G5
National Museum, Collins Barracks 66 A3
National Transport Mus 25 D3
Naul Rd 8 B1
Navan Rd *Dublin 7* 30 B2
Navan Rd *Dublin 15* 29 E1
Navan Rd (Blanchardstown) *Dublin 15* 16 B2
Navan Rd *Clonee* 13 E3
Navan Rd *Dunb.* 12 A2
Navan Rd *Mulh.* 14 C1
Neagh Rd 47 E2
Neillstown Av 38 B3
Neillstown Cres 38 B3
Neillstown Dr 38 B2
Neillstown Gdns 38 B3
Neillstown Pk 38 B3
Neilstown Cotts **2** 38 B4
Neilstown Rd 38 B2
Neilstown Shop Cen 38 A3
Neilstown Village Ct **1** 38 B3
Nelson St 32 A4
Nephin Rd 30 C3
Neptune Ter **4** 60 B2
Nerano Rd 60 C3
Nerneys Ct 32 A4
Neville Rd 48 A2
Nevinstown La 6 C4
New Bawn Dr 53 E2
New Bawn Pk 53 E2
New Bride St 67 E6
New Br 15 D4
Newbridge Av 43 D3
Newbridge Dr 43 D3
New Brighton Ter **9** 64 B3
Newbrook Av 23 D4
Newbrook Rd 23 D4
Newbury Av 21 E2
Newbury Dr 21 E2
Newbury Gro 21 E2
Newbury Lawns 21 E2
Newbury Pk 21 E2
Newbury Ter **1** 21 E2
Newcastle Rd 26 C3
New Ch St 66 C3
Newcomen Av 32 C4
Newcomen Br 32 C4
Newcomen Ct
off North Strand Rd 32 C4
Newcourt 7 D1
Newcourt Av 64 C4
Newcourt Ms **3** 7 D1
Newcourt Rd 64 C4
Newcourt Vil **6** 64 B4
New Gra Rd *Dublin 7* 31 E3
New Gra Rd *Black.* 50 B4
Newgrove Av 43 E3
New Gro Est 23 D3
Newhall Ct 52 A3
New Ireland Rd 41 D3
Newlands Av 44 C2
Newlands Business Cen 44 B2
Newlands Dr 44 B2
Newlands Manor 44 A3
Newlands Manor Ct 44 A3
Newlands Manor Dr 44 A3
Newlands Manor Fairway 44 A3
Newlands Manor Grn 44 A3
Newlands Manor Pk 44 A3
Newlands Pk 44 B2
Newlands Retail Cen 44 B2
Newlands Rd *Clond.* 44 B2
Newlands Rd *Lucan* 27 D2
New Lisburn St
off Coleraine St 66 D2
New Lucan Rd 28 B4
Newmarket 66 C6
Newmarket St 66 C6
New Nangor Rd 38 A4
New Pk Lo **7** 58 B1
New Pk Rd 50 B4
Newport St 66 A5
New Rathmore Ter **16** 64 A2
New Ravenswell Row **17** 64 A2
New Rd (Inchicore) *Dublin 8* 40 A3
New Rd *Dublin 13* 25 F4
New Rd *Clond.* 44 B1
New Rd *Grey.* 65 E1
New Rd (Killincarrig) *Grey.* 65 E4
New Rd **1** *Swords* 7 D2
New Rd, The 17 F2
New Row S 66 D6
New Row Sq 66 D5
New St Gdns 66 D6
New St S 66 D6
Newtown Av *Dublin 17* 22 A3
Newtown Av *Black.* 50 C2
Newtown Cotts 22 A4
Newtown Dr 22 A4
Newtown Glendale 15 F1
Newtown Ind Est 22 A3
Newtown Pk *Dublin 17* 22 A3
Newtown Pk *Dublin 24* 53 F1
Newtown Pk *Black.* 50 B4
Newtown Pk *Leix.* 15 F1
Newtownpark Av 50 B3
Newtown Pk Ct **5** 50 B4
Newtown Rd 22 A3
Newtownsmith 60 A1
Newtown Vil 50 C2
New Vale 63 D3
New Vale Cotts 63 D4
New Vale Cres 63 D3
New Wapping St 42 C1
Niall St 66 A1
Nicholas Av
off Church St 66 D2
Nicholas Pl
off Patrick St 66 D5
Nicholas St 66 D5
Ninth Lock Rd 44 B1
Nore Rd 31 D2
Norfolk Mkt
off Parnell St 67 F1
Norfolk Rd 31 F3
Norseman Pl 66 B2
North Av 49 E4
Northbrook Av 42 B4
Northbrook Av Lwr
off North Strand Rd 32 C4
Northbrook Av Upr 32 C4
Northbrook La 42 B4
Northbrook Rd 42 A4
Northbrook Ter 32 C4
Northbrook Vil
off Northbrook Rd 42 A4
Northbrook Wk 42 B4
North Circular Rd *Dublin 1* 32 A4
North Circular Rd *Dublin 7* 32 A3
Northcote Av 51 E3
Northcote Pl 51 E3
North Dublin Docklands 43 E1
Northern Cl 21 F1
Northern Cross Business Pk 18 C2
North Gt Clarence St 67 H1
North Gt Georges St 67 F1
Northland Dr 31 E1
Northland Gro 31 E1
North Pk Business & Office Pk 18 C2
North Quay Extension 43 D1
North Rd *Dublin 8* 30 A2
North Rd *Dublin 11* 18 C2
North Rd Number 1 43 E1
Northside Shop Cen 21 E2
North Strand Rd *Dublin 1* 32 C4
North Strand Rd *Dublin 3* 32 C4
North St 7 D1
North St Business Pk 7 D1
Northumberland Av 51 F3
Northumberland Pk 51 F3
Northumberland Pl
off Northumberland Av 51 F3
Northumberland Rd 42 C3
North Wall Quay 42 C1
Northway Est 18 C2
Nortons Av 31 F4
Norwood 63 E1
Norwood Pk 48 B1
Nottingham St 32 C4
Novara Av 64 B2
Novara Ms **15** 64 B2
Novara Pk **10** 64 B3
Novara Ter **11** 64 B3
Nugent Rd 56 A1
Nurney Lawn 22 C3
Nurseries, The **4** *B'brack* 61 E2
Nurseries, The *Bray* 64 A4
Nurseries, The *Grey.* 65 D3
Nurseries, The *Mulh.* 16 B1
Nurseries, The *Swords* 6 B3
Nutgrove Av (Ascal An Charrain Chno) 55 F1
Nutgrove Cres 56 A1
Nutgrove Enterprise Pk 56 A1
Nutgrove Office Pk 56 A1
Nutgrove Pk 48 C3
Nutgrove Shop Cen 56 A1
Nutgrove Way 56 A1
Nutley Av 49 D1
Nutley La 49 E2
Nutley Pk 49 E2
Nutley Rd 49 D1
Nutley Sq 49 D2

O

Oak Apple Grn 47 F2
Oak Av 20 C2
Oak Cl 39 D4
Oak Ct 20 C2
Oakcourt Av 39 D1
Oakcourt Cl 39 D1
Oakcourt Dr 39 D1
Oakcourt Gro 39 D1
Oakcourt Lawn 39 D1
Oakcourt Lawns 39 D1
Oakcourt Pk 39 D1
Oak Cres 20 C1
Oakdale Cl 54 A4
Oakdale Cres 53 F4
Oakdale Dr *Dublin 24* 54 A4
Oakdale Dr *Corn.* 59 E2
Oakdale Gro 54 A4
Oakdale Pk 53 F4
Oakdale Rd 53 F4
Oak Dene 60 A4
Oakdown Rd 56 A1
Oak Downs 44 A2
Oak Dr *Dublin 9* 20 C2
Oak Dr *Dublin 12* 45 D1
Oakfield 38 B4
Oakfield Ind Est 38 B4
Oakfield Pl 41 F3
Oak Grn 20 C2
Oak Gro 20 C2
Oaklands 65 E2
Oaklands Av 7 D2
Oaklands Cres 48 A2
Oaklands Dr *Dublin 4* 43 D4
Oaklands Dr *Dublin 6* 48 A2
Oaklands Pk *Dublin 4* 43 D4
Oaklands Pk *Swords* 7 D2
Oaklands Ter *Dublin 4*
off Serpentine Av 43 D4
Oaklands Ter *Dublin 6* 47 F2
Oak Lawn *Dublin 9* 20 C2
Oak Lawn *Dublin 15* 29 D1
Oak Lawn *Castle.* 29 E1
Oaklawn *Leix.* 15 E2
Oaklawn Cl 15 E2
Oaklawn W 15 E1
Oakley Gro 50 B3
Oakley Pk *Dublin 3* 34 A4
Oakley Pk *Black.* 50 B3
Oakley Rd 42 B4
Oak Lo 29 E2
Oak Pk Av 20 C3
Oak Pk Cl 20 C3
Oak Pk Dr 20 C2
Oak Pk Gro 20 C2
Oak Ri *Dublin 9* 20 C2
Oak Ri *Clond.* 44 A2
Oak Rd *Dublin 9* 33 D2
Oak Rd *Dublin 12* 45 D1
Oak Rd Business Pk 39 D4
Oaks, The *Dublin 3* 34 B4
Oaks, The *Dublin 14* 56 B1
Oaks, The *Dublin 16* 56 B3
Oaks, The (Cookstown) *Dublin 24* 44 C4
Oaks, The **16** *Abb.* 63 E1
Oaks, The **5** *Lough.* 63 D1
Oaks, The (Hilltown) *Swords* 6 B3
Oakton Ct 59 F4
Oakton Dr 59 F4
Oakton Grn **2** 59 F4
Oakton Pk 59 F4
Oaktree Av 28 C1
Oaktree Dr 28 C1
Oaktree Grn 28 C1
Oaktree Gro 28 C1
Oaktree Lawn 28 C1
Oaktree Rd 57 F3
Oak Vw 20 C2
Oakview Av 14 C3
Oakview Cl 14 C3
Oakview Ct 14 C3
Oakview Dr 14 C3
Oakview Gro **1** 14 C3
Oakview Lawn 14 C3
Oakview Pk 14 C3
Oakview Ri 14 C3
Oakview Wk 14 C3
Oakview Way 14 C3
Oak Way 44 A2
Oakwood Av *Dublin 11* 19 E3
Oakwood Av *Swords* 6 C2
Oakwood Cl 19 E2
Oakwood Gro Est 38 A4
Oakwood Pk 19 E2
Oakwood Rd 19 E2
Oatfield Av 38 B2
Oatfield Cl 38 B2
Oatfield Cres 38 B2
Oatfield Dr 38 B2
Oatfield Gro 38 B2
Oatfield Lawn 38 B2
Oatfield Pk 38 B2
Obelisk Ct **6** 50 B4
Obelisk Gro 50 B3
Obelisk Ri 50 B4
Obelisk Vw 50 A4
Obelisk Wk 50 B3
O'Brien Rd 46 B1
O'Brien's Inst 33 D2
O'Brien's Pl N 32 A2
O'Brien's Ter
off Prospect Rd 31 F3
Observatory La
off Rathmines Rd Lwr 42 A4
O'Byrne Rd 64 B4
O'Byrne Vil **7** 64 B4
O'Carolan Rd 66 C6
Ocean Pier 43 E1
O'Connell Av 31 F4
O'Connell Br 67 F3
O'Connell Gdns 43 D3
O'Connell St Lwr 67 F2
O'Connell St Upr 67 F2
O'Curry Av 66 C6
O'Curry Rd 66 C6
O'Daly Rd 32 A1
Odd Lamp Rd 30 B3
O'Devaney Gdns 41 D1
O'Donnell Gdns **9** 51 F4
O'Donoghue St 40 A3
O'Donovan Rd 41 F3
O'Donovan Rossa Br
off Winetavern St 66 D4
O'Dwyer Rd 46 B1
Offaly Rd 31 E3
Offington Av 24 C2
Offington Ct 24 C3
Offington Dr 24 C3
Offington Lawn 24 C3
Offington Pk 24 C2
O'Hogan Rd 40 A2
Olaf Rd 66 B2
Old Ballycullen Rd 54 A2
Oldbawn 53 E3
Old Bawn Av 53 D2
Old Bawn Cl 53 E3
Old Bawn Ct 53 E2
Old Bawn Dr 53 E2
Old Bawn Pk 53 D3
Old Bawn Rd 53 E2
Old Bawn Ter **1** 53 E3
Old Bawn Way 53 D2
Old Belgard Rd 44 C3
Old Belgard Rd Business Pk 44 C4

Pinewoods 44 A2
Pinewood Vil 19 F3
Pinnockhill Roundabout 6 C3
Plaza Shop Cen, The 7 D2
Pleasants La 67 E6
Pleasants Pl 42 A3
Pleasants St 67 E6
Plums Rd 57 D3
Plunkett Av *Dublin 11* 18 C2
Plunkett Av *Fox.* 58 B2
Plunkett Cres 18 C2
Plunkett Dr 18 C2
Plunkett Grn 18 C2
Plunkett Gro 18 C2
Plunkett Rd 18 C3
Poddle Pk 47 D2
Polo Rd 30 C4
Poolbeg St 67 G3
Poole St 66 B5
Poplar Row 32 C3
Poplars, The *D.L.* 50 C3
Poplars, The *Grey.* 65 D3
Poppintree Ind Est 19 E2
Poppintree Pk La W 19 E2
Porters Av 16 B4
Portersfield 16 B4
Porters Gate 14 B4
Porters Gate Av 14 C4
Porters Gate Cl 14 B4
Porters Gate Ct 14 C4
Porters Gate Cres 14 B4
Porters Gate Dr 14 B4
Porters Gate Grn 14 B4
Porters Gate Gro 14 C4
Porters Gate Hts 14 C4
Porters Gate Ri 14 C4
Porters Gate Vw 14 B4
Porters Gate Way 14 C4
Porters Rd 16 A4
Porterstown Rd 16 A4
Portland Cl 67 H1
Portland Pl 32 A3
Portland Rd 65 F3
Portland Rd N 65 E3
Portland Row 32 B4
Portland St N 32 B4
Portmahon Dr 41 D3
Portmarnock 11 F3
Portmarnock Av **2** 11 F2
Portmarnock Br 11 E4
Portmarnock Cres 11 F2
Portmarnock Dr 11 F2
Portmarnock Gro 11 F2
Portmarnock Pk 11 F2
Portmarnock Ri 11 F3
Portmarnock Sta 11 D4
Portmarnock Wk 11 F2
Portobello Br 42 A4
Portobello Harbour 42 A4
Portobello Pl 42 A4
Portobello Rd 41 F4
Portobello Sq *off Clanbrassil St Upr* 41 F4
Portside Business Cen 33 D4
Port Side Ct 32 C4
Potato Mkt *off Green St Little* 66 D3
Pottery Rd 59 D2
Pound St 15 F2
Powers Ct *off Warrington Pl* 42 C3
Powers Sq *off John Dillon St* 66 D5
Prebend St 66 D2
Preston St 67 H1
Price's La *Dublin 2* 67 F3
Prices La *Dublin 6* 42 A4
Priestfield Cotts 41 E3
Priestfield Dr *off South Circular Rd* 41 E3
Priestfield Ter *off South Circular Rd* 41 E3
Primrose Av 31 F4
Primrose Gro 22 A3
Primrose Hill 51 E3
Primrose La 26 C2
Primrose St 66 D1
Prince Arthur Ter 48 A1
Prince of Wales Ter *Dublin 4* 43 D4
Prince Of Wales Ter **16** *Bray* 64 B2
Princes St N 67 F3
Princes St S 67 H3
Princeton 49 D4
Priorswood Rd 21 F2
Priory, The *Dublin 7* 30 C2
Priory, The *Dublin 16* 55 F2
Priory Av 50 A2
Priory Ct **1** 55 F3
Priory Dr 57 F1
Priory E 30 C2
Priory Gro 57 F1
Priory Hall 57 F1
Priory N 30 C2
Priory Ri **3** 65 D3
Priory Rd 47 E1
Priory Way **4** 65 D3
Priory W 30 C2
Proby Pk 60 A3
Probys La 67 E3
Proby Sq 50 B3
Promenade Rd 33 E4
Prospect Av *Dublin 9* 31 F2
Prospect Av *Dublin 16* 55 D3
Prospect Cem 31 F2
Prospect Ct 55 D4
Prospect Dr 55 D3
Prospect Glen 55 D4
Prospect Gro 55 D3
Prospect Heath 55 D3
Prospect Hts 55 D4
Prospect La 48 C2
Prospect Lawn 59 D3
Prospect Meadows 55 D3
Prospect Rd 31 F3
Prospect Sq 31 F2
Prospect Ter (Sandymount) *off Beach Rd* 43 E3
Prospect Vw 55 D3
Prospect Way 31 F2
Protestant Row 67 E6
Prouds La 67 F5
Prussia St 31 E4
Puck's Castle La 62 B3
Purley Pk 11 F2
Purser Gdns 48 A1
Putland Rd 64 B4
Putland Vil **10** 64 B4

Q

Quarry Dr 46 B2
Quarryfield Ct 44 C2
Quarry Rd (Cabra) *Dublin 7* 31 E3
Quarry Rd *Grey.* 65 E3
Queens Pk 50 C3
Queens Rd 51 F3
Queen St 66 C3
Quinns La 67 G6
Quinn's Rd 63 E4
Quinsborough Rd 64 B2

R

Racecourse Shop Cen 23 E3
Radlett Gro 11 F2
Rafters Av 40 C4
Rafters La 40 C4
Rafters Rd 40 C4
Raglan La 42 C4
Raglan Rd 42 C4
Raheen Av 52 B2
Raheen Cl 52 B2
Raheen Ct 52 B2
Raheen Cres 52 B2
Raheen Dr *Dublin 10* 39 E3
Raheen Dr *Dublin 24* 52 B2
Raheen Lawn 64 C4
Raheen Pk *Dublin 10* 39 E3
Raheen Pk *Dublin 24* 52 B2
Raheen Pk *Bray* 64 C4
Raheen Rd 52 B2
Raheny Pk 34 C2
Raheny Rd 34 B1
Raheny Sta 34 B2
Railway Av *Dublin 8* *off Tyrconnell Rd* 40 B3
Railway Av (Inchicore) *Dublin 8* 40 A3
Railway Av *Dublin 13* 24 A2
Railway Cotts *off Serpentine Av* 43 D4
Railway Ms 23 D3
Railway Rd *Dublin 13* 23 E3
Railway Rd **5** *Dalkey* 60 B3
Railway St 67 G1
Railway Ter *off Grattan St* 42 C2
Rainsford Av 66 B4
Rainsford La **3** 61 E2
Rainsford St 66 B4
Ralahine 59 F4
Raleigh Sq 40 C4
Ralph Sq **1** 15 F2
Ramillies Rd 39 F2
Ramleh Cl 48 C2
Ramleh Pk 48 C2
Ramleh Vil 48 B2
Ramor Pk 16 C4
Ranelagh Av 42 B4
Ranelagh Rd 42 A4
Raphoe Rd 40 C4
Rathbeal Ct **1** 6 C1
Rathbeale Cres 6 C1
Rathbeale Ri 6 C2
Rathclaren **2** 64 A3
Rathdown Av 47 E3
Rathdown Cl 65 E1
Rathdown Ct *Dublin 6W* 47 E2
Rathdown Ct *Grey.* 65 D1
Rathdown Cres 47 E3
Rathdown Dr 47 E3
Rathdown Gro **6** 57 D3
Rathdown Pk *Dublin 6W* 47 E3
Rathdown Pk *Grey.* 65 D1
Rathdown Rd *Dublin 7* 31 F4
Rathdown Rd *Grey.* 65 D1
Rathdown Sq 31 E4
Rathdown Ter **7** 57 D3
Rathdown Vil 47 E3
Rathdrum Rd 41 E4
Rathfarham Gate 47 E4
Rathfarnham Castle 47 E4
Rathfarnham Mill 47 E4
Rathfarnham Pk 47 E3
Rathfarnham Rd *Dublin 6W* 47 E3
Rathfarnham Rd *Dublin 14* 47 E3
Rathfarnham Shop Cen 47 D4
Rathfarnham Wd 47 F4
Rathgar Av 47 F1
Rathgar Pk 47 F2
Rathgar Rd 47 F2
Rathingle Rd 6 B3
Rathland Rd (Bothar Raitleann) 47 D2
Rathlin Rd 32 A1
Rathlyon 54 A3
Rathlyon Pk 54 A3
Rathmichael 62 C3
Rathmichael Dales 62 C3
Rathmichael Haven 62 C3
Rathmichael Hill 62 C3
Rathmichael La 62 C3
Rathmichael Manor 63 D2
Rathmichael Pk 63 E3
Rathmichael Rd 62 B3
Rathmichael Wds 63 E3
Rathmines Av 48 A1
Rathmines Rd Lwr 42 A4
Rathmines Rd Upr 48 A1
Rathmintan Cl **3** 52 A3
Rathmintan Ct 52 A3
Rathmintan Cres 52 A3
Rathmintan Dr 52 A3
Rathmore Av 57 E2
Rathmore Pk 34 C2
Rath Row 67 G3
Rathsallagh Av 63 E2
Rathsallagh Br 63 E2
Rathsallagh Dr 63 E3
Rathsallagh Gro 63 E2
Rathsallagh Pk 63 E2
Rathvale Av 22 A4
Rathvale Dr 22 A4
Rathvale Gro *off Rathvale Av* 22 A4
Rathvale Pk 22 A4
Rathvilly Dr 18 C4
Rathvilly Pk 18 C4
Rathvilly Rd 18 C4
Ratoath Av (Ascal Ratabhachta) 18 B4
Ratoath Dr 18 B3
Ratoath Est 30 C2
Ratoath Rd *Dublin 7* 31 D3
Ratoath Rd *Dublin 11* 18 B4
Ratra Rd 30 B2
Ravensdale Cl 47 D2
Ravensdale Pk 47 D2
Ravensdale Rd 33 D4
Ravens Rock Rd 57 E3
Ravenswell Rd 64 B2
Ravenswood 14 B2
Ravenswood Av 14 B3
Ravenswood Cres 14 B3
Ravenswood Dr 14 B3
Ravenswood Grn 14 B3
Ravenswood Lawn 14 B3
Ravenswood Ri 14 B2
Ravenswood Rd 14 B3
Ravenswood Vw 14 B3
Raverty Vil **3** 64 A2
Raymond St 41 F3
Redberry 26 C4
Red Brick Ter **3** 50 B3
Redcourt Oaks 34 B4
Red Cow Business Pk 45 E1
Red Cow Cotts **3** 29 D4
Red Cow La 66 C2
Redesdale Cres 57 E1
Redesdale Rd 57 E1
Redfern Av 11 F2
Redford Pk 65 D1
Redmonds Hill 67 E6
Redwood Av 45 E4
Redwood Cl *off Redwood Av* 45 E4
Redwood Ct *Dublin 14* 48 A4
Redwood Ct *Dublin 24* *off Parkhill Rd* 45 D4
Redwood Dr 45 D4
Redwood Gro 50 A2
Redwood Hts *off Redwood Pk* 45 E4
Redwood Lawn 45 D4
Redwood Pk 45 E4
Redwood Ri *off Redwood Pk* 45 E4
Redwood Vw *off Redwood Av* 45 E4
Redwood Wk 45 D4
Reginald Sq *off Gray St* 66 C5
Reginald St 66 C5
Rehoboth Av 41 E3
Rehoboth Pl 41 E3
Reillys Av *off Dolphin's Barn St* 41 E3
Reuben Av 41 D3
Reuben St 66 A6
Rialto Br 41 D3
Rialto Bldgs *off Rialto Cotts* 41 D3
Rialto Cotts 41 D3
Rialto Dr 41 D3
Rialto St 41 D3
Ribh Av 34 A2
Ribh Rd 34 A2
Richelieu Pk 49 E1
Richmond 50 B4
Richmond Av 51 D3
Richmond Av N 32 C3
Richmond Av S 48 B2
Richmond Cotts *Dublin 1* 32 B4
Richmond Cotts (Inchicore) *Dublin 8* 40 C2
Richmond Cotts N *off Richmond Cotts* 32 B4
Richmond Ct 48 B3
Richmond Cres 32 B4
Richmond Est 32 C3
Richmond Grn 51 D3
Richmond Gro 51 D3
Richmond Hill *Dublin 6* 42 A4
Richmond Hill *Black.* 51 D3
Richmond La *off Russell St* 32 B4
Richmond Ms 42 A4
Richmond Par 32 B4
Richmond Pk 51 D3
Richmond Pl 42 A4
Richmond Pl S *off Richmond St S* 42 A4
Richmond Rd 32 B2
Richmond Row 42 A4
Richmond Row S *off Richmond St S* 42 A3
Richmond St N 32 B4
Richmond St S 42 A3
Richmond Ter **19** 64 C3
Richview Office Pk 48 C2
Richview Pk 48 B2
Ridgeford Apartments 56 C2
Ridge Hill 63 E1
Ridgewood Av 6 A3
Ridgewood Cl 6 A3
Ridgewood Ct 6 A3
Ridgewood Grn 6 A4
Ridgewood Pk 6 A3
Ridgewood Pl 6 A3
Ridgewood Sq 6 A3
Rinawade Av 15 D2
Rinawade Cl 15 D2
Rinawade Cres 15 D2
Rinawade Downs 15 D2
Rinawade Glade 15 D2
Rinawade Gro 15 D2
Rinawade Pk 15 D2
Rinawade Ri 15 D2
Rinawade Vw 15 D2
Ringsend Br 43 D2
Ringsend Pk 43 D2
Ringsend Rd 42 C2
Ring St 40 A3
Ring Ter 40 B3
Ripley Ct 64 A4
Ripley Hills 64 A4
Rise, The (Drumcondra) *Dublin 9* 32 A1
Rise, The (Ballinteer) *Dublin 16* 56 B4
Rise, The (Ballyboden) *Dublin 16* 55 D3
Rise, The (Cookstown) *Dublin 24* 44 C4
Rise, The (Kilnamanagh) *Dublin 24* 45 D3
Rise, The *Dalkey* 60 B3
Rise, The *Kins.* 7 E3
Rise, The *Leix.* 15 E1
Rise, The (Robswall) **3** *Mala.* 11 F1
Rise, The *Manor.* 14 C2
Rise, The *Still.* 49 F4
River Cl **2** 63 E2
River Ct **1** 12 B3
Riverdale 15 F2
Riverfield 65 D3
River Forest 15 F1
River Gdns 32 A1
River La *Bray* 64 A2
River La *Lough.* 63 E2
River Rd *Dublin 11* 30 B1
River Rd *Dublin 15* 30 B1
Riversdale 56 C2
Riversdale Av *Dublin 6* 47 F3
Riversdale Av *Clond.* 38 B4
Riversdale Av *Palm.* 28 C4
Riversdale Ct 28 C4
Riversdale Cres 38 B4
Riversdale Dr 38 B4
Riversdale Grn 38 B4
Riversdale Gro *Dublin 6W* 47 D2
Riversdale Gro *Palm.* 28 C4
Riversdale Ind Est 39 F4
Riversdale Pk *Clond.* 38 B4
Riversdale Pk *Palm.* 28 C4
Riversdale Rd 38 B4
Riverside **3** 38 B4
Riverside Av 21 E2
Riverside Cotts 47 D4
Riverside Cres 21 E2
Riverside Dr *Dublin 14* 47 F4
Riverside Dr *Dublin 17* 21 E2
Riverside Dr *Palm.* 28 C4
Riverside Gro 21 E2
Riverside Pk 21 E2
Riverside Rd 21 E2
Riverside Wk 48 C2
Riverston Abbey 30 C2
Rivervale Apartments **1** 64 A3
River Valley Av 6 C2
River Valley Cl 6 B2
River Valley Ct 6 B2
River Valley Dr 6 B2
River Valley Gro 6 B3
River Valley Hts 6 B2
River Valley Lawn 6 C3
River Valley Pk 6 B3
River Valley Ri 6 B3
River Valley Rd 6 B2
River Valley Vw 6 B2
River Valley Way 6 B2
Riverview *Dublin 24* 53 E3
Riverview *Palm.* 29 D4
Riverview Business Cen 39 D4
Riverview Ct 39 F1
Riverwood Chase 28 A1
Riverwood Cl 28 B1
Riverwood Copse 28 A1
Riverwood Ct 28 B1
Riverwood Cres 28 B2
Riverwood Dale 28 B1
Riverwood Dene 28 A1
Riverwood Dr 28 B1
Riverwood Gdns 28 B2
Riverwood Glebe 28 A2
Riverwood Glen 28 B1
Riverwood Grn 28 B1
Riverwood Gro 28 B1
Riverwood Heath 28 A1
Riverwood Lawn 28 B1
Riverwood Pk 28 B1
Riverwood Pl 28 A2
Riverwood Rd 28 B1
Riverwood Ter 28 A1
Riverwood Vale 28 B1
Riverwood Vw 28 B1
Riverwood Way 28 B1
Road, The 14 C2
Road Number 1 43 E1
Road Number 2 43 E1
Road Number 3 43 E1
Robert Emmet Br 41 F4
Robert Pl *off Clonliffe Rd* 32 B3
Robert St *Dublin 3* *off Clonliffe Rd* 32 B3
Robert St *Dublin 8* 66 B5
Robinhood Business Pk 45 E1
Robinhood Ind Est 45 F1
Robinhood Rd 45 F1
Robinsons Ct 66 C5
Robin Vil 29 D4
Robswall 11 F1
Rochestown Av 59 E2
Rochestown Pk 59 E2
Rochfort Av 27 F3
Rochfort Cl 27 F3
Rochfort Cres 27 F4
Rochfort Downs 27 F3
Rochfort Grn 27 F3
Rochfort Pk 27 F3
Rochfort Way 27 F4
Rockfield *Dublin 14* 56 C2
Rockfield *Lucan* 26 C4
Rockfield Av 46 B3
Rockfield Cl 28 B1
Rockfield Dr *Dublin 12* 46 C2
Rock Fld Dr *Clond.* 44 B2
Rockfield Dr *Cool.* 28 B1
Rockfield Pk 16 B4
Rockford Pk 50 C3
Rockfort Av 60 C3
Rock Hill 50 B2
Rockingham Av 15 E1
Rockingham Grn 15 E1
Rockingham Gro 15 E1
Rockingham Pk 15 E1
Rocklands **2** 60 C2
Rock Lo 60 A4
Rock Rd 49 F2
Rockville Cres 50 C3
Rockville Dr 50 C3
Rockville Pk 50 C3
Rockville Rd 50 C3
Rockwood 26 C4
Rocwood 58 A1
Roebuck Av 49 F4
Roebuck Castle 49 D3
Roebuck Downs 48 C4
Roebuck Dr 46 B2
Roebuck Hall 49 D4
Roebuck Rd 48 C3